SOCIAL LIFE AND DEVELOPMENT IN HONG KONG

SOCIAL LIFE
AND DEVELOPMENT
IN HONG KONG

Edited by

Ambrose Y. C. King
and
Rance P. L. Lee

The Chinese University Press
Hong Kong

International Standard Book Number: 962-201-337-6

First edition 1981
Second printing 1984

The Chinese University Press
The Chinese University of Hong Kong
SHATIN, N.T., HONG KONG

Typesetting by The Chinese University Press
Printing by Caritas Printing Training Centre

Acknowledgements

The papers in this collection result from research sponsored by the Social Research Centre of The Chinese University of Hong Kong. Since its inception in November 1969, the Centre has been directed by Burkart Holzner (1969-70), Jiri Nehnevajsa (1970-71), Robert Chin (1971-72), Ambrose Y. C. King (1972-73), and Rance P. L. Lee (1973-present). Throughout its course of development, the Centre has enjoyed the unfailing support and sagacious advice of C. K. Yang. The editors particularly wish to thank him for contributing an Introduction to this volume. Gratitude is also due to Barbara E. Ward and Michael Bond for their valuable assistance in the editorial process. To the clerical staff and research assistants of the Social Research Centre, we owe thanks for typing the manuscripts and putting together the research materials.

THE EDITORS

Contents

Appendices

Introduction

The emergence of Hong Kong as a major industrial metropolis from a sleepy commercial entrepot tucked away on the South China coast undoubtedly constitutes a spectacular postwar development in the world. The understanding of this phenomenal development poses a complex problem for the social sciences; papers in this volume address selected aspects of this challenging subject.

What makes this development seem even more striking is that it represents the combined product of a host of seemingly contradictory forces: the continuation of British 19th-century colonialism in the postwar world of nationalism and socialistic tendencies, the massive human and economic exodus from the Chinese Communist revolution of 1949, the stability of the colonial social and political order, and the practice of an almost unbridled Victorian *laissez faire*, forces which together permitted the generating of extraordinary vigour among the desperate immigrants spared from a violent socialist revolution. In 30 years the quiet colonial outpost of Hong Kong exploded from being a city of some 600,000 population to becoming a throbbing metropolis of almost 5,000,000. In common with the rapid growth of other great urban centres in the industrialized world, the new Hong Kong gained its population largely from in-migration and its high rate of natural increase. What did these newcomers from a revolutionary land bring into the shaping of the socio-political order and the phenomenal economic progress and prosperity besides their disciplined labour force, technical skills and financial resources? In the rise of new Hong Kong we see not only the ecological phenomena of rapid urban growth common to the industrialized world, but we also confront the proverbial intriguing problems of East-meets-West and old-meets-new. What features from the traditional Chinese culture continue to survive under the colonial polity and modernized economic environment? What changes have been induced?

These are some of the problems that provide a broad socio-political background for the papers in this volume as they take up selected aspects of the development of Hong Kong society. The research for these papers spanned a period of ten years, and they were undertaken by almost a dozen scholars who joined in the effort at varying periods of time, each with different individual specializations. Hence, there is no planned systematic attempt to give comprehensive coverage to the problem of Hong Kong's emergence as a metropolitan community.

The transformation of Hong Kong from a Victorian colonial city to a modern industrial metropolis will be discussed here from the viewpoint of community analysis. We shall view the Hong Kong community as an ecosystem within which functions a network of social institutions. In the present context, the ecosystem includes the demographic morphology and the ecological structure of Hong Kong as a metropolitan community, and the system of social institutions is taken in the usual sociological sense. The papers in this collection will gain a sense of theoretical coherence as we cluster them around these two components of community structure: the ecosystem and the institutional network.

Metropolitan Structural Development

In ecological structure, present-day Hong Kong differs most distinctly from old Hong Kong of the pre-World War II era. Old Hong Kong was a largely commercial city confined to the main island of Hong Kong, with the southern tip of the Kowloon peninsula across the habour as an outer-fringe. The rest of Kowloon, all of the extensive New Territories, and the outer islands, constituted the rural zone or countryside. Thus, its ecological components were the city of Hong Kong and the politically attached rural areas which retained a high degree of economic autonomy apart from the city, as indicated by the prevalence of self-sufficient paddy farming. But present-day Hong Kong consists of a high-density central city, a band of industrial and commercial satellites, and an urbanized countryside economically integrated to the central city and its satellites. This fits closely into the general structural pattern of metropolitan communities in the industrialized world. (Cf., for example, the definition of the SMSA or Standard Metropolitan Statistical Area in the U.S. Census.)

This structural pattern of central city-satellites-urbanized rural zone represents three phases of development of the Hong Kong metropolitan community. The first phase was the population influx into the central city and its industrial development which began in the 1950s. The second phase was the development of large industrial and commercial satellites to house the overflow of industries and population from the central city in the subsequent two decades. The third phase, rural urbanization, took place simultaneously with central city expansion and satellite development. Selected aspects of these three phases of development are treated in several of the papers in this volume.

Rance Lee (Chapter 1) aptly utilizes Philip Hauser's paradigm of population "explosion, implosion and diversity" to introduce his paper "High-density Effects in Urban Areas." The expansion of the central city of Hong Kong and the subsequent development of satellites is a dramatic result of population implosion from China's Communist revolution. The implosive impact takes the form of appalling density figures. Sample studies show a per capita living space of 38 to 43 square feet and the congestion of Mongkok area reached the proportion of 155,000 persons per square kilometre in the 1970s. This condition applied to both the central city and many newly developed satellites.

Such overcrowding naturally leads to the problem of the health of bio-psychic conditions and family life. Lee's paper on "High-density" is addressed specifically to this point. In spite of the many inconclusive interpretations, there is clearly positive correlation between overcrowding and parent-children relations, which affects the vital problem of the healthy growth of the young generation raised under such congested conditions. But the problem seems to go far deeper than the biopsychic indicators can measure, and the basic designs of studies of overcrowding obviously require further improvement. Lee's paper directs our attention to Sheelah Millar's concept of density tolerance. This is a significant point of progress in the problem. Together with E. N. Anderson's and Barbara Ward's studies of "coping mechanisms" with high-density living among Chinese, Lee's paper seems to bring forth ideas relevant to the problem of the relative biopsychic normalcy of the Chinese people living under the strain of enormous density pressure.

Chinese in the mainland have long lived under overcrowded conditions. Their hierarchical kinship structure, their tradition of sharing scarce resources (including space), their interactional pattern which facilitates intimate relations within small primary groups, and their willingness to accept limitations on personal activities as imposed by social circumstance and poverty, all contribute toward their ability to maintain normal social relations and relative degrees of emotional balance under the stress of overcrowding. This is what the mainland Chinese brought when they migrated into Hong Kong, enabling them to contribute toward a relatively stable social order when the community was undergoing a dizzy speed of expansion. For those accustomed to individual privacy in relatively ample living space, it is shocking to see the depressing congestion in the resettlement estates that line the fringe of the central city, and gives cause to wonder how residents in these congested slums can manage to keep their psychic equilibrium and conduct a normal social life.

If Lee's discussion of his data suggests ideas on this problem, they apply mainly to first-generation immigrants from the mainland; they are the primary carriers of the Chinese tradition, and they are willing to accept the inconvenience of overcrowding in view of their recent escape from the mainland hardships and dangers. It may be different with the children of these immigrants who assume a sense of security in the new environment of Hong Kong and are inclined to make efforts to emerge from the stressful conditions of over-congestion. This is pointed out by John T. Myers' "Residents' Images of a Hong Kong Resettlement Estate: A View from the Chicken Coop" paper (Chapter 2). When members of the second generation become the main residents of the congested estates, their adaptability to the overcrowded living will pose a further research problem.

Beyond the overcrowded central city of Hong Kong lies the zone of satellites, each with several hundred thousand population, the size of primate cities, commensurate with the capacity needed to contain the massive influx of immigrants from the mainland. The rapid development of satellites since the 1950s, together with the central city's highrise skyline, give observers the most dramatic impression of Hong Kong as a new metropolitan community.

In 1969, I took a group of sociology colleagues up the Black Hill for a panoramic view of Kwun Tong, a new satellite of about one-half million population which had risen with high speed from an unpopulated trash dump, in less than 15 years. The view was sociologically exciting, with all the ecological components plainly displayed like a toy city under our feet. The size seemed manageable for a field study of a Hong Kong satellite. Soon the Kwun Tong field project was set up as a part of the research plan of the Social Research Centre. As a result, many papers in this volume represent studies of different aspects of Kwun Tong as a sample community.

From the hills, the visibility of Kwun Tong's boundaries and its ecological components suggests a self-contained community. The paper "The Development of New Towns" by Y. K. Chan (Chapter 3) discusses the nature of Kwun Tong's self-containment and comes to the conclusion that the town is an integral part of Hong Kong.[1] This agrees with the general knowledge of metropolitan communities. The fully autonomous community is a matter of the past as Robert Redfield demonstrated in his *The Primitive World and Its Transformation* (Ithaca, N. Y.: Cornell University Press, 1953). Kwun Tong and other Hong Kong satellites may have been planned to offer a self-containing

[1] For more details, see Ambrose Y. C. King and Y. K. Chan's "A Theoretical and Operational Definition of the Community: The Case of Kwun Tong" (July 1972) and Y. K. Chan's "The Rise and Growth of Kwun Tong: A Study of Planned Urban Development" (August 1973). Both papers are occasional publications of the Chinese University's Social Research Centre.

complement of facilities and institutions to meet the social and economic needs of its inhabitants, but these facilities and institutions do not operate in isolation as an independent entity.

To provide the convenience and living requisites, the Hong Kong planning authorities arranged for the uses of industrial, commercial and residential lands, for the erection of housing estates and commercial centres, for the construction of transportation and public utilities, for the development of community services including education, medical care, recreation, and social welfare. These cover the development of a sustenance base to provide employment and income to the inhabitants, and a service structure to meet their physical and social needs. With a sustenance base and a service structure, inhabitants could meet their basic requirements within the community of Kwun Tong.

However, this is but a "part-community," as Robert Redfield would have it in his *The Little Community* (Chicago: University of Chicago Press, 1955), not an autonomous "whole-community." Structurally, Kwun Tong is part of the complex web of institutions of the Hong Kong metropolitan region. Its political life is firmly a part of the Hong Kong political apparatus. Kwun Tong operates as part of the Hong Kong economy including a wholesale-retail relationship, the marketing of local products, contract and subcontract arrangements, financial facilities. Educational institutions above the secondary level lie beyond Kwun Tong. Formal and informal networks of interpersonal and inter-organizational relations tie Kwun Tong to all parts of Hong Kong, as indicated in the busy operation of the modern transportation and communication systems. Large complex organizations, economic and otherwise, impose on Kwun Tong, as on communities elsewhere in the industrialized world, the vertical system of control which binds branch or sublevel agencies to headquarters of central decision-making, thus depriving local communities of their autonomous roles.[2] There is also the demographic consideration that Kwun Tong in the 1970s is largely a "first generation city" in terms of its adult population who moved in from other parts of Hong Kong, and the social and economic umbilical cords still tie them to the old bases in other parts of the city, particularly the central city. We find in Kwun Tong three sets of populations: those who live there but commute to work in other parts of Hong Kong, those who work there but commute to residence elsewhere, and those who both live and work in the town. The proportion of these three sets is yet to be ascertained, but each of them appears numerically sizable. Structurally, it is the greater metropolitan Hong Kong that functions as an autonomous community in a limited sense, not Kwun Tong which operates as a part-community.

[2] Roland L. Warren, *New Perceptives on the American Community*, Chicago: Rand McNally, 1977, pp. 260-264.

But the planning for self-containment by providing the ecological complement of a sustenance base and a service structure, the operation of which is analysed in Angela W. S. Kan's paper on "Implications of Concentrated Utilization of Local Facilities and Services in Public Housing Estates" (Chapter 4), performs an important function in the development of Hong Kong as a metropolitan community. Huge modern metropolitan communities, with their sprawling space and massive population, suffer from loss of efficiency because of the spatial differentiation among work, residence and consumption. Living in a modern metropolis imposes inordinate amounts of transportation time and cost (witness the New Yorkers commuting daily to distant points of Connecticut and New Jersey), and the financial burden of the transportation system on the government becomes ruinous. Development of self-contained satellites with a sustenance base and a service structure would reduce the negative effects from the residence-work-consumption differentiation brought on by modern specialization of functions as a main factor. The successful planning and operation of Kwun Tong and other part-communities in this direction would contribute toward the development of the efficiency and economy of Hong Kong as a complex metropolitan community.

The development of the sustenance base is analysed in Victor Mok's paper "The Small Factories: Problems and Strategies for Development" (Chapter 5). The small factories play an important role in Hong Kong's rapid industrialization. While many immigrants brought large capital and advanced technical experience from the mainland, the vast majority brought little or none of either. Relying on meager financial and technical resources, the vast majority of the "common refugees" work with ingenuity and dedication to set up small workshops, just as others eke out a living by small businesses of peddling and sidewalk stalls. Taking up small enterprises is a tradition the immigrants brought from their mainland as a means of survival in the face of adverse circumstances.

But in Hong Kong they have to operate in an environment of rapid technological modernization, in contrast to their tradition-bound homeland, and their meager financial resources and low technical level pose a difficult problem, as Mok's paper indicates. The tenacity of conservative tradition discourages change, and their low financial capacity causes aversion to innovation which, if unsuccessful, could lead to bankruptcy and starvation. This has been the obstacle to progress with small industrial and agricultural enterprises in mainland China, and the immigrants brought this with them to Hong Kong. In Hong Kong, however, the promotion of education is a means available to encourage progress, and government assistance in technical development can assume the risks of innovation, for only successful processes and techniques will be passed on to the industries. The modern channel of banking finance

can also be opened to small industries through private or government programmes to remedy the limitation of capital shortage for an industrious,
disciplined immigrant population eager for independence and success. (Take
the case of a scarcely educated peasant from the vicinity of Canton who
rowed a boat under cover of evening darkness straight to the shores of Kowloon in the mid-1960s, and ten years later became the owner and operator of
a successful luggage factory employing 50 workers and marketing products in
Europe and Latin America.) Mok's paper touches upon these points directly
or indirectly.

The development of satellites and their industrial and commercial enterprises, large or small, brought urban services, non-agricultural employment,
and a market for rural products and opportunities for economic enterprises
to the rural villages of the New Territories. This led to the urbanization of the
rural vicinities of Hong Kong, the third sector of development of Hong Kong
as a metropolitan community. Rance Lee's paper "The Fading of Earthbound
Compulsion in A Chinese Village" (Chapter 6) represents a case in point. Also
partly touching upon the same subject is the paper "Planned Development
and Political Adaptability in Rural Areas" by H. C. Kuan and S. K. Lau
(Chapter 9).

The village in Lee's paper is Taipo Tau, within earshot of the town of
Taipo, a fledgling satellite of commerce and small industries. The Taipo Tau
village study has the longest history among all the projects of the Social
Research Centre. The project began in 1965 under the directorship of S. L.
Wong, former chairman of the Sociology Department of Chung Chi College of
The Chinese University of Hong Kong, in an attempt to locate a village as a
site for field practice for sociology students. Part of the data accumulated
over the years is analysed in this paper. The major findings consist of commercialization of agriculture and the eclipse of agriculture by non-agricultural
employment in nearby urban centres as well as within the village. This trend of
commercialization of agriculture and the rising importance of non-agricultural
employment has changed the basic earthbound nature of rural life, and it is
observed not only in Taipo Tau but also in other villages in the New Territories.

The countryside is being integrated to the Hong Kong metropolitan
economy by urbanized utilization of its manpower and resources, in contrast
to the previous self-sufficient farming which formed a relatively inactive
adjunct to the old city of Hong Kong. The New Territories had raised rice as
a main crop, and the surplus from home consumption was shipped to the
city. But paddy culture drastically declined as it became unprofitable in
competition with truck farming, raising poultry and livestock and non-
agricultural employment. The huge metropolitan population must now draw
its grain and other food supplies from the mainland and foreign sources. This

food dependency strengthens the economic tie with the mainland and other parts of the world, making Hong Kong a link in the chain of international economy.

Institutional Characteristics and Their Change

The transformation of Hong Kong from a quiet, relatively homogeneous colonial city to a bustling and heterogeneous metropolitan community follows an ecological pattern with considerable universal features in common with metropolitan communities elsewhere in the industrial world. The institutional characteristics of Hong Kong society are, however, far less universal than its ecological framework. In many respects Hong Kong society in the final quarter of the 20th century developed institutional features somewhat unique to itself. Here the British political power interacts with many streams of social forces of the Chinese population from the mainland. With a numerical dominance over the natives of pre-1949 old Hong Kong, the bulk of the new population brought with them not only social institutions of traditional China, but also values and attitudes which were developed under the Communist revolution, including the Cultural Revolution. Papers in this collection discuss institutional aspects of Hong Kong polity, kinship system, health care, religion, and "face-saving" tradition as a social interaction pattern.

The most striking institutional feature of Hong Kong is its colonial polity which provided socio-political stability for the industrialization and metropolitan community development. The stability and prosperity of colonialism poses a contradiction to the postwar decline of empires and the rise of socialistic revolutions. The success of alien rule in Hong Kong appears so much the more striking in light of the fact that the British colonial masters returned as a defeated force in 1945, and that it sits at the door step of a victorious giant of nationalistic and socialistic revolution which eradicated all foreign concessions and leased territories as landmarks of a political era in China. Ambrose King's two papers, "Administrative Absorption of Politics" (Chapter 7) and "The Political Culture of Kwun Tong" (Chapter 8) represent incisive analysis on this challenging subject.

The first of these two papers deals with the relationship between the British colonial power and the Chinese population under its rule. To enhance legitimacy and acceptability of colonial rule by the Chinese population, the British used elite cooptation to integrate the established rich and the new rich into the decision-making structure as symbols of Chinese representation. The inclusion of a few wealthy and influential Chinese in the colonial power structure may alleviate the discontentment among the local leadership, but it still leaves the common man, the vast majority, alienated.

In the pre-War era when the Chinese population, overwhelmingly born and raised or long settled in Hong Kong, were politically inert, this elite-mass gap, in King's characterization, did not threaten the stability of the colony's socio-political order. But a century of political tranquility in Hong Kong was soon to face the gathering storm of political agitations as nationalistic and socialistic movements spilled over from the China mainland. The well-organized city-wide strike of 1926, involving workers of all trades, even domestic female servants and sanitary workers, brought Hong Kong almost to a stand still for months. Colonial dignity suffered another set back when Japanese invaders dislodged the British forces in 1942. In 1946, the alert and adaptive British declared a localization policy which rapidly expanded the Chinese participation in lower-echelon civil service positions so that, by 1972, one out of every fifty of the total population in Hong Kong was employed in some subordinate civil service position, as King notes in his paper. Though subordinate to the British rulers, the vast number of Chinese employees in the government services undoubtedly increased the feeling of participation in the polity among the Chinese population.

But elite cooptation and involvement in subordinate government service were insufficient to enlist Chinese civil loyalty to rebuild Hong Kong's political stability, as indicated by the riots of 1966 and 1967. The influence from China's Cultural Revolution was obvious. Recognizing that times were different, the colonial authority devised the City District Officer (CDO) Scheme as a means of bridging the elite-mass gap. The concept was to decentralize the colony's extensive bureaucracy by setting up city district offices for direct contact with the local people. The CDO and his staff would explain to the people government policies and operations; they would transmit people's grievances and opinions to the government for consideration; they would help settle conflicts and local problems, and organize community recreation and festivities to promote community spirit, in much the same way as the gentry once functioned in traditional China. Basically, as King points out, the CDO performs an "output" function of rendering government administrative services; he does not mobilize the people to participate in political power, to share in decision-making as in the case of integrating Chinese elites into the decision-making mechanism.

To broaden the population coverage of its services, the CDO extended the rural communication channel from the Village Representative system to organizations of new mainland immigrants who have numerically surpassed the indigenous natives, but their interests have not been represented by the Village Representative for redressing of grievances or requests of assistance. This shows the adaptability of the colonial administration, but, again, it is a measure to facilitate administrative output with similar implication for CDO functions elsewhere in Hong Kong. That the colonial administration can also evince a high level of adaptability in the execution of planned development projects in rural Hong Kong is shown in the paper "Planned Development and Political Adaptability in Rural Areas" by Kuan Hsin-chi and Lau Siu-kai (Chapter 9). Through the manipulation of the indigenous rural elites and the official induction of outsider elites into the political process (as exemplified in the installation of the District Advisory Boards in the New Territories), resistance toward planned development in the rural areas has been effectively subdued.

This leaves the elitist, paternalistic foundation of the colonial government untouched, with the vast majority of the Hong Kong Chinese population alienated from political power. Would this be conducive to continuation of political stability which provided an important factor for Hong Kong's development into a modern metropolitan centre, a development which justifies the continuation of Hong Kong's colonial rule? This depends significantly on the people's political consciousness or the degree to which the post-war population has become politicized. Ambrose King's paper on the nature of Kwun Tong's political culture (Chapter 8) addresses this question.

Political culture, or political consciousness as the central point here, is a complicated problem, and King analyses it by using the cognitive-affective-evaluative scheme to measure the three aspects of the Kwun Tong people's politicization.

To measure the cognitive aspect, King quotes figures of frequency with which respondents follow accounts of public and government affairs. Among ordinary people, 6.6 per cent did so regularly, 42.5 per cent, from time to time, but 50.0 per cent never did. The figure for ordinary people who follow political accounts in the category of "from time to time" or occasionally, lacks clarity for it embodies a wide range of possible frequencies. The high figure in this category, together with 50.0 per cent who never paid attention to political accounts in the media, give a clear indication of political apathy as a dominant phenomenon among the common people. Why? King's data on the affective and evaluative aspects suggest some hints.

In a sample of common people of Kwun Tong, 41.3 per cent felt free to talk politics with anyone, 6.2 per cent felt not free to do so, 31.2 per cent took "0" or neutral position, while 21.3 per cent replied "don't know" or gave no answer. Those who gave "don't know" or no answer, King notes, were among a significant number of people who prefer "not to talk of the very concept of 'politics'." The significant percentage of this category, together with the rather ambiguous category of "0" which suggests lack of positive interest, indicate a degree of "fear" of the government. King further comments that there would have been a high percentage of negative answers if the question were changed from "free to discuss public affairs" to "Do you think that people in Hong Kong are free to criticize the actions of the Hong Kong police force without fear of punishment?"

This lack of trust and faith in the colonial government among a considerable proportion of the common people receives collaboration from two other indications in King's Kwun Tong data. In a sample of local organizational leaders on the amount of government consideration they would expect for their opinions and suggestions, 16.3 per cent replied "to be ignored", and 41.6 per cent answered "depends" which implies uncertainty and suspicion. With similar implication, King points out in his data on the evaluative aspect of Kwun Tong polity that 81.9 per cent of the ordinary people believed that they can do nothing at all about an unjust government regulation, and 13.1 per cent thought they can do something "but not much". An additional note of similar significance is that, 32.6 per cent of the common people in Kwun Tong agreed that "The primary reason for being a government official is 'to make money'," only 25.1 per cent disagreed with the statement.

These data evince no signal of patriotism or loyalty and pride toward an alien colonial ruler, nor a political system which encourages or promotes the development of a government by the people. As such, it is a British government by an integrated elite through cooptation of wealthy and influential Chinese who achieved success in the stability which marked the Hong Kong polity in contrast to the century of constant political disturbance in mainland China. But the vast majority of the common people remain deprived of political power, thus leaving an elite-mass gap in which lives a populace with widespread political apathy, a general unwillingness to talk politics, and a deep feeling of political impotence and alienation. It is a picture of general political inertness, avoidance, submissiveness.

This picture reflects a continuity of the tradition of the Confucianist tradition of benevolent paternalism from the mainland. In fact, King's data on the general unwillingness to talk politics recalls signs seen on restaurant walls in Canton in the 1920s warning customers: "Please do not talk politics", for fear of bringing in the police or gendarme. But social injustice, political discontent, effective propaganda and organization by the Communists has led to the rise of a politicized population and the termination of the Confucian tradition in the mainland. The Chinese experience shows that a politically apathetic and submissive population provides no guarantee for continued political stability in an age of revolutionary mass movements, particularly when a victorious socialist China maintains an intricate and intimate relationship with every aspect of Hong Kong society. The riots of 1966 and 1967 suggest political instability which could rise from the elite-mass gap and a politically untutored population. Neither can we draw unquestioned comfort from Hong Kong's miraculous economic prosperity as assurance against instability among a population which recently escaped from mainland hardships. It remains a problem for further research just how economically serious the issue of ferry fare increase actually was, or whether it was a triggering mechanism for pent-up social and political discontent. At that time Hong Kong was well on its way on its course to an economic boom. In a more distant way, the French Revolution occurred when France was leading Europe in economic prosperity. The points King raises on the nature of Hong Kong polity deserve serious attention.

In addition to elite cooptation, another factor in Hong Kong's political stability and submissive polity is the fragmentation of the Chinese population into "utilitarianistic" familial groups which hampers mass organization for political action. The self-centred nature of kinship groups renders it difficult for the Chinese to achieve political unification. Lau Siu-kai elaborates on this issue in his paper, "Utilitarianistic Familism: The Basis of Political Stability in Hong Kong" (Chapter 10). The primacy of familial interest among the Chinese is also noted by Ambrose King, F. M. Wong, Rance Lee, and Pedro Ng in their papers in this volume.

Familism as a socially and politically divisive force has been noted by Sun Yat-sen who called upon the Chinese people to transform their familism into nationalism in order to overcome the liability of 400 million Chinese existing as "a tray of loose sand". Political and social leaders in mainland China have echoed this call for over half a century. "Down with familism" (打倒家族主義) has been a persistent slogan in Chinese social movements ever since the May 4th Movement of 1919. And Chinese Communists launched repeated, and at times violent, campaigns against the practice of familial nepotism.

The tradition of familism, integrated on the basis of materialistic interests among the members, is too deep-seated to change substantially among the Chinese in Hong Kong. In fact, in Hong Kong it found a conducive environment to develop with renewed vigor. The rapid progress of Hong Kong as an industrial metropolis feeds on the nourishment of social and economic specialization which promotes impersonalism and consequently materialistic utilitarianism in social relationships, as long noted by Georg Simmel in his characterization of metropolitan mental life. Politically British colonialism has been practicing non-interference with native cultural traditions so long as they do not endanger the political order. The divisive effect of materialistic familism is obviously conducive to the stability of British elite rule, and it thus enjoys complete freedom from political discouragement. And the social and political campaigns against familism in the mainland are an empty echo from beyond the Hong Kong border.

In this political and economic environment "utilitarianistic familism" thrived unrestrained. The primacy of materialistic interest as a criterion in intra-kinship relations is most dramatically expressed in a case in New Territories where the spiritual tablets in an ancestral temple are arranged in hierarchical tiers by generational seniority as well as by the economic achievement of certain deceased individuals, in contrast to the traditional use of generational level and age as the sole criteria of hierarchical placement of spiritual tablets, excluding worldly success from any consideration. A similar case was reported in a Chinese ancestral temple in Singapore, attesting to the possible existence of a general trend of materialistic familism in the modern metropolis. The use of materialistic criteria in the "recruitment" process is a long Chinese matrimonial tradition which severely discouraged any transgression of class line, a popular theme in the traditional literature of romantic tragedy. Circles of "skirt strings" (marital relationship) played a prominent part in Chinese politics in the Republican period, and charges of this nature are still common against Communist functionaries. But in Hong Kong such practice continues with full respectability and strength.

But the Chinese family system has not remained unchanged in Hong Kong. If it is not the colonial policy to generate change in the family institution, economic and social pressures in an industrialized metropolitan environment would compel certain alterations. Dealing with this aspect are two papers, one by F. M. Wong, "Effects of the Employment of Mothers on Maternal Role and Power Differentiation in Hong Kong", and one by Pedro Ng, "Family Planning, Fertility Decline, and Family Size Preference in Hong Kong".

Data on Wong's paper (Chapter 11) indicates the numerical dominance of the nuclear family structure (about three-fourths) and the tendency toward an egalitarian relationship among its members. Wong measures the egalitarian pattern by quantitative indicators in husband-wife distribution of household decision-making and task performance in four major areas: economic activities, social activities, child care and control, and household duties. His indices exhibit a relatively egalitarian relationship in all major sectors of family life. This presents a drastic departure from the hierarchical authoritarian pattern of husband-wife relationship which has been a benchmark of traditional Chinese culture.

The egalitarian trend in husband-wife relationship draws support from Wong's systematic data. The dominance of nuclear family structure is certainly a contributing factor,[3] for the presence of senior members (parents of husband or wife) as in a stem or joint family would introduce the hierarchical dominance by the senior generation, which is a part of the traditional Chinese

[3]For an elaborate discussion on the rise of the nuclear family, see Fei-ming Wong, "Industrialization and Family Structure in Hong Kong," *Journal of Marriage and The Family*, November 1975, pp. 985-1000.

family kinship system. It has often been observed that, in a stem or joint family in Hong Kong, not only the husband's father and/or mother exercise hierarchical authority over the young couple, but also fosters continuation of the husband-dominance tradition. Another supporting influence in Wong's data is the prevalence of neolocality which raises the wife's status in the family. Locality rule has been a rigid feature of the Chinese traditional patrilineal kinship system, for it draws the boundary of rights and privileges between the paternal and maternal lineages, particularly with regard to property inheritance. Patrilocality is a supporting part of patrilineality, and the widespread practice of neolocality undermines the entire patrilineal system so basic to the traditional kinship structure.

Maternal employment, the subject of Wong's papers, is probably the strongest influence in the development of husband-wife egalitarianism as measured by decision-making and task performance in the four sectors of family activities indicated above. In all of the four sectors, maternal employment exerts a visible influence on the uplift of the wife's status and the development of a "collaborative" type of relationship with her husband.

Wong notes that the vast majority of his Kwun Tong population sample were first-generation immigrants from the mainland. This has a vital bearing on the prevalence of nuclear type families, for such immigrants came largely alone or at times with children, but seldom with parents. Siblings might come, but usually separately and not as a household. Thus, the prevalence of nuclear families is mainly a product of population movement in the development of the Hong Kong metropolitan community. A problem is whether some of these nuclear families will develop into stem or other forms as the second generation grows into maturity, or whether the second generation members will move away to establish their nuclear families, leaving the aged parents completely alone, as is generally the case in the American urban environment.

Maternal employment as a factor in the emergence of an increasingly egalitarian family is clearly a product of Hong Kong as an industrialized metropolitan community providing wide accessibility of remunerated work, both in towns and in the villages. Working mothers are not new to Chinese womanhood, for the vast majority of Chinese mothers have always worked, but they did it as unremunerated activity within the family economy. Accessibility to remunerated work came with the urban economy which provides the mother with extra-familial gainful employment and consequently changes her family role.

One notable feature of Hong Kong's nuclear families is its size. Wong's Kwun Tong sample shows a prevalence of households with about six members. This is higher than the average size of households of traditional China, which centred around the figure of 4.5 members, and urban families were smaller than rural ones. Family size in traditional China tended to expand with the progress of family economic status, and it is likely that the economic prosperity of postwar Hong Kong spurred the increase in family size.

But a seemingly universal trend of decreasing family size in industrial communities is asserting itself in Hong Kong where the family size preference for the young generation is for two to three children, making for a family size of four to five, much in congruence with the mainland situation before 1949. This essentially is the theme advanced by Pedro Ng's paper "Social Factors Contributing to Fertility Decline" (Chapter 12). This preference for smaller family size collaborates with the general acceptance of contraception by young couples, and the decline of the crude birth rate from 25.0 per thousand in 1961 to 17.7 in 1976. Ng's systematic data and competent analysis converge on the trend toward an anticipated smaller family size among the younger generation. Ng attributes this trend to a set of complex socioeconomic influences including the rising educational standard of the young Hong Kong population, the preference for delayed marriage, the rise of women's employment, the desire for improved quality of life, and the changed sense of value in having children (less than 10 per cent of a sample retained the old belief in perpetuation of the family lineage, and for assuring old-age economic security by having children).

The prevalence of nuclear families, the trend toward an egalitarian family structure, and the distinct preference for smaller-size families, are reversing some of the central features of the traditional Chinese family ideals which once accounted for many of the fundamental characteristics of traditional Chinese society. Save for the encouragement of family planning, these developments have not been the result of policy encouragement from the British colonial government, but rather the product of impersonal forces generated by the development of industrialization and urbanization of the metropolitan community of Hong Kong. It is notable that the prevalence of nuclear families, the egalitarian trend of intra-family relationship pattern, and the reduced size of families, have been a general common feature in metropolitan communities in the industrialized world, and their prevalence in Hong Kong shows the influence of this universal trend, regardless of the ideological intentions of the colonial policies.[4]

Beyond the polity and the kinship system, papers in this volume cover other institutional characteristics of the Hong Kong metropolitan community. Rance Lee's "Chinese and Western Health Care Systems" (Chapter 13) discusses the formal status discrepancy between Western and Chinese medicine,

[4] This point has been elaborated by Rance Lee and Pedro Ng in their paper "Social Environmental Bases of Fertility Motivation: A Dynamic View," an occasional paper of the Social Research Centre, The Chinese University of Hong Kong, October 1974.

the informal co-existence of which constitutes a unique feature in the British colony. Through either British ignorance or disdain, Chinese medicine is denied any formal status in the colonial system of health care, receiving neither legal recognition nor educational and economic support for its development. Traditional Chinese medicine became an underprivileged profession in Hong Kong in contrast to its continued importance in mainland China. But traditional medicine remains important to the Hong Kong Chinese for technical reasons. The political downgrading of the Chinese medical profession could re-inforce the inferiority feeling among the Chinese population under alien rule, thus further widening the elite-mass gap which marks the Hong Kong polity. For its development, traditional Chinese medicine must rely on its own economic and social resources without the benefit of government support.

The religious institution of the Hong Kong community is discussed in John T. Myers' paper "Traditional Chinese Religious Practices in an Urban-Industrial Setting" (Chapter 14). Myers' analysis shows that ancestor worship and the cult of deities have declined in vitality, but that a few temple cults are flourishing by serving as focus for solidarity of some minority groups.

The loss of vitality of ancestor worship and the cult of deities results partly from the secularization trend in the Hong Kong metropolitan development which came with high levels of technological, scientific and educational progress. The decline of ancestor worship also appears to be a function of the increase in nuclear families in postwar Hong Kong, as indicated in many of the papers discussed in the foregoing pages. Ancestor worship is a diffused religion embedded in the family institution, and would change as the host institution undergoes alteration.[5] The vital function of ancestor worship is to sanctify the values of lineage perpetuation and the building of the numerical strength of kinship groups. Both of these two values lose function when the lineage continuity and the numerical size of families are adversely affected by the prevalence of nuclear families. Ancestor worship drew much of its strength from the large size of lineage groups in rural China, the size of which implies economic and psychological support for the system. But lineage organizations among indigenous natives in the New Territories have been declining in vitality in recent decades, as demonstrated by the disrepair of the ancestor temples in the villages, and the new immigrants who have become the majority of the population have failed to build ancestor temples either in the rural or urban areas for many reasons, including the diversity of kinship among the immigrants. The weakening of ancestor worship is, therefore, a concomitant to the

[5] For the nature of diffused religion, see C. K. Yang, *Religion in Chinese Society*, M.I.T. Press, 1961, Chapters II, XII and XIII.

change of the kinship institution in the process of development of Hong Kong as an industrial metropolitan community.

The flourishing of certain temple cults as focus of minority group solidarity reaffirms the functional theory of religion. The annual colourful festivities dedicated to the patron gods are vivid demonstrations of the continuity of similar cults in traditional China. Hong Kong's metropolitan development brought in ethnic diversity, and the temple cults' function in fostering minority group solidarity contributes to the integration and stability of Hong Kong's heterogeneous metropolitan social order.

The paper "Face Saving in Chinese Culture" by Michael H. Bond and Peter W. H. Lee (Chapter 15) deals with face-saving as a social interactional pattern so much emphasized in traditional Chinese culture. It is a device for maintaining group cohesion in traditional Chinese society which functioned with harmony and hierarchy as central concepts. Hong Kong's complex social order obviously relies much on the continued operation of this traditional device.[6]

The foregoing collection of papers represents part of the work accomplished by the Chinese University's Social Research Centre. Modern social science faces the problem of universal, cross-cultural validity, for it draws its theoretical conclusion from data in culture-bound facts. The validity of Western social science theories and the use of Western texts in social science education in Oriental societies demands research, verification and reformulation in the light of the native environment. The Social Research Centre was established primarily with this goal in view—to acclimatize social science to the Oriental soil. It is a creditable achievement that within ten fleeting years, a group of nascent scholars have developed the research institute, assembled a staff, formulated work plans, won financial support, organized field work and turned out results as partly presented in this volume.[7]

In the foregoing pages, I have added much of my own interpretation to the data presented in the papers, and I take full responsibility for any errors or inaccuracies I may have committed.

C. K. Yang
University of Pittsburgh

[6] For more discussions, see Ambrose Y. C. King and John T. Myers, "Shame as an Incomplete Conception of Chinese Culture: A Study of Face," an occasional paper of the Social Research Centre, The Chinese University of Hong Kong, August 1977.

[7] For an account of the historical development of the Social Research Centre, see Rance P. L. Lee, "Growth and Limitations of Social Science Research Institutions in Asia: The Hong Kong Experience," an occasional paper of the Social Research Centre, The Chinese University of Hong Kong, March 1975.

PART ONE
Metropolitan Structural Development

PART ONE
Metropolitan Structural Development

Chapter 1

High-Density Effects in Urban Areas: What Do We Know and What Should We Do?*

Rance P. L. Lee

Contemporary society has been undergoing what Philip Hauser has called the "social morphological revolution".[1] This revolution includes a remarkable increase in the rate of world population growth, an increasing concentration of the world's peoples on urban areas, and an increasing heterogeneity of populations sharing the same geographical area and life space. There are now over 4 billion people in the world, of whom about 38 per cent are living in towns and cities. The population explosion and implosion have resulted in not only high-density living in urban areas but also diversity of urban populations in ethnicity, language, cultural traditions, and social organizations.

A major source of the social morphological revolution is the accelerated tempo of scientific and technological development. It is scientific and technological progress that has substantially reduced the death rates and also permitted the ever larger agglomerations of different kinds of people in urban areas. The question arises: what are the human implications of the population increase in urban areas, which is partly, though not entirely, a result of scientific and technological development? The object of this paper is to focus on the social and health implications of high-density living in urban areas. Special reference will be made to the case of urban Hong Kong.

A Review of Social Science Knowledge

It has been widely belived that as a city becomes increasingly crowded, it is bound to have a number of social problems including crimes and delinquency, family conflicts, and illness, etc. Such a belief has been confirmed by many,

*The author wishes to thank Drs. Y. K. Chan, Stuart Valins and Kazuo Yamamoto for their valuable comments and suggestions. An earlier version of this paper was presented at the Asian Working Group Meeting on the Human Implications of Scientific and Technological Development, Australia, 2-7 October, 1978.
[1]Philip M. Hauser, "The Chaotic Society: Product of the Social Morphological Revolution," *American Sociological Review*, V. 34, 1969, pp. 1-18.

though not all, of the animal studies.[2] Biologists have conducted a number of studies on a great variety of animals such as mice, rabbits, rats, deer, chicken, primates, and wolves. It was generally found that high-density situations produce behavioral deviations and physiological pathologies among animals, such as less maternal care, higher mortality rates, greater hostility, lower fertility, and more sexual deviance. Various explanations have been suggested, including, for instance, the territorial needs and the increase of adrenal activity of the animals. The question is: can these findings from animal studies be extended to human populations?

Numerous theories have been proposed and a large number of empirical studies have been conducted by social scientists in the last two decades dealing with the human implications of high-density living.[3] Most studies—experiments and sample surveys—follow the tradition of animal research. Their conceptual framework is basically a stress model. It is postulated that high-density living produces stress, which in turn leads to deviant behavior. There are quite a few propositions specifying why high density is stressful to the individuals. For instance, it has been argued that high density is stressful because (1) it produces excessive stimulation or information overload; (2) it imposes behavioral restriction; and (3) it makes the supply of resources less than the demand.

Let us briefly review what has been learned from these empirical studies. Psychologists have carried out a number of laboratory as well as field experiments. In a nutshell, most experiments dealt with three major types of behavioral consequences; they are (1) interpersonal affection and attraction, (2) aggression and hostility, and (3) cognitive skills and task performance. Up to now, the experimental findings are rather inconclusive. There are so many contradictory findings that it is uncertain whether high density has adverse effects on human beings.

The experimental approach has some limitations. First, most studies dealt with a special group of individuals in an institutional setting, such as students in schools and patients in hospitals; these findings may not be generalizable to

[2] For a concise review, see Jonathan L. Freedman, *Crowding and Behavior*, San Franciso: W. H. Freeman & Company, 1975, Chapters 2 & 3.

[3] For literature reviews, see H. H. Winsborough, "The Consequences of High Population Density," *Law and Contemporary Problems*, V. 31, 1965, pp. 120-126; M. Choldin & M. McGinty, "Bibliography: Population Density, Crowding and Social Relations," *Man-Environment Systems*, V. 2, 1972, pp. 131-158; Jonathan L. Freedman, "The Effects of Population Density on Humans," in James Fawcett, ed., *Psychological Perspective on Population*, N. Y.: Basic Books, 1973; C. Loo, "The Psychological Study of Crowding," *American Behavioral Scientists*, V. 18, 1975, pp. 826-842; and S. C. Choi, A. Mirjafari & H. B. Weaver, "The Concept of Crowding: A Critical Review and Proposal of an Alternative Approach," *Environment & Behavior*, V. 8, 1976, pp. 345-362.

other groups of people. Second, many studies were conducted in an artificially created laboratory environment; people under high-density situations in a real-life setting may not behave in the same way as in an artificial setting. Third, most experiments dealt with short-time effects of high density; the long-term effects may not be the same. All these reservations about experimental findings point to the need for research on the long-term consequences of high-density living on the general populations in real-life settings. In recent years, many psychologists and more sociologists have responded to this research need and have accumulated a substantial number of research findings. Most of the studies are conducted in the form of social surveys, with the exception of a few field-experiments.[4]

Numerous surveys have been conducted on both ecological and individual levels. Ecological studies use aggregates as units of analysis. There have been comparisons between cities or metropolitan areas, and between census tracts within a city. In addition to ecological studies, there have also been a number of individual-level studies which use individuals as units of analysis. The individuals under study are normally selected through random sampling procedures.

Both ecological and individual-level surveys have been conducted in a variety of urban contexts, such as Baltimore, Boston, Chicago, Detroit, Indianapolis, Honolulu, New York, Toronto, Hong Kong, Singapore, and Manila. There have also been studies in France, Italy, New Zealand, Netherlands, and Taiwan, etc. In these studies, a wide range of behavioral consequences of high density have been examined, including, for instance, (1) *health status*, e.g., overall mortality, infant mortality, accidental death, mental disorders, stress symptoms, infectious diseases, and venereal disease, (2) *aggression*, e.g., juvenile delinquency, adult crimes, homicide, and suicide, (3) *family relations*, e.g., husband-wife conflict, sibling rivalry, parent-child conflict, and divorce, (4) *social participation and alienation*, e.g., organizational affiliations, and contacts among relatives, neighbors, and friends, (5) *political disorder and civil strife*, (6) *child development*, e.g., play patterns, intellectual ability and school performance, aggression, and health, (7) *fertility behavior*, e.g., number of pregnancies, use of contraceptives, illegal births, and abortion, (8) *sexual behavior and deviance,* e.g., the rate of sexual intercourse, homosexuality and extramarital affairs.

Regarding the concept of physical density, a number of measures have been developed. An important development is the distinction between house-

[4] Such as D. Stokols, T. E. Smith & J. J. Prostor, "Partitioning and Perceived Crowding in Public Space," *American Behavioral Scientists*, V. 18, 1975, pp. 729-814; and A. Baum & S. Valins, *Architecture and Social Behavior: Psychological Studies of Social Density*, N. J.: Lawrence Erlbaum Associates, 1977.

hold density and neighborhood density. Some examples of the measures of household density, which refers to density within the dwelling unit, are the number of rooms per housing unit, the number of families per housing unit, the number of persons per housing unit, the number of persons per room, and the amount of space per person within the housing unit. Neighborhood density refers to the density situations outside the dwelling unit. Some of its measures are the number of people per unit area, the number of dwelling units per unit area, the number of dwelling units per structure, the number of structures per unit area, and the amount of open space per person.

In the social surveys, it is generally hypothesized that high-density living will produce adverse effects on the health and social behavior of individuals. In examining the hypotheses, survey researchers typically control certain background variables, such as sex, age, education, socioeconomic status, migration, and ethnicity. Like the experimental findings, however, the results from survey studies are also inconclusive. Most studies found that there are slight or no relationships between high density and various behavioral items, especially when some background variables are held constant.

In sum, neither the psychological experiments nor the social surveys have produced significant and consistent findings about the human implications of high-density situations. After years of research, we seem to have come to the conclusion that high density as such may have little effect on human beings. Let us now focus on the case of Hong Kong, as it is undoubtedly one of the most densely-populated cities on the earth.

High Density in Hong Kong

At the end of World War II, there were about 600,000 people in Hong Kong. It was estimated that at the end of 1978 the total population had increased to about 4.6 million persons. As the total area is 1,049 square kilometers, the overall population density in Hong Kong is about 4.4 thousand people per square kilometer.

Like other parts of the world, the people in Hong Kong are unequally distributed between the urban and the rural sectors. The urban areas—Hong Kong Island, Kowloon, New Kowloon, and Tsuen Wan—constitute about 14 per cent of the total land in Hong Kong, but their share of the total population is over 90 per cent. The population density in the urban areas is thus nearly 26 thousand people per square kilometer. There are, of course, variations among the various districts of urban sector. According to the 1971 census, the district of Mongkok in the peninsula of Kowloon had a population density as high as 155 thousand people per square kilometer. It cannot be overstated that wherever we go in urban Hong Kong, we are surrounded by thousands of people and by hundreds of high-rise buildings. High density has, in effect, become the normal way of life in Hong Kong.

The people in Hong Kong have diverse ethnic and cultural backgrounds. Although more than 98 per cent of the population are Chinese in origin, the Chinese are not homogeneous among themselves. About a half of them were born in Hong Kong; the others came from different regions of China such as Canton, Sze Yap, Chiu Chow, and Shanghai. The non-Chinese include people from Britain, India, America, Australia, Portugal, Pakistan, The Philippines, Singapore, Canada, Japan, Indonesia, and West Germany, etc. Cantonese and English are the major languages in Hong Kong, but a wide variety of local dialects and other languages are still used by many ethnic and racial groups.

In Hong Kong the morphological revolution—population explosion, implosion and diversity—is certainly associated with scientific and technological development. In the past few decades, Hong Kong has been rapidly transformed from a commercial entrepot to a cosmopolitan industrial city-state. From 1951 to 1975, the total consumption of electricity increased from 354 million to 6,424 million kilowatt-hours, and the number of registered motor vehicles increased from 15 thousand to 188 thousand. During the same period, employment in manufacturing industries increased from 94 thousand to 679 thousand employees. Moreover, it has been estimated[5] that the Gross Domestic Product per capita at current market prices increased from HK$1,695 in 1960 to HK$6,764 in 1973, and that if we exclude the element of inflation, then the Gross Domestic Product per capita at constant price (the level of 1964) increased from HK$1,784 in 1960 to HK$3,978 in 1973. These statistics indicate that the technological and economic growth in Hong Kong has been phenomenal. It has attracted people from many places, especailly mailand China. At the same time, the death rate has fallen and thus facilitated the natural increase of population. From 1951 to 1975, the crude death rate increased from 10.2 to 4.9 per thousand, and the crude birth rate increased from 34 to 18.2 per thousand. Apparently there have been more births than deaths in Hong Kong.

Technological advances and a fast-growing economy have given Hong Kong the ability to absorb this rapid growth of population. Nowadays, neither unemployment nor under-employment is a major issue in Hong Kong. However, the problem that Hong Kong has grown up with is the shortage of living space. What is of great concern to the Hong Kong people today is the social and health implications of high-density living.

[5] T. Y. Cheng, *The Economy of Hong Kong*, Hong Kong: Far East Publications, 1977, Chapter 8. It should also be reported that according to the estimates by Chase Manhattan Bank (*Time*, February 5th, 1979, p. 29), the G.N.P. per capita in Hong Kong was US$2,904 in 1978, which was second only to Japan ($8,324) and Singapore ($3,205) in the entire Far East region.

In the early 1960s, an American scholar, Robert Schmitt, came to Hong Kong and was impressed by the fact that although Hong Kong was more densely populated than many cities in the United States, it had lower rates of death, disease, and social disorganization.[6] However, Hong Kong is different from American cities in many respects. Schmitt's observation cannot be taken as the conclusive statement about the effects of high density.

In the late 1960s, another American scholar, Robert Edward Mitchell, came to Hong Kong and directed the Social Survey Research Centre of The Chinese University of Hong Kong. He and his staff conducted a Study of Family Life in the urban areas of Hong Kong. A total of 3,966 individuals aged 18 and over were interviewed in 1967. Data were also collected through self-administered questionnaires from a 10 per cent sample of all Form 3 and 5 students in secondary schools.

Using part of the family life survey data, Mitchell investigated the effects of household densities on emotional health and family relationships in urban Hong Kong.[7] Household density was measured by the amount of floor space per person within the dwelling unit. Emotional health was measured by two indicators of superficial levels of strain (happiness and worry) and two indicators of more severe levels of strain (emotional illness and hostility). Family relations were indicated by husband-wife relationships (the frequency of husband-wife communications, tension in husband-wife relations, and marital happiness), parent-child relationships (the degree to which children are forced out of the house and away from the control of their parents), and the family's relationships with kin and nonkin living elsewhere.

From the survey data, Mitchell estimated that the median size of dwelling units in the urbanized areas was 400 square feet, and the median number of square feet per person was 43. Apparently, in the late 1960s urban Hong Kong had a very high degree of household density. However, it was found that high-density living within dwelling units was not associated with the more severe forms of emotional strain, and that it was associated with superficial strain for people in low-income families only. Although high-density living by itself (i.e., after controlling for income and education) apparently had little effect on emotional health, Mitchell noted that if people had to share the dwelling unit with non-related households and especially if these people could not easily escape each other by retreating outdoors, then high-density living was associated with stressful situations. Under such conditions, people were more likely to complain about the shortage of space and the lack of privacy, and

[6] Robert C. Schmitt, "Implications of Density in Hong Kong," *Journal of the American Institute of Planners*, V. 29, 1963, pp. 210-217.

[7] Robert E. Mitchell, "Some Social Implications of High Density Housing," *American Sociological Review*, V. 36, 1971, pp. 18-29.

to express emotional difficulties.

Regarding family relationships, Mitchell found that high-density living within the dwelling unit had no apparent effect on husband-wife relationships, but it had a clear impact on the relationships between parents and children. Children in high-density housing were more likely to be away from home, thus reducing parental control. Moreover, it was difficult for these young people to find a place to study, and their educational development was thus adversely affected. Mitchell also reported that high-density living within dwelling units affected the family's relationships with non-family members, because it discouraged the entertaining of neighbors and friends at home.

On the basis of the above finding, Mitchell came to the conclusion that high-density living has very little effect on individuals and families in Hong Kong. However, it is my impression that according to Mitchell's findings, high density within dwelling units is more likely to have adverse effects on family relationships (especially parent-child relationships) than on the psychosomatic state of individuals. Mitchell's conclusion seems to be overstated and should be qualified.

Mitchell's findings about the zero relationship between high density and the relatively severe forms of emotional strain are rather striking. In the study, the index of emotional illness was measured by eleven items from Langner's Twnety-Two Item Psychiatric Screening Scale. As Sheelagh E. Millar has remarked,[8] "it is questionable whether the procedure of extracting a few items from such a carefully constructed and validated scale is useful, and Mitchell does not, in fact, present evidence for a validation of his own scale of psychiatric distress." Moreover, six psychosomatic symptoms were used in the index of hostility; but, again, the index was not validated. We are, therefore, not sure to what extent Mitchell's findings on the relationship between densities and emotional strain can be trusted.

In the early 1970s, Sheelagh E. Millar of the Human Ecology Group of the Australian National University worked with Y. K. Chan of the Social Research Centre of The Chinese University of Hong Kong in conducting a Biosocial Survey. This survey was part of the Hong Kong Human Ecology Program directed by Stephen Boyden. Its major objective was to assess the long-term effects of high-density living on the biopsychic state of individuals in the urban areas of Hong Kong. The research findings were fully reported by Millar.[9] The study was based on a conceptual model consisting of the following postulates:

(1)   High-density living may produce in the individual a feeling of being crowded.

[8] Sheelagh E. Millar, *Health and Well-being in Relation to High Density Living in Hong Kong*, Doctoral Dissertation, Australian National University, 1976, p. 124.
[9] Sheelagh E. Millar, *op. cit.*

(2)   If the sensation of being crowded is not resolved, a state of frustration may develop.

(3)   The unresolved state of frustration may develop into a state of stress.

(4)   If the stress is excessive or prolonged, the individual may suffer from a state of biopsychic maladjustment.

On the basis of the above postulates, Millar hypothesized that high-density living would result in biopsychic maladjustment, but since each stage in the pathway from high density to maladjustment is subject to adaptive intervention, it was to be expected that the effects of high density would be relatively weak. To test the hypothesis, a random sample of 3,983 urban residents between the ages of 20 and 59 years were interviewed in the summer of 1974. In addition, over 200 adults from five isolated village communities were selected for interviews for the purpose of making a comparison between rural and urban responses to conditions of population density.

In the Biosocial Survey, both household and neighborhood densities were considered. The former was measured by the amount of effective floor space per person in the dwelling unit. The latter was measured by the number of persons per hectare in the census tract. The census tract used is the Tertiary Planning Unit as defined by the Government's Census & Statistics Department, and there are 111 such units in the urban area. It was found that about 43 per cent of the respondents lived in census tracts with densities of over 1,000 persons per hectare, and that only 14 per cent lived in areas with a density of less than 250 persons per hectare. Moreover, nearly a half of the respondents were residents in dwelling units with a density of less than 38 square feet of effective floor space per person. Some persons even lived in no more than a bed-space of about 10 square feet. Only 29 per cent of the respondents lived in a home with one or more rooms per person. Apparently, the survey confirmed that both the neighborhood and household densities were exceedingly high in urban Hong Kong. In subsequent analyses, Millar combined the two types of density into a composite index of physical density.

In the survey, the biopsychic state of each individual was measured by four indices: (1) general physical health, which was measured by the self-reported experience of pains and mild infectious disorders in the recent months, (2) personal distress, which was measured by Langner's Twenty-Two Item Scale taking four or more symptoms to indicate psychic maladjustment, (3) personal well-being, which was measured by Bradburn's positive affect, negative affect, and affect balance scales, and (4) enjoyment of life, which was measured by a single question concerning the extent to which the respondents found their lives generally enjoyable.[10] It should be emphasised that

[10]For Langner's scale, see T. S. Langner, "A Twenty-two Items Screening Score of Psychiatric Symptoms Indicating Impairment," *Journal of Health and Human Behavior*,

these various indices were found to have an acceptable degree of reliability and validity.[11] According to the indices, the people of urban Hong Kong tended to have relatively good health and a rather high degree of well-being, especially those with higher social and economic status. The question is: was the bio-psychic state associated with physical densities?

The survey data showed that there was a positive but relatively weak relationship between high density and biopsychic maladjustment, and that this was the case regardless of the sex, age, economic status, or educational level of the individuals. In other words, people living at a higher level of physical density were somewhat more likely to suffer from psychic distress, a poor state of general physical health, a low degree of personal well-being, and a lack of enjoyment of life. It should be noted that the adverse effect of physical density was strengthened when those with a relatively high level of education were considered alone.

Millar did not compare the effect of household density with that of neighborhood density. Reading her report, I have the impression that household density was relatively more important than neighborhood density in the determination of the biopsychic state of individuals. This impression is partly supported by Y. K. Chan's study.[12] Using part of the Biosocial Survey data, Chan found that life satisfaction was negatively correlated with household density but not with neighborhood density.

An important contribution of Millar's study was the development of the concept of density tolerance. The index of density tolerance was measured by combining the scores on two questionnaire items concerning the individual's feeling about being surrounded by a great number of people.[13] It was found that less than a third of the respondents were intolerant of high-density living, and that intolerance was unrelated to high physical density but was clearly a major source of biopsychic maladjustment. The adverse effect of intolerance of high density on maladjustment was stronger among those with low social-economic status.

Since people with tolerant attitudes were less likely to suffer from maladjustment, it is important to find out what kinds of people could develop such attitudes. It was found that the tolerance of high density was more prevalent (1) among older people, (2) among people living under high-density

---

V. 3, 1962, pp. 269-276. For Bradburn's scales, see N. M. Bradburn, *The Structure of Psychological Well-being*, Chicago: Aldine, 1969.

[11] See Sheelagh E. Millar, *op. cit.*, pp. 163-168.

[12] Y. K. Chan, "Life Satisfaction in Crowded Urban Environment," an occasional paper of the Social Research Centre, The Chinese University of Hong Kong, April 1978.

[13] See Sheelagh E. Millar, *op. cit.*, pp. 348-350.

conditions, and (3) among people of lower economic and educational status. Tolerance is also more prevalent (4) among people from the Kwangtung Province of China than those who were born in Hong Kong, and (5) in the isolated village communities than in the urban areas of Hong Kong. On the basis of these results, Millar suggested that the traditional Chinese culture might be conducive to the development of tolerant attitudes toward high-density living. On the other hand, the adoption of modern Western ideas and practices might create discontent with high-density conditions.

Millar focused merely on the biopsychic consequences of high density. She did not touch on the social implications. In a recent paper, Chan used part of the Biosocial Survey data and examined the effects of both household and neighborhood densities on attitudes toward interacting with others and on social involvement with kin, friends, and neighbors.[14] He concluded, however, that neither household nor neighborhood densities had a significant bearing upon social attitudes and relations.

Contributions to Planning and Development

Population density in the urban areas of Hong Kong is exceedingly high. As Millar has shown,[15] both household and neighborhood densities in urban Hong Kong are higher than in most other cities in the world. On the whole, however, the people in Hong Kong appear to have a rather high degree of biopsychic and social well-being.[16] Of course, this does not mean that the varying densities within urban Hong Kong do not have a differential impact on the people. Robert E. Mitchell's Family Life Study and Sheelagh E. Millar's Biosocial Survey are the two best-known studies that are concerned with the human implications of high-density living in urban Hong Kong. However, their findings are not entirely consistent with each other. In general, we may say that high-density living in urban Hong Kong does tend to have adverse effects on the biopsychic state of individuals and the relationships among family members, but the effects are relatively weak. It should be pointed out that Singapore is another modern industrial city-state in Asia with a majority of people who are Chinese in origin. Studies in Singapore have also come up with inconsistent findings, but it seems that high density per se has remarkably little effect on biopsychic maladjustment or social disorder in the Singapore populations.[17]

---

[14] Y. K. Chan, "Urban Density and Social Relations in Hong Kong," *Journal of The Chinese University of Hong Kong*, Vol. 5, No. 1, 1979, pp. 315-322.

[15] Sheelagh E. Millar, *op. cit.*, Chapter 5.

[16] Robert C. Schmitt, *op. cit.*; and Sheelagh E. Millar, *op. cit.*

[17] For a review, see Peter S. J. Chen, "Socio-psychological Implications of High-

The question arises: in terms of planning and development, what can we learn from these research findings about the effect of high-density living? In my opinion, the findings suggest that there are research needs as well as needs for improving the housing plans and development.

I. Research Needs

(1) Policy-makers and funding agencies should encourage more scientific studies to identify the adaptive or coping behavior under conditions of high density. Previous studies in Hong Kong and other countries were mostly concerned with the "causal" relationship between high density and human behavior. After years of research, we seem to have come to the conclusion that high density by itself has little effect on people. It could be that different peoples have their own special ways of coping with high-density situations, and thus do not have the feeling of being crowded. As both Mitchell and Millar have shown,[18] most people in urban Hong Kong are quite tolerant of high density. They have made few complaints about the shortage of space. Unfortunately, there have been very few social science studies aimed at identifying and probing into coping behavior. In the case of the Chinese people, I found only two such studies: one by Barbara E. Ward and another by E. N. Anderson. Ward observed the child socialization in a fishing village in Hong Kong.[19] She suggested that the early habituation to frustration and interference and the inculcation of self-control of aggressive behavior and of emotional self-reliance during childhood experience are some of the possible factors contributing significantly to the success with which Chinese adapt themselves to conditions of overcrowding. From his personal experience with a few traditional Chinese households in Hong Kong and Penang, Anderson discovered several coping mechanisms in Chinese culture, such as a stress on the desirability of several generations sharing the same dwelling unit, a definition of privacy in terms of primacy groups rather than individuals, a conformity to a hierarchy of seniority (e.g., the rule of "elders first" or "men first"), and an avoidance of social or emotional interactions among non-related persons in public spaces.[20] Although the insightful observations of Ward and Anderson have yet to be elaborated and confirmed by systematic data, their studies open

---

Density Living: With Special Reference to Hong Kong," in Peter S. J. Chen & Hans-Dieter Evers, eds., *Studies in ASEAN Sociology*, Singapore: Chopmen Enterprises, 1978.

[18] Robert E. Mitchell, *op. cit.*; and Sheelagh E. Millar, *op. cit.*

[19] Barbara E. Ward, "Temper Tantrums in Kau Sai: Some Speculations Upon their Effects," in Philip Mayer, ed., *Socialization: The Approach From Social Anthropology*, London: Tavistock, 1970.

[20] E. N. Anderson, Jr., "Some Chinese Methods of Dealing With Crowding," *Urban Anthropology*, V. 1, 1972, pp. 146-151.

up a fruitful area for future research. There are social-cultural mechanisms other than those suggested by Ward and Anderson, such as the time-scheduling of activities, the cultural habit of using the same space for multiple purposes (e.g., sleeping, dining, reading, and entertaining), the popular use of compact furniture in the household (e.g., futon in Japan, sofa-cum-beds in Indian cities, and double-deck beds in Hong Kong), the first-come-first-served principle in public service, the cultural acceptance of a relatively close spatial distance between individuals, the custom of entertaining friends in restaurants rather than homes, the establishment of hourly-rate hotels for couples or lovers to make love, and the popularization of "space-intensive" games (e.g., majong in Hong Kong and pachinko in Japan).

Besides the social-cultural mechanisms, there are physical defenses such as walls, curtains, fences, doors, windows, pictures, color of enclosing walls, and shape of the room. There are also internal psychological devices, such as perceptual and cognitive withdrawal, day dreaming, and fantasy.[21]

The various kinds of coping mechanisms—physical, social-cultural, and psychological—have to be discovered. And once they are discovered, they should be systematically verified. It is noted that very few anthropologists have been engaged in the study of high-density living. It might be that anthropologists are traditionally more concerned with rural or tribal communities than the densely-populated urban societies. Perhaps it is time to invite anthropologists to come and search for coping behaviors through some form of participant observation. Their insights can then be verified by sociologists or psychologists in a more controlled setting or with more representative samples.

The size of population and its concentration in urban areas will continue to increase. In Hong Kong, for instance, despite the success of the family planning program the population is now growing at the rate of about 2 per cent a year. Moreover, the number of women in the fertile age group is expected to increase substantially in the coming ten years. The identification of coping mechanisms in the various population groups would have many policy implications. It could tell us how to increase people's ability to survive and even enjoy themselves under conditions of high density. In particular, I would like to press for more studies of coping behavior in Asian cities, as they generally have a very high level of density living. Perhaps coping with high density is one of the beneficial kinds of knowledge and experience that people in the West can learn from the East.

(2) There are research needs on the long-term effects or recurrent

[21]For more discussion, see A. Rapoport, "Toward a Redefinition of Density," *Environment & Behaviour*, V. 7, 1975, pp. 133-158; and S. C. Choi, A. Mirjafari & H. B. Weaver, *op.cit.*

experience with high-density in non-residential areas. Previous studies in Hong Kong and elsewhere have mostly dealt with the effect of household or neighborhood densities. However, many people do not spend that much time at home or in the immediate surroundings of home. They have to go and work in factories, commercial concerns or government offices, to go and study in schools, to go and shop in markets and department stores, and to go and watch films or live shows, etc. Their recurrent experiences with traffic congestion and with high density in the various non-residential settings may have their own implications for their health and social well-being. Are there adverse effects? And what are the coping mechanisms? These questions have to be systematically studied.

(3) The possible positive effect of high density should not be ignored and should be researched. Previous studies in Hong Kong and elsewhere have mostly been based on the stress model, which tends to emphasize the adverse effects of high-density living but neglect the possible positive effects. Quite a few scholars have suggested that high-density living may be good rather than bad. For instance, it has been argued that (a) high density is a pre-requisite to the development of the division of labor and specialization, because it provides more talents and abilities of different kinds and also it reduces the time and cost for the exchange of goods and information; (b) dense living provides more chances for mutual stimulation and is thus conducive to technical and cultural innovations; and (c) dense living allows more opportunities for access to supportive and intimate relationships, and is thus good for social integration.[22] In an extensive study of American cities, Galle and his associates in fact found that high density was inversely related to homicide and suicide rates.[23] Freedman also reports that within poor neighborhoods in New York city, density is negatively related to juvenile delinquency.[24] Recently, Freedman formulated his "density-intensity" theory, arguing that high density by itself has neither good nor bad effects but that it merely serves to intensify the normal reaction, making a bad experience worse and good experience better.[25] In a series of experiments, he demonstrated that if people like each other, placing them in a crowded situation increase their friendliness. These various arguments and empirical studies clearly indicate a

[22] See E. Durkheim, *The Division of Labour in Society*, G. Simpson Translation, Free Press, 1933; H. H. Winsborough, *op. cit.*; A. Hawley, "Population Density and the City," *Demography*, V. 9, 1972, pp. 521-529; and Jonathan L. Freedman, 1975, *op. cit.*, Chapter 9.

[23] O. R. Galle, J. D. Megarthy & W. Gove, "Population Density and Pathology," a paper presented at the Annual Meeting of the Population Association of America, New York, 1974.

[24] Jonathan L. Freedman, 1975, *op. cit.*, Appendix 2.

[25] Jonathan L. Freedman, 1975, *op. cit.*

need for studies of the possible positive effects of high density and especially the conditions under which the positive effects of high density can be strengthened.

II. Needs for the Improvement of Housing Plans and Development

(1) No matter what the results of such studies may be, however, there is no doubt that residential space should be increased. In a very densely populated city like Hong Kong, the adverse effect of high-density living on people may be relatively weak but, nevertheless, there are effects. Mitchell's Family Life Study has demonstrated the adverse effect of high household density on family relationships and especially the parent-child relationships, and Millar's Biosocial Survey found some effects of high physical density (especially household density) on biopsychic maladjustment. More important, as Millar has observed, education plays an important role in the effect of high-density living. The better-educated are more likely to suffer from high-density situations and they also tend to be less tolerant of high density. An important trend in Hong Kong as well as other parts of the world is the expansion of formal education. An increasing number of people are able to receive an increasingly higher level of schooling. In the years to come, therefore, people are likely to demand more living space. Failure to meet this increasing demand may create stressful situations. It is not only desirable, but also a matter of necessity, that housing plans should allocate more space for residential purposes.

An important strategy of the Hong Kong Government for the alleviation of high densities in urban areas is the development of new satellite towns on the periphery of existing city areas and the construction of public housing estates in these new towns.[26]

Currently, public housing accommodates about 46 per cent of the total population in Hong Kong. In the public housing estates, the minimum floor space per person within the dwelling unit has increased from 24 square feet in 1954 to 35 square feet in 1970. Such an increase is good, but in view of the probable concomitants of expanding education, the trend should continue.

The development of new towns provides not only better housing, but also more services and open space in the surrounding areas. However, research findings seem to indicate that although the alleviation of neighborhood density is obviously desirable, nevertheless relatively speaking it is not as urgent as the widening of the living space within dwelling units, since it has been demonstrated that household density appears to be more likely than neighborhood

[26]C. Y. Choi & Y. K. Chan, "Housing Policy and Internal Movement of Population: A Study of Kwun Tong, A Chinese New Town in Hong Kong," an occasional paper of the Social Research Centre, The Chinese University of Hong Kong, February 1977.

density to have adverse effects on human beings.

How do we increase household space? In view of the limited ground area in Hong Kong and other cities, the construction of multi-storey buildings should not discouraged. What is important is that each household should have more space in which to live. Under the condition of space shortage, only high-rise blocks can provide more space to the households. It should here be noted that, as Freedman has argued and as Mitchell and Chen have testified, in Hong Kong and Singapore high-rise living by itself does not seem to have adverse effects on residents.[27] It is the social, rather than the physical, features of high-rises that affect people. As I shall discuss later, what is most needed is the development of close interpersonal relations among the residents.

(2) Social planning should be included in housing development. Like some other countries, Hong Kong's development of new towns and housing estates primarily based on physical plans. In the planning process, the buildings and the physical surroundings are thoroughly considered, but not the people who will make use of the physical facilities. The stress on physical planning has resulted in a low degree of community consciousness, a lack of neighborly interactions, and an under-utilization of public space and facilities;[28] even worse, it seems likely that such undesirable social conditions may well strengthen the adverse effects of high-density living.

In his study of Hong Kong family life, Mitchell found that a high-density of living within the dwelling unit is a source of stress only if the people are unrelated to each other.[29] In other words, if the people develop close interpersonal relationships, they are less likely to suffer from the high-density situation. Mitchell's finding is, in a way, consistent with Freedman's theory of density-intensity discussed earlier. This theory states that high density by itself has neither good effects nor bad effects on people but rather serves to intensify the individual's typical reactions, whatever they are.[30] Hence, if a person ordinarily finds the circumstances pleasant, he would have a more positive reaction under conditions of high density; otherwise, he would have a more negative reaction.

Mitchell's finding and Freedman's well-formulated theory indicate the

---

[27] Jonathan L. Freedman, 1975, *op. cit.*; Robert E. Mitchell, *op. cit.*; and Peter S. J. Chen, *op. cit.*

[28] Y. K. Chan, "The Rise and Growth of Kwun Tong: A Study of Planned Urban Development," an occasional paper of the Social Research Centre, The Chinese University of Hong Kong, August 1973; and Angela W. S. Kan, "Implications of Concentrated Utilization of Local Facilities and Services in Public Housing Estates in Hong Kong," an occasional paper of the Social Research Centre, The Chinese University of Hong Kong, April 1975.

[29] Robert E. Mitchell, *op. cit.*

[30] Jonathan L. Freedman, 1975, *op. cit.*, Chapter 8.

importance of social planning in housing and new town development. If we can mobilize the residents and organize them into meaningful social networks, then high density may not have adverse effects and may even have some positive effects. In the case of multi-storey buildings, social planning in even more essential. As Mitchell has shown, residents on the upper floors are more likely to be adversely affected by high density because they are forced to interact with non-related persons. If we develop social plans to turn the "strangers" into friends, high-density living in high-rises may not affect the residents adversely.

The Hong Kong Government has taken the initiative formulating Mutual Aid Committees in public housing estates and Owner's Corporations in private multi-storey buildings. The major function of these organizations at the grass-root level, however, has been limited to managing the building and upholding environmental standards. In my opinion, the function of these ogranizations should be strengthened, and they should also aim at creating close social networks among residents. If the residents become friends with each other, they would unlikely be disturbed by their high-density situation.

Furthermore, whenever possible the social backgrounds and the previous relationships among applicants should be taken into consideration when allocating public housing units. If the new residents in the same estate have similar occupational and ethnic backgrounds and if they have previously had some friendship or kinship ties, then it will be easier for them to communicate with each other and to organize themselves into meaningful social groups.

In short, one of the ways to alleviate the possible adverse effects of high density is to foster close interpersonal relationships among residents. A purely physical plan, no matter how thorough, cannot ensure the emergence of a sense of community or neighborliness. Social plans have to be formulated. Perhaps, the government should institute a social planning body within the housing or new town development office for the specific purpose of building up community spirit and creating strong social networks.

(3) When the housing estates are designed, it is the biosocial implications rather than the time and cost that should be borne in mind. As Hong Kong has been under such great pressure from the housing shortage, the government and the private investors have been constructing buildings as cheaply and quickly as possible. The design of the buildings, however, are bound to have some implications for the well-being of the residents. In their well-conducted study of student dormitories in the United States, Baum and Valins observed that residents in suite-type buildings were less likely than those in corridor-type buildings to manifest a syndrome of stress, and that on the contrary they were more likely to form friendship groups.[31] Baum and Valins therefore proposed

[31] A. Baum & S. Valins, *op. cit.*

that a building should be designed so as to permit the clustering of residents in smaller groups around semi-private or controlled-access public spaces. It is noteworthy that Freedman made a similar proposal, on the basis of his own empirical studies.[32] He proposed that the anonymity of high-rise housing would be reduced by breaking up the corridors into separate units, and by providing small play areas and social areas for each floor or set of floors. It should be recognized that the modification of the social features of housing is an important mechanism for alleviating the ill effects of high-density living, but the extent to which we can modify the interpersonal relationships is at least largely dependent on the physical layouts. Moreover, as Mitchell learnt from his Hong Kong family life research, some social features of housing affect individuals only if they are under certain physical conditions.[33] For instance, he found that sharing arrangements only affect residents on the upper floors, because these people are forced into close interaction with non-related persons while those on the low floors can easily escape each other by retreating outdoors.

We suggest, therefore, that housing design itself can play an important part in alleviating the adverse effects of high-density living. Housing in Hong Kong has been designed in many forms, such as H-shape, L-shape, U-shape, twin-cross shape, twin-tower shape, and corridor-shape, etc., but these differences have mostly been considered from an architectural point of view and their implications for the health and social well-being of the people living under the conditions of high density they provide have not been systematically assessed. The government and funding agencies should, therefore, encourage social science studies of these matters so that buildings may be designed in such a way that the negative effects of high-density living are minimized while the positive effects are maximized. As the population will certainly continue to grow and concentrate increasingly in urban areas, so the problems are likely to increase steadily and scientific studies of the social concomitants of various types of housing would have many policy implications for Hong Kong.

[32] Jonathan L. Freedman, 1975, *op. cit.*, Chapter 10.
[33] Robert E. Mitchell, *op. cit.*

Chapter 2

Residents' Images of a Hong Kong Resettlement Estate: A View from the "Chicken Coop"*

John T. Myers

Introduction

Low-cost public housing complexes as life settings have a decidedly negative image in the urban literature. American housing projects as portrayed in the well-known works of Moore (1969), Rainwater (1970), and Yancey (1971) are almost indelibly linked with social breakdown and anomie. A common image of Third World public housing is that of an environment where traditional social institutions which flourished in and bound together not only rural villages but urban squatter districts as well have atropied without being replaced by viable alternatives, see Safa (1974), Marris (1960), and Muller (1975). It may be surprising therefore to discover that the negative image of public housing as a life environment is not universal. There exists a type of lower-income housing complex that enjoys a markedly positive image in the urban literature, the Hong Kong resettlement estate. Accommodating approximately one million of that Colony's four million plus population in structures with minimal amenities and maximal densities the estates share in Hong Kong's general image as a location where seemingly intolerable densities have failed to issue in social breakdown (Michelson 1976:154-155) and where poverty has yet to generate a culture of poverty (Glazer 1969:30-31). That positive image has not only provided a substantive counterexample to the axiomatic association of social ills with public housing but has also provided foundation for the assertion that the Hong Kong model, complete with minimal spatial standards and amenities, be applied to other Asian communities (Wheaton and Wheaton 1972:150-151).

My aim here is to examine the empirical and theoretical basis of that positive image in the light of field research, 1972-1976, in one of Hong Kong's

*The research on which this paper is based was supported by an Andrew Mellon Pre-Doctoral Fellowship from the Department of Anthropology, The University of Pittsburgh, and grants from the Social Research Centre and the Institute of Chinese Studies, The Chinese University of Hong Kong. I also wish to thank Ivan Karp and Judith Hansen for helpful comments on earlier versions of the paper.

older and more populous resettlement estates, the Kwun Tong Resettlement Estate. To do this I will discuss the foundations of the positive image suggested by existing literature and then consider the images of the housing estates as life environments expressed by the residents. I will argue that the image dominating the urban literature suffers crucial weaknesses arising from the analytic and temporal limitations of its data base. The field research upon which this article is based reveals that the resettlement estate experience is too complex for adequate representation in a discretely positive or negative image. I suggest that the nature and source of that complexity can be understood through careful examination of the life experiences of residents and their personal assessments of the estates as life environments.

The Positive Image

A search for the scholarly origins of the positive image enjoyed by Hong Kong's public housing begins and virtually ends with an article by Schmitt (1963) entitled "The Implications of Density in Hong Kong." Although the article deals with urban Hong Kong in general and many facets of man's reaction to density special mention is included of the viability of social life in Hong Kong's, then, recently constructed resettlement estates. The importance of that article is apparent when one recognizes that it is the sole source cited by Michelson (1976:154-155) and Glazer (1969:30-31) in their respective discussions of the benign implications of Hong Kong's high density and its lack of a culture of poverty. My concern in the present paper will be solely with the data and arguments presented by Schmitt (1963) to support his positive assessment of social life in the resettlement estates.

As proposed by Schmitt (1963:215-216) the social dimension of the positive image is predicated on the comparison of selected indicators of social "disorganization": in contrast to American congested areas Hong Kong is seen as less prone to disorganization. Schmitt (1963) makes no effort to formulate indicators of social "organization" and the only indicators of "disorganization" used are official statistics on juvenile delinquency and adult crime. Writing several years later Hopkins (1972:202-203) enhances the image of the resettlement estate by using the same indicators to illustrate that crime rates in the resettlement estates are lower than in private housing sectors of the Colony. In both Schmitt's (1963) and Hopkins' (1972) articles crime rates are treated both as inter- and intra-cultural constants without sufficient allowance for the possibility that the rates themselves may be variables embedded in and thus reflective of local coding and reporting procedures. Criminologists increasingly recognize official crime statistics as indicators of a society's selection and enforcement priorities rather than a useful device for measuring social disorder, see Philipson (1974:90-106). The possible effect of cumbersome reporting procedures on crime statistics is indicated by the dramatic 17% rise in the number of reported crimes that occurred in Hong Kong during 1973. That rise followed a revision of the reporting process which included simplification of paperwork and the opening of local reporting centres in resettlement estates and other poorer districts in the Colony (Hong Kong 1974:107-108).

Even if one were to suspend criticism and allow for the possibility that a comparatively favourable crime profile denotes a viable social system the task remains of identifying the factors that account for the existence of low crime rates in Hong Kong. To explain that phenomenon Schmitt (1963:216) relys on the recitation of well-known anecdotes about the influence on the local population of "long established Chinese traditions," "natural gregariousness," and "family cohesiveness." The above factors are neither defined nor related to a substantive body of data testifying to their influence, they are simply presented as featureless forces controlling the behaviour of the population.

The positive image which has been so critical in shaping the presentation of the Hong Kong public housing experience in the urban literature is an image constructed single-handedly by a scholar using only his unverified perception of the critical features which characterize a viable social setting. That analytic image is akin to Spradley's (1972:44) concept of the "sociological model" of the urban drunk. It is a model that may reveal more about the analyst's world than the drunk's. The image of life in the Hong Kong resettlement estate that we seek is more akin to Spradley's "ethnographic model" which "aims at discovering the insider's view of his social world" (1972:44). Our concern is with the image of the resident users, a view long neglected by analysts but one that must be dealt with in future attempts to assess the Hong Kong resettlement estate experience and to utilize that experience for cross-cultural comparison.

Another weakness of the positive image is its continued reliance on data reflecting only the initial years of the resettlement estates' existence. Cooper's (1975) longitudinal study of Easter Hill Village vividly illustrates the dramatic changes that can occur over a period of slightly more than a decade in a public housing setting. Since the basic data for this paper was collected in an estate opened over a decade before the research was undertaken it is possible to test for possible changes that may have occurred over time in the residents' evaluation of their estate environment.

Hong Kong and Its Resettlement Estates

The resettlement estates exist in a spatio-political entity that is a living, thriving anachronism; a colony on the sovereign territory of one of the world's most vocally anti-colonial nations, The People's Republic of China. Established in 1841 as a consequence of the First Opium War, Hong Kong was intended by the British to serve as a "factory" in the East Indian sense of the term. It was to be primarily a commercial centre, not a residential settlement (Endicott 1973:14-25). Ideally it was envisioned as host to a small transient European community with only enough Chinese to service the commercial and domestic needs of the European residents. Almost from the moment of its inception that plan was destined for frustration. The Colony became a haven attracting Chinese seeking refuge from political and/or economic unrest in 19th and 20th century China.

The Colony's territory and its population expanded rapidly. In 1860 the 4.3 sq. miles of the Kowloon Peninsula were added to Hong Kong Island's 29.2 sq. miles. 1898 witnessed the addition of the 370 sq. miles of rural and insular New Territories leased from China for 99 years. With the subsequent addition of reclaimed seabed the Colony achieved its present land mass of 390 sq. miles (Hong Kong 1976:192-194). The population increased rapidly in the last half of the 19th and early decades of the 20th century until the Japanese occupation, 1941-1945. The Japanese judging Hong Kong to be vastly overcrowded systematically reduced a pre-occupation population of 1,200,000 to a 1945 figure of barely 500,000. The most dramatic population increase in the Colony's history occurred between 1946 and 1952. Returning prior residents and migrants from China swelled the total to over 2,000,000, the great majority of whom settled into the dense urban sectors of Hong Kong Island and Kowloon. Hundreds of thousands found the only available residence to be in squatter camps ringing the urban districts (Pryor 1973).

The early 1950s was an especially critical period in Hong Kong's history. Not only was the Colony inundated with homeless migrants but its economic survival was threatened by the United Nations embargo on its trade with China which was imposed because of the Korean War. To cope with that situation Hong Kong officials undertook a programme of rapid industrialization relying on the technical skills and capital of displaced Shanghainese businessmen and the plentiful supply of cheap labour represented by the urban squatters. A crucial ingredient in the programme was the resettlement of squatters into multi-storeyed housing estates near planned industrial complexes. Since the squatter districts were regularly plagued by fires during Hong Kong's dry winters and landslides amidst the summer monsoons, it is hardly surprising to discover that the squatters offered little objection to the resettlement programme.

The master plan for industrial development included the establishment of residential-industrial "new towns" on unsettled land adjacent to the Colony's built-up urban sector. Kwun Tong, a district located on the eastern tip of the

Kowloon Peninsula, was designated the first "new town" to be developed. Situated on land formerly used as Kowloon's main garbage dump Kwun Tong has in the 21 years of its existence, 1957-1978, become a residential community of 500,000 almost 80% of whom reside in the district's eleven major public housing estates. Of the remainder approximately 13% live in low-cost private tenements or medium priced apartments while the rest reside in squatter camps, small cottage districts, or industrial buildings (Chan 1973:20). The first resettlement estate constructed in Kwun Tong opened in 1959. Officially designated the Tsui Ping Road Resettlement Estate it is known colloquially by residents and non-residents alike as Kaai Liu 雞寮 —The Chicken Coop. That label is not generally interpreted by residents as derogatory since it denotes the use the land served prior to the estate's construction rather than an overt judgment on the estate itself or its population. It is this estate that served as field site for my research.

The "Chicken Coop" and Its People

During the field research period the estate's population numbered slightly over 57,000 individuals. Residency is assigned by the government and is limited to those previously located in urban squatter camps or condemned tenements. The Tsui Ping Road Estate consists physically of twenty residential blocks. Each block is composed of six-storey residential wings joined at the centre by a connecting corridor giving an H-shaped appearance when viewed from above. There are no elevators, access to the individual living units is by way of balconies on the outside of each residential floor. Spatial allotments are 24 sq. feet per adult and half of that for children ten and under. Plumbing facilities are not included in the individual living units. Communal washrooms and toilets, segregated according to sex, are located in the connecting corridors of each floor. Cooking is ordinarily handled on the balcony passage-way of each unit. The roof-tops of selected blocks are fenced and used as primary schools for local children. The ground floors are given over to specialty shops, markets, and restaurants serving the local populations. The Tsui Ping Road Estate represents one of the last complexes to be built according to the architectural design described above. After 1961 the government began introducing new types providing more amenities for residents (Commissioner For Resettlement 1972-1973:28).

Approximately 75% of the estate's work force is employed in Kwun Tong's factory district within easy walking distance of the estate. The remainder find employment in low-level service occupations or as labourers elsewhere in the Colony's urban sector. Average salaries range between $100 and $125 U.S. per month. Rents average about $4 U.S. per month for a family of four.

Few families rely on a single salary, and it is common for children at age 15-16 to leave school and seek menial work in the local factory district. The greater portion of their earnings is regularly handed over to the parents for the family purse. Even the elderly try to remain economically productive by collecting take home piece-work from local factories. Residents are in general agreement that their present economic circumstances are better than in the early years of resettlement. That current sense of relative prosperity is borne out in the government's 1975 statement that the real wages, i.e. adjusted for inflation, of the industrial workforce had risen 46% since the early 1960s (Hong Kong 1974:38).

Since an ill-defined "family cohesiveness" plays a significant explanatory role in Schmitt's (1963) rendition of Hong Kong's positive image it is appropriate to briefly consider the Tsui Ping Road Estate family. Structurally, the estate is composed exclusively of nuclear families with the occasional addition of a grandparent. The traditional Chinese extended joint family, *daih ga teng* 大家庭, which represented in Levi-Strauss' (1967:275-281) terminology the "mechanical" if not always the "statistical" model of Chinese family organization, is simply not possible in the estate setting. More important than the "de facto" prevalence of the nuclear family, *siu ga teng* 小家庭, is the fact that residents questioned about their concept of the ideal residential family unit, tended to favour the contemporary format rather than the traditional *daih ga teng*.[1]

Another important change is in the pattern of intra-familial relationships. Hsu (1972:516) posits that relationships within the traditional nuclear unit are patterned by the influence of a dominant father-son dyad. The absolute authority of the male parent over his son sets the tone for his authoritative relationship with other members of the family as well. Changes in the traditional pattern of paternal authority are difficult to document statistically because few fathers dare risk "loss of face" through public discussion of such a sensitive issue. As I became on familiar terms with male household heads it was unusual to find one who did not admit that the exercise of his traditional male authority was becoming increasingly difficult in the estate. Informants were virtually unanimous in attributing the problem to the increased availability of employment for younger members of the family. Typical is one father's remark: "My son and daughter are now working at the textile factory and making a decent salary. This is good for the family pocketbook but bad for harmonious relationships within the family. Since my children have

[1] In a 1972 survey conducted by the Social Research Centre of The Chinese University less than 10% of 450 respondents indicated a preference for an expanded family (Shively 1972:25). My own extended questioning of selected informants revealed few instances where the traditional family remained an ideal.

become wage-earners they've also become more demanding and simply don't pay attention to my wishes anymore."

It is impossible to determine whether the above changes in attitude and behaviour are recent developments or can be traced as far back as the earliest period of the estate's habitation. That lack of evidence coupled with recent data on key changes in family structure and relational patterns renders questionable attempts to account for the estates' social characteristics in terms of the assumed strength of traditional institutions and the general notion of Chinese family cohesiveness. It would be unwise, however, to write off the family as an important contributor to the social environment as perceived by residents. In fact, it is in terms of the family as a source of both individual and social identity that residents express their images of the estate.

The Residents' Image

During the initial months of field research I was concerned primarily with religious practices within the estate, but, toward the end of the usual schedule of questions were several inquiring directly about the quality of estate life and the residents' opinions about the estate. One was a simple query asking whether or not in their view the estate was a good place to live. Subsequent questions elicited their judgments about the major good points and the most bothersome negative features of their local public housing environment. Among my initial thirty informants there was an almost unanimous positive response to the question asking whether the estate was a good or bad place to live. Subsequent questions revealed that the most important positive points were the low rents and the basic improvement in life quality and safety that the estates offered compared to their previous habitats. The most commonly cited negative features were the noise, the lack of ventilation, and the frequent occurrence of petty crime. When asked to describe the estate as succinctly as possible the most common expression was, "A place where ordinary families live"—*po tung ga teng deih fong* 普通家庭地方 .

A subsequent comparison of the above data with survey results obtained by sociologists studying wider Kwun Tong revealed that in their sample of several hundred estate residents about one-third offered a negative response to questions about their local environment (Shively 1972:103). An analysis of that survey's negative responses revealed that a majority were from younger residents, i.e. twenty-five years and below. Since my previous informants had all been in their 30s or older I then put my same set of questions to a group of younger informants. As their elders had dwelt on the benefits of the estate so the younger informants emphasized negative features. None gave a firm positive response to the question asking whether the estate was a good place to live. When requested to characterize the estate succinctly the most common expression used was, "A place where problematic families live"—*maan taih ga teng deih fong* 問題家庭地方 .

The continued importance of family membership as a source of social identity is evidenced in the use of *ga teng* 家庭 (family) rather than *yahn* 人 (individual) to define the estate and its inhabitants. The relationship between the two definitions and their respective implications for the residents' social identity can be understood in the context of the resettlement estate dweller's conceptual model of Hong Kong society.

Hong Kong Society: A Resettlement Estate View

To the average resident of the Tsui Ping Road Estate Hong Kong society is divided into two major segments only one of which is of active importance in his or her everyday existence. The unimportant segment is the one designated as *saiyahn she hwui* 西人社會 or "Western society." This segment is composed of and patterned by Europeans and other Westerners who are viewed as temporary sojourners on Chinese soil. Although the Western segment is numerically small, i.e. approximately 3% of the total population, its members occupy most of the important decision making positions in Hong Kong official-dom. Resettlement estate residents, however, have only the rarest and most instrumental of contacts with that segment of society. The second major component of society is simply termed *bundei she hwui* 本地社會 or *jungkwok she hwui* 中國社會 —"local (native) society" or "Chinese society." It is this segment that is of immediate and personal concern to the estate dweller.

Traditional Chinese society consisted of two major ranked groupings; the gentry families, and the *baai sing ga teng* 百姓家庭 —the ordinary families. In Hong Kong as well as in post-imperial China the gentry as a socially recognized category has ceased to exist. Inquiries about the major components of Hong Kong Chinese society drew a variety of responses from resettlement estate residents. Some schemes accentuated linguistic group and native region identities while others emphasized educational attainment and occupation as critical features. The scheme most relevant to the present analysis is one in which estate residents placed themselves in a single category. Its most distinctive criteria are economic and residential. That particular scheme offers insight into the Hong Kong public housing experience as well as a conceptual framework for comparing it with public housing experiences in other ethnographic settings.

The scheme consists of four categories differentiated according to relative wealth and residential setting: *daih fu ga teng* 大富家庭 ; *siu hong ga teng* 小康家庭 ; *po tung ga teng* 普通家庭 ; *maan taih ga teng* 問題家庭 .

Daih fu ga teng: This group translates literally as "families with great wealth." These families are identified as those of the successful Hong Kong business entrepreneur. They are characterized by conspicuous spending and residence in the palatial mansions within the Colony's elite districts. *Daih fu* families are chauffered in or drive expensive European cars, send their children abroad for schooling, and sit on the boards of Hong Kong's Chinese hospitals and charitable organizations. The resettlement estate population has few direct contacts with individuals from that sector of Chinese society, but those that do exist are carefully nurtured. An example is the "Honorary President" of a temple in the estate who is treated with great deference and ceremony on his occasional visits to the temple. He, in return, is expected to act as patron through financial generosity and/or use of influence when the temple needs either commodity (Myers and Leung 1974).

Siu hong ga teng: This group translates as a "family with some wealth." Their residence in the newer and more expensive private apartment districts of the city is judged as a reliable indication of their possessing a moderate economic surplus. The life style of this family type includes ownership of a moderately priced European or Japanese automobile, private school for the children, a household servant, and frequent dining at better restaurants. It is not unusual to find estate residents with relatives who fit into this particular category which is composed largely of moderately successful businessmen, teachers, managers, and professionals.

Po tung ga teng: This category refers literally to "ordinary families." The ordinary families of Hong Kong, as defined by estate residents, live in public housing, densely populated private tenements, and some of the better maintained squatter districts. Although especially in recent years, the ordinary family may possess some surplus and an active savings account it does not manage to accumulate enough for substantial purchases nor to achieve economic security against illness or loss of employment. Seldom, however, is the contemporary "ordinary family" on the brink of financial desperation, most can afford television sets, small household appliances, and occasional visits to local restaurants. The older estate residents view themselves and the majority of Hong Kong's Chinese population as included in the *po tung* category.

Maan taih ga teng: This expression translates as the "family with problems." This type of family is considered a failure in the sense that it is consistently unable to meet its ordinary and necessary economic obligations. The exact source of the problem may vary, in some instances it is attributed to "bad luck," i.e. sickness or death of a key wage-earner; in other instances it is occasioned by "moral weakness," e.g. drug addiction, laziness, or excessive gambling. The *maan taih* household is forced to rely on relatives, neighbours, the government, or private relief agencies for essential support. The *maan taih* image is perceived as a stigma of failure and it was fear of acquiring that stigma which led some older estate residents to ignore the government's recently introduced old age allotment of $15 U.S. per month for those over 75. An 80-year-old informant explained her refusal to register for the allotment, "If I go to the government for the money it would be like telling the world that my son is unable to adequately support me. It would cause him to 'lose face' and make his household appear *maan taih*." Adult residents of the estate recognize that there are some *maan taih* families in their midst but add that their numbers are small. Estate residents aver that a greater portion of such families are apt to be found in squatter districts.

A crucial disagreement emerges between the judgments expressed by older and younger informants about the category into which estate residents fit. The middle aged and older, unlike their American public housing counterparts, view the estate population as "ordinary people" without a stigma of failure. The estate's drawbacks as a physical setting are recognized but are judged favourable against the remembered conditions in squatter camps as well as the situation in China prior to migration. For this group the image of the estate is basically a positive one, to borrow Rapoport's (1976:10) metaphor, their image of the physical setting is "filtered" through their accumulated past experiences and their image of themselves and place in wider Hong Kong society.

The above image of the estate and its population is not the only one expressed by Tsui Ping Road residents. For many in the younger age group, especially those in their teens and early twenties, the estate image as well as their familial based self-image differs markedly from that of their elders. The images of the young tend to be decidedly negative. That negative image is not purely a locally produced and held phenomenon, I suggest that it also reflects an image of the estate and its population that is becoming widely accepted among the more well-to-do segments of Hong Kong society both Chinese and Western. This image is reflected in local newspapers and other media that no longer emphasize the tremendous rehousing feat accomplished by the estate programme but rather the problems of unsightly, crowded, and crime-infested resettlement estates. The Government itself recognizing that conditions in the estates have deteriorated has in recent years instituted programmes aimed at countering some of the more obvious problems like uncleanliness and over-crowding (Commissioner for Resettlement 1972-1973:11-14).

Since the early 1970s the government's involvement with public housing construction no longer centres on the rehousing of urban squatters but has centred on the construction of a more expensive variety of public project known as the Low Cost Housing Estate. These complexes are architecturally more attractive, contain basic plumbing and cooking facilities within each unit, and rent for three to four times more per month than do the resettlement estate units. In the last several years approximately two hundred families from the Tsui Ping Road Estate have moved to the new complexes. When asked the reasons for their move former estate residents invariably listed as one of their primary reasons the pressures exerted by younger family members for a more attractive and comfortable home. Among the younger generation of the estate there is a trend toward reassessment of their elders' definition of the *po tung* category as including only Low Cost housing families and private housing dwellers with the resettlement estates viewed as the habitat of *maan taih ga teng*.

Reaction to the changing image of the estates takes variant forms among the younger generation. For the more upwardly mobile and better educated the primary reaction tends to be embarrassment. That feeling is expressed in the tendency of young job applicants seeking positions outside of the estate to list on their application forms the address of a relative or close friend residing in a more "respectable" setting. Young estate residents dating outsiders will often arrange their meetings at more acceptable addresses. Among the poorly educated whose future is perceived as bleak there is an increasing tendency toward involvement in petty and locally organized crime. Whether or not borne out by official statistics the local residents are convinced that there has been a marked rise in crime among the young in the last several years. Petty triad societies modelled on the secret brotherhoods of traditional China (Ho 1972) are reported by police and local residents as plentiful in the estate. Often divided according to linguistic group identity and led by accomplished criminals the triads are composed in the main youngsters in their teens and twenties. The triads engage in a variety of activities such as extortion from local merchants and control of illegal gambling. Lack of confidence in the police and a reluctance to become involved with authorities have led residents of several estates to organize vigilante societies aimed at combating petty criminals. The relationship between the vigilante groups and the police is not a totally happy one since the vigilantes feel that the police are too lenient and therefore take the prerogative of administering instant punishment. The vigilante groups in the Tsui Ping Road Estate are organized and manned mainly by the middle-aged and elderly who define crime as a youth problem occasioned by a permissive society. The youth define the problem in terms of their immediate life setting which offers little dignity and a social system that renders mobility, especially for the poorly educated, little more than a dream. It is in the point of view expressed by the young that one notes a convergence with the image of failure that dominates the American public housing project (Moore 1969:11).

The competing ethnographic images of the estate as a *po tung ga teng* or a *maan taih ga teng deih fong* reflect more than simple disagreement over fine points of definition, rather, they flow from crucial differences in life experiences, expectations, and self-image. D. Karp *et al.* (1977:81) reminds us that "we don't so much live in communities as we do live in our interpretations of the community within which we live." Interpretations of a community as a life environment are not simply the product of exposure to its physical characteristics; if that were the case then the images of the estate held by younger generations should be more positive than that of their elders. In recent years there have been improvements in the physical setting, i.e. the addition of new recreational facilities, improvement of sanitation, and the steady process of enlarging living quarters through assignment of large families to two adjacent units rather than a single unit. The pivotal change, however, is in the interpretation of the estate population's relationship to wider society. Younger estate residents have few memories of the squatter camps and of a Hong Kong where most residents live in resettlement estates, crowded tenements, or squatter huts. Their world includes the Low Cost Housing Estate whose very name and physical attractiveness denotes success of a modest nature. The resettlement estates are increasingly judged to be the habitat of the "failed" and the "problematic."

I do not mean to imply that all members of the younger generation share in the negative judgment but I am suggesting that it represents a trend of the present that will increase as the young estate dwellers become more and more aware of their relative position in Hong Kong society. This trend also illustrates the danger of any attempt to portray the estate experience in unitary terms. Neither a positive nor a negative image alone does justice to the complexity of Hong Kong's resettlement estate experience. It should also provide a cautionary note to planners who suggest Hong Kong's minimal standards as a model for other Asian localities. They do well to heed the warning given by Epstein (1972:57-58) to those who envisioned the solution to Brasilia's housing shortage as the increased construction of squatter camps. He posits that what the new residents of such quarters may see today as a basic improvement in life situation may be entirely lost in the next generation. What is viewed as an initial solution may in fact heighten the long-term problem of providing adequate housing for the less well-to-do segment of the population.

Conclusion

Exclusive research reliance on a synchronic time frame presents analytic problems well known to anthropologists. Fortes (1966) has ably argued the importance of a diachronic approach to the description and analysis of domestic groups. I. Karp (1978) has recently demonstrated that there is no such thing as a normal Iteso neighbourhood in a synchronic or static sense, the neighbourhoods experience a developmental cycle which can only be understood through diachronic analysis and description. Public housing communities like the societies in which they are sited are also subject to change. Willmott (1963) and Cooper (1975) in their respective monographs on Dagenham, England, and Easter Hill Village, U.S.A., illustrate the crucial need for incorporating the temporal dimension into studies of public housing. Each monograph attests to the dangers of making hard and fast decisions about positive or negative images of a public housing complex on investigations conducted shortly after initial settlement. In the case of Dagenham an initial negative image has evolved over several decades into an image that is dominantly positive, Easter Hill Village once celebrated by residents and outsiders alike as an ideal public housing community has in the course of a decade been radically reevaluated by both parties and is now widely judged an environmental and social failure.

When we set the analytic image of the resettlement estate as "a good place to think about" against its residents' image as "a good or bad place to live" we find the residents' image to be more complex than that of the scholar. The scholarly image is based on impersonal criteria that can be measured and coded apart from the noise of human life, the residents' images are imbedded in that noise and reflect images of the environment assessed against their own situated self-image. Self-images are seldom *sui generis* products of isolated musings on one's place in society. As Cooley (1972) reminds us they are influenced by the images expressed by others and one's experiences as a social being. It is precisely in the area of self-image and social identity that one locates the crucial differences and emerging similarity of the Hong Kong and the American public housing experiences.

In Hong Kong, the early estates were settled by individuals who viewed themselves as extraordinary neither in achievement or failure. They were the ordinary members of a society in which a relatively few could obtain the comfort of a spacious and attractive residential setting. In the United States the public housing complex has long been branded as the refuge of those who cannot achieve the American median standard of home ownership or a comfortable private rental. The stigma is apparent in the previously cited works of Moore (1969), Rainwater (1970), and Cooper (1975) as well as in Cuomo's (1974) account of efforts by a "liberal" American community to thwart construction of a federal project adjacent to their district.

The positive self-image characteristic of the original Hong Kong resettlement estate resident was transferred to their community which was defined in terms of people rather than physical setting. Although Hong Kong has changed and more attractive residential alternatives are available to the *po tung ga teng* the images of the original settlers have undergone little change. The change that is most evident is in the differing perceptions of the young who were born and/or nurtured in the estate setting. Their personal self-image and social identity is influenced by the judgments of peer groups and the media organs of wider society. It is a self-image affected by awareness of alternatives to the estate, alternatives whose realization require of their elders a set of values and a degree of financial achievement, either or both of which may be absent. It is in the perceptions of the younger group that one finds indication of an increasing similarity in the American and Hong Kong images of the public housing experience.

References

Chan, Ying-Keung (1973)
   The Rise and Growth of Kwun Tong: A Study of Planned Urban Development. Kwun Tong Industrial Community Research Programme Report, No. A30-07-6-3. The Social Research Centre, The Chinese University of Hong Kong.
Cooley, Charles (1972)
   "Looking-glass Self," *Symbolic Interaction: A Reader in Social Psychology*, pp. 231-233, edited by Jerome Manis and Bernard Meltzer. Boston: Allyn and Bacon.
Cooper, Clare (1975)
   Easter Hill Village. New York: Free Press.
Cuomo, Mario (1974)
   Forest Hills Diary: The Crisis of Low-Income Housing. New York: Random House.
Endicott, G. B. (1973)
   A History of Hong Kong, 2nd edition. Hong Kong: Oxford University Press.
Epstein, David (1972)
   "The Genesis and Function of Squatter Settlements in Brasilia," *The Anthropology of Urban Environments*, pp. 51-58, edited by Thomas Weaver and Douglas White. The Society for Applied Anthropology Monograph 11.
Fortes, Meyer (1966)
   "Introduction," *The Developmental Cycle of Domestic Groups*, pp. 1-14, edited by Meyer Fortes. Cambridge: Cambridge University Press.
Glazer, Nathan (1969)
   "The Culture of Poverty: The View from New York City," *The Poor: A*

Culture of Poverty or a Poverty of Culture?, pp. 29-48, edited by J. Alan Winter. Grand Rapids, Mich.: Eerdmans.

Ho, Fuk-Cheung (1972)
"Chinese Triad Societies: Classical Models and Hong Kong Forms," *Hong Kong: The Interaction of Traditions and Life in The Towns*, pp. 97-109, edited by Marjorie Topley. Weekend Symposium of The Royal Asiatic Society; Hong Kong Branch, November 1972.

Hong Kong (1974)
Hong Kong 1974: report for the year 1973. Hong Kong: Government Printer.

———(1976)
Hong Kong 1976: report for the year 1975. Hong Kong: Government Printer.

Hsu, Francis L. K. (1972)
"Kinship and Ways of Life: An Exploration," *Psychological Anthropology*, pp. 509-572, edited by Francis L. K. Hsu. Cambridge, Mass.: Schenkman.

Hopkins, Keith (1972)
"Public and Private Housing in Hong Kong," *The City as a Centre of Change in Asia*, pp. 200-215, edited by D. J. Dwyer. Hong Kong: Hong Kong University Press.

Karp, D., *et al*. (1977)
Being Urban: A Social Psychological View of City Life. Lexington, Mass.: D. C. Heath.

Karp, Ivan (1978)
Fields of Change among the Iteso of Kenya. London: Routledge and Kegan Paul.

Levi-Strauss, Claude (1967)
Structural Anthropology. New York: Anchor Books.

Marris, Peter (1960)
"Slum Clearance and Family Life in Lagos," *Human Organization*, 19, Vol. 3, pp. 123-128.

Michelson, William (1976)
Man and His Urban Environment: A Sociological Approach With Revisions. Menlo Park, Ca.: Addison-Wessley.

Moore, William (1969)
The Vertical Ghetto: Everyday Life in an Urban Project. New York: Random House.

Muller, Maria (1975)
Action and Interaction: Social Relationships in a Low-income Housing Estate in Kitale, Kenya. Leiden: Afrika Studien Centrum.

Myers, John and D. Leung (1974)
  A Chinese Spirit-medium Temple in Kwun Tong: A Preliminary Report.
  Kwun Tong Industrial Community Research Programme Report, No. A44-
  7-11-2. The Social Research Centre, The Chinese University of Hong
  Kong.
Phillipson, Michael (1974)
  Understanding Crime and Delinquency. Chicago: Aldine.
Pryor, E. G. (1973)
  Housing in Hong Kong. Hong Kong: Oxford University Press.
Rainwater, Lee (1970)
  Behind Ghetto Walls. Chicago: Aldine.
Rapoport, Amos (1976)
  "Introduction," *The Mutual Interaction of People and Their Built Environ-
  ment: A Cross-Cultural Perspective*, pp. 7-36, edited by Amos Rapoport.
  The Hague: Mouton.
Resettlement, Commissioner For (1972-73)
  Hong Kong annual report by the commissioner for resettlement, 1972-
  73. Hong Kong: Government Printer.
Safa, Helen (1974)
  The Urban Poor of Puerto Rico: A Study in Development and Inequality.
  New York: Holt, Rinehart and Wilson.
Schmitt, Robert (1963)
  "The Implications of Density in Hong Kong," *Journal of The American
  Institute of Planners*, Vol. 29, pp. 210-217.
Shively, Aliza (1972)
  Kwun Tong Life Quality Study Data Book. Hong Kong: The Social
  Research Centre, The Chinese University of Hong Kong.
Spradley, James (1972)
  "Adaptive Strategies of Urban Nomads: The Ethnoscience of Tramp
  Culture," *The Anthropology of Urban Environments*, pp. 21-38, edited
  by Thomas Weaver and Douglas White. Society for Applied Anthropology
  Monograph 11.
Wheaton, William and Margaret Wheaton (1972)
  "Urban Housing and Economic Development," *The City as a Centre of
  Change in Asia*, pp. 141-151, edited by D. J. Dwyer. Hong Kong: Hong
  Kong University Press.
Willmott, P. (1963)
  Evolution of a Community. London: Routledge and Kegan Paul.
Yancey, William (1971)
  "Architecture, Interaction, and Social Control: The Case of a Large-scale
  Public Housing Project," *Environment and Behaviour*, Vol. 3 (1), pp. 3-21.

Chapter 3

The Development of New Towns*

Ying-keung Chan

Introduction

Certainly, Hong Kong is "one of the most fascinating economic curiosities in the world today."[1] Facing problems of unparallelled migration influx and economic stagnation caused by trade barriers against China in the early 1950s, Hong Kong successfully developed its manufacturing industry, and in a few decades, has emerged as a world centre of trade and industry.

Apart from the economic expansion, Hong Kong has also experienced rapid urbanization in the last 25 years, with its rapid changing urban landscape and booming new towns.

Searching into the factors which operate in the processes of urbanization and industrialization and the "causal relationships" between them may be of great interest; however, the focus of this paper is on the common product of both processes—the industrial new towns, with special reference to Kwun Tong, the first new town in Hong Kong.

Background for Rapid Development

By the early 1950s, land in inner-city areas around the harbour for domestic or industrial uses had long been exhausted. Industrial development and the invasion of small industries into domestic tenements were not the only causes for deterioration of the environment of inner-city areas. The unprecedented refugee influx and the rapid natural growth of the population had caused serious housing shortage.[2] Older tenement buildings in the urban areas

*The present study was part of the Kwun Tong Industrial Community Research Programme, which was coordinated by Ambrose King and was funded by the Harvard-Yenching Institute and The Chinese University of Hong Kong. Institute support was given by The Chinese University's Social Research Centre. The author would like to acknowledge the suggestions from Siu-kai Lau and Pedro Ng.

[1] N. C. Owen, "Economic Policy in Hong Kong," in K. Hopkins (ed.), *Hong Kong: The Industrial Colony*, Hong Kong: Oxford University Press, 1971, p. 141.

[2] C. Y. Choi and Y. K. Chan, "Housing Policy and Internal Movement of Population:

were facing intolerable overcrowding. Those who could not afford living quarters which might be of unimaginably small size began to occupy hill slopes in northern Kowloon and on Hong Kong Island. "At its peak in 1953, a belt of squatter camps each containing up to 50,000 people and comprising in all over 300,000 squatters enveloped Northern Kowloon."[3]

Feeling the pressure from increasing demand on spaces for further urban development and from the need to amelioration the urban environment, the government gradually began to give up the official laissez-faire policy towards the use of land. Large scale reclamations have been carried out, planned layouts have been imposed to further urban development and thus emerged the industrial new towns.

The rapid inflow of population into new towns is mainly due to the building of large public housing estates. Most of these people belong to lower income groups. They moved into new towns either because they previously lived under intolerable housing conditions or because their former residence had to be demolished. However, most of these new town dwellers are relatively passive; instead of actively creating their own "community" (in the social sense), they tend to mind only their own business.[4] But on the other hand, the contributions from private enterprises and voluntary bodies have their special importance to the new towns.

Taking Kwun Tong as an example. Manufacturers have made enthusiastic investments, as can be seen from the applications for land. Up to 1965, land applied for was 4½ times the land available; and, without counting the large amount of capital for land and equipment, the cost of construction up to the end of 1971 was more than 4 times the estimated cost for the government in the reclamation and preparation of Kwun Tong.[5] It was the investments from private enterprise that have caused the manufacturing industry to flourish, provided job opportunities, and made Kwun Tong one of the most important industrial areas of Hong Kong.

Voluntary bodies, both religious and secular, have been important contributors to the new towns and have played a very important role in their development. Their contributions are always magnificient, particularly in the three major sectors of social services—education, medical and health, and

---

A Study of Kwun Tong, A Chinese New Town in Hong Kong", occasional paper, Social Research Centre, The Chinese University of Hong Kong, 1977, pp. 10-28.

[3]D. J. Dwyer, "Introduction", in D. J. Dwyer (ed.), *Asian Urbanization: A Hong Kong Casebook*, Hong Kong University Press, 1971, p. 4.

[4]Y. K. Chan, "The Rise and Growth of Kwun Tong: A Study of Planned Urban Development", occasional paper, Social Research Centre, The Chinese University of Hong Kong, 1973, pp. 10-19.

[5]*Ibid.*, p. 14.

social welfare services. In Kwun Tong, 83% of the students have enrolled in subsidized/grant schools run by voluntary bodies (Education Department, unpublished data, 1975); and, 81.8% of the social welfare agencies and 34.3% of the clinics in the area were also operated by voluntary bodies.[6] The effort which voluntary bodies have made in rendering social services in new towns have certainly weakened the environmental push factors and strengthened the pull factors to migrants from old urban areas.

Contributions from both private enterprise and voluntary bodies undoubtedly have been important throughout the developmental history of new towns, but what is the role played by the government?

Government as Policy Maker, Planner, and Entrepreneur

It is the government that initiates and plans the new town development. The governmental bodies mainly responsible for planning are the Town Planning Board (chaired by the Director of Public Works and comprising 8 official and 8 unofficial members), and the Land Development Policy Committee (chaired by the Secretary for the Environment and comprising 6 official members). The Town Planning Office of the Public Works Department services these two bodies and their sub-committees, prepares plans and also provides planning advice for the New Territories Administration and Advisory bodies. General planning concepts and policies are set out by the Hong Kong Outline Plan which is based on the findings of six interdepartmental working committees and a data bank. It provides a framework for the preparation of the Town Planning Board statutory outline zoning plans and departmental plans. The statutory plans indicate a broad pattern of land use and provide a guide to public and private investment. The departmental plans, subject to the approval of the Land Development Policy Committee or the New Territories Development Progress Committee, are detailed "action" plans to enable land to be prepared and released for public or private development.[7]

Though plans are prepared under the supervision of various committees, it is the Town Planning Office which does the actual planning work in the urban area. For new towns in the New Territories, the newly set up New Territories Development Department, also within the Public Works Department, is charged with the planning, coordination and implementation of the Department's effort. In addition, planning and development are under the control of a Project Manager who is responsible to the Director of New Territories Development.[8]

[6]*Ibid.*, pp. 16-17.
[7]*Hong Kong Annual Report 1977*, Hong Kong Government, pp. 99-100.
[8]See Hong Kong Government, Public Works Department, New Territories Develop-

All new towns in Hong Kong, including Kwun Tong in the New Kowloon, and Tsuen Wan, Tuen Mun and Sha Tin in the New Territories, are developed under the guidance of governmental plans. Apart from working out the "plans", the major contribution of the government has been to provide industrial land under more favourable lease terms, public housing, services and utilities. It is good for the lower income groups to be accommodated in public housing estates, and maybe it is profitable for industrialists to invest in new towns owing to the favourable terms of leasing and a sufficient labour supply, but it may even be more profitable for the government.

Take land provision as an example. During the period of 1955-1972, the total non-recurrent expenditure of public works done in the Industrial Zone of Kwun Tong was estimated to be about HK$50 million, but industrial land auctioned off in the Kwun Tong Reclamation gave the government a return of HK$120 million. Thus in comparison, Kwun Tong Reclamation alone gave the government a profit of more than 100% in 17 years, without taking into account the returns from outstanding premia, lands not yet auctioned off, direct and indirect taxes from industrial establishments, etc.[9] In other words, the government may also be doing good business in the new town development.

The Development Pattern

All new towns in Hong Kong go through a similar planning process, and traits of planning can be easily discovered from the physical layout of the areas. To provide housing and industrial land in every new town, public housing estates are built and new factory sites are created; also, commercial centres are erected and public utilities and social services are provided. Hereunder are the major common characteristics.

(A) *High density development*

New towns in Hong Kong are all of considerable size in terms of population. In Kwun Tong the population size has reached 575,000 in 1976 (according to By-census, 1976), and in Tsuen Wan, Tuen Mun and Sha Tin, the population has been estimated to be 885,000, 486,000 and 524,000 respectively in the 1980s. In these new towns, a high population density and a high degree of overcrowding can be expected, since a large population has to be transplanted into a limited space. The gross population density of Kwun

---

ment Department, *Hong Kong's New Town, Tsuen Wan*, undated p. 30; *Hong Kong's New Town, Tuen Mun*, undated, p. 24; and *Hong Kong's New Town, Sha Tin*, undated, p. 24.

[9] Y. K. Chan, 1973, *op. cit.*, p. 13.

Tong is 1,459 persons per hectare at present; for Tsuen Wan, Tuen Mun and Sha Tin which are in the New Territories and cover much larger areas, the population density is estimated to be 349, 442 and 301 persons per hectare respectively. Again, if we calculate the population density for the residential area only, for example, in Kwun Tong the density will be over 3,000 persons per hectare, and in the Housing Authority Estates of Sha Tin, will also be as high as 2,500 persons per hectare.[10] Moreover, in new towns the majority of the population will be housed in public housing estates when completed—in Kwun Tong, 80%, Tsuen Wan, 75%, Tuen Mu, 70%, Sha Tin, 60%, all higher than the Hong Kong average of 43%.[11] As the standard set so far for public housing estates is 35 to 40 sq. ft. of space for each occupant, there is reason to believe that in new towns, a high degree of overcrowding will be observed.

Besides the high residential density, flatted factories are also predominant in new towns. As a planning standard of 864 workers per gross hectare (350 workers/acre) of industrial land has been set for new towns,[12] intensive use of industrial lands can be expected.

(B) *More space for industry*

Industrial development has vital importance to the Hong Kong economy, and space is always in great demand for its development. Therefore, in all new towns, important portions of land have been reserved for industrial use. From the outline development plans, we can find more space has been reserved for such usage in Tsuen Wan and Tuen Mun (more recently developed) than in Kwun Tong, both in terms of acreage and percentage (e.g., Kwun Tong 15.7%, Tuen Mun 21%). And for Sha Tin, which was originally planned to be a residential new town, the development plan has been revised and industries, particularly light industries, will be developed in the township.

(C) *Employment*

The provision of development is a crucial factor for the residents in a new town, particularly for those who would much prefer working in the same locale to commuting to the city every day. This may be particularly true for the new towns in Hong Kong which accommodate mainly people from lower and lower-middle classes. In Hong Kong, the major economic activity in new towns is manufacturing industry which provides important working opportunities for blue-collar workers and it can be assumed that the manufacturing

[10] *Hong Kong's New Town, Sha Tin*, p. 16.

[11] Choi and Chan, 1977, *op. cit.*, p. 23; also see the reports listed in Note 8.

[12] Hong Kong Government, Public Works Department, Crown Lands and Survey Office, Planning Branch, *Tsuen Wan and District Outline Development Plan*, Hong Kong Government Printer, 1966, p. 2.

industries can attract workers from the vicinity. However, taking Kwun Tong
as an example, nearly half of the blue-collar workers were working outside,
and moreover, the proportion is even higher for white-collar workers of the
lower income group, as there is a lack of working opportunities nearby.[13]
Therefore, a commuting problem is unavoidable, and many residents even
have to spend nights away from home frequently (13% households have at
least one member doing so).[14] Since (1) the authority is aiming at developing
industry in all other new towns (as in Kwun Tong) for the provision of employment, (2) still little attention has so far been paid to the employment opportunity for white-collar workers, and (3) the attractiveness of local factories to
the residents is uncertain, very probably these industrial new towns may face
the same commuting problems, regardless of the fact that there may be
sufficient blue-collar jobs provided in the area.

(D) *Community services*

The provision of various community services, e.g., education, social welfare,
medical and health services, etc., in a new town has typically been estimated
on the basis of some facility-population ratio which may be purely arbitrary.
Not that arbitrary rations are necessarily undesirable, but the allocation of
facilities on such basis alone may be quite inadequate.

Development outline plans so far published show that sufficient spaces
have been reserved for these purposes; and eventually welfare buildings and
schools will be built by the authority in public housing estates or crown lands.
However, taking Kwun Tong as an example again, many schools, clinics, and
social welfare agencies are found under the auspices of voluntary bodies, and
the provision of these services always lags behind the needs of the people.[15]
In other new towns, though enough space has been reserved for the development of community services, again, there is no clear indication whether more
of these organizations providing services to the community will be under
government sponsorship. In Tsuen Wan, for example, two of the four main
social welfare buildings will be under private sponsorship.[16] If we must wait
until voluntary bodies to take up the responsibility of developing these
services, very likely the obvious time lag between supply and demand (as in
Kwun Tong) will appear again.

(E) *Other facilities*

Besides the above-mentioned necessities, there are many other facilities

[13] Y. K. Chan, 1973, *op. cit.*, p. 44.
[14] Choi and Chan, 1977, *op. cit.*, p. 65.
[15] Y. K. Chan, 1973, *op. cit.*, pp. 49-50.
[16] *Hong Kong's New Town, Tsuen Wan*, p. 21.

which are indispensable for each area under development—e.g., recreation/entertainment, commercial/business, transportation and public utilities.

On the plans, adequate open space for new towns has been reserved. (In Kwun Tong over 50 hectares, Tsuen Wan 47, Tuen Mun 44, Sha Tin 53.) But experience in Kwun Tong shows that the fulfilment of requirements cannot catch up with the need created by a rapidly growing population. Therefore, in the new towns under development, open space, green belt and recreation facilities should be developed before an urgent need is created by the occupants.

The 5.7 hectares central area for business and commercial undertakings in Kwun Tong was too small and it lacked space for expansion, yet district outline development plans show there are larger central areas in other new towns (Tsuen Wan 46 hectares, Tuen Mun 31, Sha Tin 17) and pressure arising from limited space for commercial undertakings can be expected to be lightened.

Among new towns, whether completed or under development, Sha Tin will most likely have the best transportation network. At present, to communicate with Kowloon, there exists already the Kowloon-Canton railway, the Tai Po Road and the highway through Lion Rock Tunnel; in 1978 a second Lion Rock Tunnel was completed and later a double-tracked railway will be laid between Sha Tin and Kowloon. As for Tsuen Wan, there are two road linkages to Kowloon, the Castle Peak Road and Kwai Chung Road, and a bridge connecting Kwai Chung and Tsing Yi. But in Kwun Tong, 20 years after the development, the four-lane Kwun Tong Road is the only land route to Kowloon, and terrible traffic congestion will continue until the completion of the tunnel linking Kwun Tong with To Kwa Wan (still under-construction). Tuen Mun may face the same problem in land transportation unless improvement, e.g., widening of Tuen Mun Road, will be carried out in time; otherwise its development will be hindered.

At the beginning of its development, factories in Kwun Tong faced many difficulties—shortage of labour supply, lack of water and electricity supply, etc., because it was industry which developed first in the area, followed later by public and private housing and other utilities. Now in the other new towns, public housing will be constructed at the early stage of development so as to stimulate industrial, commercial and private housing development—e.g., Sun Fat Estate in Tuen Mun, Lek Yuen Low Cost Housing Estate in Sha Tin, and low cost housing estates of Kwai Chung in Southern Tsuen Wan. In Tuen Mun, before the completion of the public housing estate, a road network, sewage system and water filtration plant were constructed;[17] others such as the construction of a hawker bazaar and "cooked food stall" bazaar in

[17] *Wah Kiu Yat Po*, March 6, 1969.

Tuen Mun, fire station and bus terminus in Kwai Chung, sewage treatment plant in Sha Tin indicate, at least to some degree, improvement in the coordination of work in building up a new town.[18]

Social Aspects

Town Planning has traditionally been concerned with such physical aspects as patterns of land-use, communication, provision and distribution of facilities, and aesthetic qualities of architectual design. Often neglected but at least equally important in planning for a new town is the social well-being of the community and its residents. Certainly the physical set-up of a new town can facilitate or hinder particular social activities. However, it is highly unlikely that the coordination of social activities, the integration of the residents and the promotion of the community's welfare can be achieved through physical planning alone. Insofar as planning takes cognizance of the social aspects of a new town, what is usually considered as socially basic includes only demographic characteristics since these are attributes of a population that can be measured statistically. What follows is typically the consideration of how facilities can be allocated most effectively. Some socially problematic issues are not tackled. With regard to the development of new towns in Hong Kong, there are some major issues which are socially important and deserved immediate attention.

(A) A balanced community and self-containment

Some planners have pointed out that in Hong Kong,

> "one cannot but recognize that the present and future development of this small city region lies directly in the path of Megalopolis rather than in any concept of a central urban area plus self-contained new development. . . . [It] would appear that Hong Kong, having achieved an urban concentration, should not, indeed probably could not, willingly change in the direction of independent new towns but should develop from the advantages so achieved, structured by modern mass transport. It would consider itself as a whole, as a system, rather than as a series of towns in a hierarchical grouping."[19]

This could be true for the cases of Kwun Tong and Tsuen Wan which are "virtual extensions of the enlarged urban area of Kowloon and New Kowloon".[20] But recently, the government has clearly stated that new towns

---

[18]*Sing Tao Jih Pao*, Feb. 8, 1971; and *Wah Kiu Yat Po*, Jan. 3, 1972.

[19]J. A. Prescott, "Hong Kong: The Form and Significance of a High-Density Urban Development", in D. J. Dwyer (ed.), 1971, *op. cit.*, pp. 13-14 and p. 19.

[20]*Ibid.*, p. 13.

should be self-contained,[21] and developed as balanced communities.[22]

However both "balanced community" and "self-containment" are not feasible town planning concepts in the case of Hong Kong, which is characterized by a high level of interdependency and interpenetration between the constituent components of the society. A "balanced community", even if achieved, may only mean "balance" in a demographic sense, because individuals belonging to different socioeconomic strata would have little interaction with each other. Similarly, "self-containment", if realized, would be tantamount to segregation between new towns and the other parts of Hong Kong. It is also doubtful whether self-containment would necessarily generate community identification; however, even if it can be generated, it is still arguable whether a high degree of localism or "parochialism" would really benefit both the new towns and Hong Kong as a whole.

In practice, contrary to the intention of the plan, new towns are not "balanced communities" even in a demographic sense—all having a younger population than Hong Kong as a whole. Furthermore, they are quasi-homogeneous working class communities—in Kwun Tong, only 30% of the households have a monthly income of HK$2,000 or over;[23] and in Tuen Mun, only 1.4% of the working population have a monthly income of HK$2,000 or over.[24] Besides, there are practical difficulties in making available a whole spectrum of services and jobs for different socioeconomic groups, in attracting sufficient amounts of industrial and commercial investment in the new town and in persuading individuals of different socioeconomic statuses to live alongside each other.

(B) Heterogeneity and segregation

Though all new towns in Hong Kong can be described as quasi-homogeneous working class communities, these new towns all have low and high density residential zones for residents of different socioeconomic backgrounds. For example, the Yuet Wah Street area in Kwun Tong, Residential Zone R3 in Tuen Mun, Residential Zones R3 and R4 in Sha Tin are for the development of low density private housing for residents of a higher socioeconomic status, in contrast to the crowded public housing estates which are mainly for people of lower incomes. In other words, new towns are planned as heterogeneous communities with block or estate homogeneity in terms of social class. This

[21] Hong Kong Annual Report 1973, Hong Kong Government, pp. 93-94.

[22] Hong Kong Annual Report 1977, pp. 100-101.

[23] Housing Policy and Migration Survey Data Book, p. 59, Social Research Centre, The Chinese University of Hong Kong, 1976.

[24] W. T. Chan, "Residents in Tuen Mun Community" (in Chinese), in The Hong Kong Council of Social Service Quarterly, No. 62, 1977, p. 7.

physical "segregation" by design may engender social alienation among certain residents, especially those of the lower classes. Some planners might believe that a multi-class community could enhance better understanding among the residents and might argue that the upper or middle classes could serve as a source of status emulation to the lower classes, thereby uplifting the latter's social and economic aspirations. However, up to now it is not sure whether frequent contacts and interactions among the residents of different social class statuses in fact take place. Even if there are frequent contacts and interactions, it is not sure whether any positive effect would ensue. Some kinds of fact-finding surveys need to be conducted in order to assess the effects of living in a planned heterogenous community.

(C) *Community consciousness*

How to create a sense of community among the residents is one of the major social issues in new town development, particularly when the new town contains a large population. In Hong Kong all new towns are designed to accommodate populations as large as several hundred thousands, which is comparable to a primate city in many countries. It is true that the new town dwellers' attitude towards participation in community affairs is rather apathetic.[25] Maybe their recent arrival has not provided the residents with enough time for the development of community consciousness, but the lack of community participation is nevertheless an obvious result of the failure of local organizations to attract local support, and of the large scale entry of external organizations which fulfil many of the community requirements.[26]

The organization of voluntary groups, mutual-aid societies, and similar activities in the community may contribute to the development of community consciousness. But considering the size of the population, local voluntary groups and associations can only be formed at the housing estate or at most the sub-district levels. Consequently, the aim of creating among the residents a sense of identification with the larger new town will be difficult to realize.

(D) *Social organization*

The ultimate success of the new towns will depend on the type of social organization established among the residents. Different types of social organization will affect the patterns of utilization of the physical facilities provided in the new town plan. Before they move into the new town, individuals and families might be already well-integrated into their former neighbourhoods,

[25] Hong Kong Council of Social Service, "Lek Yuen Estate community affairs and citizen participation" (in Chinese), in *Hong Kong Council of Social Service Quarterly*, No. 62, 1977, pp. 30-31.

[26] Choi and Chan, 1977, *op. cit.*, pp. 103-105.

largely through a conglomeration of formal and informal interpersonal relationships. They are probably able to satisfy their physical and social needs
through these relationship. Once relocated in the new town, however, they
will find themselves living in a social vacuum. A survey in Tuen Mun showed
that 37.8% of the respondents made very few friends in the area, and 46.1%
seldom interacted with other residents.[27] Another survey in Kwun Tong also
found that satisfactory neighbourhood relations were felt by only a small
proportion of households, and community activities were rare and insignificant, thus hindering neighbourhood/community interactions. Furthermore,
community organization projects have been externally initiated and supported,
local motivation for organization has been weak as have the linkages between
organization.[28]

Even though forms of social organization among the residents may emerge
spontaneously as time goes by, it is nonetheless the responsibility of planners
to facilitate and to structure these processes if improvement of the general
quality of life is a desired goal.

Discussion

Through close examination of the development of new towns, we can see
that besides the task of physical planning, the government's involvement in
building up new urban areas has to some extent been limited. Many deficiencies
prevailing in older urban areas—such as overcrowding, high building density,
lack of environmental beauty, traffic congestion, shortage of suitable sites for
certain institutions, insufficient supply of services and facilities also exist in
the new towns.

To deal with overconcentration in large cities, the two most propagated
theories are suggesting the erection of high-rise buildings *or* the development
of satellite towns.[29] However, in Hong Kong, it is not a question of choice
between building high-rises in central urban areas and developing satellite
towns. Hong Kong has no choice but to accept both alternatives, i.e., constructing high-rise buildings in the inner-city and at the same time developing
new towns with such unusual features as high-density living and proximity to
industrial sites.

Actually, the patterns adopted so far can be justified by (1) within such
a limited surface of about 1,000 sq. km., land is too valuable and it is not

[27]W. T. Chan, 1977, *op. cit.*, p. 9.
[28]Choi and Chan, 1977, *op. cit.*, p. 101.
[29]L. Hongladarom, "High-rise Building versus Satellite Towns", in K. Suwanagul, et
al. (eds.), *Social Science Research for Urban Development in Southeast Asia*, Social
Science Association Press of Thailand, Bangkok, 1972, pp. 159-186.

possible to develop dispersed suburban residential areas; (2) industrial establishment should be city-oriented or close to existing urban areas, otherwise,
enormous investment would be required for transportation facilities and other
public utilities; (3) what must be developed as a first priority is housing for a
lower class population, rather than upper class residences located in a "green
belt"; (4) to minimize the commuting problem, housing for workers would
best be located close to factories; (5) high-density urban development is
possible since "Hong Kong has had the advantage of taking a large agrarian-
based immigrant population and converting it into an urban multi-storey
densely-packed community. The population had little preconception of what
urban life meant or would mean and has adapted to whatever it found."[30]

Though the twin purposes of providing housing and industrial sites have
been attained, the physical and social infrastructures of new towns are still
far from satisfactory. For example, even though sufficient jobs have been
created in the vicinity, they have not met the need of the new town residents;
therefore large scale commuting has not been avoided. While the plan for
industrial development in a new town should provide considerable occupational opportunities for blue-collar production workers, sufficient opportunities for white-collar workers should also be provided for residents of different
occupational interests. Of course, the latter type of work would have to
withstand competition from similar opportunities available in the city. While
there will always be some residents of the new town who for various reasons
want to or have to work in the city, some minimum variety of job opportunities (most of which will have to be comparable in rewards with those of
the city) will be necessary in order to satisfy a fairly heterogeneous working
population in the new towns. This situation would also have favourable
implications for reducing the load on the transportation system between the
new towns and the inner-city.

In the case of Kwun Tong, the community services and facilities provided
have been inadequate, either because of limited government involvement or
because the provision of such services and facilities was not actively considered
until urgent needs had been created.[31] Future planners must consider whether
the provision of services and facilities can keep pace with the rapid population
influx. It is also necessary to examine deliberately whether the proposed
services and facilities will in fact serve their purposes, whether there might be
differences in the pattern of use among different types of residents, and
whether the needs of some particular groups of residents might have been
totally neglected. If too much attention is paid to the physical and quantitative

---

[30] Prescott, 1971, *op. cit.*, p. 18.
[31] Y. K. Chan, 1973, *op. cit.*, p. 63.

aspects of community services and facilities, it may turn out that some of them are ill-used or under-used while certain other needs remain unsatisfied.

Therefore, instead of talking about a "balanced community" and "self-containment" in general terms, the plan must be more specific. What needs to be "balanced" and what needs to be "self-sufficient"? Obviously, as a minimum, the working population and the non-working population must be balanced, and those urgently needed facilities and services (e.g., hospitals, schools, clinics, law-enforcement agencies) must be self-sufficient. A list of these specific items of "balance" and "self-containment" must be carefully spelled out as relatively feasible goals for the plan to achieve.

Moreover, planned social intervention is particularly necessary in the early stage of implementing the new town plan. This planned social intervention should aim at mobilizing the new residents to form informal and semi-formal networks of interpersonal relationships, and at coordinating these networks. These networks can serve both the expressive function of catering to the psychological and social needs of the residents, and the instrumental functions of social welfare provision, social control, cooperative actions and collective decision-making.

In many case of town planning, the profession of planning sees itself as planning for the community, but deals with only a portion of that community, and city planning has concerned itself primarily with buildings and the physical environment, and only secondarily with the people who make use of that environment. Moreover, it sometimes even pays no attention to the social structures, institutions, culture and subcultures; the people are seen only as occupants of dwellings, offices, factories and moving vehicles. Not much attention has been paid to how they use these facilities; the people are little more than artifacts.[32] That is also a rather appropriate description of the philosophy of the planning authority in Hong Kong. It cannot be denied that in societies undergoing rapid social change, social objectives become very difficult if not impossible to define, let alone to quantify with relatively clear directions for planning. That being the case, any attempt to strengthen and coordinate "community" efforts in dealing with emergent social issues, either during the planning process or after the new town has come into being, will remain highly problematic. As a first step, the planners should listen to the people, investigate and help the people in order to solve their problems instead of just imposing professional expertise and values on the people assuming that these former squatters and rural dwellers are totally ignorant of what life in a new urban area should be.

[32] H. J. Gans, "Planning for People, Not Building", in M. Steward (ed.), *The City: Problems of Planning*, Penguin Books, 1972, pp. 363-364.

Chapter 4

Implications of Concentrated Utilization of Local Facilities and Services in Public Housing Estates*

Angela W. S. Kan

Introduction

1. *Neighbourhood as a planning concept*

The essence of the neighbourhood principle is that of building townships into smaller, more manageable units in the form of neighbourhoods, containing population sharing facilities and services that are conveniently accessible to the individual households. However, the question "Is the neighbourhood unit socially valid?" has been discussed for decades by students of urban planning who appear to be still sharply divided on the issue.[1] The adequacy of the neighbourhood theory as a planning concept has also been strongly opposed as promoting specialization, segregation and as an attempt to recreate an idealized form of village-life which is essentially anti-urban. In spite of the opposition, the neighbourhood concept has continued to be applied to a large extent. A study made by Goss on British new towns concluded that,

*The data of the present paper were collected during my term of office in the Social Research Centre, The Chinese University of Hong Kong, under the Kwun Tong Industrial Community Research Programme financially supported by the Harvard-Yenching Institute. I am grateful for the cooperation and information given by the Housing Department in general and the Shek Kip Mei and Tsz Wan Shan Housing Estate Offices in particular. I would like to thank my former colleagues, Mr. H. K. Tsoi, Miss F. K. Wan and Mr. Z. K. Kwok for their collaboration in designing the surveys. The invaluable assistance rendered by Miss S. L. Suen in computerizing of the data, Miss Ann Marshall in the English editing, and Mr. K. W. Mok in typing and printing the paper are also gratefully acknowledged.
[1] Supporters are represented by Lewis Mumford, C. A. Doxiadis, Clarence Stein and Frank Llyod Wright. Critics include scholars as Reginald Isaacs, Jane Jacobs, Catherine Bauer and others. For some of their views, see, for example, Reginald R. Isaacs, "The Neighbourhood Theory: An Analysis of its Adequacy," *Journal of the American Institute of Planners*, V. 14, No. 2, 1948, pp. 15-23; Catherine Bauer, "Social Questions in Housing and Community Planning," *Journal of Social Issues*, V. 7, No. 1 & 2, 1951; Lewis Mumford, "The Neighbourhood and the Neighbourhood Unit," *Town Planning Review*, V. 24, 1954, pp. 256-270; and Jane Jacobs, *The Death and Life of Great American Cities: The Failure of Town Planning*, Random House, 1961.

"Despite the shortcomings of many neighbourhood units, there is little doubt that most of the new neighbourhood units in British new towns represent a qualitative advance over most pre-war housing estates. The neighbourhood units built in Britain were the first real attempts on a nation-wide scale to plan residential areas comprehensively with shops, schools, community buildings and open spaces fitted into residential areas as part of a planned pattern."[2]

Snow and others were probably right to state that,

"The question is not whether or not the neighbourhood ideal should be fostered, but what is the best approach in terms of planning, to bring about the realization of the neighbourhood ideal."[3]

Most of the recently built new towns in Hong Kong are designed as fully integrated self-contained townships with residential accommodation, employment opportunities and a range of community facilities provided—shop spaces, schools, clinics, nurseries, youth centres and children's clubs. In the more recent housing estates, primary schools, welfare and community organizations are being concentrated in specially designed buildings. The inevitable trend of future development in Hong Kong will be in the direction of moving the urban population to these new towns hopefully bringing forth the "neighbourhood ideal".

2. *The use of the local neighbourhood*

Undoubtedly, there is always a gap between an ideal and its realization. It is a well-established fact that the local neighbourhood is more important for some groups than for others.[4] Its importance varies according to the resources of the residents themselves. These resources may be economic, psychological, cultural or ecological. The immobile young or old, the disabled, the overburdened and the isolated need the neighbourhood most. They cannot venture very far from their immediate dwellings. They are no more than 'block-dwellers', whereas the relatively better-off, the better-educated and the mobile are 'city-dwellers' and 'city-users'.[5] The 'block-dwellers' need the local neighbourhood for the basic necessities of goods and services, as well as for the intangible need of friendship, neighbouring, mutual aid and attachment;[6] the

[2] Anthony Goss, "Neighbourhood Units in British New Towns," *Town Planning Review*, V. 32, No. 1, 1961, pp. 66-82.

[3] David A. Snow, Thomas Fuller and Ashok K. Dutt, "Neighbourhood Planning: A Historical and Critical Analysis," *Greek Review of Social Research*, No. 14, 1970, p. 195.

[4] H. L. Ross, "The Local Community: A Survey Approach," *American Sociological Review*, V. 27, No. 1, 1962, pp. 75-84.

[5] Alvin L. Schorr, *Slums and Social Insecurity*, Washington D. C.: U. S. Department of Health, Education and Welfare, 1963, p. 41.

[6] See Angela W. S. Kan, "A Study of Neighbourly Interaction in Public Housing: The

'city-users' have different needs. Other factors that may affect the local use of the facilities and services are the types and functions of the facilities, their adequacy and accessibility, the degree of isolation of the neighbourhood and the accessibility of nonlocal facilities. Any or all of the local facilities or services may thus turn out unexpectedly 'over-utilized', 'under-utilized' or 'mis-utilized' from the original design of the planners. But, the under-use, over-use, or misuse cannot be explained by such local factors as these alone, one important explanation lies in what critic Herbert Gans has called "the planner's physical bias". He puts it in the following way,

> "In planning land uses, the location and design of buildings, streets, other transportation facilities, utility lines and open spaces, the profession sees mainly the natural and man-made physical artifacts of the city. It aims to arrange and rearrange these artifacts to create an orderly—often even static—efficient and attractive community . . . . the planner ignores almost entirely the people who live in the community, and without whom there would be no buildings or land uses. He does not plan for them either as individuals or as members of groups. . . . Indeed he does not even pay much attention to how they use these facilities. For the planners, people are little more than artifacts. They are expected to function within the housing, land uses and other community arrangements which he provides, and are supposed to subordinate their personal and familial interests to the needs of the neighbourhood, the community and the community plan, and to share the planner's goals of order, efficiency and beauty for their community."[7]

It is the purpose of the present paper to discuss in detail the need for and concentrated use of local facilities and social services, and the factors behind the non-use of such facilities. General observations will be based on the findings of surveys carried out in two resettlement estates in Hong Kong. The paper may raise more questions than it answers; however, with the following preliminary findings as guidelines, further research into this area should bring about sounder planning principles and more appropriate physical environment to meet the needs of the people concerned.

Provision of Facilities and Social Services in Resettlement Estates in Hong Kong

When the Resettlement Department came into being in April 1954, it was stated very clearly that squatter clearance and resettlement was not in any sense a welfare operation and that the Department was not a welfare agency.[8]

Case of Hong Kong," in *Housing in Hong Kong,* edited by Luke S. K. Wong, Heinemann Educational Books (Asia) Ltd., 1978, pp. 160-182.

[7]Herbert Gans, "Planning for People, not Buildings," *Environment And Planning,* V. 1, No. 1, 1969, pp. 33-46.

[8]"What was required was not primarily to improve the living conditions of that section of the community which happened to be breaking the law relating to the occupation

On the contrary, if the resettlement estates were to be successful, the persons who were becoming the direct tenants of Government had to be "assisted to build up an orderly community; they had to learn self-respect and respect for the rights of their neighbours; they had to be taught to make the best of the simple accommodation provided, to forget the defeatist attitude towards dirt and disease which pervades the squatter areas, to make their small contribution to the Colony's revenue, and to take advantage of such social services as the Colony is able to offer to her people."[9]

It was recognized that the process of integration can never be made effective merely through restrictive rules and regulations. There must be a positive side to the process of teaching the people what it can mean to be a citizen. Thus, despite the original intention of the resettlement scheme, Resettlement Assistants in fact have to be part-welfare officers, part-teachers, part-health inspectors and part-rent-collectors. Almost inevitably it was believed that much more was needed than could be accomplished by the administrative staff. For this reason, voluntary agencies were encouraged by the Social Welfare Office and the Resettlement Department to undertake welfare work of all kinds in the estates.

1. *Education and welfare*

In the early (Mark I and II) blocks, the Resettlement Department had no sites to offer to the voluntary agencies to run boys' and girls' recreation centres, milk distribution centres or reading rooms. These agencies could either rent rooms for their activities at the normal rate of $14 a month for a single room or have the free use of large roof playgrounds, with large penthouses at either end of the arms of the H-shaped blocks. The urgent need for schools was met by allocating the rooftops to be used for primary schools, the penthouses at either end being enclosed and converted into classrooms, while the open spaces in between became school playgrounds.

The housing estates built later, with their still large concentrations of people, presented greater needs and opportunities for welfare work of all types. Since the rooftops were insufficient to meet the need for schools and welfare facilities in the early estates, ground floor rooms in selected blocks of both Mark I and II designs were reserved for these purposes. Structural limitations in the newer designs of resettlement blocks precluded the use of the

---

of Crown land: the task was to devise a rapid and practical method, at a cost at least less than prohibitive, of removing, in the interest of the whole community, the fire risk and the threat to public health and public order presented by the worst squatter areas." Commissioner for Resettlement, *Annual Departmental Report 1945-55*, p. 30.

[9]*Ibid.*, p. 40.

rooftops for these purposes; and in the Mark IV, V and VI estates, it was likewise impossible to have schools on the ground floors. Specially modified top-floor accommodations have been provided for schools in a number of the Mark III blocks, while free-standing school buildings, each having six storeys with 24 classrooms, have been built to serve the Mark IV, V and VI blocks.[10]

As to welfare work in the Marks I, II, and III estates, rooftop and ground floor rooms are used as nurseries, clubs, clinics, casework centres and for many other welfare purposes. In the Mark IV, V and VI estates, however, although some ground floor rooms are available for welfare activities which require little space, these facilities are largely accommodated in separate Estate Welfare Buildings. One building to every 50,000 persons is the norma-tive standard used. These Welfare Buildings house a variety of services, both government and unofficial, planned and coordinated by the Social Welfare Department and the Hong Kong Council of Social Service.

2. *Parks and playgrounds*

Recreation areas are included in all resettlement estates. These may take a variety of forms: fields for football, basketball and other forms of active recreation, children's playgrounds equipped with swings, slides and other attractions, or rest gardens and sitting-out areas. The areas are allocated, surfaced and fenced during the construction of the estate, and then banded over to the Urban Services Department to equip and manage.

3. *Medical clinics*

For some years, medical services in the resettlement estates were carried out in a number of vans converted into make-shift mobile clinics run by a variety of agencies. At the end of 1967, the Medical and Health Department introduced a scheme to replace the mobile units by low-cost clinics in charge by qualified medical practitioners located on the ground floors of domestic blocks. Hospitals and polyclinics are planned on the district level.

4. *Commercial premises, shops and cottage industries*

Squatters who had been operating shops and workshops were allocated spaces on the ground floors of the domestic blocks to continue their businesses

---

[10]One classroom for every 450 persons was laid down as the standard for planning of primary schools. If one class consists of 45 students, then 1 seat is reserved for every 10 persons (or 2 seats for 10 persons when the classroom is used both for morning and afternoon sessions). In other words, the standard is set on the assumption that among 10 persons in the population, there will be one or two persons of primary school age. The secondary school is planned on the district level and the standard is one classroom for every 600 persons.

after resettlement. The modification introduced in the later blocks built from 1961 onwards produced a variety of shop sizes. These have a wide miscellany of business such as restaurants, retail stores, shops for fresh meat and fish, hairdressers, and dry-cleaners. Ground floor workshops also accommodate a great variety of enterprises, and tenants have always been allowed to carry on certain simple and inoffensive cottage industries such as tailoring, assembling plastic goods, and knitting, in their upper floor domestic rooms.

In the above, we have seen glimpses of the general provision of facilities and services in most of the resettlement estates. We may now note a few characteristics related to the planning and managing of these facilities and services.

First, facilities and services are described as adequate or inadequate in terms of acreage ratios per thousand of population (as in the number of schools and number of Estate Welfare Buildings to be provided to such and such numbers of population on the estate level or district level). Such an approach tells us something about the methods of planners, but nothing about the employment or value of the facilities and services.

Second, most of the facilities and services of the estates of Mark I and II blocks were not planned in the strict sense. Spaces were allocated for facilities and services only after the buildings were occupied when there were needs felt by the concerned religious bodies or welfare organization to set up services for the residents. Government did not take the lead in providing social services and welfare facilities. Only with increasing demand in the later years were these facilities and services included in the planning stage.

Third, the management and control of the facilities within the housing estates are sometimes unnecessarily split among different governmental departments, i.e., the management of parks and recreational grounds within the boundary of the resettlement estate is in the hands of the Urban Services Department rather than the Resettlement Department. This complicates the problems of estate management and may consequently lead to improper surveillance of the facilities.

These observations and others will be discussed in the later chapters. In the meantime, we will turn to the two resettlement estates on which the arguments are to be based.

Shek Kip Mei and Tsz Wan Shan Resettlement Estates

The data used in this paper are drawn mainly from small-scale community studies of two resettlement estates—Shek Kip Mei Resettlement Estate and Tsz Wan Shan Resettlement Estate—conducted during the period May to

July 1973.[11] A brief description of the geographical location, historical development, numbers and kinds of facilities and services of the two Resettlement Estates will be given in the following.[12]

1. *Description of the two Resettlement Estates*

The Shek Kip Mei Resettlement Estate (hereafter abbreviated as SKM) is centrally located in the built-up areas of Shamshuipo in Northwestern Kowloon. It was the first multi-storey estate built at the public expense for general resettlement purposes. The construction of the first eight 6-storey blocks, H-shaped in plan, was undertaken during the last three months of 1954 as an experiment for a long-term program to solve the grave squatter problem facing the Colony. The whole estate was originally composed of 23 H-shaped and 3 I-shaped, six- or seven-storey Mark I blocks with a total population capacity of 62,000. Communal wash-places and lavatories are located in the cross-piece of the H. An access balcony runs all the way around the outside of each floor and back-to-back rooms open off it. Due to the central location, SKM is easily accessible by public transportation.

Since October 1972, when the Shek Kip Mei Rehousing Scheme was started, SKM has been undergoing a period of transition. This involves the removal, in five phases, of the domestic tenants, shops and workshops, roof-top schools, welfare organizations and hawkers so as to enable the 29 blocks to be converted or redeveloped to provide self-contained accommodation units. The moving of the tenants of the first phase of rehousing to new accommodation in Pak Tin Estate was completed by the end of March 1973. The total population residing in SKM when the Survey was undertaken, was estimated to be 51,000.

Tsz Wan Shan Resettlement Estate (hereafter abbreviated as TWS) is the largest resettlement estate in Hong Kong, and is planned to house a total population of 170,000. It is situated on the southern slope of the Temple Hill located on the northeastern part of Kowloon. At the time of the Survey, it was served by five bus and two mini-bus routes. The Estate consists of four types of blocks, Mark III (8 storeys), Mark IV, V and VI (all 16 storeys), built in various shapes. Construction work has been carried out in stages, the first

[11] The Surveys were designed by H. K. Tsoi, F. K. Wan, Z. K. Kwok and the author. The two samples were selected through multi-stage (blocks, floors, households) random procedures. About 2 per cent and 1.2 per cent of the estimated number of households in Shek Kip Mei and Tsz Wan Shan, respectively, were sampled. As a result, we collected data from 200 households in Shek Kip Mei and 302 households in Tsz Wan Shan. The former consists of 1,231 individuals and the latter consists of 2,031 individuals.

[12] For the sake of convenience, the old term of 'Resettlement Estate' (re-named as the 'Group B Estate' after April 1, 1973) will be used in the present paper.

block being completed in April 1964. By March 1973, the total population was about 146,000 occupying 63 blocks in the Estate.

The blocks are of a completely different design from that of the SKM Resettlement Estate, with room access from an internal corridor. Each room is a self-contained unit with its own private balcony, water-tap and toilet (for Mark III blocks, toilets are shared between two rooms).

For administration and management purposes, the TWS Resettlement Estate was divided into six sections, each under the charge of an Assistant Resettlement Officer assisted by a certain number of Resettlement Assistants. The entire estate has been under the charge of two Resettlement Officers until the turn of this year (1975).

2. Provisions of facilities and social services in the two Estates

Tables 1 and 2 show the number of primary schools and welfare services in SKM and TWS for a period of six years. The contrast between the two Estates is obviously shown in the drastic displacement of rooftop schools and boys' and girls' club in SKM and the steady growth of these facilities and services in TWS.

TWS has a younger population than SKM.[13] Children who moved with their parents into SKM twenty years ago are grow-ups now, and for various reasons (such as marriage and congestion) out-migration has been taking place continuously. The movement of population and change of age structure over the years inevitably renders functionless some facilities and services that might have served the area previously.[14] Nevertheless, in May 1973 SKM still had 11 rooftop schools, 5 children's clubs, a welfare centre, a vocational training centre, a library and a nursery. In the vicinity, a government primary school had been opened in 1959, and a polyclinic constructed in 1958. The Kaifong Welfare Association also has a long history of serving this neighbourhood.

In TWS, 14 annex schools, including one for handicapped children, had been completed by 1973 to provide a total of 24,780 primary school places. Three day nurseries and eight kindergartens provide places for over 3,000 children. As to welfare organizations and facilities, there are the Savings and Loans Association, Family Planning Association, youth centres, libraries, reading rooms and twelve medical clinics run by different welfare agencies.

[13] From our sample surveys, about 39.9 per cent of the population in TWS was under the age 15 while 29.1 per cent in SKM was under that age.

[14] Besides, the standards of these facilities are incomparably lower than those offered by the ones built later. The rooftop schools which were so popular in the 60's are now almost at the end. The same situation is also facing many of the youth centres. The number of youth centres had declined from 13 to 5 in SKM within the space of five years.

Table 1

Primary schools in Shek Kip Mei and
Tsz Wan Shan Resettlement Estates

(As at 31st March of each year)

Year	No. of schools	No. of classrooms	No. of places	No. of enrollment
		SKM		
1967-68	18	78	—	—
1968-69	—	—	—	—
1969-70	18	83	5,758	4,462
1970-71	16	—	4,350	4,621
1971-72	12	—	3,616	2,518
1972-73	11	—	3,094	1,893
		TWS		
1967-68	8	192	—	—
1968-69	—	—	—	—
1969-70	11	240	21,180	20,411
1970-71	11	—	21,180	20,885
1971-72	14	—	24,740	24,470
1972-73	14	—	24,780	24,489

Source: Commissioner for Resettlement, *Annual Departmental Reports* 1967-68 to
1972-73.
Note: All schools included in SKM are rooftop schools and those in TWS are annex
schools.

Table 2
Welfare services in Shek Kip Mei and
Tsz Wan Shan Resettlement Estates
(As at 31st March of each year)

	1967-68	1968-69	1969-70	1970-71	1971-72	1972-73
			SKM			
Clinics	—	1	2	2	2	2
Kindergartens	—	—	—	—	—	—
Nurseries	—	—	—	—	—	1
Family Planning Association	—	—	—	—	—	—
Library & Reading Rooms	1	1	1	2	1	1
Children & Youth Centres*	13	13	11	10	6	5
Welfare Centres	1	1	—	—	5	1
			TWS			
Clinics	6	6	10	11	10	12
Kindergartens	—	—	—	4	8	8
Nurseries	2	3	2	3	2	3
Family Planning Association	1	1	1	1	2	2
Library & Reading Rooms	—	1	3	3	2	3
Children & Youth Centres*	1	2	1	1	4	4
Welfare Centres	—	—	1	1	1	6

Source: Commissioner for Resettlement, *Annual Departmental Reports* 1967-68 to 1972-73.

*Include boys' & girls' clubs, youth centres, play and recreation centres.

The TWS Kaifong Welfare Association has been established to promote the welfare, recreation and sporting facilities of the neighbourhood, and a six-storey Estate Welfare Building has been providing coordinated social welfare services to the residents.

Concentrated Utilization of Local Facilities and Services

As noted earlier, the extent of utilization of neighbourhood facilities is an important criterion for the delineation of a neighbourhood. In this section, we shall see if the neighbourhood unit functions to provide convenient services to the community. We shall first discuss the ecological pattern of the two Estates, and then give a presentation of the basic services such as shopping for daily commodities and medical services. The ecological parameters and basic services are both considered as 'primary' in the sense that they are indispensable to the residents. We shall then move to a discussion of the usage of 'secondary' facilities and services such as parks and playgrounds, libraries and reading rooms. Finally, we shall consider secondary groups such as youth centres, Estate Welfare Building and Kaifong Welfare Association, which are equally important in enriching the dullness of life in these vertical slums.

The area being served varies for the different facilities. A resident may have children attending schools in the Estate, may shop and go to clinics in the Estate. He may also have other children going to secondary schools in distant areas and may go for entertainment in other districts. Similarly, the usage pattern of parks and playgrounds, youth centres, libraries and reading rooms in the neighbourhood may take different forms. Some facilities may be completely ignored by the residents. Some people may never use the facilities despite their knowledge of them because of the absence of need; others may have hidden demands, but for one reason or another they may never make use of the facilities.

1. *Ecological patterns*

Seven parameters have been chosen to assess the ecological networks of the two Estates under study. They are shown in Table 3. They include the percentage of primary school and kindergarten attendance, percentage of secondary school attendance, percentage of employment, percentage of people living within walking distance to school/to work, percentage spending less than 15 minutes to go to school/to work. The districts in which the Estates are situated are used as the geographical boundaries for delineation.[15]

----

[15] The aged SKM and the middle-aged TWS are residential complex with no planned provision of employment opportunities within the Estates. Therefore it is more meaningful to extend the boundary to their adjacent areas. The district in which SKM is located

Table 3

Ecological patterns among respondents in SKM and TWS

Ecological Parameters	*SKM*	*TWS*
Primary school and kindergarten attendance in the district	93.8%	98.3%
Secondary school attendance in the district	50.0%	49.7%
Walking to school	84.7%	73.5%
Spending less than 15 minutes to go to school (one-way)	50.0%	47.4%
Employed in the district	52.5%	39.6%
Walking to work	42.5%	18.1%
Spending less than 15 minutes to go to work (one-way)	16.5%	6.4%

The high percentage of primary school and kindergarten attendance indicates that these neighbourhood facilities are very well utilized. As to secondary education, about half the secondary students in both Estates go to schools in other districts. With so many intertwined factors in the educational system, the provision of secondary schools is a Colony-wide problem, and distribution of enrollment by district of residence can hardly be accomplished by simply planning the number of schools in the district. Overall, there is not much difference in schooling offered by the districts in which the two Estates are located.

Whether or not the housing estate is centrally located bears on the provision of employment opportunities. This is clearly shown in the three ecological parameters associated with employment. 52.5 per cent of economically active members in SKM compared with 39.6 per cent of those in TWS are employed in the district. In addition, a great proportion of the former (42.5 per cent) can go to work on foot and 16.5 per cent of them can reach their place of work within 15 minutes. Because of the relatively isolated location of TWS, a number of those employed in the same district have to take public transportation and have to spend hours queuing and squeezing before they can reach their place of work. Not surprisingly, almost half of our respondents living in the comparatively isolated and populously inhabited TWS considered the transportation services as inadequate, and almost three-quarters thought that new bus routes should be opened.

This raises the question of communication between the planned com-

includes Shamshuipo, Cheung Sha Wan and Lai Chi Kok. The district in which TWS is located includes Wong Tai Sin, Wang Tau Hom, San Po Kong and Chuk Yuen. The district delineation is based on the boundaries of the government's administrative districts.

munity and the urban built-up areas. It is evident that complete self-containment is beyond the potential of many planned communities or new towns. Even in the large new town of Kwun Tong, where various housing schemes provide the labour force and industrial sites provide job opportunities, there is a tremendous amount of manpower exchange with other districts.[16] Self-sufficiency is difficult to realize in practice. Therefore, linkage with and accessibility to other districts are two of the crucial factors that determine the viability of the neighbourhood with respect to employment.

2. *Primary facilities and services*

Our limited data indicated positively that the two Estates are viable functional entities as regards shopping for daily commodities and the use of medical services. Over 80 per cent of the households in both Estates utilize the local medical services; 98.5 per cent in SKM and 73.0 per cent in TWS buy their medicines and drugs in the Estates; 97.0 per cent and 87.0 per cent in SKM and TWS respectively purchase their daily commodities in the Estates.

Unlike those in Government Low-cost Housing Estates and the Estates of the former Housing Authority where commercial shops are let on contract to approved trades only, shops in the resettlement estates are allowed to operate any trades or services, and the tenants are free to sublet or to alter their businesses at will. In such cases, we may expect that without any formal control, in due course, the supply may naturally strike a balance with the needs of the area. It has been nearly twenty years for SKM and ten years for TWS since their construction. Therefore it is not surprising that the businesses have adjusted themselves well to suit the needs of the residents.

On the other hand, a problem of inadequate provision of primary services is usually found in new estates. Shops that provide various types of goods for the residents move in rather late. Pioneer settlers often find an empty estate when they first move in. They may have to go back to their former districts where all commodities and services are provided, or else they may have to suffer the high prices charged by the occasional shops that have so far opened locally.[17]

---

[16]See Ambrose King and Y. K. Chan, "A Theoretical and Operational Definition of Community: The Case of Kwun Tong," an occasional paper of the Social Research Centre, The Chinese University of Hong Kong, July 1972; and Y. K. Chan, "The Rise and Growth of Kwun Tong: A Study of Planned Urban Development," an occasional paper of the Social Research Centre, The Chinese University of Hong Kong, August 1973.

[17]A survey conducted in the new Upper Pak Tin Estate in the summer of 1974 by the Neighbourhood Advice Council reveals that residents of Pak Tin have been waiting two-and-a-half years for Government to supply them with clinics, nurseries, playgrounds, traffic lights and supermarkets. See *Hong Kong Standard*, 20 November, 1974.

3. *Secondary facilities and services*

Five parameters were chosen to indicate the usage of secondary facilities and services in the two Estates. They were the patronage of playgrounds and recreation areas, libraries and reading rooms, activities and services provided by the Kaifong Welfare Association, the Estate Welfare Building and the youth centres. Various reasons were given by the respondents for not using the different types of local facilities and services. These may help us to understand the functioning of the present facilities and services and their implications for future planning in new housing estates.

Generally speaking, the degree of patronage of secondary facilities and services is unexpectedly low as compared with that of the primary facilities and services in these Estates. The percentages of nonusage due to absence of knowledge or need (know but never go) are very high for all the listed facilities and services.

An average of 60 per cent of the children of the respondents in both SKM and TWS do not use the playgrounds, recreation areas, libraries or reading rooms in the Estates (See Table 4). Because of easier accessibility to other districts, a higher percentage of children in SKM than in TWS diffuse their patronage to nonlocal facilities. 'Environmental insecurity' (i.e., the sense of insecurity caused by the belief that the area is infested with bad elements) and 'fear of their children falling into bad company' are the most stated reasons for parents' not allowing children to use these facilities. Over half the respondents (54.4 per cent in SKM and 62.6 per cent in TWS) forbid their children to go to the playgrounds and recreation areas, and the majority (33.6 per cent in SKM and 49.3 per cent in TWS) discourage their children's using the libraries and reading rooms in the Estates for these two reasons. The excuses that their children are too small and that no elder ones in the family can accompany them to the playgrounds (18.1 per cent in SKM and 18.4 per cent in TWS) or the worry about the absence of porper supervision in the libraries and reading rooms (18.0 per cent in SKM and 17.6 per cent in TWS) are similarly fear-laden statements.

Though we do not have enough solid data to show that the resettlement estates have turned into 'crime-trodden slums', we cannot deny the fact that the people are extremely 'fear-stricken' and the sense of insecurity has developed into a sort of phobia which is intensively disturbing the peace of mind of the residents. This 'crime-phobia' accounts for the considerable desertion of public places where strangers are likely to be encountered; and has robbed many children of their chance of enjoying the facilities and services provided for them. The problem of security will be further discussed in the next section.

In the same manner, activities and programs sponsored by the secondary

Table 4

Concentrated usage of secondary facilities and services among respondents in SKM and TWS

Facility and service usage parameters	Estate	Usage of local facilities and services	Usage of nonlocal facilities and services	Nonusage due to absence of need or knowledge	Total	No answer or inapplicable
Playground and recreation area	SKM	32.5%	2.4%	65.1%	100.0% (166)	(34)
	TWS	49.6%	—	50.4%	100.0% (254)	(48)
Library and reading room	SKM	12.2%	26.1%	61.7%	100.0% (115)	(85)
	TWS	29.3%	10.0%	60.7%	100.0% (229)	(73)
Kaifong Welfare Association	SKM	4.1%	—	95.9%	100.0% (197)	(3)
	TWS	4.0%	—	96.0% (47.2%)** (48.8%)***	100.0% (301)	(1)
Estate Welfare Building*	TWS	30.0%	—	70.0% (44.0%)** (26.0%)***	100.0% (300)	(2)
Youth centre*	TWS	6.6%	—	93.4% (64.5%)** (28.9%)***	100.0% (290)	(12)

*   No data for SKM
**   Absence of knowledge
*** Absence of need (know but never go)

groups such as the Kaifong Welfare Association, the youth centres or the agencies in the Estate Welfare Building are indifferently received. Over 90 per cent of the respondents in both SKM and TWS are not using the services at all (see Table 4). An exceptionally high percentage of respondents (47.2 per cent, 44.0 per cent and 64.5 per cent respectively of the respondents in TWS) do not even know that there are such facilities provided, despite the fact that they have been living alongside them for almost ten years.

With greater length of residence, the majority of the respondents in SKM might have heard about the Kaifong Association; however the participation rate is as low as that of TWS (only 4 per cent of our respondents in SKM and TWS has ever joined the activities). 'No time' and 'no interest' account for as many as 72.2 per cent of the stated reasons in SKM and 32.7 per cent in TWS. As a matter of fact, these are the main reasons for respondents who have never been to the Estate Welfare Building in TWS as well. Were it not for the clinic being located in the Building, the situation would surely be worse.[18] Again, 'environmental insecurity' and 'the fear of children falling into bad company' are repeatedly stated as factors hindering the full utilization of youth services in TWS (accounting for 39.4 per cent of the excuses). Other commonly mentioned reasons for the low participation rate in youth centres are the 'time factor' and 'the worry of having no elder ones to accompany their children to these centres'.

This is indeed a gloomy picture. It is sad to see some of the facilities and services not functioning to their full capacity. It is depressing to learn that the children are deprived of their opportunities for outdoor activities, and for meeting people of their own age and enjoying group life. It now seems time for social engineers to pause and reconsider the real meaning of the existence of these facilities and services and to search for a new approach to make them work effectively.

Lack of publicity is often cited as the explanation for the under-utilization of secondary group activities such as those sponsored by the Kaifongs, the youth centres and other organized community activities. Undeniably, publicity or promotion is important, but is this the root-cause? Can we really drag the people out of their dwellings when they have no time? And no interest? Will any people send their kids over to 'receive' our services when they perceive the environment as insecure and they are genuinely frightened? Have we ever sincerely asked ourselves when a program is designed, 'what good is it?' or

[18]Among the 90 respondents in TWS who said that they have ever gone to the Welfare Building, half of them go there for medical services provided by the clinic situated in the Building; a quarter of them go to the library; 8 per cent go for the family welfare services, 4 per cent go for the youth activities and 3 per cent go for the family planning services.

'who wants it?'. Did we ever find out what 'images' have been created in the minds of the ordinary people about the youth centres, and Kaifongs, playgrounds and reading rooms?

Admittedly, not all the resettlement estates are bad neighbourhoods, and not all the playgrounds are 'under-utilized' or 'misutilized'. Many welfare services are meaningful and should be brought to the knowledge of more potential recipients. Nevertheless, just as one would not hesitate to find out the cause and the cure whenever there are symptoms of a malignant disease and try to prevent its growth and spread to other parts of the body, so when the accusation of malfunctioning of neighbourhood facilities and services is justified, it should be treated as a symptom of social disease and prompt action should be taken to look into the matter.

Major Causes for the Nonuse of Facilities and Services

The concern of this section is to analyse the major causes for the nonuse of facilities and services provided in the housing estates. A number of points have to be made clear at the outset.

First, we shall limit our discussion to the nonuse of what we have called secondary facilities and services (namely the playgrounds, recreation areas, libraries, reading rooms and secondary activities run by youth centres and Kaifongs). These are usually referred to as leisure activities. Second, 'nonuse' stand for 'under-utilization' (that is, facilities and services not fully used by the desirable number of persons) and 'mis-utilization' stands for facilities and services not being properly used by desired kinds of persons. Third, our purpose is not to pinpoint precisely which basketball court in TWS has been trespassed upon by certain gangs, neither are we interested in tracing the particular reasons why a certain rooftop in SKM is infested by drug addicts. Rather, we are hoping to generalize the experience of SKM and TWS to a higher level of interpretation. This leads to our last point; that though we discuss only the general and major causes of the nonuse, readers are reminded that other minor factors such as location and accessibility may also be important in affecting the success of certain facilities in the neighbourhood.

1. *The overall picture*

Whether or not the potential users possess appropriate 'needs' or 'hidden needs' is decisive to the usefulness and the justification for the existence of these facilities and services. When the secondary facilities and services provided do not coincide with the leisure preferences and satisfactions of the majority of potential users, needs for such facilities and services will not benefit and facilities and services other than those provided by the planners and social engineers will be exploited instead. One striking example is the competitive pressure mounting from the flourishing televison programs which have become so popular in Hong Kong during the past decade.

Nevertheless, competing activities and their advantages cannot explain completely the reasons for the nonuse of the existing facilities and services. Besides, nonuse does not necessarily mean that there is no 'hidden need' for these services. Other environmental and institutional factors must be examined to give us a more comprehensive picture. As we have already seen, the reasons most often mentioned for the nonuse of facilities like playgrounds and recreation areas, libraries and reading rooms, are 'environmental insecurity' and 'the fear of falling into bad company'. For the nonuse of services like the Estate Welfare Building, Kaifong Association and youth centres, 'no interest' and 'no time' are the most often verbalized reasons.

Environmental insecurity has become an acute problem in Hong Kong during recent years. Law and order must be maintained to ensure that people can use the public places and community activities at leisure without concern. Only in this way can we save our neighbourhoods from deterioration and enable the people to have safe homes and peace of mind.

The insecurity of the environment and failure of the secondary group activities are also explained by other institutional factors. These involve management practices, the maintenance levels of the facilities, the relevance of the program and service to the need of the people, and, above all, the relationship between the management and the people.

2. *The security problem in the neighbourhood*

The prevalence of crime prompts many people to stay away from public places, to avoid strangers, and to keep away from groups or organized activities. The public image of the resettlement estates especially to the outsider (someone who does not live there) is frightening and stigmatized. With their overall physical shabbiness, the high degree of congestion and the heterogeneous population from all walks of life, they are commonly believed to be cradles for the nourishment of gangs, triad societies, drug addiction and other evils.

A considerable proportion of the residents themselves consider that their neighbourhood is crime-ridden. Over half of the respondents (57.3 per cent in SKM and 56.3 per cent in TWS) said that they thought that their neighbourhood was insecure. The majority of them (58.2 per cent in SKM and 76.3 per cent in TWS) felt worried or frightened when coming home late at night. One-third of the respondents in SKM and half in TWS believed that their neighbours had been victims of some criminal offense.

As to the types of crime that occur in the Estates, our data show that vandalism and gang fights account for 61.7 per cent of the crimes in SKM;

whereas in TWS, robberies, account for 44.9 per cent of all the crimes. Robberies, thefts, and sexual assaults are crimes that require direct confrontation of the victim by the offender (or offenders). They usually take place in the quiet corners of the staircases, corridors, inside the elevators and the garbage disposal rooms. For crimes like vandalism, gang fights and drug addiction, the residents may not be directly involved, but mere onlookers. A gang of teenagers may be loitering in the corridors or tarrying on the vacant rooftops. They cause disturbances to the residents who dare not say a word for fear of vengeance. Organized gangs from two different housing blocks may have a big gang fight in order to decide which one should control a certain playground or recreation area in the Estate.

Generally speaking, many crimes are crimes of opportunity rather than premeditated. And few criminals will operate within the buildings where they live for fear of being easily recognized. Crime rates are high in resettlement estates because most of the public areas are under incomplete surveillance by the residents themselves, and this provides good opportunities for offenders to commit crime. When we run down the list of crimes, we find that the crimes typical of each Estate are reflections of the physical structure and management of the housing blocks and their surroundings.

The 'single-loaded corridor' design of the blocks in SKM provides a higher degree of neighbourliness among the residents,[19] and also gives ready opportunities for natural surveillance of the corridors and the public areas, such as communal bathrooms and lavatories. By contrast, the 'double-loaded corridors' in TWS are devoid of surveillance opportunities.[20] On top of that, the gigantic blocks (sometimes adjacent blocks are linked togehter by common corridors) in TWS have several exits and thus provide good opportunities for offenders to escape. As reflected in our data, robberies, thefts and sexual assaults in public areas like corridors, staircases and lavatories are much fewer in SKM than TWS. The present proposition that a housing project composed of high-rise double-loaded corridor buildings is much more vulnerable to criminal activities than its walk-up counterparts will have to be confirmed by further research.

In addition, these estates have many deserted and unmanaged areas like the vacant rooftops and playgrounds where crimes can take place.[21] Without proper management and surveillance they are often made use of by undesir-

[19] See Angela W. S. Kan, *op. cit.*

[20] Oscar Newman, *Defensible Space: Crime Prevention through Urban Design*, The MacMillian Co., New York, 1972.

[21] After the closing down of many rooftop schools and welfare centres in Mark I and II blocks, many of the rooftops, left unlocked and deserted, have been used by drug addicts or have served as gathering places for teddy boys and girls.

able people and as a result the ordinary citizens avoid them. The final outcome would be encroachment upon and mis-utilization of these facilities and services by certain groups of people, and their under-utilization by the persons for whom they were originally designed. Above all, they may serve as black spots where illegal transactions may take place and new members be recruited into the group.[22] Unpopular facilities are troubling not only because of the waste and missed opportunities they imply, but also because of their frequent negative effects of 'malfunctioning', a consequence that town planners may never have considered.

3. *The behavioural patterns and the displacement of facilities and services*

A. Playing habits

No systematic studies have ever been made in Hong Kong to ascertain the playing habits of children and teenagers in order to plan facilities and services according to the orientation of the users rather than that of the planners. Children need a variety of places in which to play and to learn. They need opportunities for all kinds of sports, games, exercise and physical skills. Planners provide their ready answers in parks, playgrounds, open spaces, youth centres and community centres. However, what children mostly need is an 'unspecialized outdoor home base' in which to play and to hang around.[23] A lot of outdoor life for children adds up from bits. It happens in a small leftover interval after lunch; it happens while they are waiting to be called for their suppers; it happens in brief intervals between supper and homework, or homework and bed. These home-base play periods occur at various times and must be sandwiched between other activities. Games, such as shot marbles, jump rope, hide and seek, play stoop ball, clapping cards, write with chalk, trot out their possessions, horseplay, role-playing games like teacher-student, doctor-patient, cooking, wedding and even talking, pushing, shoving and climbing on rails etc. are most often seen being played near the home. Corridors in the high-rise public housing estates (which are in a sense streets piled up in the sky), and the spaces around the corners and the staircases are the most convenient places for such unspecialized home-base play.

The fear-stricken parents would rather have these sorts of unspecialized home-base games in the corridors or spaces near the staircases so that they can

---

[22]This can be confirmed by the data of the survey of juvenile delinquency in Hong Kong in 1974 (see Agnes Ng, "Social Causes of Violent Crimes among Young Offenders in Hong Kong," an occasional paper of the Social Research Centre, The Chinese University of Hong Kong, May 1975). In that survey, it was found that about one quarter of the respondents who associated with triad societies had had their first contact in the playgrounds and other empty places in the neighbourhood.

[23]Jane Jacobs, *op. cit.*, p. 91.

keep watch on their children every now and then than have the children playing in the streets, playgrounds or joining any organized programs run by secondary groups. It is not unusual to find cases where parents have bought television sets, despite their knowledge of their hindrances that they would cause to their children's study in the unpartitioned and congested dwelling units, in order to keep their children at home.

B. The influence of television

Television is a strong competitor to the playgrounds, youth centres, reading rooms and other secondary and specialized activities in the neighbourhood. Respondents in SKM and TWS were asked about the usual kinds of leisure activities they thought their children would undertake after school or after work. Though we do not know from the simple question whether these are the activities desired by the parents or actually practiced by their children, the answers can still serve as rough indicators. An average of as many as three-quarters (77.1 per cent of those in school and 61.3 per cent of those working in SKM; 86.3 per cent of those in school and 80.2 per cent of those working in TWS) of their children stay at home after school or work. The great majority of these children pass their time by watching TV while the number playing in parks and playgrounds and joining of secondary activities is relatively low. It is evident that television programs have become a significant part of the life of the people in Hong Kong.

C. Displacement by demographic change of the population

The demands and standards of people are subjected to change. A ready example is the displacement of rooftop schools in the Mark I and II blocks. With the aging of the population in the older estates and the building of new ones with higher standards, more and more of these primary schools became unnecessary. Similar situations were faced by welfare centres with somewhat out-dated services such as sponsorship and foster-parent schemes, distribution of milk and provision of meals. The displacement of older services is a natural consequence of the changes in social and economic structure of society under industrialization and economic development. However, services of different types and higher standards are still needed. The deserted rooftops of the older resettlement estates should be made use of, rather than being left to lie empty or turn into spots that are dangerous to the block. Because of their proximity, convenience and familiarity, the use of the now deserted rooftop for the re-creation of appropriate services under good management might be much better received and trusted than the setting up of separate youth centres which require youngsters to walk through dangerous neighbourhoods.

4. *Institutional factors*

It has been repeatedly emphasized that ignorance of people's needs and lack of surveillance are the major factors contributing to the under-utilization of facilities and services. These in turn have to do with the maintenance levels, the relevance of the program, the management practices and the relationships between the staff of the institution and the people. The last two points will be elaborated in what follows.

A. Attitudes towards the services

Services in a neighbourhood are different in function and in the way that the people relate to them. At one extreme, services such as work, education and medical care are so vital to the individual and the neighbourhood that people have little choice but to accept them. Services that agencies from outside offer to the residents (notably the family welfare services, youth centres, programme's for the aged, neighbourhood and community development organizations and so forth) are treated with a mixture of curiosity and suspicion. Since they are not basic necessities, they are essentially ignored. At the other extreme are the law, the management, the bureaucracy, the police and the government. They are usually conceived of as agencies that exist to exploit people. Ambivalent as to their usefulness and skeptical as to their authority, residents view these agencies with considerable hostility. If possible, contact with them is minimized or avoided.

B. Management practices towards facilities

Good planning and good management should always go hand-in-hand in serving a good neighbourhood. Inadequate management may be caused by a number of factors ranging from the quality and training of the managing staff and the problem of inter-organizational coordination within the Estates to the inter-departmental functions and coordination on the higher or district level. In the following paragraphs, attention will be drawn to a few points concerning management which need to be further investigated.

The provision and management of facilities and services in each housing estate are delegated to several governmental departments such as the Police Department, the Urban Services Department, the Social Welfare Department, the City District Office, and to certain private agencies such as the welfare organizations, the bus company, the Kaifong Association and others. Understandably, clashes of interest may arise among these various agencies. While the Estate manager is thinking of the welfare and convenience of the residents in the Estate itself, the outside agencies have to think and plan in terms of the overall situation in the Colony. For instance, the Estate manager may fight on behalf of the residents to open more bus routes from the Estate to other districts, but be defeated simply because of the insufficient profit made to cover the additional expense by the bus company. Similarly, the Estate manager may request an additional police depot in the neighbourhood, but be denied because of the much more urgent need in other districts than the Estate.

Another point needs to be considered further here: Is there any unnecessary splitting of functions among administratively independent departments in the management of certain facilities? Until the setting up of a 'tidiness team' in the Resettlement Department,[24] the responsibility for controlling hawkers rested solely with the Urban Council and the Urban Services Department. Since then, the control and resiting of hawkers within the Estates have been gradually assumed by the former Resettlement Department. In the same manner, the management of open spaces such as playgrounds and rest gardens is still officially under the Urban Services Department, but the cleaning of these areas is delegated to the staff of the Housing Department. This splitting of functions between two Departments may lead to some technical problems. Unexpected negligence may sometimes arise through incompleted supervision or unclear demarcation of tasks. There may be negligence caused simply by the problem of distance and communication between the central office and the staff who are stationed in various Estates to control the facilities. Administrators should note that some facilities are more efficiently managed on the Estate level while others are better fostered on the district level.

Another point worth drawing to the attention of policymakers is that management problems have to be handled with care. Because of the accumulation of historical mistakes due to improper management in the first place and the subsequent intrusion of bad elements and their growth, some facilities can hardly be managed at all. In some places they are managed not by rules laid down in black and white, but by the rules of 'human relationship'. Occasionally, illegal actions such as gang fights and drug trafficking can be prevented because 'face' (respect) has to be given to the person who has visible or invisible power in that neighbourhood. That person may be a renowned housing manager, a respectable Kaifong leader or even a notorious gang leader in the neighbourhood. Some gangs may even give 'face' to the gardener who has looked after the playground for a long time. Through their influence, the residents of the neighbourhood can have peace and security. On top of that, there is always a hidden danger when the authority and management system have to rely on one person who may be transferred to other neighbourhood or whose power may decline in the course of time. It is not that human or public relations are unimportant in the field of management,

[24]Tidiness teams were set up at the beginning of September 1969. The first three teams each consisted of 20 labourers led by two gangers and a chargeman were centrally based and were on call by any estate to demolish new illegal structures. By 1972, the number was increased to a total of 17 and 11 posts for Resettlement Assistants to act as team leaders were created.

but too much dependence on this resource can hinder the movement of the whole system and may lead to malpractices as well. This is another field that needs to be further examined before any definite solution can be discovered.

Summary and Implications

1. *Summary*

In this paper, we have accepted the concentrated use of an area's facilities and services as an indication of the viability of the neighbourhood concept in the planning of housing estates in Hong Kong. Facilities and services are divided into two broad types, namely primary and secondary. The former involves a number of ecological parameters related to daily activities such as working and schooling, and basic services such as medical care and shopping outlets. The latter is represented by the facilities and services for leisure activities such as parks and playgrounds, libraries and reading rooms, and such secondary groups as the youth centres, Estate Welfare Building and Kaifong Welfare Association.

On the average, the indicators for primary facilities and services pointed to a high level of utilization. The inadequacy of employment opportunities provided within the district gave rise to transportation problems acutely faced by the isolated and populous housing estates. Motivated by the unexpectedly low utilization of neighbourhood facilities and participation in secondary group activities, we attempted to analyse the real causes accounting for their nonuse.

Environmental insecurity has produced creeping fears and negative feelings towards public areas where strangers might be encountered. With the rapid development of television in the last decade, people would rather retreat to their homes for leisure activities than endanger their lives in the neighbourhood. They rear their children under close scrutiny. They do not trust places that are visually inaccessible. In most cases, children are only allowed to associate with others on the same floor and games in the corridors are the only 'outdoor' activities provided. These points are enlightening as to the evaluation of the usefulness of the facilities and services that are planned to be located at a distance from the residences.

Institutional factors in general, and management practices and the attitudes of the people in particular contribute to the nonuse of services and the creation of distorted images in the minds of the potential users. They call for the re-examination of the basic philosophy and attitudes upheld by town planners, housing managers and social workers. They also ask for a comprehensive interorganizational review of the interrelated policies governing the sphere of management of the housing blocks and the adjoining environment.

2. *Some theoretical implications*

A. The facility-centered theory of social change[25]

Many of the early urban reformers believed that if poor people were provided with a set of properly designed facilities, ranging from housing and better work places to parks and playgrounds, they would not only give up their slum abodes but also change themselves in the process. The founders of the playground movement believed that if the poor could be provided with playgrounds and community centres, they would stop frequenting the cafes, brothels, and movie houses in which they spent their leisure time and would desert the street corner gangs and clubs which they had created for social life. On the contrary, these beliefs have turned out to have no true basis in reality.

One mistaken assumption of the physical planners is the importance of facilities in everybody's life. For most people community facilities are relatively unimportant. The number of people who use such public facilities as playgrounds and libraries is always small and limited to a selected group of people. Although a few may be so attracted to the facilities that their life is changed by them, the majority of people use a facility only rarely, and it becomes important to them only when it becomes part of their *social environment*. For example, teenagers may not loiter around playgrounds as individuals, but a gang may come in as a group and make it its gathering place. That the existence of community facilities is a guarantee of their proper utilization and thus desirable for the people, is another wrong supposition. Planners have overlooked the fact that the facilities might be mis-utilized and turned into an evil for the neighbourhood, despite their own original good intentions.

What affects people is not the raw physical environment, but the social and economic environment in which that physical environment is used. If the planner wants to affect people's lives, it is an integrated social, economic and political environment for which he must plan. To be successful, the concept of urban renewal must embrace the notion of human renewal. Jane Jacobs puts the matter in a vivid way:

> "It is fashionable to suppose that certain touchstones of the good life will create good neighbourhoods—schools, parks, clean housing and the like. How easy life would be if this were so! How charming to control a complicated and ornery society by bestowing upon it rather simple physical goodies. In real life, cause and effect are not so simple. . . . Good shelter is a useful good in itself, as shelter. When we try to justify good shelter instead on the pretentious grounds that it will work social or family miracles we fool ourselves. . . . Reinhold Niebuhr has called this particular self-deception 'the doctrine of salvation by bricks'."[26]

---

[25] The term is employed from Herbert Gans, *op. cit.*

[26] Jane Jacobs, *op. cit.*, pp. 122-123.

B. User-oriented facilities and services

Why are there so often no people where the facilities are and no facilities where the people are? How does one go about planning for people? Very often normative standards are set in terms of acreage ratios per thousand of population. Planning standards are applied for housing, schools, playgrounds, hospitals, clinics, libraries and other recreation facilities. The standards themselves are not based on expert knowledge or empirical analysis. Quantity is used as the yardstick for adequacy and advancement. As we know all too plainly, a good school building does not necessarily generate a good education.

Instead of being oriented to how people live, what they want and what problems they have that need to be solved, the facilities and services designed often reflect the vested interest, cultural values and biases of the planner himself. It is a debatable question whether or not we should give people whatever they demand. To a certain extent, the government should have the responsibility to enlighten the people as to their needs and to change the lives of the people by giving them what they should have. However, this involves a long process of social education and cannot be achieved by simply granting them the facilities patriarchally and telling them "Here is something for you," and then saying contentedly "Isn't it wonderful! Now the poor have everything!"

C. The unit of planning

We go back to the question we asked in the beginning, "Is the neighbourhood unit socially valid?" The orthodox neighbourhood unit theory in its pure form posits a neighbourhood composed of several thousand persons, a unit supposedly of sufficient size to populate an elementary school and to support convenience shopping and a community centre.[27]

The study of SKM and TWS enables us to draw the preliminary conclusion that the planning of primary facilities and services (such as schools, clinics and shops etc.) in Hong Kong, using the housing estate as a unit of planning, is both theoretically and practically feasible. However, in view of the employment patterns, the ideal of a completely self-sufficient, supposedly cozy, inward-turned neighbourhood cannot be realized locally.

Turning to the secondary facilities and services that cater for leisure activities of the residents, it seems likely that smaller planning units would be more practical. The centralization of facilities and services in one building (such as community centres and Welfare Buildings) will serve only a limited number of people.

Jane Jacobs advocates using the 'street neighbourhood' as a planning unit,

[27]Clarence A. Perry, "The Neighbourhood Unit Formula," in *Urban Housing*, edited by W. Wheaton, G. Milgram and M. Meyerson, Free Press, New York, 1966, pp. 94-109.

". . . . to weave webs of public surveillance and thus to protect strangers as well as themselves; to grow networks of small-scale, everyday public life and thus of trust and social control; and to help assimilate children into reasonably responsible and tolerant city life."[28]

Reflecting upon the prevalence of environmental insecurity, the fear of residents to leave their dwellings, and the playing habits of the children, it seems to be more realistic to consider using the blocks or even the individual floors of the high-rise projects as units for the planning of services for leisure activities.

3. *Some practical implications*

A. Restoration of neighbourhood security

It is argued that the restoration of security in one neighbourhood will only succeed in displacing crime from one area to another. When a vigorous police effort is concentrated in one district, criminals respond by moving into adjacent areas. This raises a new question: is a pattern of uniformly distributed crime preferable to one in which crime is concentrated in particular areas? There are serious moral implications to the question of displacement which is a phenomenon yet to be understood and a means for coping with it yet to be developed.

Meanwhile, disregarding the question of crime displacement, the feeling of security at home and in its environs is of primary importance for the development of a healthy neighbourhood. As short-term measures, additional police manpower, equipment and depots are only palliatives to the crime problem. The creation of surveillance opportunities would decrease crime in the neighbourhood. This can be achieved by encouraging both the management and the residents themselves.

(1) Strengthening the official surveillance through the following steps may prevent some crimes from happening:

(a) Prohibit any usage by strangers, or even residents, of the areas like vacant units, garbage-disposal rooms, meter rooms by adding locks and frequent checking;

(b) Extend the caretaker system to each block;[29]

(c) Check frequently the unused rooftops, especially those of the Mark I and II blocks. Gates and locks to be added to block the exists.[30]

[28] Jane Jacobs, *op. cit.*, p. 129.

[29] A few blocks in TWS have adopted the caretaker system and the response of the residents in those blocks to the management and to the security of the block seems to be more positive. In addition to the placement of caretakers, these blocks are fenced, providing distinguishable boundaries.

[30] However, the rooftops are frequented by the residents in order to fix their TV antennae that are usually stored on the rooftops. Better solutions have to be discovered.

(2) Strengthening of natural surveillance by the residents themselves may be achieved in the following ways:

(a) Through the manipulation of building, spatial configurations and territorial definition, (applicable only to the new buildings under planning) one can create "surveillance opportunities to allow the citizen to achieve control of his environment and to make him instrumental in curtailing others from destroying his habit, whether the others are criminals or a reactionary authority."[31] Huge and linking blocks with many exits should be avoided in the future design of housing. It is worth applying the popular concept of 'defensible space' which has been studied in other countries, to the local scene for detailed examination of its feasibility. Planners have to be cautious in the future designs of housing. For once the block is inhabited, the residents have to take whatever consequences the design will bring to them. From her rich experience of the past in the building industry, Hong Kong cannot afford to commit more mistakes.

(b) At the same time, natural surveillance can be created by the development of a cooperative spirit among neighbours on the same floor and in the whole block. The provision of play facilities for children at each floor level may bring families out to use them and may further enhance the formation and development of friendships. This may lead to a shared effort to maintain the facility, to prevent intruders using public areas for mal-practices and to help neighbours in case of danger. The establishment of the Mutual-Aid Committees are positive signs along these lines. Indeed we do need genuine and committed citizens to form strong neighbourhoods.

B. Program planning of services

The housing estates with their large concentration of people offer both a great need and a great opportunity for welfare work. Successful programs that aim to raise the people's social horizons and to realise 'human renewal', have to break through the barriers and gain the trust of the people. Unfortunately, there the prevalent image of welfare services among the people is distorted. They usually look upon these services with a mixture of curiosity, suspicion, and indifference.

As we have seen, the lack of confidence in services such as youth centres, reading rooms, and libraries is reinforced by feelings of environmental insecurity and the belief in the prevalence of bad elements in the neighbourhood. This being so, the services should design programs that are not only

[31] Oscar Newman, *op. cit.*, p. 204.

relevant to the immediate needs of the families, but that can also be brought to their households or their immediate neighbourhoods. Some agencies are already offering services along this line. Among the most popular programs are student guidance schemes, tutorial classes, neighbourhood organizations and other community development activities. They are operated usually either at the floor or the block level.

Since it will take years before any change can occur for most of the Mark I and II blocks, the deserted rooftops in these estates should be re-opened for welfare purposes. The Housing Department should encourage agencies that are interested to take control of the rooftops. This may save these places from the hands of bad elements, on the one hand, and may offer programmes for the benefit of the residents, on the other.

The influence of television has a great impact on the lives of the people. One point we have to note is that having a television set in the unpartitioned and congested dwelling unit is detrimental to the children's homework. Unless an increase of space can be allocated, which seems to be very unlikely, the demand for a quiet place for studying is great. Bringing well-supervised library and reading room services up to the floors of the blocks or to the rooftops are promising measures worth considering.

C. Other implications

It has been pointed out that for relatively isolated and populous housing estates, considerations of the transportation network must have top priority. Close coordination should be maintained between the Housing Department and the bus companies to keep a constant check on the demand and the supply.

The problem of the inadequate provision of primary services such as shops, markets, medical clinics calls for better timing in the early phase of moving into the new estates. The provision of services should be synchronized with the moving of the people into the estate as residents.

Another point that has been raised is the policy underlying the management practices. In the sphere of the management of housing and its environment, there are inter-organizational and inter-departmental tensions that require further examination. This is particularly necessary for those areas of management were functions are shared between departments. Where are the operational difficulties? Is there any ambiguity and confusion of tasks that may lead to negligence in management? Is the objective inadequately realized because of these divided responsibilities?

A number of questions have been raised in this paper. Some are answered but some are not. Immediate actions are called for in some respects while further research and discussion are required in others. The problem of housing is not an isolated one; it is closely linked with the economic, social, political and technological development of society; it is a topic for multi-disciplinary research and multi-sectoral planning. We need a mutual understanding and working relationship between the physical and social sciences. The result might then be that when new towns are developed, social planning for the social well-being of people and their social development as people is given a recognized place alongside planning for land use and the physical structure of buildings and roads. Then vital communities will materialize.

Chapter 5

Small Factories in Kwun Tong:
Problems and Strategies for Development*

Victor Mok

Hong Kong's small scale factories are threatened by a series of grave problems—trade barriers, keen competition, rising costs and labour shortage —all of which have become more acute in recent years. Hong Kong has come to the point where a fresh look at this sector and a reassessment of policy towards it are needed.

It is true that at an earlier stage of economic development Hong Kong did provide a most favourable climate for the Schumpeterian entrepreneur. Under a laissez-faire policy, with well-established transportation and communication facilities, cheap labour and access to overseas markets, many small scale enterprises did grow up into respectable sizes. Many an entrepreneur, after learning the tricks of his trade, scraped up some savings of his own together with those of his friends and relatives, started modestly by himself, ploughed his profits back and established himself in business. But the further development of Hong Kong has certainly worked against him. For one thing, the emerging labour shortage means that he can no longer rely on low wages to compensate for his relatively low efficiency. What is more, increasingly keen competition in the world market for labour-intensive products necessitates Hong Kong's production moving into high quality and more capital-intensive lines. We should note that many small factories in Hong Kong are also export-oriented. In a world of trade barriers and international negotiations, increasingly dependent on long-standing contacts, small factories are at a great disadvantage. Our survey indicates that small factories here have relatively slow rates of growth in terms of production, export value, and employment. They can only pick up what is left to them by the large ones. With respect to employment too, we should not over-emphasize their importance. Our survey shows that 73.9% of the factories in our sample are small, but they employ

*The present paper is produced for the Kwun Tong Industrial Community Research Programme, which was coordinated by Dr. Ambrose Yeo-chi King and was financially supported by the Harvard-Yenching Institute and The Chinese University of Hong Kong. The study was under the auspices of the Social Research Centre, The Chinese University of Hong Kong.

only 14.5% of the labour force.[1] In many aspects, we find these small factories constitute the traditional sector. Admitting that they do have advantages, it is not their smallness that causes our concern. Perhaps it is not even their proliferation per se. It is their continued reliance upon traditional ways while the rest of the economy has changed that is the core of the problem.

If they are to continue to play an active role in the development of Hong Kong, the small factories must be integrated into the rest of the economy. But it has become clear that from now on their full integration will depend increasingly upon their modernization. They need up-to-date technical knowhow, rational management and organization, efficient marketing, and modern means of financing. A policy which simply distributes indiscriminate assistance to "lame ducks" will only generate their further proliferation and continued inefficiency. What is needed instead is a programme that will seek out those small firms which show promise and encourage them to modernize successfully. This paper is offered as a possible contribution to such a programme.

The first step must be to define the subject. Unfortunately, there is no generally accepted definition of a "small factory". Size alone is not the only criterion, for there are also such functional considerations as relatively little internal specialization, rudimentary technical competence, and management based on close personal contacts.[2] For our present purpose, however, we have decided to retain a numerical standard and define a small factory as one having less than 50 workers. We readily admit that this is an arbitrary figure, but our analyses show that it does seem to be associated with the other characteristics that go to make small factories a distinctive class in Hong Kong at the present time.

Our survey was carried out in the District of Kwun Tong—a newly developed industrial-residential town—in the summer of 1971. From information supplied by the Department of Labour, a sample of 35 per cent was taken from the population of 1,552 factories in our survey.[3] Sampling was stratified according to industrial type, and the survey was conducted by interview with pre-coded questionnaires. Out of a total of 546, there were 200 unsuccessful interviews.[4] Thus we have an actual sample of 346 factories,

[1] See Victor Mok, "The Nature of Kwun Tong as an Industrial Community: An Analysis of Economic Organization," an occasional paper of the Social Research Centre, The Chinese University of Hong Kong, August 1972, p. 15.

[2] J. E. Walsh, Jr., *Improving Productivity in Small and Medium Scale Manufacturing Enterprises,* Asian Productivity Organization, 1969, pp. 4-5.

[3] Even though 58 factories were listed as "not in operation", in fact a number of them were operating during the time of our survey. Therefore they were included in our sampling process.

[4] The reasons for unsuccessful interviews are: factory moved or closed, manager not in, reject, can't find address, promised to answer by mail but actually did not, etc.

or 22.3% of the population. The factories in our sample were all "registered" and "recorded", meaning that they either had more than 20 workers or used power machinery, gas, petroleum, or other inflammable materials. Thus we had already eliminated a large part of what Staley and Morse have called "non-factory" forms of manufacture[5] and the small factories we studied were "factories" in a genuine sense. All were located in the urban area. The questionnaire asked about each factory, the owner and his ideas, its management and organization pattern, products and markets, inputs and sources, its relationships with other factories, and so forth.

In the summer of 1972, 48 of the small factories owned by Chinese were selected from our previous sample for re-study by interview. We were able to make 30 successful contacts—the rest had either moved or been closed or simply could not be located. This fact alone gives us some idea about the fast changing scene in this sector. The textiles, plastic products, garments, wigs, and fabricated metal products industries were represented in this sample, which provided us with information about production, marketing, finance and management problems. Previous studies of Kwun Tong have demonstrated that it is very much an integral part of Hong Kong's economy as a whole, and has much in common with other areas.[6] Thus we have some confidence in asserting that the problems of the small factories in Kwun Tong are common to this sector in Hong Kong in general.

Production

In both our original survey and the re-study,[7] we were amazed to find that respondents admitted to few problems in production. In the second study, out of the 30 answers to the question whether they had technical difficulties, 19 stated that they had none, 5 expressed no opinion, and only 2 complained about their equipment. A number of possible reasons can be given. First and on the face of it, one could argue that the small factories really were doing a good job and had little to complain about. Second, it is possible that in accordance with the spirit of individualism prevalent in Hong Kong, respondents were confident about taking care of themselves. Even if they had difficulties they would not want to tell any one except close friends; they just wanted to be left alone. Third, it could be that factory owners were simply

[5] E. Staley and R. Morse, *Modern Small Industry for Developing Countries*, Free Press, 1965.

[6] See Mok, 1972, *op. cit.*

[7] The original survey was reported in Mok, 1972, *op. cit.*, and his "The Organization and Management of Factories in Kwun Tong," an occasional paper of the Social Research Centre, The Chinese University of Hong Kong, June 1973.

complacent and had little desire to change what they had been doing for some time. If this were the case, then contradictory to the Schumpeterian image of the venturesome entrepreneur, these small industrialists appear to have been satisfied with marginal profits and reluctant to initiate changes. Fourth, it seems possible that because of his lack of knowledge and limited economic horizon, the average small factory owner had few future plans at all. Instead, he conducted what was basically a hand-to-mouth operation whose problems were so deep-rooted that the lack of complaint is rather a sign of stagnation.

Even though theoretically the small factory needs a shorter period to raise capital and so can be more adaptable to new technology, our survey showed that these small factories tended to use older equipment.[8] What is more, when asked in the re-study whether they had made important technical improvements in the past three years, 21 out of a total of 30 respondents stated that there had been none whatsoever, and only 6 had purchased new equipment. With respect to their products, more than two-thirds of the small factories had had no changes during the same period. This lack of product improvement was mainly due to the fact that the majority of them produced according to ordered specifications—less than one-third of them had made any effort in respect of product design and improvement. In our survey, only 22.7% of the small factories had increased their product lines since their establishment, with an overwhelming majority of them remaining in a one-product operation. Compared to the factories of larger sizes, in which nearly one half claimed that their product lines had increased, there is ample indication of stagnation in this sector.

Regarding personnel, our survey indicated that the percentage of technical to all workers decreased slightly as factory size increased.[9] By no means should this be interpreted as showing that there was a higher level of technical expertise in the smaller factories. On the contrary, this finding is no more than an indication of little internal specialization. So often in these factories, not only has the owner-manager himself to assume other duties, but also the technically more advanced workers have to do many other chores as well. In our re-study, two-thirds of the factories had no people specializing in product design and improvement or in technical innovation. The same percentage showed that technical personnel were interchangeable with others—they also worked as foremen, buyers, salesmen or plain workmen. Under these conditions, the technical expertise in small factories just cannot be compared with that in the larger concerns.

[8] Mok, 1972, *op. cit.*, p. 56.

[9] Mok, 1973, *op. cit.*, p. 28. By our definition, technical workers include engineers, craftsmen, technicians and skilled workers.

Nevertheless, the simple nature of their lines of production and the lack of internal specialization could be considered as advantages to the small factory. To work otherwise might just be too complicated and expensive. If a small factory has a good working relationship with a large firm, be it another manufacturer or exporter, it can concentrate its efforts on the improvement of production efficiency. This we shall discuss when we come to the subject of sub-contracting. Another way is to solicit specialized services from public or private organizations at low cost. Productivity centres in many developing countries have been founded for this purpose, and Hong Kong is no exception. However, the relationship between the Hong Kong Productivity Centre and the small factories does not seem to be encouraging despite its many activities. In our re-study, 13 respondents (out of a total of 30) said that they had never heard of it at all; 11 said that even though they had heard of it, it had made little impression on them. Only 2 claimed that they had had contacts with it. When asked to express their opinion about the Productivity Centre, the overwhelming majority had none.

The way the small factories react to changing production requirements also gives us some idea about their operations. In booming seasons, the majority tend to work overtime and hire more temporary workers; in slack seasons, they slow down and hire less temporary help. A few of them even turned to laying off workers. The large factories react in the same way except that they have a much higher percentage of production workers which *allows for a bigger adjustment* in terms of employment.[10] This was evidenced by the fact the larger factories did have higher turnover rates in their production workers.[11] The lower turnover rates of the small factories were accounted for by reasons such as closer personal relations, less rigid organizational structure and the general interchangeability of the work force. In this respect, we have to reconsider the "flexibility" of the small factory which is so often claimed to be its advantage. In terms of capital overhead and internal organization, it may be quite true. But there seems to be an assymetry in its adjustment to changing production requirements. In times of prosperity, a small factory can adapt itself readily in the same way as its large counterpart, or perhaps even more so. It is in a period of low activities that it may face serious adjustment problems. Its low overheads in terms of equipment may well be more than counter-balanced by its disadvantages in having a more rigid "establishment".

In one of our reports we found that the large factories tended to have higher capacity use.[12] As Hong Kong is an export-led economy, it is under-

[10] Mok, 1972, *op. cit.*, pp. 28-29.
[11] Mok, 1972, *op. cit.*, p. 42.
[12] Mok, 1972, *op. cit.*, p. 33.

standable that the large factories would be first in line to reap the benefit of their established connections. But there is also another plausible explanation. Since the large factories have more capital equipment and make wider adjustments in their employment of production workers, they tend to report their use of capacity in relation to their capital investment. The small factories, with fewer overheads, tend to relate their capacity use to the utilization of their existing manpower. Here the small factories may not be as flexible as they first appear. In normal times, their excess capacity may still be tolerable; but in times of adversity when they are especially hard hit, they will have a difficult time in making cost adjustments. The small factories, acting as a buffer, might add some flexibility to the economy as a whole by the fact that they are easy to set up and close down. But this is quite different from saying that small factories are individually flexible in weathering a storm.

The low productivity of the small factories is reflected in low wages. In our survey of the average monthly wages of production workers, we found that in larger factories wages were approximately 18 per cent higher than in small ones.[13] On top of this, the larger ones also had better working conditions and provided more benefits such as medical care, transportation, insurance and occasional entertainment.[14]

All these facts give us a general picture of small factories as being beset with serious problems. Low in productivity, stagnant, and especially vulnerable to external changes, they are very much occupied with their daily operation and have little time to plan for the future. We are not saying that they have not shared in and contributed to Hong Kong's continuing economic growth, but it is clear that their performance bears no comparison to that of the larger ones. Our surveys show that since the establishment of Kwun Tong up to 1971, the value of production of about three quarters of the small factories there had less than doubled while that of over half of the larger ones had more than doubled, with more than one quarter of them chalking up increases in excess of 200%. The same pattern can be found in the relative increases in the employment of production workers, though the disparity was much less. These facts alone suggest that the productivity increase in the small factories was much slower.

One further factor affecting the production of small factories is the acute housing shortage in Hong Kong. Dwyer has lamented the chaotic land-use pattern in the city where small factories are located in tenement building.[15]

[13] Mok, 1972, *op. cit.*, pp. 69-72.

[14] Mok, 1973, *op. cit.*, pp. 54-57.

[15] J. D. Dwyer, "Problems of the Small Industrial Unit," in J. D. Dwyer, ed., *Asian Urbanization: A Hong Kong Casebook*, Hong Kong University Press, 1971; and J. D. Dwyer & Lai Chuen-yan, *The Small Industrial Unit in Hong Kong: Patterns and Policies*, University of Hull, 1967.

This is the result of the lack of urban planning and general housing shortage. In Kwun Tong, the situation is somewhat better as it was planned with zoning. However, many of the small factories were resettled there in low-cost government flatted factory buildings. No wonder that in our re-study we found that 20 (out of 30) small factory owners declared themselves satisfied with the housing and rent situation. It would have been quite different if they had had to pay the market price. Their dependence on low-cost housing is such that since their establishment only one quarter of the small factories had increased their space, compared with one half of the larger ones which had been able to do so. Without low-cost housing, the problems would be much aggravated.

It is true that the Hong Kong Productivity Centre has made efforts to interest factory owners in new techniques by arranging exhibitions and providing technical consultation services. But we wonder how many of these have really been useful to the small factories. For one thing, the equipment which they are interested in buying is not the same as that required by large factories; for another thing, the types of technical information and advice they seek are also different. Moreover, the small factories need basic training as well as mere advice. Therefore, what is needed is an agency created specifically for them. The first task of such an agency would be to convince the small factory owners that they must and can modernize. For instance, a mere display of low-cost automation units would only leave the small manufacturers confused and would soon be forgotten. As Groot put it, ". . . we have to break the vicious circle where a lack of knowledge about the equipment does not create the demand that is necessary to get the equipment which in turn is required to get the knowledge".[16] Factory owners must be induced to realize that such equipment is well within their reach and that the change-over can be a gradual one. Another area in which such an agency could be of use would be in providing technical information, testing and quality control and consultation in general. Some of these points are elaborated below.

Although rationalization by consolidation in this sector could also help improve efficiency, many more problems are involved. A frontal attack by means of the open promotion of mergers would most probably fail. We have ample evidence that Hong Kong is still a strong bastion of rugged individualsim: an overwhelming proportion of the small factories in our re-study were interested neither in taking partners nor in being absorbed. They would rather stay the way they were or even engage in hit-and-run operations than commit themselves permanently in a bigger joint venture. The rationalization of this sector must therefore be indirect and more subtle.

[16]R. de Groot, "The Application of Low-cost Automation in Small Manufacturing Plants," in *Small Industry Bulletin for Asia and the Far East*, No. 7 ECAFE, 1970, p. 97.

One thing that could be done would be to create a physical environment favourable to more cooperation among factories of all types and sizes. Here we are especially referring to the development planning of new industrial areas. More flatted low-cost factory buildings should be built for small factories in these areas in order to foster more complementarity and interdependence. This would not only make it much easier for the government to conduct studies and carry out its training and consultation programmes, but it would also facilitate the spreading of information and the use of common facilities. In addition, such a relatively convenient environment might foster the development of a sense of common interest in he collective tackling of problems such as joint marketing and purchase of raw materials. A further step would be to promote sub-contracting between large and small factories. This we shall discuss in the following section. But it should be noted that sub-contracting can be much more than just a marketing relationship, for it can help small factories to improve their efficiency through specialization.

Marketing

It is well known that in Hong Kong the majority of factories are more related to overseas than domestic markets. They also depend heavily on foreign suppliers for their equipment, intermediate products and raw materials.[17] Our survey showed that small factories were somewhat less export-oriented than large ones,[18] but it is interesting to find that those which were export-oriented indulged in direct exporting, instead of using middleman exporters to an extent similar to other size groups.[19] Either they were actively doing their own trading, or the larger ones depended just about as much on the export merchants.

Relatively little is known about the overall pattern of the export merchants in Hong Kong, especially the small ones who presumably serve the small factories. It is our general impression that this sector of small traders is about as individualistic as the sector of small factories. A person with some capital, having some knowledge of overseas markets through friends and relatives or even his previous employer, hires a couple of clerks, may or may not have a regular office, has some connection with a couple of small manufacturers, and he is in the export business. Hong Kong is by no means short of one-man exporting firms. With much ingenuity and effort, they look for small markets throughout the world and shop around for local manufacturers to fill their orders. Like the small factories, they eke out a marginal profit and are

[17]See Mok, 1972, *op. cit.*, pp. 29-30, 55-59.
[18]See Mok, 1972, *op. cit.*, pp. 24-25.
[19]See Mok, 1972, *op. cit.*, pp. 25-26.

vulnerable to external changes. Needless to say, these traders do only a relatively small amount of trading, but they certainly contribute a great deal to
the confusing marketing pattern.

In our re-study of the small factories, we found no clear pattern of marketing channels. Export merchants, other manufacturers, direct local sales,
direct exports and local distributors were all reported to be major outlets.
Asked how they had contacted their customers in the first place, respondents
gave a great variety of answers ranging from making use of existing overseas
connections or agents, being approached by customers and doing their own
market research on the one hand to connections with the Trade Development
Council on the other. Opinions were also divided on the question whether
there was regular cooperation with various types of buyers. The whole set of
answers adds up to a very complicated picture of the overall marketing network. Given the highly individualistic nature of the market, both on the
supply and demand side, this is what we would expect. Even though there is
no consensus among the small factories about the degree of competition, the
overwhelming majority of them pointed out that competition came mainly
from within their own ranks and in the price rather than the quality of their
products, so much so that more than half of them admitted that they kept
their own secrets and had little to do with their peers.

Indeed the small factories are engaged in a close struggle for survival.
Even though many of them do have standing connections with their buyers
and produce according to specification, yet their large number makes it
necessary for them to resort to price-cutting in order to fend off competition.
At the same time, they also shop around for buyers just as much as the buyers
shop around for them. The way in which they cluster into certain new
opportunities is also against their interest. It is a common scene in Hong Kong
that whenever there is demand for some new product which can be produced
on a relatively small scale, many small factories will flood into its production.
It does not take long for the market to become saturated. Of course, there
will always be a few who get in first and reap a handsome profit; but the rest
find it increasingly difficult to meet the competition. If, on top of this, the
industry is confronted with external adversities, such as a suddenly reduced
foreign demand or material shortage, many of them will face bankruptcy. The
history of Hong Kong's industrial development is littered with examples—the
rise and fall of the wigs industry being the classic case. As early as 1962, a
report on the industry of Hong Kong concluded:

". . . the multiplicity of firms engaged in manufacturing and exporting, the
tendency towards a limited view of management, the inadequate equipment, and
under-capitalisation of large parts of industry, the habit of waiting for the buyer
to place his orders and the ceaseless struggle to attract the largest possible volume

of trade, add up to Hong Kong industry's most serious problem—disorderly marketing. In these conditions the unhappily familiar tale of fierce internal competition, price-cutting, deterioration in quality, over-expansion and collapse is bound to be repeated time and again."[20]

Over the years, the larger factories in a number of industries have taken steps to conduct their marketing in a more organized manner, but what the report says is still very true with respect to the small ones. Indeed while a large segment of the market is getting more organized, those who are left in the open will be bound to find life more difficult.

In the previous section, we suggested that in the process of Hong Kong's further economic development the small factories should complement rather than compete with the larger ones in production as well as in marketing. Complementarity in production can take two forms. One is in the provision of different kinds of products to cater for different markets. Here the small factories can fill a gap by producing goods and services which the large factories may not find profitable. The other is in cooperation and specialization in the process of producing the same kind of product. Our basic concern here is with complementarity of this second type. We have shown that in their marketing the small factories can be described as disorderly, and that at the same time they subject themselves to excessive competition within their own ranks (and even with large factories) thus duplicating efforts which are then wasted in the struggle for merely marginal gains; they are also inefficient because of distraction from production matters and irregular input and output flows. Consequently they suffer a high rate of failures. Hong Kong has come to the point where these basically irrational trading and marketing practices have to be changed. It is expensive to rely on the invisible hand which takes a high toll in eliminating many small factories and yet cannot prevent them from coming back a second time around just to go through the same cycle again. What is needed is a more integrated industrial structure in which the small factories have a regular role to play instead of indulging themselves in hit-and-run activities.

It is clear that either a horizontal or a vertical integration of factories could go a long way in the desired direction of providing more resources, finer specialization, better bargaining power, more stable relationships and less irrational competition. Unfortunately any kind of complete integration seems to be too much for many small manufacturers to stomach. Probably the best one could do would be to promote collective action in sales and purchases, and perhaps to strengthen sub-contracting relationships.[21]

[20] Economic Intelligence Unit, *Industry in Hong Kong*, The Federation of Hong Kong Industries, 1962, p. 9.

[21] An expert group from ECAFE has given a definition of sub-contracting as follows: "A sub-contracting relationship exists when a company (called a contractor) places an

It is true that many small factories already carry on production according to the specifications of larger factories and export merchants. To have real substance, however, such relationships must be regular and long-standing, valued and honoured by both sides, and, as a final resort, obligations must be accountable at law. Under such conditions a good working relationship going far beyond the mere contract to purchase can develop as the manufacturing industries of Japan, which have developed an elaborate system of sub-contracting, have shown.[22]

There are many benefits a small factory can derive from sub-contracting. First of all, a steady off-take of output by its contractor(s) lessens the pressure of competition, especially in price-cutting and gives a better chance of survival. Second, with a standing relationship, many matters in which the small factory is in a disadvantage can be delegated to its contractor. These include marketing and market research, bulk purchase and regular supply of materials, product design and general information which the contractor can better handle. Third, a good working relationship extends to purchases. The contractor can provide much valuable guidance in technical know-how, product lines, quality inspection and control as well as management efficiency. And finally, the contractor can also render useful financial assistance in the form, for example, of trade credit and regular payments. All these matters could save the small factory a great deal of time and effort, both of which could be better spent on realizing its comparative advantages through specialization. From the standpoint of the economy as a whole, the result would be less waste in duplicated efforts, a better division of labour, a more stable market, and generally higher efficiency.

It is conceivable that there would be little immediate incentive on the part of the large factories to initiate such a move. The ever-changing scene of the small factories, their inefficient management and the low quality of their products would be the major reasons for their anxiety. On the other hand, the

---

order with another company (called a sub-contractor) for the production of parts, components, sub-assemblies or assemblies to be incorporated into a product to be sold by the contractor. Such orders may include the processing, transformation or finishing of materials or parts by the sub-contractor at the request of the contractor." (See U. N., *Small Industry Bulletin for Asia & the Far East*, No. 8 ECAFE, 1971, p. 51.)

[22] In the Japanese system, the majority of sub-contractors are "captive firms" which sell nearly all their products to their "mother" firms. It might not be feasible for others to follow exactly the Japanese pattern, but as Vepa has pointed out, "There is no doubt . . . that at an early stage of development, sub-contracting helps industry to grow rapidly and to produce goods at a lower cost than is otherwise possible. For this reason, a widespread, but judicious, adoption of such a system in developing countries is likely to produce immense benefits to the growth of small industries" (see R. K. Vepa, *Productivity in Small Industries—Some Lessons from Japan*, Asian Productivity Organization, 1969, p. 74).

short-sightedness of the small manufacturers and their reluctance to abandon their independence may prove equally fatal to the idea. However, we should not be too pessimistic about this, and, in fact a considerable amount of sub-contracting is already taking place in Hong Kong. If we accept the idea that it is a necessary step for Hong Kong's economic growth and in the long run to the interest of all parties concerned, we must find ways of promoting its development on a more organized and regular basis.

We have mentioned earlier that in order to have real substance a system of sub-contracting must imply legal obligations; but too much legislation and too many formalities might well prevent the idea from being accepted in the first place. The best we could do would be to set up a public body which could bring all interested parties together for the purpose of exploring sub-contracting possibilities. This body should not limit its functions to being merely a clearing-house. In addition to supply publicity and information, it should also be able to provide consultation, especially to the small factories which presumably will have many questions to ask and show signs of reserve at the beginning. Once the ice was broken, discussions could be left to the parties concerned until they were ready to formulate more concrete proposals. Then such a body could render services in the more formal aspects of sub-contracting, such as advising on sub-contracting schemes, the formalities of contracts and other relevant legal matters, which must include provisions to guard against the non-fulfilment of contracts and other abuses so that both parties can be assured of deliveries and payments on schedule and so forth.

A discussion of the marketing problems of the small factories would not be complete without further mention of the trading sector, which has the same basic characteristics. Clearly an active trading sector has much to contribute to the small factories. By specializing in marketing, it could help arrange contacts with buyers and exhibitions and could work as a buffer by carrying stocks. It is unfortunate that the small exporters in Hong Kong, who deal heavily with the small factories, are not performing these functions satisfactorily. Instead, they behave in more or less the same manner as the factory owners themselves and only succeed in adding more disorganization to the already unorganized marketing structure. Rationalization of the sector of small traders requires a separate study. It suffices to say here that the better integration of the small industry sector with the rest of the economy by promoting sub-contracting relationships is likely to prove one way of forcing the small traders to rationalize too.

On the promotion of exports, the Trade Development Council has contributed much in seeking overseas markets, introducing Hong Kong products, arranging for the participation of exhibitions and strengthening trade negotiations. However, there is much doubt as to how much the small factories benefit directly from these activities. In our re-study 20 respondents (out of 28) who answered this question stated that they either had never heard of it or had no impression at all. Since the amount of exports by the small factories is relatively small and fragmented and the activities of the Trade Development Council overseas are costly, it would seem to be uneconomical for it to expand its activities into this area. It would be much better to promote their exports through the larger firms by a better system of sub-contracting.

Finance

Until recently, when merchant bankers and finance companies began to flourish, the financial scene in Hong Kong was completely dominated by commercial banks which had over a century's history of development. Although the shares of some well-established companies were traded, the stock exchange was not utilized as a means of raising capital from the public. There was no industrial bank or anything close to it in nature. Thus, aside from internal sources and other traditional means of small financing, the commercial banking sector was the source of finance for Hong Kong's industries. In the late fifties, the increase in the number of banks and the spread of branch banking contributed a great deal to the development of the financial sector. This growth was made possible by the out-dated Banking Ordinance, which was then so lenient that there were neither capital nor reserve requirements and no regulations at all governing lending activities. Nevertheless, being what they were, the commercial banks were still limiting their operations to short and intermediate term loans. There was an expressed need for the establishment of an industrial bank to cater for the long term capital requirements of the industrial sector.

The Chinese Manufacturers' Association had long been a champion of this idea. Its outcry prompted the government to appoint an Industrial Bank Committee in 1959-1960, but this only advised the government that there was no such need after all. The banking crisis in the early sixties resulted in an amended Banking Ordinance which, among other things, imposed upon the commercial banks a minimum requirement of a 25% liquid assets to total deposits ratio. Naturally, this compulsory liquidity ratio only made the banks more reluctant to make long term commitments. The plea for an industrial bank was revived and later took a change in its direction. This time the emphasis was on the small factories which were believed to have special difficulties in financing. Because they were unable to put up collateral in order to obtain bank financing, they were subject to exploitation by alternative channels which were either expensive or very limited in scale, and they were normally the first victims of any credit squeeze. The controversy continued in public and private quarters, and finally, with some reluctance, the government handed the matter to the Trade and Industry Advisory Board for a study in 1968. The Department of Commerce and Industry conducted two sample surveys, one among factories with less than 100 employees and the other among those with 100-200 employees. The results were quite astonishing. The bulk of the capital investment needed to start the factories came from the owners themselves, some were loans from friends and relatives, private money-lenders and hire-purchase firms, but little came from banks because of the lack of adequate collateral. Moreover, neither were the loans from private channels extraordinarily expensive, nor had the small factories in general found financing to be a major constraint upon their growth plans.

In our survey, high percentages of factories of all sizes agreed that there was need for an industrial bank financed out of public funds.[23] In view of the fact that more than three quarters of the small factories were under single or family proprietorship, we expected that they would have a more urgent need for such an institution because of their limited capability. But the evidence was not so. Even though a government industrial bank might provide additional finance, the small factories were not particularly enthusiastic about it.[24] They might be sceptical about getting the government involved in their business; or, limited by their narrow horizons and having relatively fewer capital investment requirements, they were satisfied with what they were and had few plans for expansion in the future. This also explains why the small factories are sometimes more interested in obtaining working capital which is more urgent as far as immediate needs are concerned. Thus, compared with larger factories, small ones depend more on themselves for financing capital expenditure.[25] This is either because bank loans are difficult to come by, or because the small factories have ingenious ways of scraping up enough funds for their more limited needs.

Our re-study only confirmed these results. Out of 34 answers,[26] the original capital of 16 factories was from the owners and their family members, 10 from friends and partners, and 7 from relatives. Only one mentioned a bank as a source of capital. The banking sector did better in providing working capital. In a total of 39 answers, friends and relatives were stated as sources by 13, the owner and his family by 11, and banks by 9. The rest mentioned trade credits and other channels. A hypothetical question was raised: where would the capital come from if they were to expand? Close to one half (12

[23]Mok, 1972, *op. cit.*, p. 54.

[24]Mok, 1972, *op. cit.*, pp. 54-55.

[25]Mok, 1972, *op. cit.*, p. 53.

[26]Respondents were asked to give up to two answers, so the total number of answers is larger than the number of responding factories.

out of 27) had no idea—they said they would consider it only when the time came. However, 6 thought they would get finance from the banks and 7 mentioned their own savings, friends and relatives.

In general, the financing problem of the small factories can be summarized as follows:

First, as far as fixed capital investments are concerned, the small factories have to rely heavily upon themselves. They may also get financial assistance from friends and relatives, but little from the banks. In fact, this is a major characteristic of small business units—they plough back their profits heavily and rely very much on personal connections. The fact that they have little finance from banks implies either that they are unable to offer collateral which proper banking practice requires, or that their capital needs are sufficiently met by conventional means. Difficulties arise only when they want to expand beyond the capability of such means.

Second, now that there is a well-established banking system in Hong Kong and ever expanding banking services, the small factories do have access to banks as an important source of working capital. For many of them, loans and advances from banks have become an accustomed business practice. However they are the first victims of a credit squeeze, with credit lines reduced and loans recalled or not renewed.

Third, for both long and short term loans it seems that for the small factories the availability of credit is more of a problem than its cost. Loan rates paid to private money-lenders may be somewhat higher than the going rate of banks; those to friends and relatives would probably be lower, if any. But it is the availability of credit in times of need that makes the big difference. The current plea for working capital to be provided from government sources well demonstrates the difficulties experienced by small firms when they are faced with an exceptionally tight money market. Again, as in production and marketing, this financial plight is just another aspect of the vulnerability of small factories to the impact of adverse conditions.

Following on the surveys made by the Commerce and Industry Department which had found an apparent lack of need for government finance, the Trade and Industry Advisory Board still considered that there might be a case for government finance for purchasing equipment. A Loans for Small Industry Scheme was approved and became effective in July 1972. In this Scheme, any manufacturing enterprise employing less than 200 workers and with the proprietor's investment amounting to less than $600,000 is qualified to apply for a loan for the purchase of machinery. The size of loans will normally range from $50,000 to $250,000 with an interest of 2% above the prime lending rate of banks on the reduced balance of loans. In fact it is the banks which have to do the actual lending; the government simply underwrites the Scheme with $30 million and carries 50% of the risk of every loan granted. In applying, the small factory has to submit audited balance sheets and profit and loss accounts for three previous years to its bank (provided, of course, that the bank has joined the Scheme). No collateral is required when a loan is granted, and screening is performed by the Hong Kong Productivity Centre for a fee of $1,000.

It was in August of the same year that we conducted our re-study. When asked about their opinion of this Scheme, 13 out of 30 respondents said that they had not heard of it, another 14 expressed no interest, and 3 thought that they would apply. When they were asked to give their comments on this Scheme, 17 of them had none to make. Of those who did have specific comments, 6 pointed out that the process was too cumbersome, 3 thought that probably they would not qualify, and 1 considered the $1,000 fee too expensive.

About a year and a half after the first implementation of this Scheme, it was found that there had been altogether only 9 applications of which 6 had been approved with total loans amounting to less than $1 million. It should be noted that under this Scheme the definition of a small factory is one with less than 200 workers, a substantially broader definition than the one we are using here. By the government's definition, more than 80% of all the registered or recorded factories in Hong Kong are qualified to apply.

The poor response is regrettable as well as puzzling. It could be attributed to a number of reasons. First of all, the requirement for submitting three years' financial records immediately disqualifies many of the small factories simply because they do not keep their accounting records systematically. Moreover, the screening fee of $1,000 which is not returnable if the proposal is rejected, is not only a burden but also a risk for the would-be borrowers. Even though it could be said that the report itself is of some use, it is still difficult to convince the small manufacturers of its worth. Furthermore, interest charges under this Scheme are not particularly attractive. Many of the small factories could probably get alternative financing at similar cost. In their efforts to promote the sale of machinery, the hire-purchase firms also provide credit schemes and other services with many fewer questions asked. In short, the poor response to this Scheme is to be ascribed to the fact that those who are qualified may not need it, and those who may need it are not qualified. It has also been claimed that what the small factories really need is working capital rather than long-term loans.

In November 1973 the Scheme was revised in order to widen its scope and make it more attractive. The maximum requirement for the proprietor's investment was raised to $1 million, the minimum loan amount was lowered to $30,000, the screening fee was reduced to $500 for loans from $30,000 to

$50,000, and only one year's audited financial statements were required instead of three. It is still too early to tell what effects will result from these revisions. Davenport has pointed out the poor results of most similar programmes and adduced a number of reasons—they are hastily conceived, allow too limited financing, are beset with administrative delays and burdensome qualifications, and their terms are often ill-adapted to the needs.[27] It is likely that many of these reasons are equally applicable here in Hong Kong.

However, the performance of such a scheme, especially in its experimental stage, cannot be measured merely by the number of loans approved, for this can be achieved by simply watering down its requirements. What is more essential is to establish the fact that it can make important contributions to the modernization of small factories and is not merely another source of ordinary business financing. In the process, the administrative organ must also train more of its personnel, for it was found in an international study by the Asian Productivity Organization that for such programmes the major common problem was not the shortage of capital but the existence of a bottleneck in administrative manpower.[28]

The major reason for setting up such programmes in so many developing countries is that their small industries are by and large excluded from the modern financial sector. In Hong Kong the problem is not so acute, especially for those factories having close to 200 workers. Most of them do in fact qualify for the present Scheme for they can submit up-to-standard proposals and financial statements. At the same time, however, they also have better access to alternative channels of financing. The government Scheme works only through the commercial banks, with which these factories would most probably prefer to deal directly because of connections already established and fewer additional procedural formalities. The efforts of this Scheme, then, should be concentrated on the lower end—the genuinely small factories. Even these factories, we have noted, have quite adequate means of internal finance, and they are not excluded from the hire-purchase arrangements provided by the private sector. If the government Scheme is to have a special contribution, it must have something additional to offer—the kind of services along with financing which the private sector does not provide. At present the Productivity Centre has already been given the responsibility of screening applications, but there are many more services it could render. It is more crucial to the success of this Scheme to provide additional services than just to revise its requirements.

[27] R. W. Davenport, *Financing the Small Manufacturers in Developing Countires*, McGraw-Hill, 1967, pp. 7-8.
[28] See *Finance Policies for Small Industries in Five Asian Countries*, Asian Productivity Organization, 1969.

There is little doubt that in the initial stage knowledge and experience will be lacking. Officials will have as much information and experience to acquire as advice to give. The job of the screening team should not be limited to approving or rejecting proposals; in the longer run, it should build up information and contacts and identify small manufacturers who have the incentive and capacity for modernization. Once a good working relationship is established, then technical, management and other advice should be provided in a single package along with financial assistance. Even after the granting of a loan, follow-up actions in counselling should continue. The demonstration of some successful examples will help dispel the scepticism about this Scheme; it will also encourage the initiative for modernization and inspire full cooperation. To do all this, the screening team must enlist the support of other services; or better still, a single specific unit should be set up with the job of coordinating all its efforts in servicing the small factories.

(Postscript: Due to poor response, the Scheme was later abolished altogether.)

Management

In the previous sections we have discussed the production, marketing, and financial problems facing the small factories and suggested certain solutions. The prerequisite for the success of these measures is that the management of these factories must be convinced of their usefulness. They must be induced to aspire to modernization and be educated on its many aspects, so that all kinds of assistance can be fruitfully utilized in a coordinated manner. In a small factory, the owner-manager is the management; he is the central figure coordinating all matters. His strategic role must be fully recognized by development policies.

The importance of management is borne out by the experience of Indonesia, which found its programme for the mechanization of small factories unsatisfactory after some years of experimentation and reported that "Management seems to be the main prerequisite for a favourable implementation of the mechanization programme. Without proper managerial skills upon the side of the entrepreneurs, we cannot see any useful purpose in continuing this mechanization programme, even with all sorts of government protection and help".[29] Some economic historians also hold that at an earlier stage of economic development capital accumulation and a more efficient use of the existing productive capacity are of equal importance in their contribution to

[29]J. E. Stepanek, *Managers for Small Industry: An International Study*, Free Press, 1960, p. 1.

growth.[30] At the present stage, Hong Kong does not seem to suffer from a lack of entrepreneurs, as the proliferation of small firms in almost every line of economic activity bears unmistakable witness. However, the sheer number of entrepreneurs, though a valuable asset, does not necessarily bring forth exactly what is desirable. We have alluded to the deplorable results of too much duplicated effort and excessive competition. What is even more important is the quality of the entrepreneurial endeavour. As Hong Kong must now move in the direction of improved production efficiency and better organized marketing, an improvement in the quality of her entrepreneurship becomes all the more important.

In our survey, we found that more than three quarters of the small factories were under single or family proprietorship; needless to say an overwhelming majority of them were owned by Chinese.[31] Most owners had had same schooling, whether at primary or secondary level.[32] In our re-study of 30 factories, we also found that more than two-thirds of the owners were in their thirties or forties. Most of them were first generation entrepreneurs.

In our analysis of the management and organization of the factories in Kwun Tong,[33] we found that the small ones constituted quite a distinctive group being much simpler in structure both vertically and horizontally. Their functional structure was also somewhat peculiar in that the "administrative personnel" constituted a substantially higher percentage in the total employment pattern. This suggests that the lack of internal specialization in smaller factories starts all the way from the top administrative level. Our re-study confirmed this hypothesis. The administrative personnel, including the owner, the manager, department chiefs, etc., had also to work as clerks, technicians, foremen, buyers, salesmen and workmen. Rarely were these people engaged exclusively in administrative jobs. Other categories of workers were also largely interchangeable. Being the size they are, it is hard to imagine that such small factories could gain anything from internal specialization, but without it good top-level management becomes even more indispensable.

It was clear from our surveys that personal contacts played a very important role in the management of the small factories. The owner-managers relied very much on their own decisions, and in their absence, they tended to leave the authority to their kinsmen or some direct appointees. In other words, many of these small factories were genuinely family businesses. The administrative personnel was not formally structured as an apparatus which could

[30] See, for example, R. Cameron, "Some Lessons of History for Developing Nations," *American Economic Review*, LVII, May 1977, pp. 312-324.
[31] Mok, 1973, *op. cit.*, pp. 3-6.
[32] Mok, 1973, *op. cit.*, pp. 9-11.
[33] Mok, 1973, *op. cit.*

assume authority in the absence of the owners. Personal relations were also an important factor in the recruitment of various categories of workers. Compared with the larger factories, the small ones relied considerably less on the market mechanism. Instead, a high percentage of them resorted to the recommendations of friends and relatives in hiring administrative, clerical and other workers. It was also found that in many other respects the small factories operated in an informal manner and depended primarily on direct personal communications, and there were few prescribed ways of tackling problems systematically.

Actually, of course, all these matters are very much as expected. The small factories do constitute the "traditional" segment of various industries, and modernization will call for gradual change. However, we should not be too hasty to brand all these ways and attitudes as irrational. On the contrary, the existence of many elements of traditionalism in small factories has great practical importance. For one thing, simple organization and close personal contacts are the natural results of smallness in size. Moreover, the lack of internal division of labour stems from the fact that their size limits their feasible degree of specialization. Even close family or kinship ties have their economic rationale. In a place like Hong Kong, highly individualistic and competitive, with so many people wanting to get independently established, loyalty without personal ascription has become a rare commodity. Any small factory owner who disregards this may well find himself making an expensive mistake. In fact, reliance upon particularistic ties is by no means confined to the small factories. We found that some large factories, especially those owned by Chinese, also relied upon similar means to safeguard the interests of the owners.[34] Any decision in striking a balance between universalism and particularism must ultimately rest upon practical considerations.

Let us now come back to the point that since the owner-manager of a small factory is its management, the modernization of the factory must start with the modernization of his ways, attitudes, ability and outlook. A management training programme should give some knowledge of all aspects of management as a start in order to arouse the interest of the small industrialists. Conceivably, a programme of this sort could consist of short courses of three categories. The first would be a management course in the narrow sense, somewhat like an introductory business course aiming at showing modern business practices, basic management and organization principles and giving some general economic knowledge to the small manufacturers. The second category would consist of a number of short courses, which could also be combined, on various specific problems facing the factory, such as finance, marketing, accounting,

[34]Mok, 1973, op. cit., pp. 47-48.

and business law etc. All these are matters of applied knowledge in various fields. Courses in the third category would be even more specific in nature. They would be courses dealing directly with the production problems of various industries, such as the introduction of new technical know-how, quality control, testing, packaging, plant layout and product design. Of course, it would not be necessary for all these courses to be structured in a single comprehensive study programme. The needs of the small managers are varied. As Lomnicky has pointed out, some entrepreneurs are technically-minded so that what they need is an orientation to management techniques, whereas others are commercially-minded and need advice on technical matters.[35]

It is true that there is no lack of courses of all these various types. The Hong Kong Productivity Centre, the Hong Kong Management Association and the Extra-mural Studies Departments of the two Universities etc. all have a wide range of courses from which an interested individual can choose. However, the following observations are worth making. First, all these courses are offered separately and there is little coordination. As a result, an interested individual may have to do a lot of shopping around and trying out in order to obtain what he needs. Second, except those dealing directly with technical matters, most courses are taught by people with more academic orientation than practical experience. The lectures thus tend to presume a certain level of academic preparation which unfortunately many small manufacturers lack. More specifically, many management courses are actually intended for the junior executives of big firms; they are theory-oriented and have little relevance for the small factories. Third, there is little or no counselling in the entire process of this type of education. Before enrolling in a certain course, the student has no way of knowing whether this is really what he needs except from what he can read in the short course descriptions. In the course of his study, he has no idea of what other programme he could benefit from in connection with what he is doing at present. Furthermore, there is little information available upon which programme designers could offer courses better tailored to the needs of the small factories. Under these conditions, an owner-manager of a small factory might be hard put to select a suitable course of study for his own improvement.

If it is desired to modernize the small factories through management training, three lines of action can be taken. At the very minimum, a central counselling service should be set up for the purpose of giving out information and publicizing the available courses which are now offered by various organi-

[35] T. W. Lomnicky, "The Training of Manager is the First Step in Developing Small Scale Industry," *Small Industry Bulletin for Asia and the Far East*, No. 7, ECAFE, 1970, pp. 69-74.

zations in a scattered manner. In addition, it could also advise interested individuals on the requirements and contents of these courses.

Furthermore, this counselling service should try to achieve coordination among these organization in designing course programmes suited to the needs of small manufacturers and paying special attention to their existing backgrounds and orientation. In this way the courses may be prepared at an appropriate level and be practical enough to lead to actual application.

Finally, an integrated programme should be worked out consisting of a series of short courses on the various aspects of management including production, lecturers and instruction. At the beginning, it has to be a pilot project limited to a manageable number of trainees with genuine interest and active participation. With a relatively small group, it is much easier to test out teaching materials, encourage the exchange of ideas through group discussion, use case studies to demonstrate the practicability of basic principles, and in case studies to demonstrate the practicability of basic principles, and in general promote a better working relationship. It is also easier to invite guest speakers, hold panel discussions and plan visits. Based on the experience of this pilot group, the programme can be expanded to include more would-be modern small manufacturers. Like financial assistance, the demonstration of successful examples is likely to inspire enthusiasm and better use of these services.

Summary and Conclusions

To a great extent, the successful industrialization of Hong Kong in the past twenty years has been due to active entrepreneurship. Even though at the very beginning there were already some large business concerns, few of them were industrial in nature. The rapid transformation of an entrepot into an industrial city must have been brought about by advances on a broad front. It was, indeed, a classic example of the Schumpeterian world. In this pageant of Darwinian industrial development, many small manufacturers did make great achievements. There is little doubt that their contribution to Hong Kong's economic growth has been very significant.

As far as the scattered activities of the small entrepreneurs are concerned, the general pattern continues to be true. Hordes of small manufacturers are still flooding into industries where and whenever there seems to be opportunity. This pattern of behaviour certainly leaves no feasible avenue unexplorded, but it is not without its disadvantages. After some twenty years of development, there are many more well-established large firms than before. In the manufacturing industries, even though small factories dominate in number the large factories are of overwhelming importance in terms of employment, output, and exports. These large factories are modern and efficient, have well-established connections here and abroad, and are in a much better position to weather a storm. With a large portion of the market already secured, the small factories can only absorb what is left. Competition is tense within their ranks. In good times, they may still be successful in carving out fragments of the market; it is in times of adversity that the real problem is revealed. Their high rate of failure shows how deplorably much ingenuity and effort has been duplicated.

On top of this, the small factories are also faced with emerging changes in Hong Kong's comparative advantage. Cheap labour, once an asset so valuable to their existence, has begun to vanish. The economic development of other regions in the world with cheaper labour, notably South Korea and Taiwan, has made their lot even more difficult. Needless to say, this situation can only be aggravated in the years to come. Looking forward, it is necessary for Hong Kong's industries to move into products of higher quality and more capital-intensive categories. With their superior know-how, financial resources, and bargaining power, the larger factories are able to make the necessary adjustments, but the small ones are just not equipped to do so. If this process is allowed to take its natural course, we can foresee a growing disparity between the large and small factories. Inasmuch as the economy requires complementarity among factories of all sizes and kinds, this development will have undesirable effects on overall economic efficiency. It can be argued that because Hong Kong is an industrial city (and juding from past experience) the market mechanism can be depended upon to weed out the inefficient. Unfortunately, this process is slow and painful, and usually results in heavy private and social losses. This kind of experience is not unfamiliar in Hong Kong; in the industrial sector alone, it has happened time and again. We need more positive attitudes and policies.

There is no doubt that the small factories must be modernized. A growing economy needs a sector of modern small factories to provide modern goods and services, some of which the large factories cannot efficiently produce for reasons of scale and locality. This is complementarity in catering to various needs. In addition, the modernized small factories can supply better and cheaper outputs which can then be used as inputs for the large factories. The development of this kind of complementarity will in turn foster the process of modernization itself, as both large and small concerns can benefit from their comparative advantages. In view of the current status of the small factories in Hong Kong, their transformation into modern ones and their fuller integration with the modern sector are of great importance to Hong Kong's economic future.

It is unfortunate that so many small factories seem to be unaware of their precarious situation. Other surveys in addition to ours have shown that many are seemingly satisfied and not enthusiastic about changes. We should not hastily take this as a sign that there are no problems. Rather, it is likely that they are so occupied with their hand-to-mouth operations that they have little chance to plan for the future. They clamour for assistance when deep-rooted difficulties materialize, but their problems are so complicated that piecemeal assistance is useless. What they really need are better coordinated services which will have mutually reinforcing effects on modernization.

Staley and Morse have developed a Principle of Combinations and Interactions which states:

> ". . . the productiveness of small manufacturing plants . . . depends on a combination of interacting factors. If a development program improves only one of these factors, the results may be quite meagre, perhaps not worth the effort and expense. To improve a properly selected combination of factors may, on the other hand, prove highly effective. The yield, in terms of the development of the country, may then be much more than the cost."[36]

As far as specialists' services go, there seems to be a sufficient supply in Hong Kong. Various official and semi-official bodies do provide courses and services in production, marketing, finance, and management. But so many of the small manufacturers are ignorant of or not interested in them either because they are not designed to cater to their special needs or because they are provided in such a way that is doubtful whether they have much real contribution to make to their special needs.

Thus, to deal with the problems confronting the small factories, there must be more coordination of effort. The best thing to do would be to create a public body exclusively for this purpose. It should be understood at the start that it is not to be a "relief agency"; put quite simply, its objective would be to foster the modernization that economic development requires.

[36] Staley and Morse, *op. cit.*, pp. 352–353.

Chapter 6

The Fading of Earthbound Compulsion in a Chinese Village: Population Mobility and Its Economic Implication*

Rance P. L. Lee

Earthbound compulsion has been widely recognized as a central characteristic of the traditional structure of peasant societies. For many centuries, for instance, village folks in China were relatively immobile. To be born and to die in the same place was regarded as most desirable. By contrast, to leave one's homeland was viewed as a tragic event.

In view of the relatively self-contained farm economy in traditional villages, persistence of the earthbound psychology appears to be a natural consequence. Urban dwellers may not be so conscious of the importance of the soil, but the livelihood of peasants is almost entirely dependent on the soil in the village. To the farmer, it is the soil that keeps him and his family members alive. Away from the soil, they may face the possibility of hunger and the threat of death. Naturally there is a close emotional tie between peasants and their homelands. In traditional peasant societies, population immobility is a "normal" phenomenon whereas mobility is "abnormal."

Industrialization and urbanization have become common processes in most countries today. The traditional social structure of peasant communities and their changes under the impact of industrial-urbanism have been well-documented (see, for instance, the various articles in Potter, Diaz and Foster, 1967; in Shanin, 1971; and in Dalton, 1971). In the case of Chinese villages there are, for example, studies by Kulp II (1925), Fei (1939), Lin (1948), Gamble (1954), Freedman (1958), Yang (1959), Osgood (1963), Myers (1970), and Pasternak (1972) in the Chinese Mainland; by Gallin (1966), Wu (1973), Wolf (1974), Wen, et al. (1975), and Cohen (1976) in Taiwan. Since the

*This is a revised version of the paper presented at the Third Asian Pacific Social Development Seminar (sponsored by the Cultural & Social Center for the Asian & Pacific Region), Taipei, June 15-21, 1976. The paper was also published as a working paper by the Development Studies Centre, The Australian National University in 1976. The present study is part of the project on "The Impact of Urban-Industrialization on a Chinese Village in Hong Kong," funded by the Asia Foundation and The Chinese University of Hong Kong. Special thanks are due to S. L. Wong and C. K. Yang for their substantial contribution to the conceptualization of the data.

work of Barbara Ward (1954; 1967), there have been numerous studies of village communities in Hong Kong, such as those by Freedman (1966), Barker (1968), Potter (1968), Berkowitz and his associates (1969), Osgood (1975), and Hayes (1977). In this paper, I shall focus on the effects of industrialization and urbanization upon the earthbound characteristic of a village in Hong Kong, and then examine the subsequent effects on the internal economic life of the village. Some of the specific questions to be raised are: (1) How extensive has been population mobility in the village under study in recent years? (2) How has it been associated with the industrial and urban growth of Hong Kong? and (3) How has population mobility under the impact of industrial-urbanism affected the material well-being of the village dwellers? Three types of population mobility will be examined; they are immigration, outmigration, and the commuting of village dwellers to work outside.

The Growth of Industrial-Urbanism in Hong Kong

Hong Kong is located on the southeast coast of the Chinese Mainland. The total land area is 1,045 square km., of which about 12 per cent are cultivated land. The mid-year population in 1975 was estimated at 4,366,600, which is about two and a half times that in 1948 (1,800,000). There has thus been a rapid growth of population size since the Communist takeover of the Chinese Mainland in 1949. Currently, an overwhelming majority (over 98%) of the total population are Chinese in place of origin.

About 88 per cent of the total population in Hong Kong are concentrated in the urban sector which comprises only 18 per cent of the total land area, whereas the rural New Territories, comprising 82 per cent of the total land area, accommodate only 13 per cent of the total population. Clearly Hong Kong has become a highly urbanized society (Dwyer, 1971).

Concomitant to population and urban growth is the rapid industrialization of Hong Kong's economy in the past few decades. For instance, the proportion of working population engaged in manufacturing has increased from less than 10 per cent in 1948 to over one half in 1975, and electricity consumption has risen from 3,499 million kilowatt-hours in 1968 to 6,424 million in 1975. Hong Kong, therefore, is a Chinese society with rapid industrialization and urbanization (Hopkins, 1971; Lin, et al., 1979). The rise and growth of industrial-urbanism has had a number of ramifications on the settlers in various villages of the New Territories.

The rural New Territories consists of about 230 islands and a large piece of the hinterland in the northern part of Hong Kong. It has been settled by the Chinese for almost ten centuries. There are currently about 900 villages, which are mostly occupied by a single clan.

The Village of Taipo Tau (大埔頭村) is the site of our study. It is located in the mid-eastern coast of the New Territories, and is about a mile northwest of a market town called Taipo Hui. A railway and a public highway are along the west side of the village site. A bus stop is nearby and the railway station is only a mile way. It takes about 45 minutes by train or by automobile to commute from the village to the urban centres of Hong Kong.

A hill lies along the northern boundary of the village, and a main pathway runs through the village from west to east. When one walks into the village from the western entrance, one sees a number of small-scale cultivated fields (a total of about 30 acres) clustering on the right hand side (i.e., the south). On the left (north), is a primary school and its playground, and a couple of retailing shops. Walking further, one sees blocks of houses constructed in traditional Chinese style with stones and bricks. These houses are arranged in a rectangular pattern, and are mostly used by the natives for residence. A few houses, however, have been turned into small factories. In the midst of the houses is the Ancestor Hall, behind which is the watch-tower. Approaching the northeastern section, one finds a group of wooden shacks inhabited by immigrants, also a number of cottage industries.

For many centuries the village was settled by a single clan of the Tangs (鄧) who were originally natives of Chi-Shui Hsien (吉水縣) of the Kiangsi (江西) Province. The clan moved to the New Territories around the year A.D. 973. They were not only first comers, but also the largest and most influential clan in the New Territories. Taipo Tau is one of the villages established by the clan; it has a history of nearly 400 years. According to our major informants, relatively self-sufficient farming and population immobility were two of the marked characteristics of the village about twenty-odd years ago. The situation, however, has changed rapidly in recent years because of the drastic changes in the larger society (Wong, 1975).

Research Procedures

Under the general directorship of S. L. Wong, our research project was begun in the autumn of 1964 by making contacts with village leaders and by collecting preliminary information from major informants. A group of sociology students at The Chinese University of Hong Kong participated in the project as fieldworkers under the supervision of several faculty members. Two village houses were rented, and were used as research office as well as dormitories for fieldworkers.

At the preliminary stage of the project, fieldworkers were mainly concerned with getting acquainted with individual families and collecting basic information through participant observation and informal interview. Seminar discussions were frequently held among faculty supervisors and student field-workers so as to exchange ideas and field experiences, to identify significant problems and phenomena, and to plan for the next task.

A complete set of demographic information was collected by the summer of 1966. A family file and a subject file were also built, where information on each family and on each topic was kept in separate folders so that the inflow of new data could be systematically compiled. Subsequently, several significant research areas were identified in the autumn of 1966. Fieldworkers were then organized into several research teams, each of which took a special area for investigation. Data were collected through various methods, such as content analysis of historical documents, depth interview of major informants, field observation, and sample surveys with questionnaires.

A number of preliminary research reports were produced by the summer of 1969. Since the village had undergone a rapid growth of population over the past years, a second census-type survey was carried out. The data were analyzed and compared with the survey findings in the summer of 1966. In the spring of 1970, an economic survey was also conducted to find out the production and consumption patterns of all village families.

The present author has been a member of the project since its inception. This paper used part of the data to shed light on the previously raised questions concerning the pattern of population mobility and some of its economic implications.

Population Composition of the Village

Since World War II, the growth of population in the village has been phenomenal. It was estimated that there were 95 people in the year 1946, almost all of whom were clan members. According to our surveys, the numbers were 557 in 1966 and 596 in 1969. The population size in 1969 is six times that in 1946. The rapid gorwth cannot be explained merely by natural increase which was estimated at only 2 per cent per year. The primary reason was the influx of immigrants to the village since the Second World War and particularly since the Communist takeover of the Chinese Mainland in 1949.

There were 169 clan members and 388 immigrants in 1966, and 156 clan members and 440 immigrants in 1969. In other words, only 30 per cent of the total population in 1966 and 26 per cent in 1969 were members of the clan. In both years, the clan group was outnumbered by the immigrant group. Moreover, a comparison of the two surveys indicates that over the 3 years, there has been a decrease of 8 per cent in the clan population, but an increase of 13.4 per cent in the immigrant population. It is evident that the population growth in the village was largely due to the inflow of outsiders.

   The 1969 survey reveals that there were then 95 immigrant families and
27 clan families. The average size of immigrant families was 4.6 persons, while
that of clan families was 5.8. There were thus more outsider families than
native families, but the average family size of the former group was smaller.
The figures about average family size, which are somewhat similar to the
findings of many other studies in Chinese villages, dispell the common mis-
conception that the Chinese always have a large family.

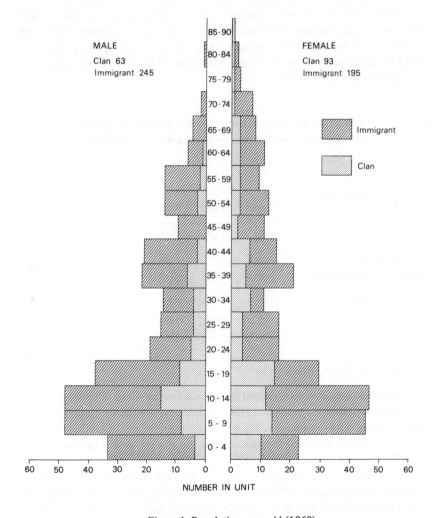

Figure 1. Population pyramid (1969)

The sex-age characteristics of the clan and immigrant groups are presented in Figure 1. The pyramid was essentially shaped by the immigrants. In almost all sex-age categories, there were more immigrants than clan members. The sex-ratio of the immigrant group was 126, while that of the clan group was 68. There were thus more men than women in the immigrant group, but fewer men than women in the clan. The median age of immigrants was 18.9, while that of clan members was 18.6. Both population groups were relatively young, mainly because of the large number of children in both groups.

Table 1 shows that both clan members and immigrants, excluding those who were under the age of 10 with no schooling, were most likely to be with primary school education or equivalent (e.g., private tutoring). In general, the level of education was lower among immigrants than clan members. In both groups, women received less education than men.

Table 1

Education among clan members and immigrants, by sex
(Excluding those under 10 years old with no schooling)

Education	Clan			Immigrant		
	Male	Female	Total	Male	Female	Total
	%	%	%	%	%	%
No schooling	1.9	25.0	16.2	3.9	27.8	15.0
Primary school or equivalent	61.5	48.8	53.7	74.5	60.5	68.0
Secondary school or more	36.6	26.2	30.1	21.6	11.7	17.0
Total (N)	(52)	(84)	(136)	(208)	(180)	(388)

Immigration: When, Where, Why

Taipo Tau has, in effect, ceased to be a single clan village. Population-wise, the clan group is rather small and is increasingly outnumbered by people from other places. Then, when did these outsiders move into the village? Where were they from? Why did they move into the village? And what do they do now?

According to our 1969 survey, about 62 per cent of the immigrant families came during the decade 1959-69, 29 per cent during 1949-58, and 9 per cent came between World War II and the Communist takeover of the Chinese Mainland. The influx of outsiders to the village was hence a relatively recent phenomenon. It started during World War II and became more massive since the civil war in the late 1940s.

In the 1969 survey, the head of each immigrant family was asked to tell the single most important reason for moving into the village. It was found that 31 per cnet reported "low cost of living in the village"; 26 per cent "work accessibility" (e.g., availability of jobs or business sites, and proximity to the place of work); 23 per cent "inducement of friends or relatives residing in the village"; and the remaining 20 per cent were in favour of the environmental setting of the village, such as "friendly and personal relationships in rural area," "fresh air and quiet atmosphere," and "availability of open space for children to play." Apparently, economic considerations were the dominant motives for immigration.

In recent years it has become rather expensive to live in city areas. The cost of living in a village community is usually lower, and thus pulls some people towards the village. An average urban family, for example, normally shares a flat with several other families, and yet has to pay a sizable portion (around 20%) of its total income for the rent. Since a family can rent more space with much less money (about 10% of the total income) in the village, a number of people have chosen to settle in rural communities especially those, like the Village of Taipo Tau, which are accessible to a market town and urban centres through public transportation routes.

Work accessibility was another important economic consideration. It was found, for instance, that some of the immigrants moved into the village because they were (1) workers in retailing shops, schools, or factories near the village, (2) business men in need of more space to store or sun-dry their goods, or of cheaper labour for industrial production, and (3) farmers who wanted to continue agricultural production in the village.

Nevertheless, it should be noted that immigration cannot be explained by economic motives alone. As indicated, a substantial proportion of the immigrants reported reasons which were not economic. These immigrants, altogether about 43 per cent, mainly considered the interpersonal relationships and the quality of the living environment in the community.

People arriving in the village at different periods of time, however, may not necessarily for the same primary reasons. In Table 2, we see a significant change of primary reasons over the past few decades. Immigrants before 1949 were primarily induced by friends or relatives residing in the village. During the period 1949-58, inducement of friends or relatives became the next important reason, while the low cost of living appeared as most important. From 1959 to 1969, work accessibility emerged as the prime reason, whereas the inducement of friends or relatives fell to the bottom of the list. Note also that environmental considerations have become more important in recent years.

112   Social Life and Development in Hong Kong

Table 2

Primary reason for settlement in village
by immigrant families, by period of time

Reasons	Period			
	Before 1949	1949-58	1959-69	Total
	%	%	%	%
Low cost of living	25.0	53.8	21.4	31.1
Work accessibility	25.0	7.7	33.9	25.6
Inducement of friends or relatives	50.0	30.8	16.1	23.3
Others	0.0	7.7	28.6	20.0
Total (N)	(8)	(26)	(56)	(90)

As regards to the place of origin, most of the immigrant families moved *directly* from urban areas of Hong Kong and other parts (mostly nearby districts) of the New Territories. Only one-fifth of them moved directly from the Chinese Mainland to the village. Table 3 shows that those who immigrated before 1949 were mostly from other parts of the rural New Territories. Since 1949, however, the proportion of immigrant families from urban areas of Hong Kong had increased rapidly.

Table 3

Place of origin of immigrant families
by period of time

Place of Origin	Period			
	Before 1949	1949-58	1959-69	Total
	%	%	%	%
Urban Hong Kong	25.0	46.2	41.0	41.1
Other parts of New Territories	50.0	30.7	42.9	40.0
Mainland China	25.0	23.1	16.1	18.9
Total (N)	(8)	(26)	(56)	(90)

The data in Table 4 reconfirm the importance of economic motivation in making people move into the village site. It was the prime reason for immigrants from different places, especially those from urban areas of Hong Kong and from the Chinese Mainland.

Table 4

Primary reason for move to village
by immigrant families, by place of origin

Reason	Place of Origin			
	Urban Hong Kong	Other parts of New Territories	Mainland	Total
	%	%	%	%
Low cost of living	32.5	27.8	35.3	31.1
Work accessibility	29.7	13.8	41.1	25.6
Inducement of friends or relatives	24.3	27.8	11.8	23.3
Environmental quality	13.5	30.6	11.8	20.0
Total (N)	(37)	(36)	(17)	(90)

On the basis of the above information, let us make an attempt to reconstruct the story of immigration to the Village of Taipo Tau. As a single clan entity, the village was exclusive of outsiders for many centuries. Soon after World War II, however, outsiders began to move into the village. The immigrants were then mostly from other parts of the rural New Territories. They were able to break the traditional rule of exclusiveness, probably because of their particularistic relationships with some members of the community. As reported by these immigrants, their primary reason for moving was the inducement of friends or relatives residing in the village.

Since the Communist takeover of the Mainland in 1949, the influx of immigrants to the village increased at an accelerated rate. A number of them came *directly* from urban areas of Hong Kong. Economic considerations became the prime motive for immigration. It was probably due to changes in the Hong Kong society as a whole. As suggested previously, since the year 1949 the growth of population and of industrial-urbanism in Hong Kong have been remarkable. Consequently the living cost and the land value in city areas have been rising rapidly. As houses were available for residence at a lower rate

114   Social Life and Development in Hong Kong

and as cheaper land and labour were available for industrial production or
commercial pursuits, it has become more profitable to move and stay in the
village rather than in the city. The question comes: Why were these outsiders
accepted by the natives? As I shall explain later in this paper, it was probably
because the newcomers brought a significant amount of economic benefit to
the clan.

It was noted that in recent years the quality of the living environment in
the village gained more weight in attracting immigrants. As city areas become
more crowded, more impersonal, and more polluted in the years to come, we
would expect that more people will come and settle in the village. It is in a
rural community that people can still find the warm and personal feelings of
the good old days, enjoy more open space, and inhale "fresh" air.

Outmigration

The rapid population growth in the village was caused largely by the influx
of outsiders. Concomitant with immigration, however, was the emigration of
some village members to other places. The growth of industrial-urbanism, plus
the village's accessibility to the outside world, has led to an increasing rate of
outmigration in the years studied.

According to our observation, there were very few cases where entire
family moved away from the village. Most often, some members of a family
emigrated while others remained. Therefore, we shall here focus on those
emigrants whose families still have some members residing in the village. The
1969 census sruvey indicates that there were 72 such emigrants, of whom 33
were males and 39 were females. They belonged to 34 families in the village.
More specifically, 23 emigrants belonged to 9 clan families, while 49 emigrants
belonged to 25 outsider families. As there were a total number of 156 clan
members and 440 immigrants residing in the community in 1969, the ratio of
emigrants to residents in the clan group was about 16 to 100, whereas the ratio
in the immigrant group was 11 to 100. The ratios suggest that natives were
more likely than outsiders to emigrate. It was, however, found that nearly one
out of four outsider families had one or more members moving away. These
once mobile people were not so easy to settle down.

Villagers were most likely to emigrate as young adults. Almost one-half of
the emigrants left the village between the ages of 15 to 29, while about one-
fourth moved at the ages 30 to 54. In other words, three out of four emigrants
left between the ages of 15 and 54. This pattern existed among both males and
females, and among both the clan and the outsider groups. The data lends
support to the proposition that villagers tend to emigrate at their most
productive ages.

As reported, outsiders began to arrive in the village after World War II. With the exception of one person who emigrated in 1932, all emigrants were found to leave the village after World War II. More specifically, 2 persons emigrated between World War II and the year 1948, 8 between 1949 and 1958, and 61 between 1959 and 1969. So the rate of emigration is seen to have accelerated over the last few decades.

Why did they leave the village? Let us first examine their educational background *before* emigration. Should we exclude those who were under 10 years old with no schooling at the time of outmigration, then 9.1 per cent of the remaining emigrants (a total of 55) were with no schooling, 58.2 per cent with primary school education or equivalent, and 32.7 per cent with secondary school education or above. As indicated previously, the corresponding figures among the current residents in the village were 15.3 per cent, 64.3 per cent, and 20.4 per cent. Emigrants thus generally possessed a higher level of education than current residents in the village, suggesting that education may be a major factor fostering outmigration. Here comes a dilemma in the area of education and manpower development. The introduction of modern education, which is needed for the development of manpower in a rural community, may encourage the young generation to desert the village.

What were the reasons for outmigration? According to our respondents in the 1969 survey, "better job opportunity" was the most important reason (54%) for male emigrants, followed by "inducement of friends or relatives" (26%). For the female emigrants, "marriage" was the prime reason (33%), followed by "better job opportunity" (22%). Economic motivation was thus a major cause of outmigration.

What did they do immediately after emigration? We found that except for one woman, none of the emigrants was engaged in farming. Of the male emigrants, most (74.4%) were engaged in industrial or commercial activities, while the rest (25.6%) went to school. Most of the female emigrants were housewives (46.1%), followed by industrial or commercial workers (28.2%), students (23.1%), and farmers (2.6%).

In recent years, a number of villagers in the New Territories have emigrated to foreign countries for the purpose of seeking better economic opportunities. In the case of Taipo Tau, we found that 33.2 per cent of the male emigrants and 24.2 per cent of the female emigrants have moved to other countries including England, Netherlands, The United States, and Canada. Most of them emigrated in the early 1960s. All these emigrants, except three in England, were members of the clan.

Moreover, about 33.4 per cent of the male emigrants and 35.2 per cent of the female emigrants left for urban areas of Hong Kong, while 33.4 per cent of the men and 40.5 per cent of the women went to other parts of the New

Territories. Within Hong Kong, therefore, the rural to rural migration was as frequent as the rural to urban migration. Should we also include the emigrants to foreign countries, the proportion of emigrants to urban places (66.6% of males and 59.5% of females) then exceeds the proportion to other rural regions (33.4% of males and 40.5% of females).

We have thus seen that people in the village were no longer tied to the soil. The number of emigrants has increased in recent decades. The rate of out-migration was relatively higher in the clan group than the outsider group. Emigrants were equipped with better education than those who remained in the village. Most of them left for urban areas of Hong Kong or other countries during their productive ages, in order to pursue better economic opportunities. Subsequently, they were mostly engaged in non-farming occupations.

The Commuting of Workers

In addition to immigration and outmigration, there is also a third type of population mobility, i.e., the commuting of village dwellers to work in places outside the community. In a traditional village, peasants normally lived there and worked there as well. There was little differentiation between the place of work and the place of residence. Under the impact of industrial-urbanism, this kind of earthbound practice has been fading away.

We conducted an economic survey of all village families in the spring of 1970. Of the 567 village dwellers being covered by the survey, 202 were found to be economically active. More specifically, 44 per cent of the 298 males and 26.4 per cent of the 269 females were economically active. Among them, only 12 men and 6 women were engaged in farming and fowl raising. About two-third of these farmers were immigrants. The remaining 184 workers were widely scattered in various types of industrial or commercial occupations such as factory worker, small business proprietor, waiter, office clerk, nurse, teacher, construction worker, bus driver, and seaman. Apparently, agricultural production has ceased to be the economic base of the village community. The economy of the village has undergone the process of sectoral reallocation from agricultural production to manufacturing production and services.

As a result of the sectoral change, members of the village do not have to be earthbound in their economic pursuits. They can choose to work outside rather than inside the village confines. It was found that among the 184 persons engaged in non-farming occupations, only one-fourth (mostly women) were employed *inside* the village as workers in the small factories, as store keepers, or as attendants in the village school. A great majority (about three-fourths) of the working population was thus engaged in jobs *outside* the village. For them, the village is a place to live but not a place to work. They have to commute to the outside world to earn their living almost everyday. This overwhelmingly large but highly mobile portion of the population has, in effect, turned the village into a *dormitory* site. The immobile characteristic of the traditional village was thus radically changed.

The question arises: Why do these people continue to reside in, rather than move away from, the village site? In an effort to answer this question, we interviewed a sample of 10 clan families and 15 outsider families which had settled in the village for 9 years or more. It was found that the primary reason for both groups was the low cost of living in the village, especially the relatively cheap rents and school fees.

The second reason concerned the quality of the living environment, such as fresh air, open space, relatively simple life and quiet atmosphere. Many villagers were quite happy with the recent improvement of public facilities in the village, such as the supply of water and electricity.

The third reason was economic opportunity. The village was considered a good place to make their living. It was observed that the village factories provided domestic handicraft work for housewives, children, and the aged, and had thus become an important source of supplementary income for many families in the village.

In short, many villagers did not emigrate because they perceived that the cost of living in the village was low, that the quality of the living environment was satisfactory, and that economic opportunities were available. Under these considerations, they remained to reside in the village site, even though many of them had to work in other places.

Economic Implication

The change from population immobility to mobility under the impact of industrial-urbanism may produce multiple effects on the social, political, and economic life of the village. To delimit the scope of discussion in this paper, I shall focus on some of the changes in family income and living standard. Our question is: How do the people in the village benefit, at least economically, from the mobility?

Before the arrival of immigrants after World War II, farmers of the village were mainly engaged in growing rice. Because of the small-scale cultivation and primitive technology, the income of farmers remained low year after year. Those who had to pay land rent were on the subsistance level of living even in a good harvest year. Under the influence of the more sophisticated immigrant group, however, the income of the farmers has been substantially improved in recent years. From some of the newcomers, the native farmers

learned some of the new technical know-how: better seeds, improved irriga-
tion and the use of more fertilizers. More important, they learned to grow
many varieties of seasonal vegetables and flowers to replace rice farming, thus
bringing in more economic return from land cultivation. On the average, the
economic return has gone up nearly ten times. To give a rather extreme
example, one of the farmers in the clan gets his major income from growing
peach blossom trees, and has become so wealthy that he recently spent 250
thousand Hong Kong dollars on building a new house. This kind of upward
mobility was utterly impossible in the old days. The livelihood of other
farmers has also generally been improved as evidenced by their consuming
pattern. Radio, television, refrigerator, electric fan and cooker were commonly found in every farmer's home.

The number of immigrants who came to the village to engage in agricultural production was relatively few. Altogether, there were 12 individuals.
A number of outsiders was found to have come to the village because of the
availability of industrial sites and labour force there. They brought with them
a good amount of capital and set up small factories in the village. In recent
years, the number of factories has increased to nearly 20, opening up more
job opportunities to people in the village. As reported, many clan members
as well as immigrants were in fact employed by these small industries either
on a full-time or part-time basis.

As jobs were available in the non-farming sectors inside or outside the
community, clan members became less reluctant to sell their land inherited
from ancestors. No less important is that the pressure of population growth
and the demand for commercial and industrial sites have boosted the land
values in Hong Kong. Because of its proximity to a market town and its
accessibility (through a railway and a public highway) to urban centres, the
land value in the village has gone up nearly 20 times in the last two decades,
although it is still considerably cheaper than the land in city areas. Under
these circumstances, the clan can hardly resist the temptation to relax the
traditional rule of exclusiveness by permitting outsiders to live in and to set
up business in the community. The native group has made a fortune by
selling their land and investing the money in other economic enterprises.

Another source of income of the clan group was the renting of land and
houses to newcomers. The total sum was estimated at some 4,000 dollars
per month. It enabled the hitherto soil-tilling farmers to join the ranks of the
rent-collecting class and also permitted them to seek additional income from
industrial or commercial employment inside or outside the village. As
reported, most clan members had, in fact, shifted to non-farming jobs.

Remittance from emigrated relatives to foreign countries or urban centres
of Hong Kong was also a significant source of income for some families in the

village. 6 clan and 19 immigrant families were found to receive remittance regularly. On the average, each of these 25 families received HK$179 per month. More specifically, it was $275 for each clan family and $148 for each immigrant family. As regards remittance, the clan group seemed to have benefited more from emigration than the outsider group.

Adding all kinds of income together, we estimated that the average family income of the clan group as a whole was HK$852 per month, while that of the immigrant group was HK$695.

Regarding the household expenditures, the major items were food (about 60% of the total income), children's education (13%), and rent (10%). Taking other expenditures into account, each family on the average spent approximately HK$480 per month. It was about $518 for each clan family and $469 for each immigrant family. The monthly balance was thus $334 for each clan family, and $226 for each immigrant family. Compared with urban dwellers of similar socioeconomic status, the people in Taipo Tau were in a more favourable financial situation. This explains why a number of people moved into, or remained to reside in, the village.

The above statistics lead to the conclusion that the livelihood of the villagers has been substantially improved. They have, however, paid a price: the previous self-sufficient farm economy has already been replaced by an economy which is highly dependent on the outside world. As an overwhelming majority of the working population have shifted to manufacturing and services, their employment opportunities have to depend upon the job market in the larger society. Those remaining in farming have changed from the production of primary food to commercial crops which are also highly sensitive to price fluctuation in the urban market.

Concluding Remarks

Traditional villages were mostly based on a relatively self-sufficient farm economy. The livelihood of peasants was primarily, if not entirely, dependent on the soil in the community. The earthbound psychology thus emerged and persisted for centuries. The village population was practically immobile.

There were at least three ways in which the earthbound compulsion was expressed. First, villagers were extremely reluctant to leave their homeland for places in the outside world. They preferred spending their lives in the place they were born. Second, the place of work and the place of residence were usually the same. People rarely just resided in the village but worked in other places. Third, the native villagers were exclusive of outsiders. Immigration to the village was a rare phenomenon. People saw the same old faces in the village almost everyday.

The rise and growth of industrial-urbanism in the modern era, however, has led to the breakdown of this long-standing practice. There are outsiders migrating into the village, and meanwhile insiders migrating to other places especially the urban centres. In addition to immigration and outmigration, there is also the daily commuting of the village's working population. A large segment of the economically active dwellers in the village have to commute to the outside world to acquire their economic ambitions, and have thus turned the village into a dormitory community. The population in the village is no longer static. Its earthbound tradition has been seriously eroded, as the people have become increasingly mobile.

The impact of industrial-urbanism is evidenced by the importance of economic motivation in guiding the various kinds of population movement including immigration, outmigration, and mobility of workers. Besides economic considerations, the expansion of school education, which is basically a product of industrial-urban growth, has also encouraged some of the young adults to leave the village in order to fulfill their occupational aspirations in urban areas. On the other hand, as the industrial-urban development makes the city areas more crowded, more polluted and more impersonal, more urban dwellers will move into the village and more rural settlers will be reluctant to move out. Inspite of the constant mobility, therefore, the residential population of the village may not decrease but may instead increase. This has been the case in the Village of Taipo Tau.

The importance of warfare in the breaking of earthbound compulsion cannot be overstated. It dislocates individuals and forces them to move. Immigrants to the Village of Taipo Tau, for instance, were found to arrive after World War II and the last civil war in the Chinese Mainland. Without the rise and growth of industrial-urbanism, however, these outsiders may not have been able to break through the wall of exclusiveness in the village. Even if they were able to find a place to settle, they would most probably have become earthbound again. There were a number of wars in the history of China, but the earthbound tradition in villages of various localities continued to survive until the modern age.

Population mobility under the impact of industrial-urbanism would cause fundamental changes in the economic structure of villages, espeically those which are located nearby the major transportation routes. The primary change in agriculture is the shift from self-sufficient farming to commercial farming such as growing vegetables and flowers and raising fowls. Agricultural production becomes sensitively tied to the outside market. More important is that farming gradually loses its importance and gives way to industrial production and services. In the case of Taipo Tau, for instance, an overwhelming majority of the working population has shifted to non-farming occupations inside or outside the village confines.

The change of economic types, resulting from the fading of earthbound compulsion under the impact of industrial-urbanism, may do more good than harm to the well-being, at least money-wise, of the people residing in a rural community. In the Village of Taipo Tau, the material conditions of its population and particularly the native group have been substantially improved. They are no longer on the subsistance level of living. To underscore the improvement of livelihood, let me code a concluding remark made by Fei (1939: 282) on the basis of his village study in the Chinese Mainland about forty years ago:

> "The essential problem in Chinese villages, putting it in the simplest terms, is that the income of the villagers has been reduced to such an extent that it is not sufficient even to meet the expenditure in securing the minimum requirements of livelihood. It is the hunger of the people that is the real issue in China."

References

Baker, Hugh D. R. (1968) *A Chinese Lineage Village: Sheung Shui*. London: Frank Cass.

Berkowitz, Morris I. Brandauer, Frederick P., and Reed, John H. (1969) *Folk Religion in an Urban Setting: a Study of Hakka Villagers in Transition*. Hong Kong: Christian Study Centre on Chinese Religion and Culture.

Berkowitz, Morris I. and Poon, Eddie (1969) "political Disintegration of Hakka Village: A Study of Drastic Social Change in the New Territories of Hong Kong," *Chung Chi Journal*, Vol. 8 2 (May), pp. 16-31.

Cohen, Myron L. (1976) *House United, House Divided: The Chinese Family in Taiwan*. N. Y.: Columbia University.

Dalton, George, ed. (1971) *Economic Development and Social Change: The Modernization of Village Communities*. New York: The Natural History Press.

Dwyer, D. J., ed. (1971) *Asian Urbanization: A Hong Kong Casebook*. Hong Kong: Hong Kong University Press.

Fei, Hsiao-tung (1939) *Peasant Life in China*. London: Kegan Paul.

Freedman, Maurice (1958) *Lineage Organization in Southeastern China*. London School of Economics.

———— (1966) "Shifts of Power in the Hong Kong New Territories," *Journal of Asian and African Studies*, Vol. 1, No. 1.

Gallin, Bernard (1966) *Hsin Hsing, Taiwan: A Chinese Village in Change*. Berkeley: University of California Press.

Gamble, Sidney D. (1954) *Ting Hsien: A North China Rural Community*. Stanford: Stanford University Press.

Hayes, James (1977) *The Hong Kong Region 1850-1911: Institutions and Leadership in Town and Countryside*. Connecticut: Archon Books.

Hopkins, Keith, ed. (1971) *Hong Kong: The Industrial Colony*. London: Oxford University Press.

Kulp, Daniel Harrison, II (1925) *Country Life in South China: The Sociology of Familism, Volume I, Phenix Village, Kwangtung, China*. N. Y.: Teachers College, Columbia University.

Lin, Tzong-biau, Lee, Rance P. L., and Simonis, Udo-Ernst, eds. (1979) *Hong Kong: Economic, Social and Political Studies in Development*. N. Y.: M. E. Sharpe, Inc.

Lin, Yueh-hwa (1948) *The Golden Wing: A Sociological Study of Chinese Familism*. London: Kegan Paul.

Myers, Ramon H. (1970) *The Chinese Peasant Economy: Agricultural Development in Hopei and Shantung, 1890-1949*. Cambridge, Mass.: Harvard University Press.

Osgood, Cornelius (1963) *Village Life in Old China: A Community Study of Kao Yao, Yunnan*. N. Y.: The Ronald Co.

———— (1975) *The Chinese: A Study of a Hong Kong Community*, Vols. 1-3. Tucson, Arizona: University of Arizona Press.

Pasternak, Burton (1972) *Kinship and Community in Two Chinese Villages*. California: Stanford University.

Potter, Jack M. (1968) *Capitalism and The Chinese Peasant: Social and Economic Change in a Hong Kong Village*. Berkeley: University of California.

Potter, Jack M., Diaz, May N., and Foster, George M., eds. (1967) *Peasant Society: A Reader*. Boston: Little Brown.

Shanin, Teodor, ed. (1971) *Peasants and Peasant Societies*. Penguin Books.

Ward, Barbara E. (1954) "A Hong Kong Fishing Village," *Journal of Oriental Studies*, Vol. 1, pp. 195-214.

———— (1967) "Chinese Fishermen in Hong Kong: Their Post-Peasant Economy," pp. 271-288 in *Social Organization: Essays Presented to Raymond Firth*, edited by M. Freedman. London: Frank Cass & Co., Ltd.

Wen, C. I., Hsu, C. M., Hchu, H. Y., and Huang, S. E. (1975) *Social Change in a Suburban Village of Taipei*. Republic of China: Institute of Ethnology, Academic Sinica. (In Chinese)

Wolf, Arthur (1974) *Marriage and Adoption in a Hokkien Village*. Ph.D. dissertation in Anthropology, Cornell University.

Wong, S. L. (1975) "A Chinese Village in Transition: Some Preliminary Findings," an occasional paper of the Social Research Centre, The Chinese University of Hong Kong.

Wu, T. S. (1973) "The Changes of Peasant Personality in the Process of Modernization," pp. 333-375 in *The Character of The Chinese*, edited by

Y. Y. Li and K. S. Yang. Republic of China: Institute of Ethnology, Academic Sinica. (In Chinese)

Wu, T. S. and Tsai, H. C. (1975) "Patterns of Agricultural Out-migration and Multiple-Crop Farming in Taiwan," *The Philippine Economic Journal*, Vol. 16, Nos. 1 & 2, pp. 127-148.

Yang, C. K. (1959) *A Chinese Village in Early Communist Transition*. Cambridge, Mass.: M.I.T. Press.

Yang, Martin (1948) *A Chinese Village: Taitou, Shantung Province*. N. Y.: Columbia University Press.

PART TWO
Institutional Characteristics and Their Change

Chapter 7

Administrative Absorption of Politics in Hong Kong: Emphasis on the Grass Roots Level*

Ambrose Yeo-chi King

Hong Kong is one of the major Asian cities which have become rapidly urbanized and industrialized in recent decades. In the last twenty years, Hong Kong has been transformed from a British colonial entrepot to a city of world significance with a population of four million.

There is a growing literature arguing that Asian urbanization has distinct characteristics and thus differs from Western urbanization. This difference is often believed to have resulted from the differing growth patterns of their seminal cities. Most students of the city use technology as the strategic variable to delineate types of cities. Indeed, the Western city differs in large measure from the Asian city in that the former resulted from technological-industrial expansion while the latter did not. However, cities in both the West and the Orient have been multifunctional, and there are very few contemporary cities so heavily committed to industrial activities that a great majority of the labor force is engaged in it. Therefore, apart from technology, other variables such as value and power, especially power, should be taken into account. More often than not, contemporary Asian cities have been created and shaped primarily by colonial powers for political and economic reasons; they did not grow out of an indigenous urban process. In this sense, Hong Kong is, using Redfield and Singer's concept, a heterogenetic city, and it fits well into McGee's description of the so-called "colonial city."[1]

*Reprinted with permission from *Asian Survey*, Vol. 15, No. 5 (May 1975), pp. 422-439. This paper is one of a series of reports produced for the Kwun Tong Industrial Community Research Programme which was financially supported by the Harvard-Yenching Institute and was under the auspices of the Social Research Centre, The Chinese University of Hong Kong. I would like to thank the people at Harvard-Yenching Institute, particularly Professor John Pelzel, for their generous and unfailing support of the above-mentioned research programme of which I was the coordinator and the principal investigator. Also I want to thank my able research assistant, Kong King-leung, who worked with me closely in my City District Officer Scheme study in 1972.
[1] Robert Redfield and Milton Singer, "The Cultural Roles of Cities," in *Economic Development and Cultural Change*, 3 (1954-55), pp. 53-73; and T. G. McGee, *The Southeast Asian City* (London, 1967), Chapters 3 and 4.

Hong Kong's urban characteristics cannot easily be described by the rural-urban continuum theory concepts which grow out of the grand tradition of dichotomous soical change. The grand dichotomous conception of social change, despite its usefulness as a heuristic model, is primarily a useful typology, rather than a theory of social change. Moreover, it is probably time-bound and culture-bound. The concept of Asian urbanization, however, it seems to us, can hardly be applied to Hong Kong. In this paper, we are primarily concerned with the political implications of urbanization. In the West, urbanization has often been linked to democracy by political theorists. Max Weber, one of the pioneering students of the sociology of the city, held that the city, as a political community, is a peculiarly Western phenomenon and the source of the modern conception of "citizenship," which itself is the source of democracy.[2] Later, Harold Laski's view that "organized democracy is the product of urban life" was further elaborated by S. M. Lipset.[3]

But it would be a gross mistake to assume that what holds true of the historical relationship between urbanization and democracy is necessarily true in the cities of the Third World. The cities of the Third World are in a situation "that is congenial not to democracy but rather to political demagoguery, or to radical movement, and to the eruption of mob violence."[4] There are many things that make the city political life of the West different from that of Third World societies. But the basic fact is that the rapid increase of population living in urban settlements in the Third World makes the city a field where the major socio-political transformation process takes place in a rather short period of time. Karl Deutsch has termed the process "social mobilization," which is "the process in which major clusters of old social, economic, and psychological commitments are eroded and broken and people become available for new patterns of socialization and behavior."[5] It is our belief that the social mobilization process is certainly not confined to the Third World city, but it is by definition more dramatically manifested in cities where people have sudden high exposure to aspects of modern life through demonstration of machinery, buildings, mass media, etc. The increased numbers of mobilized population tend to increase their demands for participation in the political system, leading to a phenomenon called "participation explosion." More often than not, social mobilization and participation explosion lead to political

[2] Max Weber, *General Economic History* (Glencoe, Ill.: Free Press, 1950), pp. 315-318.

[3] Harold Laski, "Democracy" in *Encyclopedia of the Social Sciences* (New York: Macmillan, 1937), quoted in S. M. Lipset, *Political Man* (Garden City, N.Y.: Doubleday Anchor Book, 1963), pp. 34-38.

[4] Brigitte Berger, *Societies in Change* (New York: Basic Books, 1971), p. 160.

[5] Karl Deutsch, "Social Mobilization and Political Development," *American Political Science Review*, 55 (September 1961), pp. 493-514.

instability in the Third World resulting primarily from, using Huntington's concept, the political gap between the rapid social and economic changes and the slow development of political institutions which have dominated the scene throughout Asia, Africa, and Latin America. The political gap is wider in the city than in the countryside precisely because rapid social mobilization takes place in the city and yet non-governmental institutions are weak or undeveloped. As a consequence "the instability of the city—the instability of coups, riots, and demonstrations—is, in some measure, an inescapable characteristic of modernization."[6]

What has been said above is indeed a rather gloomy view of the political aspect of urbanization in the Third World. However, we are not ready to accept the view that the pattern of political development in Asian cities and other cities in the developing countries is a "deviant" pattern of the Western model. In our view, the reason why Asian political urbanization does not fit the Western model can be explained in two equally valid ways: either it is the particularistic nature of the Asian political urbanization, or it is simply the parochial nature of the Western model itself. The positive political role of cities in Asia can be better understood by viewing the city as a center of change that has contributed to nation-building because urbanization serves to undermine primordial sentiments, loyalties, and identifications with subnational entities and thus helps to make the development of new and larger political communities possible. Indeed, the Asian cities' political function must be understood in terms of the relation between the parts (cities) and the wholes (national societies). This, however, cannot apply to the Hong Kong case. Hong Kong is a city-state: it is a total entity itself. And this makes Hong Kong a special variant of the Asian city, or the colonial city. What concerns us in this paper is the way Hong Kong's political system has coped with the problem of stability and, especially, the way it has been coping with the "crisis" of political integration resulting from rapid urbanization in recent decades.

Participation, Synarchy, and Elite Integration

In large measure, Hong Kong is an urban polity relatively free from riots and political cleavages. It has achieved a kind of equilibrium in a very intricate political situation. It certainly has not experienced violence on the same scale as many cities in the Third World. It is the argument of this paper that the kind of equilibrium this colonial city has thus far achieved is largely due to a process which might be called the "administrative absorption of politics."

[6] S. P. Huntington, *Political Order in Changing Societies* (New Haven, Conn.: Yale University Press, 1969), pp. 4, 77.

By this we mean a process by which the government co-opts the political forces, often represented by elite groups, into an administrative decision-making body, thus achieving some level of elite integration; as a consequence, the governing authority is made legitimate, a loosely integrated political community is established.

Hong Kong is not a democracy. The British colonial government has never attempted to follow Western democratic models. It has from the very beginning tried to adopt a unique brand of politics of its own. To characterize politics in Hong Kong is far from an easy job. The most widely quoted concept of "governemnt by discussion" is given by Endacott:

> An examination of the working of the Hong Kong constitution shows interested opinion is consulted continuously prior to any important government decision, . . . and that on occasion . . . the general public at large is invited to express its views. Indeed, consultation as practiced by the Government is so extensive that the term "government by discussion" aptly describes one of its leading characteristics.[7]

Endacott's arguments certainly have some insight and validity. However, it is our view that conceptually and empirically the concept of "synarchy" is the key to understanding the art of government and politics in Hong Kong. "Synarchy," to borrow the concept of J. K. Fairbank,[8] implies a joint administration shared by both the British rulers and non-British, predominantly Chinese, leaders. The kernel of synarchy is a form of elite consensual government; it is a grass-tops approach to the problem of political integration. The British have, consciously or unconsciously, governed the colony on the synarchical principle by allowing, though limiting, non-British participation in the ruling group.

Synarchical rule has both formal and informal faces. Before proceeding to discuss the formal face of synarchy, it should be noted that the constitutional structure of Hong Kong's political system is in the typical colonial pattern. The British Crown is represented by a Governor who is "the single and supreme authority responsible to and representative of the Queen." The office of the Governor is the central feature of the Government of Hong Kong. The Governor is in a real sense the head of the Government. Strictly speaking, the Governor can govern the colony, if he wishes, with his own will without regard to what the people in the colony think. But the Government does not seem to have an unlimited image of authority; it has tried to gain legitimacy for its authority not from the Crown but from the consent of the ruled by

[7]G. B. Endacott, *Government and People in Hong Kong: 1841-1962* (Hong Kong: Hong Kong University Press, 1964), p. 229.

[8]John K. Fairbank, "Synarchy Under the Treaties," in John K. Fairbank, ed., *Chinese Thought and Institutions* (Chicago: University of Chicago Press, 1957), pp. 163-203.

claiming to conform to democratic values, if not to a democratic form of government. It is under this normative "democratic" or consensual framework that the system of synarchy is practised.

The formal face of synarchical rule can be analyzed through discussing the operation of the three Councils and the civil service system. On April 5, 1843, Hong Kong was granted a Royal Charter which declared Hong Kong a separate Colony. Among other things, the Charter established a Legislative Council and an Executive Council. The Governor is advised by the Executive Council and is bound to legislate through the Legislative Council. These two Councils are not elected bodies; they are composed of both "official members" and "unofficial members." As of now, the total membership of the Executive Council is 14; six are "official members," of whom five are ex-officio members, eight are "unofficial members." The Legislative Council has 29 members in total, with 14 "official members," of whom four are ex-officio members, and 15 "unofficial members." And 15 out of the total 23 unofficial members are Chinese. All members, with the exception of ex-officio members, are appointed by the Queen or by the Governor on the instructions of the Secretary of State. These two Councils are the top governmental organs through which the people from the community participate in the policy-making and management of public affairs in the Colony. The precise degree of the unofficial members' influence in the Councils is difficult to assess, but in large measure "on important issues, their opinion has obvious weight and their opposition is avoided," and "in deference to local Chinese opinion, Chinese custom is safeguarded and legislation concerning it is unlikely to be proposed except on the initiative of the Chinese unofficial members."[9] What concerns us is not only the question of whether the unofficial members have influence in the policy-making process, but also the question of who the unofficial members are and whom they represent. It is true to say that the great majority of the appointed unofficial members are men of caliber and that they are sensitive to the needs of the community as a whole. But the undeniable fact is that the appointed unofficial members were and still are established or emerging socio-economic elites who are order-prosperity minded and come from a very narrow sector of the population.

With a few exceptions, the Unofficial Members are men of wealth. Among the Chinese Unofficial Members, prior to 1964, over 90% are from "established rich" families and are among the small circle of elite in the Chinese community. After the mid-1960s, another category of persons has been rising—the "new rich," representing the ever-increasing industrial forces. And among the non-Chinese Unofficial Members, about 75% are chief executives or managing

[9] Endacott, *Government and People in Hong Kong*, p. 231.

directors of commanding economic institutions.[10] It is worth noting that in the very beginning of the Colony's history, the British ruling group seemed not too much concerned about the problem of Chinese participation. Although the two Councils were assembled as early as 1844, the first Chinese, Ng Choy (or Dr. Wu Ting-fang) was appointed to the Legislative Council only in February 1880, due to the belief of the Governor Sir John Pope Hennessy that since the Chinese outnumbered the foreigners in Hong Kong, they should be allowed a share in the management of public affairs. And it took another 46 years to appoint Sir Shouson Chow as the first Chinese member of the Executive Council in 1926. It seems that the concept or practice of administrative absorption of politics is not out of grand design by any person, but rather it grows out of a need to cope with the problem of legitimacy. In the words of a Chinese informed on Hong Kong politics, the appointment of Sir Shouson Chow was not made simply on personal grounds, "it was evident that political considerations also came in, viz., to pacify anti-British sentiment in China and further encourage the loyalty of local Chinese towards Hong Kong."[11] Chinese participation in the two Councils has steadily increased since World War II. This is clearly shown in the Legislative Council: the Chinese Unofficial Members were less than 50% between 1945-50, 62.5% from 1960-63, 70% from 1964-67, 77% from 1968-69, and 84% from 1970. The steady increase of Chinese participation in the Councils is a reflection of the growing strength and vitality of the Chinese community on the one hand, and the sensitive responsive capability of the government to absorb the socio-economic leaders on the other. The British are not attempting to create a mass-consensual community; they are, however, attempting to create an elite-consensual polity. The normal pattern in elite-consensus building is to co-opt the men with a power base into the polity.

Below the Legislative and Executive Councils, there is the Urban Council, which is the only government organ with a partially elected membership. Prior to April 1, 1973, there were 26 members on the Council—six were ex-officio members and twenty were unofficial members, ten of whom were appointed and ten elected. Despite the fact that the Urban Council's elections are the only occasions for the general public to participate in the formal political process, they have never interested the average person. The striking thing is that ever since the Urban Council elections were reinstituted in 1952, the rate of registration for election has never exceeded 1% of the total population and, although up to 30-40% of those who register eventually turn up at

[10] Data compiled from *Hong Kong Who's Who (1970-73)*, Joseph Walker, ed.
[11] T. C. Cheng, "Chinese Unofficial Members of the Legislative and Executive Councils in Hong Kong up to 1941," in *Journal of the Royal Asiatic Society*, Hong Kong Branch, 1971, pp. 7-30.

the polls, only 0.5% or less of the total population turn out to vote.[12] The poor turnout in voting is often deplored as a lack of civic spirit and as an exhibition of political apathy. One reason for political apathy, it seems, must be the traditional Chinese Confucian political culture which is more parochial-subject than participant in nature; the ordinary people lack an active self-orientation towards politics in Hong Kong.[13] A more basic reason for the low participation, however, could be found in the political system of Hong Kong itself; that is, the Urban Council is an organ without teeth. It is perceived as involved in a "politics without power," "completely divorced from the dynamism of Hong Kong's economy."[14] It would appear that the Hong Kong Government does not hold that modern democratic politics has to be politics of mass participation. The foremost goal of the Government is to achieve a maximum level of political stability in order to foster economic growth. And the key to that goal is the "administerization" of politics; it is the antithesis to politicization.

Bearing in mind the notion of the "administerization of politics," we will be in a better position to understand the role of the government bureaucracy in Hong Kong. Insofar as Hong Kong's real and day-to-day governing power is concerned, it lies in the hands of the civil service, headed by the Chief Secretary who, under the direction of the Governor, carries on the general administration. At present, there are 40 government departments. The growth of the bureaucracy has been phenomenal: there were just over 17,500 officers in 1949; this increased to 45,000 in 1959; and now its present strength is over 84,500. The bureaucratic expansion is, in short, primarily due to the pressures of urbanization.[15] It is no exaggeration to say that Hong Kong, despite its claim to a laissez-faire philosophy, is, in fact, an "administered city" governed by "departmentocracy."

Strictly speaking, there are no politicians in Hong Kong. Gabriel Almond, expressing a functional view, has distinguished four input functions in any political system: political socialization and recruitment, interest articulation,

[12] Aline K. Wong, "Political Apathy and the Political System in Hong Kong," *United College Journal*, 8 (1970–71), pp. 1–20.

[13] Ambrose Y. C. King, "The Political Culture of Kwun Tong: A Chinese Community in Hong Kong," a research paper, Social Research Centre, The Chinese University of Hong Kong, June 1972; and J. S. Hoadley, " 'Hong Kong is the Lifeboat': Notes on Political Culture and Socialization," *Journal of Oriental Studies*, 8:1 (January 1970), pp. 206–218.

[14] J. S. Hoadley, "Political Participation of Hong Kong Chinese: Patterns and Trends," *Asian Survey*, XIII: 6 (June 1973), p. 616.

[15] *Hong Kong: Report for the Year 1972* (Hong Kong: Government Printer, 1973), p. 209.

interest aggregation, and political communication.[16] Since there are so few political structures outside of government for the performance of these four input functions in Hong Kong, the bureaucracy of necessity plays a "political" role. And, as a matter of fact, the old orthodoxy of the politics-administration dichotomy is purposefully broken down in Hong Kong; the administrators, especially those at the top level, are encouraged to play the political role. A point should be noted here that the Government is the largest employer in Hong Kong. By January 1972, there were 84,565 officers in total, of which 82,662 were local officers, and 1,903 overseas officers.[17] The data indicate that one in every fifty of the total population was employed within the civil service. Because of this very fact, the bureaucracy has contributed a great deal to the stability of Hong Kong by serving as a mechanism for assimilating the potential "discontented" into the governing machinery. The government bureaucracy has been fairly open to Chinese intellectuals, especially since the 1950s. And it is mainly in the area of administration that the synarchical rule has been put into practice. From 1952 onward, the local officers, who are predominantly Chinese, have constituted over 95% of the total number of officers. However, the quantitative figures do not give us the whole picture; if we look at the qualitative side of the picture, a rather different conclusion will emerge. Although localization of the government bureaucracy has been the publicly stated policy of the Government since 1946, it has proceeded slowly and very unevenly. The pattern of localization is that the lower the categories of officers, the faster the localization; and the reverse is true. The obvious evidence is that in the Administrative Grade, 64% were British, while only 36% were local officers in 1970 (although, as compared to 2.3% in 1950 and 16.27% in 1960, the progress cannot be ignored). On the other hand, in the Executive Grade, 73.4% were local officers, while 26.6% were British. Insofar as the top rung of the bureaucracy is concerned, the Government is still dominated by British expatriates.[18] In a sense, Hong Kong's administration is a lop-sided synarchy, with much Chinese "participation" but little "joint rule." Synarchy has never become fullfledged.

The discussion of synarchical rule cannot be completed without mentioning the informal side. Synarchical rule does not stop at the direct or formal co-option of political elements into administration; it also reflects indirect or informal co-option.

[16] G. A. Almond, "Intorduction: A Functional Approach to Comparative Politics," in G. A. Almond and James Coleman, eds., *The Politics of the Developing Areas* (Princeton: Princeton University Press, 1960), pp. 3-64.

[17] *Hong Kong: Report for the Year 1972*, p. 209.

[18] David Podmore, "Room at the Top," *Far Eastern Economic Review*, 65:29 (1969), pp. 180-182.

When the British took over Hong Kong in 1842, Hong Kong was a rural community without a great gentry. However, by the end of the 19th century a viable and rapidly developing community of Chinese had come into being. Because of the ingenuity and great organizational ability of the Chinese merchant class, they were able to build up an autonomous power base outside the polity of the British Government. The wealthy Chinese have demonstrated extreme adaptive capacity in creating high-power associations of various kinds for the purposes of mutual assistance and self-advancement in a rapidly urbanized settlement under alien rule. The Tung Wah Group of Hospitals, the Po Leung Kuk and the Kaifong are all indigenously developed. The key figures in these Chinese associations are civic-minded men of achievement respected by their community. They have developed an informal system of power and influence parallel to the formal system of the British. The Hong Kong Government has never failed to appreciate the fact that these prominent Chinese could well perform a boundary role between the Government and the community, much like that played by the Chinese gentry in traditional society. The last thing the British want to see is the development of powerful opposi- tional forces by Chinese or other non-British leaders. In this connection, the British have wisely and successfully absorbed Chinese leaders into the official political circle by either giving them formal membership in the Councils and in the bureaucracy or bestowing on them honors (e.g., Justice of the Peace) and involving them in more than 130 consultative and advisory committees at various Governmental levels. Here again we find that the great majority of unofficial Justices of the Peace among Chinese are successful men in the economic field. The Chinese members of consultative and advisory committees are also by and large successful businessmen. The significant boundary role of the leaders of Chinese associations is well recognized by the Government. It is beyond doubt that the formal and informal administrative absorption of Chinese leaders of important associations is one of the major factors contri- buting to the stability of the urban community of Hong Kong.

The Integration Crisis and Its Response

What we have said thus far should give us a fairly clear picture of how the continuous stability of Hong Kong is secured through the willingness and ability of the British to change and enlarge the elite circle by co-opting emerging leadership groups. The best example is shown in the Government's readiness to accept the industrial "new rich" into the Legislative Council since the mid-1960s, because from then on the industrial sector has become the backbone of the economy.[19] But it is our contention that elite integration can

[19] Since 1964, the Chinese "established rich" (old families) have decreased their weight in the Legislative Council, while the Chinese "new rich" (industrial elite) have

work relatively well only in a society in which the masses are primarily apolitical, and it probably would not work as well in a society which has undergone the process of social mobilization. This was not fully recognized until two major riots occurred in 1966 and 1967. The 1966 riot, lasting for several days, resulted from a rise in the first-class fare for the ferry between Kowloon and Hong Kong Island. In 1967, a series of uprisings against the colonial Government were triggered, as it is widely perceived, by the Cultural Revolution in mainland China. The riots were controlled and died out rather quickly. What is significant is that these episodes indicate that Hong Kong's equilibrium is rather precarious, and there are underlying factors which are predisposed to react to stimuli for violent and mass behavior. After the 1966 riot, the Government realized that the basic political structure of Hong Kong had been changed with the rising young generation entering into the political strata.[20]

According to the findings of the Government, the cause for the 1966 riot was a "failure of communication" between the Government and people.[21] This finding admits in fact, implicitly or explicitly, that the structure of "government by discussion" which had succeeded in elite-to-elite communication had failed in providing an effective channel for elite-to-mass communication. In a way, Hong Kong's current problem is not so much the gap between the British and the non-British as the gap between the elite and the masses. The riots were symptoms of malintegration between the rulers and the ruled in this rapidly urbanized city.

It seems quite legitimate to view the riots as a kind of communication crisis or, more accurately, integration crisis. The basic reason for the integration crisis can be found in the political structure, which has few political structures performing the basic political functions for the masses in Hong Kong. At present, there are only seven associations which are political in nature. Four

---

increased their weight rapidly. The percentage distribution of the Chinese "established rich" and "new rich" in the composition of the Unofficials of the Legislative Council from 1964 to 1971 is as follows:

	1964	1965	1966-67	1968-69	1970-71
"established rich"	66.0%	41%	46%	38.5%	30.8%
"new rich"	18.5%	25%	23%	38.5%	53.7%

For the composition of the Legislative Council, see Stephen Tang's senior thesis entitled, "The Power Structure in a Colonial Society—A Sociological Study of the Legislative Council in Hong Kong (1948-1971)," unpublished, Department of Sociology, The Chinese University of Hong Kong (May 1973).

[20] *Report of the Working Party on Local Administration* (Hong Kong: Government Printer, 1966), pp. 11-12.

[21] *Kowloon Disturbances 1966—Report of the Commission of Inquiry* (Hong Kong: Government Printer, 1967), pp. 110-111.

of them are registered as political parties: the Democratic Self-Government Party, the Hong Kong Socialist Democratic Party, the Labour Party of Hong Kong and the Liberal Democratic Party, but none of these are of any political significance. Three are registered as "clubs" and "associations": the United Nations Association of Hong Kong, the Reform Club of Hong Kong, and the Hong Kong Civic Association. Of the seven, the Reform Club and the Civic Association, which claim a membership of 30,400 and 10,000 respectively, have dominated the Urban Council elections. But both of these are more concerned with social and economic reforms and are, by nature of their limited resources and organizational ability, hardly effective articulators or aggregators of the interests of the masses. In addition, at the bottom there are seldom any strong grass-roots associations which can perform a role as interest articulators for the masses. It is small wonder that, on the whole, ordinary urban dwellers have the tendency to express their sentiments and demands through "anomic" political structures—i.e. riots, demonstrations, strikes, teach-ins, sit-ins, and sleep-ins, etc. Indeed, this becomes increasingly a form of political participation in Hong Kong.

The gap between the elite and the masses is not unique to Hong Kong; it is a very common probelm among new nations. Edward Shils is probably the scholar who has given this problem most attention. For Shils, the political integration of the new state depends primarily on the closing of the elite-mass gap, and he suggests that the gap be bridged by the dispersion of initiative. The solution suggested by Shils is, in short, political democracy.[22] In fact, in late 1966, the Working Party on Local Administration appointed by the Governor took a similar view by suggesting the creation of a strong Hong Kong Municipal Council. It in effect proposed a political democratic solution. However, the proposal was not implemented at that time; instead, a City District Officer Scheme was instituted in April 1968 as a "stop gap" mechanism in lieu of local government.

Political Absorption at the Grass-roots Level: The City District Officer Scheme

After the 1966 and 1967 riots, the government decided that it needed a political machinery to cope with the ever-increasing politicized life of the urban dwellers, especially at the local level. It is here that we see that the City District Officer Scheme carries a basically political spirit, for the government's diagnosis of the riots of 1966 and 1967 reflects a belief that the basic problem lies not in the colonial system as such but in a metropolitan government structure that is too big to manage and too complex and bureaucratized to be

[22] Edward Shils, "Political Development in the New States," *Comparative Studies in Society and History*, 2:3 (April 1960), pp. 265-292; and 2:4 (July 1960), pp. 397-411.

138 Social Life and Development in Hong Kong

intelligible to the ordinary people. Therefore, what the CDO Scheme tries to accomplish is a decentralization and a debureaucratization of the metropolitan Government.

The Ideology, Goals and Structure of the CDO Scheme

The CDO Scheme was launched with great fanfare and publicity in mid-1968, immediately after the climax of the 1967 riots. A government-sponsored intensive image-building campaign was successfully carried out to convince the public that the CDO Scheme is something which is genuinely of and for the people. The ideology of the CDO Scheme is a "service ideology": service for the Government; service for the community; and service for the individuals. These are explicitly stated in the Directive to City District Officers.[23]

The explicit goals of the CDO Scheme are many-sided. It is designed to be a political communication agent, a community organizer, a trouble-shooter for the people. To put it in more general terms, the CDO Scheme is aiming to counteract the tendency of the metropolitan Government toward centralization and departmentalization. The establishment of the CDO Scheme is to make one person or one office which the residents could recognize as "the government" in their district.

The CDO Scheme was approved by the Hong Kong Government in early 1968. It was decided that ten CDOs would be established in the whole metropolitan area. By the end of the same year five CDOs had been established: Eastern, Western, Wanchai, Mong Kok, and Yau Ma Tei. The other five, subsequently opened by the end of 1969, were Central, Kwun Tong, Sham Shui Po, Kowloon City, and Wong Tai Sin.

The CDO Scheme is under the general supervision of the Secretariat for Home Affairs. Directly under the Secretary for Home Affairs are two deputies. One is in charge of the traditional duties of the former Secretariat for Chinese Affairs—newspaper registration, trust fund, liquor licensing, tenancy matters, etc. The other is responsible for the CDO Scheme. Under him are two City District Commissioners, one responsible for the four CDOs on Hong Kong Island, and the other for the six CDOs in Kowloon.

The organizations of the ten CDOs are the same. The City District Officer is the head of the office. Under him are two sections: Internal and External, each headed by an Assistant City District Officer. The Internal Section deals mainly with administrative matters, and the External Section with field or "liaison" duties. The number of other staff varies with individual offices. There are usually five to eight Liaison Officers assigned to each office. One

[23] *The City District Officer Scheme,* hereafter referred to as *CDOS.* Report by the Secretary for Chinese Affairs, Hong Kong Government, January 24, 1969, pp. 12, 18, 21.

is invariably assigned to the Public Enquiry Counter, and a greater part of the rest to the External Section. There are two to four Liaison Assistants in each office to assist the LOs.

The CDO at Work in Kwun Tong Community

How has the CDO Scheme actually performed at the district level? How has the idea of the CDO Scheme been transformed into action? We have selected Kwun Tong District for our study. Kwun Tong District, one of the ten City Districts of metropolitan Hong Kong, is one of the most rapidly developed urban communities in Hong Kong.

The CDO is not an ordinary functionally-specific administrative organization; rather, it is a multifunctional political structure. What are the functions of the CDO in the Kwun Tong District? According to our findings, during the three-month period of June to August 1971, the CDO's activities involve such things as commenting on the District's development planning; helping to clear out huts and hawkers; building a playground for children; helping in relief of typhoon victims; organizing festival celebrations: administering the Fat Choy Special Aid Fund; handling "individual and family cases"; answering public enquires; and administering statutory declarations, etc. The CDO's activities are indeed highly functionally-diffuse. They involve just about everything occurring in any local community, ranging from political to very mundane affairs.

One of the CDO's major functions is to facilitate communication between the governors and the governed, including the input of intelligence about "public opinion" to the decision-makers in the government. The CDO is required to produce a report entitled "The Anatomy" of his District within six months of his appointment. In the "Anatomy" thorough information about the peculiarities of the social and economic structure of the district as well as its personalities is expected to be included. The CDO is often asked by various departments to give comments on intended actions, such as the Development Town Plan of the Public Works Department, and other Government organizations ask it to gather information on social needs for decision-making. For example, the CDO has conducted a "survey" on the needs of the ferry service on behalf of the UMELCO (Unofficial Members of the Executive and Legislative Councils). The methods used to gather intelligence, besides "survey" conducting, are the District Monthly Meeting, the Study Group and "Town Talk."

The CDO holds regular Monthly Meeting which involve a fairly stable group of local leaders, leaders of Kaifong Associations, Multi-Storey Building Associations (MSB), District Associations, the business and industrial sector, etc.; the representatives of field agencies of Government departments are also present. The Monthly Meeting is the primary mechanism of the CDO for collecting the opinions of local leaders on any issue concerning the Government and the public. From the minutes of the meetings, we find that members present voice their opinions on the procedure of reporting crime to the police, on the improvement of recreational facilities in the district, etc. The CDO is designed to extend the Government's consultation circle at the center to a much wider circle at the peripheral and district level.

The Study Group is rather ad hoc in nature. The people invited to discuss in the Study Group vary from one occasion to another, depending on the topics discussed. The discussants include industrialists, school principals, hawkers, shop owners, taxi-drivers, factory workers, students and others. Sometimes the subjects discussed might include not only matters of a specific nature but also matters of common concern such as traffic problems, corruption, petty crimes, smoke from restaurants, clearance of refuse, Chinese as an official language, etc.

The "Town Talk" mechanism is not officially included in the CDO Scheme, but it is believed to be one of the most important channels for soliciting public opinion by the CDO. It is probably true that the Monthly Meeting or the Study Group are, in practice if not in theory, geared primarily to reach local leaders rather than the ordinary man. The Town Talk is in a sense more oriented toward the "man in the street." The CDO has no specific instructions on whom to consult. As one respondent reported, comments were noted down from casual conversation with whomsoever they happened to talk to, on official or private terms. It emphasizes not the quantitative but the qualitative aspect of the opinions expressed by the people. The key word is "people"; several officers interviewed repeatedly and spearately asserted that the present "trend" was towards contacting the "man-in-the-street."

A second function of the CDO is to articulate the demands made known to them through the Monthly Meeting, the Study Group and Town Talk by people from different walks of life, as well as demands channelled through newspapers and outside "requests." Moreover, interests are articulated by the CDO's self-initiative, based upon its knowledge of the needs and attitudes of the residents of the community. The interests articulated by the CDO are both minor in nature and all-embracing. According to our findings in the period under analysis, the CDO made comments on multi-storey building car parks, cooked food stalls, hawker bazaars, a mini-bus station, a refuse collection center, and a clinic with regard to the Kowloon Bay Development Plan. The CDO's interest articulation is limited in the sense that it has only a recommendation function.

With respect to the redressing of grievances, it has been expressly denied by the Chairman of the Urban Council that the CDOs are ombudsmen.[24]

[24] *Official Proceedings*, The Urban Council, XII: 5 (March 1969), pp. 473-474.

The CDO is certainly not an ombudsman in the original Scandinavian sense which guarantees his independence as an instrumental officer of the legislature. The CDO is not independent. However, the public image of the CDO as an ombudsman is prevailing, and it is, furthermore, clearly stated in the Report of the CDO Scheme.[25] The CDO's grievance redressing activities can be classified into two major types: redressing of grievances for groups and for individuals. The first type arises out of events affecting a large number of people, such as a clearance operation. This type of grievance redressing is relatively rare; in Kwun Tong District there were only two instances. One was the Shun Lee Chuen Clearance in which villagers whose huts were due to be demolished demanded compensation from the Government through the CDO; the other was the Typhoon Rose case in which the victims of Sam Ka Chuen demanded a reassessment of the decisions of the Resettlement Department. By contrast, the individual cases in the same period were very large in number, totalling 256. Of these, family disputes accounted for 152, housing 37, and traffic accidents and compensation 24. In all cases it was the clients who took their complaints to the CDO for assistance.

The CDO referred the two group cases for consideration by the departments responsible but they were not favorably reviewed because the departments concerned thought their demands were not in compliance with government policies. In this respect, the CDO could do very little, but it did "explain" the government policies to the two groups in a more personal way. As for the individual cases, 204 out of 256 cases received were recorded to have been settled. In handling individual cases, the CDO acted as a middleman between parties in disputes. When individual grievances arose from a Government decision, the CDO could not reverse the original decision, but it had the "power" to bring the case to the responsible departments for a second look, although often all that the CDO could do was "talk things over," and "give advice."

Another function of the CDO is a special set-up called the Public Enquiry Service Counter, usually manned by an Executive Officer, a clerk, and clerical assistants. The PES set-up is designed to familiarize people with the government bureaucracy. The Hong Kong metropolitan Government has become more and more technical, complicated, and fragmented; the ordinary people are often bewildered by the intricacy of governmental operation. There exists a kind of "information gap" between the Government and the people. The PES is apparently a useful mechanism to bridge this "information gap," and this is evinced in its enormous use by the people. The number of enquiries received per month by the CDO's PES counter increased from 991 in Septem-

[25]*CDOS*, p. 3.

ber 1970 to 5,472 in April 1971. The enquiries cover a wide range of information concerning personal documents, land and housing, employment, taxes, duties and fees, family welfare, education, traffic, medical, and other miscellaneous things.

Another important political function of the CDO may be called political socialization and recruitment. The CDO, in this regard, provides a framework for participation by "responsible" local sectors. Most of the CDO's efforts are geared to structuring the channels of participation for two major categories of people—youth and "local leaders." Different institutional mechanisms have been created to co-opt and socialize them in CDO-sponsored community activities. The Monthly Meeting is the most formal forum. During the three months under study, other mechanisms and activities relating to socialization and recruitment were used. For example, with the help of the Lion's Club and the Army, student volunteers were mobilized to assist in constructing a playground and jetty at Kowloon Bay; they initiated and sponsored, with the support of local prominent people from Kaifongs, schools, and business firms, district-wide sports activities; they worked through voluntary associations in organizing and promoting recreational and festival activities. All these activities were apolitical in terms of their manifest functions; they were primarily recreational in nature. However, these activities were not sheer structuring of leisure time for the local leaders and the youth; they served to channel participation in a "right" way, to develop community-oriented civic consciousness, to transform the young people into "good citizens" and future community leaders, and to create a political culture which is supportive of the political structure of Hong Kong.

An Evaluation of the CDO Scheme

The CDO of Kwun Tong has played a fairly successful boundary role between the Government and the society: as a multi-functional political structure, it has by and large provided institutional channels for political inputs and outputs. The most effective function of the CDO is in political communication, especially the "information output" from the Government to the people. The Public Enquriy Service has undoubtedly performed a vital role in transmitting and spreading knowledge of the aims and purposes of the government to the people, and has helped to make the government more intelligible and relevant. The "information gap" between the governors and the governed has been substantially removed. But the CDO has not been as successful in its "information input" as in "information output." Despite its efforts to reach people in the street, it has thus far not been very successful in penetrating the masses in a structured way, although it has been fairly successful in securing the views and attitudes of local leaders towards government policies and actions before they are put into effect. In this respect, the CDO acts as a feedback mechanism for the government to detect the acceptability of its actions, or as a political barometer for the government to detect early symptoms of any public dissatisfaction. It is in this political communication function that the CDO has been referred to as the "eyes and ears" of the government. Regarding the interest articulation function of the CDO, it is often unrecognized or underestimated. It is interesting to note that, according to the Kaifong leaders of Kwun Tong, "to represent people's interest to government" was ranked as the last among all functions of the CDO. However, the CDOs' self-imate is very different; they have a strong sense of mission that they are not only the "eyes and ears of the government" but also the "tongues of the people." It is here that we have found tension developing between the CDO and other local organizations, especially the Kaifongs, who also claim this as their foremost function.

Whatever the relationship between the CDO and other local organizations, the CDO is involving local leaders in consultation at the Monthly Meeting and other mechanisms. But that is as far as the CDO is willing to go. The CDO is not ready to accept the local leaders' views at face value; and, more often than not, views of the local leaders tend to fade into faint echoes. Probably because of this, we found that quite a few local leaders were dismayed and frustrated; more than one of them even went as far as to say that "the CDO was a waste of money. . . . The Monthly Meetings were 'a child's game'." It seems to us that local leaders and non-leaders alike often fail to appreciate the fact that the CDO has only recommendatory powers. Although the CDOs can and often do apply pressure on other Government agencies for their recommendation, there is a genuine structural weakness in the CDO. A City District Officer normally spends only two to three years in the post, with the rest of his career spent in other government departments. He cannot afford to alienate himself from his home base; he cannot push too far or too hard because he is after all a bureaucrat within the same bureaucratic structure.

The grievance redressing function of the CDO is gradually becoming more appreciated by the community. This function was the Kaifong's monopoly in the past, and is now being taken over by the CDO. The kind of grievance redressing the CDO does is often no more than just giving the complainant a "human-to-human talk." Some critics point out that the CDO's power in this respect is limited in that it cannot reverse the original decision, when the individual grievance arises from a government decision. However, in spite of the limited power the CDO has, it usually enables the individual to have a "fair hearing" in a very personal way. The CDO is no dragon-slayer; he cannot afford to be. But the significance of the "human touch" in the modern imperial bureaucracy cannot be underestimated. While grievance at local government

level may often be trivial, the small issues are of substantial importance to
the citizens. This function of the CDO has rendered good service for the poor
and inarticulate ordinary man. In no insignificant degree, this function of the
CDO has served as a "safety valve" for the release of people's imaginary or
real grievances.

In analyzing the last political function of the CDO, political socialization
and recruitment, we must bear in mind that generating a favorable and supportive attitude and behavior toward the Government was one of the basic reasons
for the inception of the CDO Scheme. The CDO, as the political agent at the
district level, is not aiming at political mobilization of the populace; in fact, it
is trying to depoliticize the political process. In short, the CDO Scheme is
primarily concerned with social stability rather than with social change. It is
our impression that the CDO has been fairly successful in absorbing and
recruiting the most active political strata—local leaders and youth—by
working with and through them is undertaking community-wide cultural and
recreational activities. Through this kind of orderly participation, community
consciousness or local identification has often been generated; a great deal of
energy has been absorbed and channelled into non-political activities; and,
above all, social solidarity has been enhanced.

Conclusion

The focus of this paper was on the political side of city life. We have
treated politics not as an epiphenomenon; it is not just the reflection of the
socio-economic structure. In the case of Hong Kong, we found that its particular brand of politics shapes and is shaped by the socio-economic structure
of the society.

We have attempted to provide a conceptual framework to describe and
analyze the nature of the political system of Hong Kong. Basically, we are
of the opinion that Hong Kong's political stability in the last hundred years
could be accounted for primarily by the successful process of the administrative absorption of politics. It is a process through which the British governing
elites co-opt or assimilate the non-British socio-economic elites into the
political-administrative decision-making bodies, thus attaining an elite integration on the one hand and a legitimacy of political authority on the other. We
have witnessed a system of synarchy, though a lopsided one, operating in
Hong Kong. However, the synarchical system is only open to a rather small
sector of the population—men of wealth, established or new. The ingenuity
of the British governing elites lies in their sophisticated response in timely
enlarging and modifying the structure of ruling bodies by co-opting or
assimilating emerging non-British socio-economic elites into "we" groups at

critical periods. Consequently, the development of any strong counter-elite groups is prevented. In short, Hong Kong has been governed by an elite consensus or integration in the last century or so. However, it is our contention that elite integration could constitute a sufficient.condition for legitimacy of government only in a society in which the political stratum is rather small. Once a society undergoes rapid urbanization or, more specifically, social mobilization whereby the apolitical strata become politicized, it is not elite integration but elite-mass integration which becomes necessary for a stable political system. Hong Kong has in the last two decades undergone that process of social mobilization. Hong Kong today is no longer just an economic city but also a political city; more people, especially the young literates, demand ever-increasing participation in the political decision-making process. The basic probelm of legitimacy in Hong Kong today lies not in elite dis-consensus but in the elite-mass gap, as exemplified by the riots of 1966 and 1967.

The Hong Kong Government's response to the political crises was not more democracy, but the creation of the City District Officer Scheme. But it should be noted that, despite the usefulness of the CDO Scheme in the district, especially as a communication facilitator, the CDO Scheme has a limited function as an administrative absorber of community politics; and this will become more evident when community life becomes progressively politicized in scale. Some fundamental features of urban life in Hong Kong seem to be working in the direction that, despite the artificial administrative-political boundaries defined by the CDO Scheme, no important socio-economic-political issue is confined to any one District. That is to say, all important political issues tend to be escalated to a level which could only be dealt with at the center of the political system. The CDO Scheme is good at handling personal problems but not political issues. Not only the image but the actuality of the limited power of the CDO has seemingly led people in the community to believe that big sensitive issues should not be left to the CDO. Instead, they feel the only effective way is to march to the center of power, ultimately of course to the Governor's House which is the symbol of the authority of the city-state.

The last point we would like to make is that the Government's diagnostic statement which sees Hong Kong's current problem between the Government and the people as an "information gap" is at best a half-truth. Another half-truth might be due to the incompatibility of goals or interests between the elite and the masses. Politics is not just who knows what and how, but also who gets what and how. The CDO Scheme is effective in bridging the information gap which results from misunderstanding or misperception of goals or interests between the rulers and the ruled. But it is too much to expect it to reconcile the conflict arising from incompatibility of goals or interests between the governors and the governed; therefore, it cannot be very useful as an administrative absorber of community politics as such. All in all, the CDO Scheme can be no substitute for sound and responsive government itself, and it certainly is no panacea for urban politics.

Hong Kong today is facing a new challenge of politics which arises basically from rapid urbanization. The kind of issues and problems of this city-state have become increasingly political. How Hong Kong can maintain a viable political system poses a question of the first order to the students of the art or the science of governing. The century-old practice of administrative absorption of politics which has contributed to the stability of the city-state up to the present is susceptible to change in form or in substance, or in both.

Chapter 8

The Political Culture of Kwun Tong:
A Chinese Community in Hong Kong*

Ambrose Yeo-chi King

This is a study of the political culture of Kwun Tong, a fast-developing industrial community of Hong Kong. Employing a set of concepts developed by sociologists and political scientists, it attempts to give a systematic explanation of data, thereby throwing some lights on the understanding of people's attitudes and orientations towards politics. This study can provide us with a theoretical and empirical base, preliminary though it may be, from which to begin to study the nature of the political system of the Colony. In analyzing the data bearing on the political culture of the Hong Kong community, empirical findings of other societies are utilized in order to provide comparative perspective. In addition, Chinese traditional political-cultural value systems have been used as a point of reference, in order to show the continuities and discontinuities of the Chinese political culture of Kwun Tong.

Before embarking on analyzing the data directly, a brief statement of the theoretical framework is in order.

Theoretical Framework

The important function of culture in systems perspective has been most adequately expounded by Talcott Parsons. He states, "the central functional exigency of the interrelations between a society and a cultural system is the *legitimation* of the society's normative order. Legitimation systems define the reasons for members' rights and for the prohibitions incumbent upon them."[1] The political scientists have singled out political culture from the general cultural system by using it as a concept to explain variations of political behavior in different political systems. According to Verba:

*Reprinted with the permission from *Southeast Asian Journal of Social Science*, Vol. 5, Nos. 1-2 (1977). This research is part of the Kwun Tong Industrial Community Research Programme which was partially funded by the Harvard-Yenching Institute during 1970-1974 and was under the auspices of the Social Research Centre, The Chinese University of Hong Kong.

[1] Talcott Parsons, *Societies: Evolutionary and Comparative Perspectives* (Englewood Cliffs, N. J.: Prentice-Hall, 1966), p. 10.

"The political culture of a society consists of the system of empirical beliefs, expressive symbols, and values which define the situation in which political action takes place. It provides the subjective orientation to politics."[2]

Almond and Powell put it more succinctly, "Political culture is the pattern of individual attitudes and orientations toward politics among members of a political system."[3] In essence, for the individuals concerned, political culture "provides the guidances of political behavior;"[4] for the political system, it provides "a systematic structure of values and rational considerations which ensures coherence in the performance of institutions and organizations."[5] The concept of political culture has merits, methodologically speaking, in that it provides us with a conceptual tool by means of which we can bridge the "micro-macro" gap in political analysis. It makes possible the transition from the study of the individual in his political context to the study of the political system as a whole and enables individual interviews and responses to be related to the aggregate statistics and group behavior patterns which reflect the course of a system's total behavior.[6]

Having discussed the concept of political culture, a few words should be said about the concept of political system. The term 'political system' is used by modern political behavioral scientists instead of the terms 'government' or 'state' as used by traditional political theorists. To substitute the term political system for government or state involves more than the mere style of nomenclature. This new terminology reflects a new way of looking at political phenomena. The old terms—state and government—are limited to legal and institutional meanings; they are limited to governmental institutions such as the legislative, the executive and the judiciary. If we employ this formal and institutional approach to study the political behavior, we are bound to be deprived of understanding the total dynamics of politics, since politics occurs also outside of governmental spheres. Moreover, if this approach is employed to study the politics of non-Western societies, the shortcomings are even more serious because some formal institutions might not even exist in those societies. And even when they do exist, they do not necessarily have the power of actual performance; there is a gap between what is prescribed and the way it

[2] Lucian Pye and Sidney Verba (eds.), *Political Culture and Political Development* (Princeton: Princeton University Press, 1965), p. 513.

[3] Gabriel Almond and G. Bingham Powell, Jr., *Comparative Politics: A Developmental Approach* (Boston: Little, Brown and Company, 1966), p. 50.

[4] Claude Ake, *A Theory of Political Integration* (Homewood, Ill.: The Domcy Press, 1967), pp. 1-2.

[5] Pye and Verba (eds.), op. cit., p. 7.

[6] Almond and Powell, op. cit., pp. 51 ff.

actually behaves, a phenomenon coined by Riggs as "formalism."[7] The advantage of the term political system is that it sensitizes us to the entire scope of political activities within a society, regardless of where in the society such activities may be located, thus enabling us to grasp the dynamics of the total polity and the intricate relationship between polity and society.[8] Moreover, it also enables us to study politics in any society, whether or not it has a government.[9]

By political system, we refer to an entity of which the component units are engaged in the processes of identifying and posing problems and in making and administrating decisions in the realm of public affairs.[10] With this definition, the boundary of the political system, separating it from the total society, is definable, and it allows us to include not only governmental institutions, but also other kinds of structures which involve political activities.

To study the political culture of a political system is to study the particular distribution of patterns of orientation toward political objects among members of the system. According to Almond and Verba, a political system can be broadly conceptualized as having four objects.[11] These four objects are (1) the system as a general object; (2) input objects (referring to something, be it structures, incumbents, or decisions which are involved in the political or input process. 'Input process' refers to the flow of demands from the society into the polity and the conversion of these demands into authoritative policies.) (3) output objects (referring to somethings, be they structures, incumbents, or decisions, which are involved in the administrative or output process. 'Output process' refers to that process by which authoritative policies are applied or enforced.) and (4) the self as an object (referring to the content and quality of norms of personal political obligation, and the content and quality of the sense of personal performance vis-a-vis the political system.)

The individual's orientation toward political objects, in the view of Almond and Verba who follow the scheme suggested by Parsons and Shils, can be analytically distinguished into three types: (1) cognitive orientation, that is, knowledge of and belief about the objects; (2) affective orientation, that is,

---

[7] F. W. Riggs, *Administration in Developing Countries: The Theory of Prismatic Society* (Boston: Houghton Mifflin Company, 1964), Chap. 1.

[8] This new way of studying politics is first articulated in Almond's "A Functional Approach to Comparative Politics" in *The Politics of the Developing Areas*, eds. by G. A. Almond and J. S. Coleman (Princeton: Princeton University Press, 1960), pp. 3-64.

[9] Lucy Mair, *Primitive Government* (Linotype Georgian: Hazell Waston & Viney Ltd., A Pelican Book, 1970), p. 16.

[10] Roy C. Macridis and Robert E. Ward (eds.), *Modern Political Systems* (Englewood Cliffs, N. J.: Prentice-Hall, Inc., 1963), p. 8.

[11] Gabriel Almond and Sidney Verba, *The Civic Culture* (Boston: Little, Brown and Company, 1965), pp. 13 ff.

the feeling about the objects and (3) evaluative orientation, that is, the judgements and opinions about the objects; that is, the combination of value standards and criteria with information and feelings. Thus conceptualized, political cultures can be differentiated into three types basing upon the frequency or different kinds of cognitive, affective, and evaluative orientations towards the four political objects. The first type is "parochial political culture" in which the frequency of orientation to political objects of the four kinds approaches zero. The second type is "subject political culture" in which the frequency of orientations toward the political system as a whole and toward the output aspects of the system are high, but orientations toward input objects and toward the self as an active participant approach zero. The third type is "participant political culture" in which there is a high frequency of orientations toward the objects of all the four kinds.

Political Culture in Kwun Tong

Kwun Tong, covering an area of more than 1,200 hectares, is a newly developed industrial community with a short history of 17 years. Kwun Tong has a population of about 500,000. Physically, the district is rather isolated; it lies at the eastern end of Victoria Harbour, separated from the Kowloon Peninsula by Kowloon Bay and Hammer Hill. The chain of Kwo Pui Shan, Black Hill and Devil's Peak forms a natural barrier and serves as the eastern and north-eastern boundaries of the district. On the north, Clear Water Bay Road separates Kwun Tong from Wong Tai Sin District. More important, there is only one land transportation route—Kwun Tong Road—connecting Kwun Tong and other districts of Kowloon. Therefore, the physical boundary of Kwun Tong as a community is rather easy to identify. However, the socio-political boundary of Kwun Tong is not congruent with the physical one. According to our findings, if we compare the intra-Kwun Tong flow of social communication with that between Kwun Tong and other districts of the Colony, there are strong indicators showing that Kwun Tong, socially, politically and economically, is more a functioning part of the Hong Kong metropolitan city than a separate community with a high degree of self-containedness.[12] Thus, we think the findings about political culture in Kwun Tong should be able to shed light on the nature of political culture in Hong Kong as a whole.

This study only attempts to get a general cognitive and psychological map of the politics of the ordinary men and leaders of Kwun Tong. What we have

[12] Ambrose Y. C. King and Y. K. Chan, "The Theoretical and Operational Definition of a Community: The Case of Kwun Tong", Social Research Centre, The Chinese University of Hong Kong, July, 1972.

tried to do is to locate special attitudes towards and propensities for political behavior among parts of the population, or in particular structures of the political system; in other words, to find out the cognitive, affective and evaluative orientations of both ordinary men and leaders towards the political objects of the four kinds listed above: system, inputs, outputs, and self as actor. The methods used in this study are mainly structured questionnaire survey and intensive interview for both ordinary men and leaders. The term 'leader' is here loosely used to refer to those with most power in a group, and we have called those who are the heads of organizations of various types leaders, though a large percentage of them are in no sense those with most power in the community as a whole.

Cognitive Dimension

In studying the political cognition of people, we are primarily concerned with their knowledge about and awareness of government and politics. What we are trying to find out is the degree of their exposure to mass media. According to the Life Quality Study[13] survey based on 1,065 cases of which 32.6% are male, 67.4% female, we have the findings as shown in Table. 1.

Table 1

Frequency with Which Respondent Follows Accounts of Public
and Governmental Affairs: by Ordinary Men

	N	%
regularly	70	6.6
from time to time	453	42.5
never	533	50.0
other	4	0.4
don't know	2	0.2
no response	3	0.3
	1,065	100.0

Table 1 shows that 42.5% of the ordinary men in Kwun Tong follow the accounts of public and governmental affairs "from time to time", and 6.6%

[13] The *Life Quality Study* was part of the Kwun Tong Industrial Community Research Programme conducted by Dr. Stanley Shively. The survey data were collected in May, 1971.

of them follow it "regularly". These two groups of people who, comprising
49.1% in all, follow the accounts of politics either regularly or from time to
time should be described as having an interest in, concern about the knowledge
of politics, and might be characterized as belonging to the "political strata"
in the political system.[14] In comparison with countries like the U.S., the
U.K., Germany, Italy, and Mexico, the percentage of people in Hong Kong,
who follow politics regularly (6.6%), and who may be labelled as the "attentive public", is considerably lower; while the percentage of people who follow
politics from time to time is rather high.[15] The fact of the matter is that the
size of the political strata is not small; the majority of people are not
necessarily politically apathetic as were often stated. In interviewing with
15 civic and governmental leaders about their view on ordinary men's concern
for current public affairs, ten of them say "moderate", one even says, "very
great", but none say "very low". People in Hong Kong often say that the
ordinary men have an extremely high degree of political apathy by referring
to the fact that at the elections for the Urban Council, the Colony's only
elective political body, the voting rates are very low. For example, in March
1971, only about 26% of the registered voters actually voted which is
equivalent to roughly 5% of the potentially qualified voters.[16]

However, voting behavior, the most important index of political participation in Western democracies, cannot be a meaningful indicator in Hong Kong

[14] Robert A. Dahl, *Modern Political Analysis* (Englewood Cliffs, N.J.: Prentice-Hall
Inc., 1963), pp. 56 ff.

[15] The frequencies with which ordinary citizens follow accounts of public and
governmental affairs in the United States, Britain, Germany, Italy and Mexico are shown
in the following table.

Following Accounts of Political and Governmental Affairs: by Nations

Percentage who report they follow accounts	U.S.	U.K.	Germany	Italy	Mexico
Regularly	27	23	34	11	15
From time to time	53	45	38	26	40
Never	19	32	25	62	44
Other and don't know	1	1	3	1	1
Total percentage	100	100	100	100	100
Total number	970	963	955	995	1,007

(From Almond and Verba, *The Civic Culture* (Boston: Little, Brown and Co., 1965), p. 54.

[16] These figures are compiled from the Annual Report of the Director of Urban
Services Department and Chairman of Urban Council for 1969/70 and 1970/71.

simply because Hong Kong is ruled by Colonial bureaucrats who are not subjected to election, and the Urban Council is in no way a really powerful rule-making body. As was pointed out by a political scientist, "apathy towards the Urban Council elections is just as likely to be the result of the limitations on the Council's powers and influence as it is to be consequence of a general lack of interest in politics or in the actions of government."[17] But political apathy does exist in Kwun Tong; Table 1 shows that 50% of the respondents never follow public and government affairs. This percentage is indeed high compared with other countries.[18] The lack of concern about public affairs is further confirmed by the Kwun Tong Health Study survey, in which 478 or 68.1% of a total of 702 cases agree with the statement: "Residents of this district are more concerned about their own (family) affairs than with the welfare of the whole district", and only 84 or 12% disagree. These data suggest that more than half the population in Kwun Tong is oriented primarily towards traditional familistic social organization, thus showing clear elements of parochial culture. Those who never follow politics and have an orientation towards parochialism can be called "politically inert", or characterized as belonging to the "apolitical strata."

As for the leaders of Kwun Tong, the political cognitive map is different. Among 13 civic leaders (heads of Kaifong and MSB), 12, or 92.3%, say they "always" or "sometimes" follow politics. In three separate surveys—the Kwun Tong Economic Organization Study (directed by Victor Mok), the Kwun Tong Religious Organization Study (directed by Joan Delaney and Y. K. Chan) and the Kwun Tong Medical & Health Study (directed by Rance P. L. Lee), we have studied the political cognition of 346 economic leaders, 45 religious leaders and 94 doctors by asking them their degree of concern about public and government affairs. The findings are shown in Table 2.

The figures in Table 2 are interesting in many ways, for they indicate that, with the exception of religious leaders, the percentage of all other leaders who are "very much" concerned about politics is very low; however, the percentage of leaders who have a "moderate" concern about politics is rather high. Moreover, among the economic and religious leaders, only 2.9% and 4.4% respectively show a lack of concern about or interest in politics. Nevertheless, 24.5% of the medical doctors showed no concern about politics. This figure is rather high, although still lower than that of the ordinary men; we tend to think that it may not be very legitimate to consider medical doctors as leaders, be they West-trained physicians or Chinese herbalists, for they are seldom heads of organizations as others are. Anyhow, the overall indication

[17]John Rear, "One Brand of Politics" in *Hong Kong: The Industrial Colony*, ed. by Keith Hopkins (London: Oxford University Press, 1971), p. 111.

[18]See Note 14.

Table 2

Degree of Concern about Public and Government Affairs:
by Leaders

Degree	Economic		Religious		Medical	
	N	%	N	%	N	%
Very much	15	4.3	13	28.9	8	8.5
Moderate	244	70.5	18	40.0	39	41.5
Little	70	20.2	9	20.0	21	22.3
Nil	10	2.9	2	4.4	23	24.5
No response	7	2.0	3	6.7	3	3.2
	346	99.9	45	100.0	94	100.0

is clear that the percentage of leaders who are politically inert or belong to the "apolitical strata" is much smaller than that of the ordinary men. In other words, leaders are more oriented toward extra-familistic objects, and thus are less parochial in outlook.

Affective Dimension

In talking about the affective dimension of politics, we are in effect looking at the state of feeling of people about government and politics. We believe that for a person to engage in political activities the thing of first importance is the feeling of its being safe to do so. Hong Kong's is not a democratic system, but it is widely believed that people in the Colony enjoy a high degree of freedom. Engaging in politics needs, first of all, freedom of expression. It is held by political scientists that talking politics with other people is an active form of political participation, while exposure to mass media is relatively passive. Talking politics with other people can indeed be viewed as having an orientation towards system, input objects and self as an active participant. That a feeling of freedom to talk politics with other people by ordinary men in Kwun Tong is empirically found is shown in Table 3.

The figures in Table 3 show that (1) 41.3% of the respondents in Kwun Tong feel moderately and/or strongly that they are perfectly free to talk politics with anyone; (2) only 6.2% of the respondents feel that they are not free to talk politics with anyone. However, a significant phenomenon emerging in Table 3 is that 21.3 percent of respondents either "don't know" or give "no answer" to the question at all. The rather high percentage (18.6%) of the

Table 3

Feeling of Freedom in Talking Politics with Anyone:
by Ordinary Men

	N	%
−2 Strongly disagree	12	1.1
−1	54	5.1
0	332	31.2
+1	373	35.0
+2 Strongly agree	67	6.3
Don't know	29	2.7
No answer	198	18.6
	1,065	100.0

Actual text of the question, 'Agree or disagree': "I feel perfectly free to discuss public affairs with anyone".

sample in giving "no answer" is something not totally unexpected. In fact, according to our interviewers, there is a significant number of people in Kwun Tong who just do not want to talk about the very concept of politics at all, even though we "skillfully" avoided using the word "politics" in the actual text of our questionnaire. Those respondents who give "no answer" should be interpreted either as being ignorant or as having no orientation towards the input object or towards the self as a political actor here.

But, the overall meaning of Table 3 is unmistakably clear that the percentage of people who feel perfectly free in talking politics with anyone is considerably higher than other countries.[19] However, a word of caution is worth mention. This rather high percentage might be attributable to one plausible factor, that is, in the actual text of the question, as was mentioned, we used the words "public affairs" instead of "political affairs". This wording was purposely used with the intention of avoiding the possibility of getting a high percentage of "no answer". However, because of this wording design, we might have created a possibility of getting high percentage in the category "free to discuss public affairs." We suspect that if we had adopted the same wording of the question as was used by Survey Research Ltd. (Hong Kong) in

[19]The percentage of ordinary men in the United States, Britain, Germany, Italy and Mexico who reported they felt free to discuss political and governmental affairs with anyone are 29%, 23%, 22%, and 19% respectively. (Almond and Verba, *The Civic Culture*, p. 83.)

1966-67: "Do you think that people in Hong Kong are free to criticize the actions of the Hong Kong police force without fear of punishment?", the percentage of positive answers would be decreased and the negative answer and/or "no answer" would be significantly increased.[20]

What interests us here is that 49.1% of the ordinary people in the political strata claim they take part in the political communication process (Table 1), and only 6.2% of the same sample feel a lack of freedom in talking about politics (Table 3). These figures should suggest that there is a high degree of openness about the political communication process in the mind of people. And this might suggest that there is a positive orientation towards the system.

What is the feeling of freedom of leaders in Kwun Tong in talking politics with others? We directed this question to 402 heads of different organizations in Kwun Tong: 346 of economic organizations, 45 of religious, 8 of Kaifong, and 3 of MSB. The results are shown in Table 4.

Table 4

Feeling of Freedom in Talking Politics with Others:
by Heads of Organizations

Percentage who say they	N	%
Feel free to talk politics with anyone	228	56.7
Feel free to talk politics with most people	34	8.5
Feel free to talk politics with a few	57	14.2
Don't feel free to talk politics with anyone	32	8.0
No answer or other	51	12.7
	402	100.1

The figures of Table 4 are of interest, for they suggest (1) that 56.7 percent of the leaders in the sample "feel free to talk politics with anyone"; that is,

[20]The results of the Survey Research Ltd. study based on a sample of 254 respondents of that particular question were as follows: only 27% of respondents said yes, while 40% refused to answer. Of the remaining 33% who answered no and volunteered supplementary comments, only one respondent indicated some actual experience with the police. The others, presumably basing on "common knowledge" rather than experience, though that criticism in a British Colony was illegal, that the police would interfere with one's business establishment, that "the Government has a right to do anything," and that Chinese people are afraid of Government officials. *The Star* (Hong Kong), 12 November, 1966, p. 1 quoted and discussed in J. Stephen Hoadley, "Hong Kong is The Lifeboat: Notes on Political Culture and Socialization," in *Journal of Oriental Studies*, Vol. 8 (January 1970), No. 1, pp. 206-218.

15.4 percent more than the ordinary men (i.e. 41.3%); (2) the percentages of leaders of Kaifong Associations, economic and religious organizations, who either follow the accounts of politics "regularly" or "sometimes," or are concerned with politics "very much" or "moderately," are very high, i.e., 92.3% of Kaifong, 74.8% of economic and 68.9% of religious organizations, and only 8% of them feel seriously restricted in talking politics. This should mean that the leaders of the political strata do have a feeling of safety in engaging in the process of political communication, and an orientation towards the system in positive way. But, a word of caution is again needed; there is no lack of cases in which the leaders said they feel there is no restriction in talking politics with anyone, yet they have shown reluctance in commenting on the policies and/or incumbents of the government.

At this juncture, a more explicit finding about the individual's orientation toward the "system" is worth comment. In the Kwun Tong Medical and Health Study, 94 doctors were asked to respond to the question: "Whether or not do you think the role of doctors will be different under different politico-economic systems?" 11 or 11.7% of them said "very different"; 17 or 18.1% said "different"; 44 or 46.9% said "not much different"; and 21 or 22.3% were "undecided"; together with 1 or 1.1% providing no answer. These figures are of interest, for they suggest that almost half of the total sample did not see the different "system effect" on the role of doctors; and more than 20 percent of them even could not give their opinions on the system object. Granted that doctors are usually less politically oriented than people in other kinds of roles, nevertheless, this is at least one valid indicator that the doctors' orientation towards the system is neither sensitive nor strong.

We also studied the feeling of the leaders of organizations towards governmental authorities by inferring from their expectation of how they will be treated by them. We asked 399 leaders of local organizations: i.e., 346 economic organizations, 45 religious organizations and 8 kaifong, how they saw government officials' reaction to their opinion and suggestions. The results are shown in Table 5.

The figures are of great significance, for they tell us that leaders of the Kwun Tong community had a fairly low expectation that consideration would be given to their point of view in the public realm by government officials; only 11% and 17.5% of them felt that their opinions and suggestions would be given serious and moderate consideration by government officials, while 16.3% of them felt that their opinions and suggestions would be totally ignored.

If we compare these figures with those of other countries in which the respondents are only ordinary citizens, we have the result shown in Table 6.

The comparative figures in Table 6 are striking, for they tell us that only

Table 5

Amount of Consideration Expected from Government Officials for
their Opinions and Suggestions: by Heads of Organizations

Percentage who expect	Economic	Religious	Kaifong	Total	
	N	N	N	N	%
Serious consideration	33	9	2	44	11.0
Moderate consideration	56	8	6	70	17.5
To be ignored	61	4		65	16.3
Depends	147	19		166	41.6
No response	49	5		54	13.5
	346	45	8	399	99.9

Table 6

Amount of Consideration Expected for Point of View from
Government Officials: by Countries

Percentage who expect	U.S.	U.K.	Germany	Italy	Mexico	Kwun Tong (Hong Kong)
Serious consideration	52.0	66.5	56.0	35.0	13.7	11.0
A little consideration	26.5	17.5	14.5	14.0	47.0	17.5
To be ignored	8.5	5.0	4.5	11.5	28.0	16.3
Depends	10.0	8.0	14.0	20.5	6.5	41.6
Others	3.0	1.5	11.0	19.0	4.0	13.5
Total percentage	100.0	98.5	100.0	100.0	98.5	99.9
Total number	970	963	955	995	1,007	399

The figures for the U.S., the U.K., Germany, Italy, and Mexico are derived from the
studies of Almond and Verba, and those figures have been recombined here for the
purpose of comparison. (Almond and Verba, *The Civic Culture*, Boston: Little, Brown
and Co., 1965, p. 72.)

11% of the leaders of organizations of Kwun Tong expect serious consideration from governmental officials, should they try to express their point of
view, in contrast with 52%, 66.5%, 56%, 35%, and 13% for the ordinary men

in the U.S., the U.K., Germany, Italy and Mexico respectively. It also tells us that 16.3% of the leaders of organizations of Kwun Tong expect that their point of view will be totally ignored by governmental officials, in contrast with 8.5%, 5% 4.5%, and 11.5% for the ordinary men in the U.S., the U.K., Germany, and Italy; this is only lower than the figure for the ordinary men in Mexico (i.e., 28 percent). These comparative figures unmistakably show that, on the whole, the leaders of Kwun Tong have unfavorable expectations of government. And we have reasonable grounds to say that the ordinary men of Kwun Tong would have much more unfavorable expectations of government authorities. The rather negative attitudes of the ordinary men of Kwun Tong towards government can be partially proved by another of our findings. Among 1,065 ordinary men interviewed, 32.6% agreed or strongly agreed with the statement that: "The primary reason for being a government official is 'to make money'," while only 25.1% of them disagreed or strongly disagreed with that statement. We might say that both the leaders and the ordinary men have some suspicions about or low affective expectation of the output objects of the political system.

Evaluative Dimension

The last dimension of the political culture of Kwun Tong we explored was men's "sense of citizen duty" and "political efficacy". His sense of citizen duty and political efficacy have a great deal to do with an individual's orientation towards the input object and towards the self as an active political role. By "sense of citizen duty" (an alternative label for it might be "sense of civic obligation"), we mean "the feeling that oneself and others ought to participate in the political process, regardless of whether such political activity is seen to be worthwhile or efficacious."[21] By "political efficacy," we mean "the feeling that individual political action does have, or can have, an impact upon the political process, i.e., that it is worthwhile to perform one's civic duties."[22] It is held by Dahl that there is "a strong relationship between a persons's sense of political efficacy (the confidence that what one does really matters) and the extent of his political involvement. The weaker one's sense of political efficacy, the less likely one is to become involved."[23] And this statement is strongly confirmed by the empirical findings of Campbell and his associates.[24]

With regard to the "sense of citizen duty" of the people of Kwun Tong, we have findings about the ordinary men from a sample of 702. When they

[21] Angus Campell, Gerald Gurin, and Warren E. Miller, *The Voter Decides* (Evanston, Ill.: Row, Peterson, and Company, 1954), p. 194.

[22] Ibid., p. 187.

[23] Dahl, op. cit., p. 61.

[24] Campell et al., op. cit., pp. 187 ff.

were asked to respond to the statement: "Improvement of the district (Kwun Tong)'s living condition is a responsibility of the Hong Kong government, not that of ordinary citizens," 168 or 23.9% of the sample said "yes", 89 or 12.7% say "no", and 445 or 63.4% were "undecided". These figures show that only 12.7 per cent of the ordinary men have an orientation towards the self as an active participant, while 23.9 percent show rather an orientation towards the self as a passive subject of the system. Moreover, 63.4 percent of the sample are either ignorant of or have no orientation towards the input object or towards the self as an active participant. Therefore, this is more a parochial than either a subject or a participant culture.

In contrast with the low degree of sense of citizen duty of the ordinary men, the leaders of Kwun Tong show a high sense of citizen duty. 13 leaders of Kaifong, MSB and district organizations, were asked: "How do you think the ordinary men should participate in the local community affairs?" All of them unanimously answered that the ordinary men should "actively partici-pate" in the local community affairs. This bit of evidence does indicate that the leaders had an orientation towards the self as an active participant. How-ever, another bit of information seems somewhat contradictory to what we have just said. Among 346 heads of factories, 67 or nearly 20 percent failed to provide their opinion on to what degree the government should control industry. And among 94 doctors, 43 or nearly 46 percent were unable to give their opinion on whether or not the government should exert more control on the medical practice of the West-trained physicians. These two figures do, in one sense, suggest that a significant number of the leaders were either ignorant or lacked orientation towards the input object or towards the self as playing an active political role. Thus, generally speaking, the sense of citizen duty of the leaders indicates that the leaders' orientation toward the self as playing an active political role was a mixed one: a mixture of parochial, subject and participant orientation.

With regard to political efficacy, we also tried to examine the ordinary men first. In the Life Quality Study, 1,065 respondents were asked to think what they could do about it if there was a government regulation which they believed to be unjust. The self-image of political efficacy of the ordinary men is shown in Table 7.

Table 7 shows that only 14% of the respondents thought they could do something about an unjust government regulation, while 81.9% of them thought that there was nothing at all they could do about it. These figures are of great significance in comparison with those of the U.S., the U.K., Germany, Italy and Mexico as shown in Table 8.

Table 8 shows that the political efficacy of the ordinary men of Kwun Tong was more than five times lower than that of the ordinary men both in

Table 7

Percentage Who Say They Can Do Something About an Unjust
Government Regulation: by Ordinary Men

Who say they can do	N	%
A great deal	10	0.9
Some, but not much	140	13.1
Nothing at all	872	81.9
Other	6	0.6
Don't know	12	1.1
No answer	25	2.3
	1,065	99.9

Actual text of the question: "Extent to which respondent thinks he/she can do something about an unjust government regulation."

Table 8

Percentage Who Say They Can Do Something About an Unjust
Government Regulation: by Nations

Nation	%
U.S.	76.0
U.K.	70.0
Germany	55.0
Italy	39.5
Mexico	45.0
Kwun Tong (Hong Kong)	14.0

(The figures for the five nations are adopted and modified from the studies of Almond and Verba, *The Civic Culture*, p. 142.)

United States and Great Britain; more than three times lower than that in Germany and Mexico; and more than two times lower than that in Italy. This phenomenon of low political efficacy indicates that the "civic competence" of the ordinary men of Kwun Tong was very limited. To state it alternatively, the ordinary men's orientations towards the input object or towards the self as an active participant is strikingly low, if not totally absent.

As for the political efficacy of the leaders of Kwun Tong, among the 12 heads of organizations interviewed, of which 8 are Kaifongs, 3 are MSB and one is a District Association, 4 said they could do "something" about it; 6 said they could do "very little"; and 2 said "nothing at all". Based on this limited sample, we can find only 4 (or 33.3%) showing political efficacy; and though it is a higher percentage than that of the ordinary men in Kwun Tong, it is still much lower than that of the ordinary men in the above-mentioned countries.

The leaders' orientation towards the input object and towards the self as an active participant is also rather low. And this statement can be further indirectly supported by the findings on 94 doctors. When they were asked to respond to the question: "Suppose there is some kind of conference held in Kwun Tong to discuss the medical and health issues and problems concerning the District, will you or will you not participate in it?" 4 or 4.3% said "definitely yes"; 61 or 64.9% said "probably yes"; 28 or 29.8% said "definitely no"; and one or approximately 1% gave no answer. This bit of evidence suggests that there exists a considerable amount of political apathy among the doctors, only a tiny proportion of them have a high input orientation and an active self-image of political role.

The findings on leaders' political efficacy unmistakably tell us that the leaders of Kwun Tong share a parochial culture, but tend to have a relatively higher subject and participant culture than the ordinary men.

Summary and Discussion

In summing up the empirical findings on the political culture of Kwun Tong, we can state briefly: First, among the ordinary people in Kwun Tong, about half of the sample of 1,065 (49.1%) have some knowledge of public and government affairs. They can be loosely characterized as belonging to the "political strata." The popular view that the people of Hong Kong are politically apathetic should not be accepted without reservation. However, the other half of the sample do lack knowledge of or concern about politics: they never follow the accounts of public affairs. They belong to what we can call the "apolitical strata." The majority of the sample of 702 indicate that the ordinary men's orientation tends primarily towards traditional familistic organization: thus showing characteristics of parochial culture. As for the leaders or heads of local organizations, their political cognition is clearly higher than that of the ordinary men. And the leaders are oriented more towards the extra-familistic larger system: thus showing less parochial characteristics.

Secondly, among both the leaders and the ordinary men, the feeling of safety or freedom in talking politics with others is comparatively high: only about 6 and 8 percent of the ordinary men and the leaders respectively feel that there is any serious restriction on engaging in the process of political communication. These figures, though not without reservation, do tend to confirm the general view that although Hong Kong is not a democracy, it has high degree of political freedom, at least freedom of expression. This finding shows, in one sense, a positive orientation towards the "system" as a whole, though the data do not allow us to say whether the people are cognizant of the nature of the system. However, the people's orientation towards the government or the "output" object is far from being positive; a significant percentage of the ordinary people tend to believe that the primary reason for being a government official is "to make money". More significantly, the leaders of the local community have an extremely unfavourable expectation of the responsiveness of government officials, should they try to explain their point of view to them. Only 11 percent of the sample of 399 expect to get serious consideration from government officials for their views. This figure which is extremely low in comparison with those of countries like the United States, Britain, Germany and Italy, should suggest nothing more than that the leaders are somewhat suspicious of and negatively oriented towards the output object.

Thirdly, insofar as the people's conception of political role is concerned, we find that the sense of citizen duty of ordinary men is very low; more than 60 percent are either ignorant of or have no orientation towards the input object and towards the self as an active participant: thus showing strong characteristics of parochial culture. As for the sense of citizen duty of the leaders, although the limited data do not allow us to make a definite statement, we do find that the leaders' sense of citizen duty is higher than that of the ordinary men. But, the fact of the matter is that among the leaders there is no lack of ignorance or absence of orientation towards the input object or towards the self as an active political role. What is unmistakably clear is that both the leaders and the ordinary men are, more or less, cognizant of and have an orientation towards the output object or the administrative side of the political system. They tend primarily to think that it is the government, not the individual citizen, that should bear the responsibility for improving the living conditions of the community. We are inclined to believe that the people in Kwun Tong still hold strong traditional, paternalistic views about government. Furthermore, according to our data, the political efficacy of the ordinary men is extremely low in comparison with that of people in countries like Italy and Mexico, not to mention the United States, Britain, and Germany. When asked what they can do about an unjust government regulation, more than 80 percent said they could do "nothing at all", and only 14 percent of them gave a positive answer. Surprisingly or not, the political efficacy of the leaders, though relatively higher than that of the ordinary men, was also rather low. The feeling of powerlessness and helplessness among both the ordinary men and the leaders is undisputably high. The data on political efficacy indicate that the orientations towards the input object or towards the self as an active participant are low among both the ordinary men and the leaders.

In conclusion, we may say that there are some indicators showing that the political culture of the leaders is different from that of the ordinary men, though the line of demarcation is far from being clear-cut. In fact, it is sometimes rather blurred; the difference is but a matter of degree. The data do not allow us to make a comprehensive and rigid statement about these two different structures' exact frequency of cognitive, affective and evaluative orientation towards all four political objects: system, input, output and the self as an active participant.

Despite these limitations it may be legitimate for us to give a rough approximation of the political culture of both the ordinary men and the leaders. The political culture of the ordinary people is predominantly a parochial one. Despite the fact that they have a fairly high degree of political cognition, and that there is no total lack of orientation towards the output, or administrative aspects of the system, or even towards the input object or the self as an active participant, yet, the majority's orientations towards the system, the input object and the self as an active role are extremely low. The political culture of the leaders is predominantly a subject culture: despite the fact that parochial orientation is not absent in some of them, and orientations towards the input object and towards the self as an active participant are also found in some others, yet, the fact of the matter is that the majority's parochial or participant orientations are relatively low, while their orientation towards the output or the administrative side of the political system is salient. Thus Kwun Tong has a mixed political culture. While the ordinary men have more parochial orientation, the leaders are more subject oriented, and both of these two sections of population share some of the characteristics of a participant culture. In general, however, it might not be too far wrong to say that the political culture of Kwun Tong is mixed parochial-subject.

At this juncture, a word of further clarification should be made. We have not in this study examined the demographic variables, such as age, sex, or even such crucial socio-economic variables as education, income and occupation. We have reason to suspect that the difference of political culture between the ordinary men and the leaders had a great deal to do with two demographic variables: i.e., sex and education, since the majority of the sample of 1,065 of the ordinary people were female (32.6% were male, 67.4% were female) and of a low level of education (31.6% had had no schooling; 45.4% were of primary school level, 18.5% were of secondary school level, and only a small percentage were above post-secondary level); while the samples of the leaders were predominantly male and of a relatively high level of education.[25]

That education is the most important variable strongly related to a political sense of citizen duty and political efficacy has been verified by empirical studies in the United States and Kwun Tong itself. And the sex variable is also crucial in the sense that men are somewhat more inclined to have a sense of political efficacy than women.[26]

In the following pages we attempt to give a plausible explanation for the mixed parochial-subject culture of Kwun Tong, which we believe to be, at least partially, the continuation of Chinese political tradition.

However, before talking about the political education of China, it is necessary to say a few words about the political system of Hong Kong. Admittedly, Hong Kong is a colonial system on the British pattern. However, the British government has in many ways tried to preserve the Chinese arts of administration, the Chinese social organizations and behavior. According to our interviews with local leaders, we are of the impression that the local leaders admire the British government's capability in manipulating Chinese cultural-political symbols and values. Behaviorally, both the leaders and the ordinary men are still living very much under traditional Chinese cultural-political values, even though there are significant signs of a break in traditional Chinese-culture.[27]

Regarding the political-cultural tradition of Imperial China, we must first

---

[25] See the following table.

Number and Percentage of Leaders in Kwun Tong by Education
(Percentage in Brackets)

Organization / Education	CDO	Kaifong	MSB	Religious	Economic	All Organization	All except Econ. Org.
Primary	0	2	0	0 (0.0)	102 (29.5)	104 (25.1)	2 (2.9)
Secondary	1	3	1	5 (11.1)	104 (30.1)	114 (27.5)	10 (14.5)
Post-secondary	6	1	2	29 (64.4)	51(14.7)	106(25.5)	38 (55.1)
University	3	2	3	9 (20.0)			17 (24.6)
Self-educated	0	0	0	1 (2.2)	15(4.3)	16(3.9)	1 (1.5)
No response	0	0	0	1 (2.2)	74 (21.4)	75(18.1)	1 (1.5)
Total	10	8	6	45 (99.9)	346 (100)	415 (100.1)	69 (100.1)

[26] Ibid., pp. 190-1; and Stanley Shively, "Political Orientations in Hong Kong—A Socio-psychological Approach", Social Research Centre, The Chinese University of Hong Kong, May, 1972.

[27] See Aliza and Stanley Shively, "Value Changes During a Period of Modernization—The Case of Hong Kong", Social Research Centre, The Chinese University of Hong Kong, May, 1972.

of all bear in mind that there is no one unitary and homogeneous Chinese "great tradition" as such. In fact, the most dominant official ideology of Chinese empire, Confucianism is, as is well known by Sinologists, a "Taoist-Legalist-Confucian amalgam." Yet, it is still correct to say that Confucianism has been the most persuasive prescriptive system for the Chinese political system in the last two thousand years.[28] Under the Confucian political-cultural system, the individuals are persuaded to be oriented towards Almond and Verba's four political objects in the following ways:-

(a) System Object: Confucianists were not, to begin with, interested in the form of government or system, rather they were more interested in the quality of officials. Indeed, they took the form of absolute monarchy as something for granted. Almost all Chinese thinkers, except those of the Legalist School, held that the moral character of the ruler was the ultimate factor in determining the nature and quality of his government; and no single philosopher ever advanced the view that a change in the form or principle of government was vital for good ruling. All the reform movements from above were, ideologically and behaviorally, nothing more than demands for changes in policies and personnel, but not in the form of the governmental system. Surprisingly or not, even all the violent mass movements from below were aimed at the change of personnel, rather than the change of form or principle of government. It was perceptively contended by Thomas Meadows that "Of all nations that have attained a certain degree of civilization, the Chinese are the least revolutionary and the most rebellious."[29] In brief, the Chinese are not too keen about the system: its form, principle, or nature.

(b) Input Objects: In the ultimate analysis, Confucian political theory is a bureaucracy-centered moralistic doctrine. The traditional Chinese political system, according to Chien Mu, was one of "trusteeship" in which the emperor and his ministers were jointly vested by the people with the authority to administer the empire.[30] And the bureaucracy had a monopoly of all political functions: input and output functions. It is small wonder that the permanent feature of Chinese society is officialdom. In the eyes of Confucianists, what is the best administration is the best government. And a good administration can be achieved if, and only if, it is run by the best people: i.e., superior men. Therefore, governing is something left exclusively in the hands of superior men, or the moral and cultural elites, while the people at

[28]S. N. Eisenstadt, *The Political Systems of Empires: The Rise and Fall of the Historical Bureaucratic Societies* (N.Y.: The Free Press, paperback ed. 1969) esp. chap. 9.

[29]T. T. Meadows, *The Chinese and Their Rebellions* (1956; reprint, Stanford, Calif., n.d.) p. 25.

[30]Chien Mu, *Kuo-shih hsin-lun* (A New Treatise on Chinese History). (Reprint, Taipei: Commercial Press, 1966), p. 35.

large are excluded; thus, we have the sayings: "You don't talk politics, if you are not in the (government) position" and "The people can be made to follow it (a policy or decision decreed from above); they cannot be made to understand it." In practice, the goal of the ruling class is to make the people submissive and subservient subjects.[31] True enough, the great tradition of Confucianism does encourage the superior men to develop an "input orientation" toward the government system in transcending their familistic identity; they are persuaded not to be exclusively concerned with cultivation of the self, but also to be committed to a total cultivation of society. This is a doctrine called "Sageliness within and Kingliness without".[32] However, the basic functional requirement of the familistic ethics of Confucianism was such that it militated against public spirit or the sense of citizen duty.

(c) Output Object: One of the most important themes in Confucianism was the doctrine, primarily owed to Mencius, of "the paramountcy of the people". The doctrine was a step short of a genuine democratic spirit in the sense that it never recognized the need for government by the people, although it does emphasize the ideal of government of and for the people.[33] Faithful to this doctrine, the Chinese literati never failed to pay attention to what the government officials do to the people. No student of Chinese history can be blind to the fact that superior men as well as people at large were, more or less, oriented toward the administrative side of the system. The whole censorial tradition bears witness to it.

(d) The Self as an Active Participant: In spite of the doctrine of either "the paramountcy of the people" or "Sageliness within and Kingliness without", the Chinese social philosophers are silent about all the people's political rights except that of rebellion.[34] The Chinese law was administrative in nature.[35] It was concerned with administrative fairness and justice rather than

[31] Hsiao Kung-chuan, *Rural China: Imperial Control in the Nineteenth Century* (Seattle, Wash.: University of Washington Press, 1967), p. 501.

[32] Fung Yu-lan, *A Short History of Chinese Philosophy* (N.Y.: The Macmillan Company, 1964), pp. 8-10; Benjamin Schwartz, "Some Polarities in Confucian Thought" in *Confucianism in Action*, ed. by D. S. Nivison and A. F. Wright (Stanford, Calif.: Stanford University Press, 1959), pp. 50-62.

[33] Derk Bodde, "Authority and Law in Ancient China," in Authority and Law in the Ancient Orient, Supplement No. 17 (1954), *Journal of the American Oriental Society*, pp. 54-55.

[34] Liang Chi-chao writes: "People's rights were unknown in the old days in China. The Legalist school emphasizes rights but not people, the Confucian school emphasizes the people but not rights, the followers of Motze and Laotze have no interest in these questions. So on the question of democracy all four schools are equally silent." Liang Chi-chao, *History of Chinese Political Thought during the Early Tsin Period*, trans. L. T. Chen (N.Y.: 1930), p. 196.

[35] A. Hulsewe, *Remants of Han Law*, vol. 1 (Leiden, 1955), p. 5.

with individual rights. As one student of Chinese law states: "The law was only secondarily interested in defending the rights—especially the economic rights—of one individual or group against another individual or group, and not at all in defending such rights against the state."[36] Herbert Franke writes: "The concept of 'citizen' as an individual possessing certain inherent or explicit subjective rights, has no roots in Chinese tradition, nor has the legal protection of social minorities."[37] The ordinary man had neither a role in national politics nor a voice in community decision-making processes. The so-called "village democracy" or autonomy was hardly a reality in its true meaning. What should be mentioned here is that the moral and cultural elites who were either bureaucrats or gentry remained "subjects" of the Son of Heaven. Fundamentally, the Confucian political culture, as Pye argues, tended to constitute a form of authority.[38] Therefore, it is legitimate for us to expect that the individual's orientation towards the self as an active participant in traditional Chinese culture would be absent.

Briefly, then, traditional Chinese political culture tended to orient the individual, ordinary people or elite, towards the output or administrative side of the political system, and to accept the system as it was without question. And it definitely did not tend to orient the individual towards the self as playing an active political role. What made the difference between the ordinary people and the elite was that the elite tended to be oriented towards the input object, and to develop a sense of "subject" duty, while about both the rights and duties of the ordinary men, traditional culture was silent. Thus, the traditional Chinese political culture was a mixed parochial-subject culture, at least at the normative level.

If the above analysis is not totally wrong, we have reason to say that the Kwun Tong's mixed parochial-subject culture is largely a continuation of traditional Chinese political culture. Nevertheless, as analyzed in the preceding pages, there is a small sector of the population of the ordinary men who have already acquired characteristics of subject culture; furthermore, a not small percentage of the ordinary men and leaders have even shown an orientation towards the self as an active participant. The trend seems to us to be moving from a mixed parochial-subject culture to a mixed subject-participant one. We do see the discontinuity side of cultural change. The influence of Western democratic ideologies on traditional Chinese political culture is not difficult to detect.

[36]D. Bodde, and C. Morris, *Law in Imperial China* (Cambridge, Mass.: Harvard University Press, 1967), p. 4.

[37]Ping-ti Ho and Tang Tsou (eds.), *China in Crisis*, Vol. 1. Book One, *China's Heritage and the Communist Political System* (Chicago: University of Chicago Press, 1968), p. 48.

[38]Lucian Pye, *The Spirit of Chinese Politics* (Cambridge, Mass.: The M.I.T. Press, 1968), p. 33.

Chapter 9

Planned Development and Political Adaptability in Rural Areas

Hsin-chi Kuan and Siu-kai Lau

In the last twenty years, the New Territories of Hong Kong, which are considered to be her rural hinterland, have been undergoing rapid and dramatic changes. They involve (a) the transformation of land-use from agricultural to non-agricultural patterns, (b) the displacement of settled, rural communities by dynamic, commercial/industrial communities, and (c) the substitution of the traditional ways of life by modern ones. Despite these fundamental changes, which have been accelerated by the planned actions of the Government, the political system of the New Territories has, surprisingly enough, remained unchanged until very recently. This system was initially devised to maintain the status quo in the New Territories, and was characterized by a version of indirect rule somewhat similar to British colonial practice elsewhere.

From the mid-1950s to the mid-1960s, the system (enlarged but not fundamentally altered) was still able to cope with the problems generated by the changes mentioned, as its main task was only to smoothen the acquisition and clearance of land so that it could be released for development purposes. The expanding administrative apparatus and the resuscitated local leadership (which otherwise would have remained more or less defunct) were instrumental both in forestalling possible collective action against planned development and in minimizing rural demands directed to the Government.[1] In the last decade or so, however, the political structure has been faced with a much more challenging task, namely, the building up of new and balanced communities in the New Territories, which is the ultimate target of the planned development. The New Territories Administration has therefore had to adapt itself to the task of cooperating in the management of an urbanizing New

[1] For more details on the political and administrative functions of the resuscitated local leadership in the New Territories, see Kuan Hsin-chi and Lau Siu-kai, "Development and the Resuscitation of Rural Leadership in Hong Kong," (Social Research Centre Occasional Paper, The Chinese University of Hong Kong, 1978). The essence of these tactics lies in the Government's deliberate effort to strengthen the position of the rural leaders so that they can serve to smoothen the process of development in their localities.

Territories with many central government departments most of which have until recently, been involved in the area only marginally. At the same time the old system which had proved effective in dealing with the rural inhabitants has had to learn how to deal also with the new residents, who are now in the majority.[2] The problem is how to mobilize the new residents in the effort to build up new communities, since lacking natural community structures, they are not organized. Existing rural organizations, elected by the original inhabitants and catering to their interests, cannot be expected to represent the new elements. In brief, a new configuration of political needs and forces has been generated by the process of development, which requires fresh thinking about the political system of the New Territories.

The Traditional Political Structure

The traditional political structure was designed primarily to cultivate a harmonious relationship between the colonial regime and the rural people, and to afford the rural interests certain measures of protection. It consisted of a system of District Officers whose main duty was the administration of land, and a system of rural representation which championed the interests of the 'original inhabitants'.[3]

As soon as the British took over the New Territories in 1898, a special New Territories Administration was established to govern the area. The backbone of the Administration was the District Officer system, as was typical in most British colonies. The essential characteristic of the system at that time lay in the concentration of political, administrative, and judicial power in the person of the District Officer. Even though the power was only delegated to him by the Centre, a District Officer was expected to exercise it with wide

[2] According to the Census, the population of the New Territories in selected years was:

1911	81,227
1921	83,163
1931	98,157
1961	409,945
1971	665,700
1976	938,440

The rapid increase in the population of the New Territories since the end of the Second World War is accounted for predominantly by immigration of persons from China and urban Hong Kong, notably from the latter. The out-migration of indigenous New Territories inhabitants to other countries further reduces the proportion of indigenous inhabitants in the area.

[3] The 'original inhabitants' are, according to Government politics and practices, those inhabitants and their descendants in the villages recognized by the Government in 1898 when the New Territories were leased to Britain by China.

discretion in the area under his administration. In 1907, there was one District Officer only. At present, there are 8 District Officers responsible for the following districts: Tai Po, Sha Tin, Yuen Long, Tuen Mun, Tsuen Wan, Kwai Chung, Sai Kung, and Islands. Originally, a District Officer was in charge of all government activities in his district, ranging from the provision of assistance to needy people to acting as a magistrate in civil and criminal cases. He was therefore the local boss in his district. In the course of time, however, many of the executive functions of the District Officer have been taken over by central Government departments and by the judiciary. Most of the functions concerned were of a technical or specialized nature, such as judicial duties, land surveying and control of buildings other than village-type houses. Others, such as police functions, were taken over because they could best be undertaken on a Colony-wide basis. The District Officer has finally become primarily a land authority, concerned with the administration of land, and a political officer specializing in the promotion of communication and understanding between the Government and the rural populace.

The New Territories Administration with its District Officers has the benefit of advice provided by a system of rural representation. At present, the lowest tier of that system comprises 900 Village Representatives who are elected or otherwise selected from amongst the heads of households in 651 villages.[4] Village Representatives are organized into 27 Rural Committees which are responsible for representing local public opinion, maintaining contact with the District Office, arbitrating in clan and family disputes, and promoting local welfare. The apex of the rural representation system is the Heung Yee Kuk, literally 'Rural Consultative Council', which is an advisory body established by statute in 1958 to advise the Government on the well-being of the people of the New Territories. From a legal point of view, the Heung Yee Kuk advises the Government in affairs which would have consequences for *all* people of the New Territories; but, quite naturally, it has displayed a well-nigh exclusive concern with the impact of development programmes on the *'original inhabitants'*, particularly when these programmes affect their land and property. The Heung Yee Kuk's records of performance, reinforced by its restrictive system of election which bars 'outsiders' (i.e., recent immigrants, not descended from the 'original inhabitants') from being

---

[4] The village representation system gradually took shape only after the restoration of British rule in the New Territories in 1945. Before the Second World War, it was the village elders who served to mediate between the colonial government and the rural people. After the War, it was felt that the inauguration of a village representation system would facilitate the rise to political power of the younger village leaders who based their authority on ability and wealth, and who were prepared to challenge the political legitimacy of their elderly counterparts.

eligible to vote or to stand as candidates, has prevented the Heung Yee Kuk from developing into a truly representative body for all.[5]

The Challenges of Development

The New Territories comprise 88 per cent of Hong Kong's 1,045 square kilometres and are separated by the Kowloon foothills from urban Hong Kong. Before the late 1950s, the area was largely undisturbed and unaffected by the progress of the twentieth century. Private development had brought about some changes in the life of the New Territories, especially in those areas adjacent to the urban centres, such as Tsuen Wan and Sha Tin. However, these changes seem very small when compared with the upheavals resulting from the planned efforts by the Government to develop the New Territories since 1950s. The major aim of development has been to create, between the mid-1970s and the mid-1980s, permanent and self-contained homes for two million people in the three new, carefully planned, towns: Sha Tin, Tsuen Wan and Tuen Mun, all of which are located in the New Territories, The operational concept of this development is not just the building of dormitories for overcrowded metropolitan residents, but the establishment of 'balanced communities' which could cater for all their social and economic needs *in situ*. Measures are being adopted to ensure a balanced development of public and private housing, job opportunities, and community facilities, and the intention is to provide these by the end of each stage of development as well as upon full completion. Such a task is the largest of its kind in the world and constitutes one of the greatest challenges the Hong Kong Government has ever had to face.

The process of development commences with planning and engineering feasibility studies. The implementation of the plan begins with the acquisition and clearance of land, which is followed by site formation and the provision of roads, drainage, water, etc. Land then becomes available for the building of public estates and private housing, factories, commercial and community facilities, all of which are to be occupied or used upon completion by people coming mostly from outside the New Territories.

The physical aspects of the development process are the province of the New Territories Development Department set up under the Public Works Department and headed by a Director. Under the Director of the New Territories Development Department, the Project Manager of each new town is responsible for the progress of public works and charged with all detailed

---

[5]This general impression can be gleaned from the minutes of the meetings of the Kuk, in which scanty attention has so far been paid to matters which are related to the welfare of the 'outsiders' in the New Territories.

planning and construction assignments. He is assisted by a Works Progress Committee.

The Secretary for the New Territories and his District Officers are primarily responsible for the social-political aspects of the development process. They conduct prior consultation, if necessary, with affected or interested parties over the development plans, and negotiate with them on the surrender of land and the terms of compensation. Evicted villagers have to be resettled. Community organizations have to be promoted in the newly urbanized areas.

In the earlier phases of development, when land acquisition constituted the major political work, the structure of administration and consultation described above demonstrated remarkable effectiveness. As development moves towards a more mature stage, it is no longer the problems of land acquisition, but rather the problems of building totally new communities that put the current political structure to the crucial test. In many parts of the New Territories, especially in the new towns, the old agricultural communities have virtually ceased to exist, owing to emigration and residential, commercial, or industrial development. The once predominant population of the 'original inhabitants' has now become a virtual minority. How can the traditional political structure adapt itself to this new social reality? Let us first take a closer look at the needs and resources of the component elements of the new political configuration.

Development and the 'Original Inhabitants'

Development in the New Territories affects first of all the 'original inhabitants'. On the one hand, they are requested to give up their land, their houses, and their traditional ways of life. On the other hand, development also brings them new wealth. Had they continued to be farmers in the absence of planned development, they would have remained living at more or less subsistance level, as was the case in the early 1950s. With planned development, they are entitled to receive attractive compensations for the land requisitioned, houses surrendered, crops given up, etc. What amounts to a sufficient compensation is, of course, a matter of contention. It remains true, nevertheless, that the value of the compensation actually paid out does exceed the proceeds that would be produced by continuing with farming the land.[6] Moreover, as the value of land tends to appreciate in the course of development, the value of

[6]When compared with the compensations meted out to 'outsider' inhabitants in the New Territories and to inhabitants in urban Hong Kong who happen to be in similar situations, it is easy to see that the Government has already been surprisingly generous toward the 'original inhabitants'. This generosity tends occasionally to draw the envy of the general public in Hong Kong.

compensation also appreciates. Therefore, there is generally speaking a positive balance of sacrifices and gains, which explains partly why the planned development of the New Territories since the late-1950s has not met with opposition in principle from the original inhabitants. As of today, what they prefer is no longer the preservation of the traditional ways of life, but the material gain deriving from the planned development. The best known claims placed by the 'original inhabitants' on the government are concerned with matters of compensation for land surrendered and villages demolished. What they want, and what the Government is reluctant to concede, are for example: (a) compensation at the rate of one house for each of the male inhabitants of a single household when it has to be evicted from its house, (b) compensation for land resumed by land *in situ* instead of by land lying elsewhere, the rationale being that the New Territories are a leased area, whereas the other parts of Hong Kong are ceded and hence permanent territories of the Colony. Compensation for land requisitioned by land is preferred to compensation by cash as the value of land appreciates at an extremely rapid rate, and hence the possession of land is likely to bring in much more monetary profit than cash receipts which can only reap fairly modest interest returns when deposited in the bank. With similar logic, compensation for land requisitioned by letters of entitlement to future land exchange (the so-called Letter B) is preferred to compensation by cash as the former will also appreciate in value, like the stocks of a successful real estate company.[7]

The less known, but by no means less important, need as perceived by the 'original inhabitants' refers to the preservation of their status as 'original inhabitants'. Ever since 1898, they have been treated as a special category of people in Hong Kong. Their customs have been respected by the Government as well as by the Courts. Their 'plight' as caused by the planned development has been well appreciated by the Government, which, in return for their cooperation in facilitating the planned development, has granted them the following privileges:

1. Each male 'original inhabitant' and his male descendants are entitled, once in their life, to build a small village house (which is not subject to the buildings regulations generally applicable in Hong Kong) on private or Crown land within a village or within a radius of 300 feet around the boundary of the village. A small village house is, by statutory definition, a building not exceeding 700 square feet in area and 15 or 25 feet in height (in the latter case no structural reinforced concrete is to be used). An 'original inhabitant' may therefore make a profit by building what is in effect a villa, without the

[7] See *Wah Kiu Yat Po*, October 11, 1979. In the same piece of information, it is reported that rich men with tens of million of dollars are numerous in the New Territories.

obligation to submit its architectural designs or pay a license for construction, and if the house is built on Crown land, he will be granted a one-third discount on the market price of the premium payments required. *Most important of all, this privilege is hereditary.* In view of the chronic housing shortage in Hong Kong, which has been exacerbated in the last couple of years, this is a very significant privilege indeed.

2. Each village is entitled to be preserved. The Government has tried its best to resettle any village affected by development (if it is so desired by the villagers) to a place as near as possible to the centre of the development areas.

For the maintenance and realization of these ascriptive privileges, the 'original inhabitants' are dependent on the system of village representation and on the Government. The system of village representation enables them to monopolize the right to gain legal administrative access to the Government and thus to have their interests represented in the decision-making circles of the Administration. Through this system, the representatives or elites of the original inhabitants are able to obtain prior knowledge about the development programmes, as well as policies and procedures of land acquisition and compensation, and to negotiate directly with the Government to promote the interests of their constituents. Evidence thus far accumulated has demonstrated unmistakably that, as a result of so many years of political maneuverings, these indigenous elites are extremely skillful in these respects.

The dependency of the 'original inhabitants' on the Government can be explained by the fact that it is the Government which has the ultimate control of the process of development and of the 'new wealth' and opportunities generated thereby. What this means is that it is the Government which decides on the construction works to be done, the location of the roads and factories, and the land to be acquired (information about which has a significant effect on land values), and so on and so forth. As these 'commonly sought-after' benefits are allocated or re-allocated by the Government, the goodwill of the Government toward the 'original inhabitants' has to be maintained. Turning to the other side of the coin, the Government is also very apprehensive of the upheavals and disturbances which might be aroused among the original inhabitants. Moreover, it is anxious to proceed at the scheduled speed set for the implementation of its development programmes, which could be slowed down should the rural leaders succeed in mobilizing the resistance of the 'original inhabitants'. In a sense, therefore, the Government is also dependent on the 'original inhabitants' and their elites, and is intent on controlling the latter by means of selective dispensation of benefits and punishments to them so that both their private interests and their leadership positions can be seriously affected if the Government deems it necessary to do so.

In the future, when most of the land required for development has been resumed and the new urban centres have been fully established, the 'original inhabitants' will become an insignificant minority in the new towns and in the New Territories as a whole. Their needs and interest would still need to be taken care of, but probably not with the same amount of administrative attention and the same priority consideration as have been given them before. The system of rural representation, as of now, is losing its representative basis, the population of the 'original inhabitants' having already dwindled to only 20% of the existing population in the New Territories,[8] and this percentage will continue to fall with time. Although the Heung Yee Kuk has, rather belatedly, claimed to represent not only the 'original inhabitants' but also the newcomers, its claims have thus far not been substantiated by deeds, as issues connected with the welfare of newcomers are seldom raised in its meetings. The right of election to the Kuk is, with the Tuen Mun and the Tai Po Rural Committees as the exceptions, still confined to the 'original inhabitants'.[9] On the part of the new residents, they do not seem to regard the rural representation system as relevant to their own interests. In a move which may prove to have significant implications for the future, the Government has also begun to obtain advice from a broader spectrum of the people than previously. It seems obvious that reform of the system of local governance ought not to be delayed any longer.

Development and the New Residents

After all, the New Territories and the new towns already contain communities of new residents and other parties having a *bona fide* interest there.

[8] According to the estimate of the Chairman of the Kuk, Mr. Chan Yat-san, the population of the New Territories is 1.25 million, among whom 250,000 are 'original inhabitants'. See *Wah Kiu Yat Po*, November 2, 1977.

[9] Reluctance to admit 'outsiders' into the Rural Committees is still strong among the 'original inhabitants'. A recent incident occurred when the Tsing Yi Rural Committee rejected the requests of the commercial and sports associations in the district to be allowed to send representative to the Committee, see *Wah Kiu Yat Po*, January 22, 1979. Tuen Mun Rural Committee seems to have adopted an exceptional policy in its relationship with 'outsiders', and gradually it has opened its door to them. For example, in its September 3, 1977 meeting, the members of the Committee decided to allow a newly established village (the Wo Ping Sun Chuen) consisting entirely of 'outsiders' to send its representatives to sit on the Committee, though they were not given the right to vote (*Wah Kiu Yat Po*, September 4, 1977). In its July 2, 1979 meeting, the Committee decided to go one step further and made it a policy to have a variety of interests and parties represented in the Committee. And, in pursuance of this stated policy, the Committee also decided to revise its constitution to that effect (*Wah Kiu Yat Po*, July 3, 1979). In its meeting on September 4, 1979, the Tai Po Rural Committee also decided to open its door to 'outsiders' (namely, commercial associations, voluntary organizations and mutual aid committees), see *Wah Kiu Yat Po*, September 5, 1979.

These people are very different from the 'original inhabitants' in terms of composition, needs, and political perceptions. Whereas the 'original inhabitants' belong to rather homogeneous groups based on family and clanship ties, the newcomers are highly heterogeneous, coming from all walks of life and from every part of the older urban centres. Accordingly, their needs are much more diversified than those of the 'original inhabitants', and many of these needs demand immediate attention.[10] The newcomers usually need guidance and assistance related to settling down in their new residences, operating shops and factories in a new environment, commuting between the new residences and the older urban centres for schooling or work (which they cannot give up, at least not in a transitional period). It is true that many of the 'original inhabitants' share some of the needs of the newcomers—for example, they may also have to move around when they choose to migrate to the older urban centres in search of jobs and opportunities—but there is a big difference. Their needs are catered for much more conveniently and adequately in the older urban centres, whereas there is an underprovision of public and community services in the emerging new towns to meet the rapidly growing needs. The general demands of the newcomers are therefore concentrated on upgrading the public and community facilities in the new districts rather than the old centres.

Finally, the newcomers differ from the 'original inhabitants' in terms of political culture. Cognitively speaking, the political horizon of the 'original inhabitants' is narrower than that of the newcomers. The former are more conscious of their interests as a group and tend to identify strongly with the New Territories, which have been their native home for centuries, whereas the latter's political passions are much less intense, and their political identification is with Hong Kong as a whole, hence they have no strong sense of regionalism. In comparison with the 'original inhabitants', newcomers are less politically

[10]From the end of the Second World War, many immigrants from China began to settle down in the New Territories. Some of them were industrialists who set up factories and workshops in areas close to urban Hong Kong; the emergence of Tsuen Wan as an industrial town is a consequence of their efforts. Other immigrants were farmers (many of them specializing in vegetable production) who acquired their farmland either by clearing barren land or by renting previously cultivated land from the 'original inhabitants'. However, the number of 'outsiders' settling down in the New Territories before the mid-1960s were small compared to the influx of immigrants which took place after that date. Though the relationship between these earlier immigrants and their hosts was not cordial, the magnitude of the problems thus generated was small, even though the 'outsiders' tended to harbour serious grudges against the 'original inhabitants' who constituted a distinctly privileged caste in the area. It is the later influx of immigrants into the New Territories as a consequence of planned development in the last decade or so that is the really crucial force in changing the political configurations of the area.

mobilized. The newcomers themselves have found no issues salient enough to justify the exertion of group political pressure on the Government, as existing organizations which can perform this function are practically nil. Contrariwise, the 'original inhabitants' have more stake in the outcome of the development process, and they can more easily be mobilized by their representatives. Without any established channels of communication, newcomers have to approach central Government departments individually for help. Inasmuch as their requests for help must be of a private nature, they seldom meet with favourable consideration from officials who are busily preoccupied with overall policy and programme results and already overburdened with the larger-scale problems generated by the process of urbanization. The ineffectiveness of the newcomers' individualistic mode of interest articulation thus contrasts sharply with the efficacy of the organized mode of the 'original inhabitants', and the disparity of political power between the two parties is readily apparent. This situation cannot be remedied simply by referring the newcomers to the District Officer for assistance as, after having been deprived of many essential executive functions in the last two decades, he is not in a position to bend the thrust of the policies of the central departments which are increasingly making their influence felt in the New Territories. The critical problem now facing the Government is: how to ensure proper appreciation and satisfaction of *local* needs when planned development has to be monitored from the centre.

Development and the Governmental Machinery

The government machinery is the most significant player in the game of development. Quite naturally, the Government as a whole is concerned with the overall impact of development programmes on the general well-being of all citizens of Hong Kong. The development of the New Territories is primarily meant to reduce population in the over-crowded older urban centres of Hong Kong island and Kowloon, to provide more and better housing for the growing population, and to provide badly-needed land for commercial and industrial development. The pursuit of these general policy goals inevitably pits the Government against the individuals and groups which are adversely affected in the process. Whenever such a situation of confrontation occurs, reconciliation of public and private interests is imperative, and it is the responsibility of the New Territories Administration to see to it that this arduous job is accomplished. The District Officers and their retinue of subordinates are expected to gauge local reactions to the development programmes, solve problems arising from the processes of development, and solicit the goodwill and understanding of the affected parties throughout all stages of the development process. Reconciliation of interests is crucial to the successful execution of planned development here, because the Government is dependent on, on the one hand, the acquiescence of the 'original inhabitants' for expediting the processes of land acquisition and clearance, and, on the other hand, on the newcomers for the building up of the new communities.

In this triangular political game the government is in an advantaged and dominant position for various reasons. First of all, it has the authority to prescribe the rules of the game and to structure the political arena to its own advantage, and this is attributable to the basically colonial underpinnings of the administrative system in Hong Kong. Second, it has the support of the majority of the Hong Kong populace, since the development of the New Territories is generally in their interest. Third, as has been mentioned before, it has the ultimate control over the allocation and re-allocation of the 'commonly-coveted' benefits. Fourth, both the affected parties—namely, the 'original inhabitants' and the newcomers—are, in the last analysis, privately pleased with the fruits which they have reaped from the development process, and in general they lack the determined will to wrench from the Government additional allotments of concessions (beyond those the Government is prepared to grant). Fifth, the elitist and non-ideological nature of politics in the New Territories, coupled with the fact that the elites themselves are far from united, makes permanent alignment of political forces impossible. In fact, it is the Government's ingenuity in manipulating the elites individually through selective dispensation of rewards and punishments that accounts in large part for the smoothness of the implementation of the development programmes. Sixth, the lack of adequate communication between the 'original inhabitants' and the newcomers prevents their forming coalitions against the Government and allows the Government to deal with each group separately.[11]

Although the Government is in an advantaged position, the management of local politics in the New Territories and the new towns is still no easy task. Traditionally, the New Territories Administration with its District Officers was designed to maintain the status quo in a rural setting. Beginning from some

[11] In a study of politics in a village in the western part of the New Territories, it was found that the Government is even willing to bypass the legal formalities of the administrative system and grant informal political recognition to organizations formed by 'outsiders'. In the case under study, 'outsiders' are able to make use of their economic associations for political purposes, and, in the eyes of the New Territories Administration, the leaders in these nominally non-political associations appear as the *bona fide* political representatives of the 'outsiders', who are thus largely relieved from the obligation to seek help from the leaders of the 'original inhabitants' (who supposedly are the legal representative of the whole village in which the 'outsiders' constitute the majority of its inhabitants). See Chau Lam-yan, "Power Bifurcation in a Changing Chinese Village in Hong Kong" (Unpublished M. Phil. thesis, Department of Sociology, The Chinese University of Hong Kong, 1979).

twenty years ago, it was called upon to adapt itself to the task of managing change. Today, a District Officer in the new towns is much less concerned about village structures, clan politics, agricultural production or *fung shui* (geomancy) than with the concepts and procedures of town planning, engineering principles and works, the attitudes and practices of private developers, provision of urban services, and promotion of commerce and industry. As is typical of rapid development, no planning, however detailed, can avoid under-administration in one area or another, such as dust pollution, inadequate transportation, etc. Although these are transitional problems which are bound or planned to subside when the whole process of development is completed, they still need to be coped with in the meantime lest public indignation may result in uncontrollable resistance to the process of development. To deal with such problems, the emergence and magnitude of which may not have been foreseen and the solution of which has not been devised, it is highly necessary to have a responsive machinery which is capable of making swift and interim arrangements. The District Officer as an administrative coordinator is handicapped by the fact that the representation of the central departments in his District is far from adequate to the task of assuring prompt provisional response to the local problems. There thus exists a loophole in the local administrative system.

The Evolving Political Structure: Administrative Reforms

As far back as 1966, a Working Party on Local Administration was established to advise the Government on the possibility of establishing local government in Hong Kong. In November of that year, the Working Party concluded its study by recommending the development of local authorities consisting of an administration and a Council. The administration would provide services or otherwise exercise responsibilities geared to meet the needs of the localities, as distinct from the needs of the population of Hong Kong as a whole. The Council was to be partly elected and partly nominated, and would be vested with decision-making power with regard to matters transferred from the central to the local level. Tsuen Wan, the most developed part of the New Territories, was included in this scheme. For other less developed areas of the New Territories, the Working Party recommended the following special arrangements:

(a) The appointment of an Administrative Officer with overall responsibility for a 'development area', including responsibility for co-ordinating the preliminary master plan;

(b) As soon as practicable, the association with this Administrative Officer of an advisory committee, consisting of persons residing or having some other *bona fide* interest in the area. The composition of this committee should change from time to time, as the area developed;

(c) Subsequently, when the population had reached approximately 150,000, or as other circumstances dictated, this *ad hoc* working body (the Administrative Officer and advisory committee) should be transformed into a local authority, with an appropriate range of powers and functions.[12]

There was no consensus among the members of the Working Party on the development of local administration. Half of the membership had reservations about the recommendations of the Working Party. Although they did not oppose the eventual establishment of a local administration with a partly elected council, they argued that the time was simply not ripe for such a venture. Instead, it was thought essential to introduce interim steps which would prepare the citizens of Hong Kong for democratic local government. They recommended, *inter alia*, a re-organization of Government departments on a district or regional basis and more opportunities for meritorious and willing citizens to participate in the affairs of their districts.

As expected, the Report of the Working Party met with strong opposition from the Urban Council as well as the Heung Yee Kuk, both of which bodies rightly perceived a grave danger to their survival. The Heung Yee Kuk promptly established a Committee for the Defense of the Integrity of the New Territories and a Study Group on the Political Structure of the New Territories. On the recommendations of the said Committee, the Heung Yee Kuk mounted campaigns to discredit the Report of the Working Party, including repeated warnings to the Government that the statutory status of the Heung Yee Kuk as the sole representative body of the New Territories should be respected, and in the ensuing ten years the Study Group produced various positions for the Heung Yee Kuk,[13] which can be summarized in chronological order (together with the reactions from the Government) as follows:

(a) The Commissioner for the New Territories be upgraded and vested with 'full' authority to deal with all matters related to the New Territories, so as to eliminate the adverse effects caused by the penetration of central Government departments, and to safeguard the distinctive interests of the people of the New Territories. This request was at first turned down by the Government which argued, first, that as the New Territories had become an integral part of Hong Kong, a great many of its affairs had to be handled by professional

[12] *Report of the Working Party on Local Administration* (Hong Kong: Government Press, 1966), p. 21.

[13] See for example, *Striving for Justifiable Rights for the People of the New Territories*, vols. I and II (vol. II in Chinese only) (The New Territories Heung Yee Kuk, 1964), and *The New Territories Community of Hong Kong Under Colonial Administration* (The New Territories Heung Yee Kuk, 1977).

departments, and second that the interests of the people of the New Territories had been thus far sufficiently safeguarded by existing arrangements. Further pressure on the part of the Heung Yee Kuk, however, resulted in 1973 in the upgrading of the Commissioner for the New Territories to the Secretary level, albeit with an authority not as 'full' as originally requested.

(b) Representatives from the 'original inhabitants' of the New Territories be appointed to the Executive and the Legislative Council of Hong Kong. The request was also turned down by the Government in the beginning, with the argument that unofficial members of the above two Councils were not appointed on any sectoral or factional basis. In 1977 however, Mr. Yeung Siu-cho, an 'original inhabitant' of the New Territories was appointed an unofficial member to the Legislative Council. In 1978, another 'original inhabitant', Mr. Wong Lam, was appointed to join the same rank.

(c) The political structure of the New Territories be fundamentally reformed to become an autonomous entity alongside the colonial structure of Hong Kong. A Political Board for the New Territories should be established as a law-making and policy-making body which was independent of the existing governmental structure of Hong Kong. Bills passed and policies decided by the Political Board should assume effect with the assent of the Governor of Hong Kong. Members of the Political Board should be appointed partly by the Special Commissioner for the New Territories who was to be the chairman and partly by the Heung Yee Kuk. The Special Commissioner was to be responsible to the Governor of Hong Kong, and under the Special Commissioner there was to be a departmental structure comprising executive Sections for Economic Affairs, Security, Housing, Environment, Social Welfare, etc. Such a revolutionary proposal could hardly be expected to be approved by the Government, which replied in 1975 that it would be unrealistic to separate the developing New Territories administratively from other areas of Hong Kong and that, given limited resources, it would also be wasteful to tear apart the administration of Hong Kong.

Although the Government of Hong Kong had accepted neither the recommendations of the Working Party concerning the establishment of democratic (i.e. electoral) local administration nor the request of the Heung Yee Kuk concerning the establishment of a Political Board for the New Territories, it did (incrementally and with low profile) follow some of the advice of the members of the Working Party. In the late 1960s, District Officers were entrusted with the overall responsibility for co-ordinating the processes of development in their Districts. In light of the earlier and more rapid development of Tsuen Wan, a Town Manager was appointed there in early 1976 to oversee the implementation of the development programmes, with special responsibilities to promote new community organizations, such as the Mutual Aid Committee, and to develop community relations. At the same time, a Town Centre Advisory Committee was appointed to give a broad specturm of the people opportunities to participate in development adminis- tration. Many other machineries of public participation were organized in the following months, such as the City Amenities and Recreational Committee. The experiment with public participation in Tsuen Wan turned out to be successful and thereafter became a model for the District Advisory Boards established in November 1977.

Another line of administrative reforms is represented by the regionalization of some governmental services. The Medical and Health Department started with regionalization in April 1977 with the aim of bringing about a better appreciation of the needs of the localities through the provision of more readily accessible services. In April 1979, success with the regionalization of this department having been proven, the Government decided to reorganize its provisions of social welfare services on a regional and district basis. At about the same time, other Government departments undertook to strengthen their presence in the New Territories by appointing commissioners or their equiv- alents for the whole area and officers for the regions and districts, though not with the wide authority and discretion required if full regionalization were to be carried out.

Up till now, the administrative structures of the districts in the New Territories have not assumed their final shape, as it is crucial for the management of development to retain structural flexibility and to allow for innovative experiments. According to the present arrangements, each District in the New Territories is headed by either a Town Manager (in Tsuen Wan only) or a District Officer, who is responsible, in close liaison with the project manager, for the overall coordination of the developmental processes, with special responsibility for developing the social-political fabric for the new community. The major Government departments—Public Works, Education, Medical and Health, Transport, Housing Authority, Urban Services, Fire Services, Royal Hong Kong Police Force, Social Welfare and Labour—are represented on a town management committee chaired by the Town Manager or the District Officer. Alongside the traditional system of rural representation, new consultative links are provided by the District Advisory Boards and by many other local branches of Colony-wide groups and organizations, such as the Salvation Army, Caritas, the YMCA, and various vocational associations, etc.

The District Advisory Boards and the New Local Politics

From the standpoints of both the 'original inhabitants' and the newcomers, the establishment of District Advisory Boards in the New Territories constitutes a drastic change in the political arena of the New Territories, even though, in view of their many divergent interests, each party has reacted to this political and administrative reform differently. For the newcomers, the District Advisory Board is an unqualified good, as it affords them the opportunity to participate in the decision-making organs in their own districts, and they have longed for this right for such a long time. To the 'original inhabitants', and especially to their leaders, the District Advisory Board represents a devastating threat to their authority and privilege in the New Territories, and, in the final analysis, it subverts the rural leaders' claim to be the legitimate representatives of all the people in their districts. When, in the past, the Urban Council of Hong Kong sought to extend its domain into the New Territories (and in the process would have taken over many of the functions of the Rural Committees and the Heung Yee Kuk), the rural leaders were able to counteract this attempted 'encroachment' with their political muscle. The District Advisory Boards, however, are beyond their means of resistance, and the (surprisingly short) history of the establishment of these Advisory Boards throughout the New Territories demonstrates vividly the determination of the Government to bring about reforms in the local political and administrative structure and the futility of the rural leaders' opposition. The New Territories are ready for political change, and once change comes, it seems that it will encounter no serious obstructions.

As soon as the Government made known its decision to extend the District Advisory Board system from Tsuen Wan (where it was established on an experimental basis in early 1976) to other Districts in the New Territories, an uproar from the rural leaders ensued. Their almost unanimous reaction to this decision was a combination of anger, frustration, and fear. The District Advisory Boards, which were to be established in all Districts in November 1977, were not meant to be a representative assembly based on electoral principles, but rather a mirror of public opinion in each District, as well as a training ground for future local elites. The future development of the District Advisory Boards is still an open question, but one thing seems to be certain: the system of rural representation is bound to suffer in terms of influence. Although the Government promised that the affairs of the Rural Committees would not be interferred with and that this would be written into the terms of reference of the District Advisory Boards, it has turned out that there is no certainty that this principle will be strictly honoured in fact. First of all, it was not written into the terms of reference of the District Advisory Boards. Second, decisions as to the allocation and utilization of the local public work funds, which come from Government coffers and are to be used for environmental and other kinds of improvements in the rural areas, are now put under the jurisdiction of the District Advisory Board whereas in the past they were controlled by the District Officers in consultation with the Rural Committees. Third, there is a catch-all article in the terms of reference for the Boards which stipulates that they shall advise on matters affecting the well-being of the inhabitants of the District. Up till now, this clause has not been put to much use by the Boards; however, if deemed appropriate, it may well be interpreted in the future to cover the 'rural' inhabitants.

For the time being, there is no serious clash of interests between the rural and non-rural segments of the population in the new towns as represented in the District Advisory Boards, and even if there were such a clash, it is unlikely that rural interests would be unscrupulously suppressed. In fact, rural leaders are heavily represented in the Boards, an arrangement that was prudently improvised by the Government in order that a transitional period should be available in which to work things through. In any case, at present, the District Advisory Boards are operating with a low profile, as they are still very young and inexperienced. The majority of their work so far has been concentrated in the fields of providing cultural, recreational, and sports services. Local public works are considered and recommended by the relevant sub-committee chaired by a rural leader whose views are generally respected by the other members of the Board.

Between the time when the proposal to extend the District Advisory Board system from Tseun Wan to other districts was made by the Government, in late 1976, and the time when the Boards were fully appointed, in late 1977 (that is, a little over twelve months), it is interesting to find that the rural leaders put up rancorous opposition to the proposal in the first several months, after which it was rapidly softened. Judging from their statements and public speeches in the initial period of stiff resistance, it is apparent that some of the rural leaders were fully aware of the political implications of the proposed administrative reforms which would seriously undermine the legitimacy of their leadership in their localities. Among the reasons put forth against the setting up of the District Advisory Boards, those from the Tai Po Rural Committee may be taken as representative of the views of the New Territories' rural elites in general:

(a) The Advisory Boards had no mass basis and therefore lacked representativeness.

(b) Many of the members of the Advisory Boards were persons in charge of occupational associations, and their goals were to promote the interests of their associations and not to serve the public at large.

(c) As the members of the Advisory Boards lacked both administrative experience and decision-making power, they would easily be turned into mere political ornaments.

(d) The District Advisory Board in Tsuen Wan had not proved to be effective.

(e) As the appointment of members to the Hong Kong Legislative Council was not based on their organizational affiliations, why should organizations in the New Territories be given representation on the Advisory Boards?

(f) Organizations in the past were only requested to participate in ceremonial and festival functions, and now they were being compelled to participate in social affairs, it was doubtful whether they could make substantial contributions.

(g) District Advisory Boards might not necessarily be more useful than the Rural Committees which they had displaced.

(h) Social organizations represented on the Boards might evince undesirable political colorations, while Rural Committees did not.

(i) Even after the status of the Heung Yee Kuk and the Rural Committees had been disparaged and they were denied respect by the Government, opposition and resistance to unfair land resumption or house demolition would still be launched by the people in the New Territories. What would be different then would be that mediation and arbitration previously performed by rural organizations and leaders (who helped maintain peace and order) would be supplanted by collective action on the part of the villagers.

(j) Some of the social organizations being co-opted by the Government were co-opted because they could replace the Rural Committees in performing the functions of organizing artistic shows to liven up the atmosphere on social and ceremonial occasions, and not because of their real contribution to public affairs.[14]

Behind the wordings of these reasons it is not difficult to detect a mood of powerlessness among the rural leaders, who were only too well aware of the political strength which the Government was able to muster and the readiness of the newcomers and their elites to enter into the political game. In a portrayal of the plight of rural organizations when the functions of the Advisory Boards were fully realized, the tone of the Peng Chau Rural Committee was acrimonious:

> From now on we shall expect to see the Advisory Boards showing off their power and taking the initiative to strengthen the services delivered to the various Districts of the New Territories, particularly in the areas of welfare and recreation. These kinds of developments will possess the full repertory of colour, fragrance and flavour and are capable of intoxicating people . . . .
>
> When this programme has advanced to another stage, . . . the functions of the District Officers will be taken over by these Advisory Boards. At that time, the administrative and political system of the New Territories will be gradually modified through the Government's trick to replace the old system with the new system. As a consequence of pragmatic considerations, the people will be attracted to the Advisory

---

[14] *Wah Kiu Yat Po*, October 13, 1977.

Boards, while the Heung Yee Kuk and the Rural Committees, which have formerly served as a bridge between the Government and the people, will be totally paralyzed and abandoned. From then on, the Government will be relieved from all constraints on its actions coming from the necessity to recognize the special status of the New Territories, and will be able to do whatever it likes. These smug calculations of the Government are certainly very ingenious.[15]

Despite the impending threat, the Heung Yee Kuk and the Rural Committees were not able to set up effective opposition apart from verbal assaults, which were generally ignored by the general populace and easily brushed off by the Government. What was more devastating to the rural leaders was that there were internal dissensions among their ranks. Even though, on the whole, a majority of the Rural Committees were in opposition, still a substantial number of them consented, though with some reservations, to the establishment of the District Advisory Boards. The Rural Committees which consented included Tuen Mun, Tai Po, Hang Hou and Sup Pat Heung, some of which (like Tai Po and Hang Hou) shifted to their present position of concurrence after a temporary period of opposition.[16] With such internal disunity, the power of the Heung Yee Kuk vis-à-vis the Government was further weakened.

As the Government's stand could not be budged, the only avenue open to the rural leaders was to force concessions from it, and this the Kuk and the Rural Committees have actively tried to do. What they wanted from the Government included: heavy representation of rural interests on the Advisory Boards, appointment of rural leaders to the vice-chairmanships of these Boards, the right of the Heung Yee Kuk to approve the decisions made by the Boards, the right of the Kuk and the Rural Committees to decide together with the Government on the appointment of individuals to membership of the Boards, and the exclusion of the Boards from interfering in the affairs which were traditionally the concern of the rural organizations. As can be noted from our previous discussion, concessions have indeed been granted, notably in the area of representation of rural interests on the Boards, to save the 'face' of the rural leaders. Nevertheless, in the future, many experienced observers expect that these concessions will gradually be withdrawn.

The establishment of the District Advisory Boards is a major event in the recent history of the New Territories. What it signifies is not only a critical change in the political policy of the Government toward the area, but also a new phase in the relationship between the 'original inhabitants' and the newcomers. In the long-term, it is also significant in that it inaugurates a process of political development in the New Territories the ultimate destination of

[15] *Wah Kiu Yat Po*, October 15, 1977.
[16] *Wah Kiu Yat Po*, November 17, 1977.

which is to set up in the area a political and administrative system which will bear a close resemblance to the system in the urban areas. From a global point of view, it is a process of political and administrative homogenization whereby former disparities between the regions in the Colony will be minimized, though not totally obliterated (as the special privileges attached to the status of 'original inhabitant' will still linger on).

In the new political context, the 'original inhabitants' and their leaders have been driven into a defensive position, which forces them to decide afresh their relationship with the newcomers and their elites. Their former attitudes of indifference, ignorance, or downright rejection will no longer suffice, as in an urbanizing New Territories they have to co-operate in one way or another with the newcomers and share in the facilities and services which are provided for common use. Besides, they constitute only a numerically insignificant minority in the new urban centres, and they have no way to seclude themselves from the political presence of their one-time 'outsider' neighbours. What these new relationships are likely to be will constitute our major concern in the next section.

'Original Inhabitants' and 'Outsiders': Patterns of Relationships

As the phenomena under study are still in an embryonic state, and our observations are far from complete, we are able to offer here only some of our tentative findings. One thing certain is that the new relationships between the 'original inhabitants' and the 'outsiders' are developing in a variety of socio-political settings which differ in their historical background, the personalities and intentions of the key political leaders, economic and occupational structures, and the balance of power between the 'original inhabitants' and the 'outsiders'. In this mélange of factors, our opinion is that the personality and insight of the political elites are of crucial importance in structuring the new relationship between the two parties, given the political passivity of the general populace and the elitist nature of politics in the New Territories. Nonetheless, because of the smallness of the area, it is the basic similarity among the various districts in the New Territories rather than their differences that is salient in any total analysis. Consequently, the local differences we have detected should not be blown out of proportion and should be considered as only minor (though still important) differences in a context of basic, general similarity.

What is interesting to note is that the three major new towns in the New Territories—Tsuen Wan, Sha Tin, and Tuen Mun—have displayed divergent patterns of relationship between the 'original inhabitants' and the 'outsiders'. In the case of Tsuen Wan, which has been developing and industrializing since the 1950s, the economic power and cosmopolitan outlook of the 'outsiders' (among whom were many Shanghainese entrepreneurs) in the past has created a situation which, structurally speaking, puts the 'original inhabitants' in an extremely disadvantaged position. As a matter of fact, conflict between 'outsiders' and the 'original inhabitants' was rare, as the powerful presence of the former enabled them to totally ignore the latter. Between the two there has been no political issue which was hotly contested, and the onus has always been upon the 'original inhabitants' to adapt themselves to an environment which was beyond their control. On the other hand, the cosmopolitanism of the 'outsider' elites drove them to enter into politics at a Colony-wide level in their quest for Colony-wide political power and influence, the result of which was that they deserted their 'home district' (i.e. Tsuen Wan) and left a leadership vacuum there, which was only partially filled up by less talented 'outsider' elites who became the responsible persons in the locally-based voluntary associations. In a situation in which 'outsiders' were not strongly organized against them, rural leaders in Tsuen Wan were given a breathing space, which, together with their monopolization of the official channels of representation to the Government, enabled them to perform very well in taking care of the interests of their constituents, and occasionally even extending their influence and patronage to some of the 'outsider' groups.[17] In recent years, however, as many incidents have demonstrated, the significance and salience of the Tsuen Wan Rural Committee have been rapidly undermined. One of the reasons for this may be that the voluntary associations of the 'outsiders' have matured and the 'outsider' (i.e. newcomer) leaders have become more politically experienced. Another reason, which is fairly obvious, is the policy pursued by the Government to administer Tsuen Wan as a full-blown city rather than as an 'urbanized village', one implication of which is to downgrade the status of the Tsuen Wan Rural Committee still further. Moreover, the setting up of mutual-aid committees in the highrise residential buildings in the district, ostensibly to promote a sanitary and violence-free Tsuen Wan, has in practice implanted a new layer of administrative bodies at the grass-root level, and thus indirectly stripped the Rural Committee of many of its residual administrative functions.[18] To consummate the whole process there is the Tsuen Wan District Advisory Committee, which spells the doom of the Rural Committee.

[17] See Graham E. Johnson, *Natives, Migrants and Voluntary Associations in a Colonial Chinese Setting* (Unpublished doctoral dissertation, Cornell University, 1971).

[18] By early 1979, the number of mutual aid committees in Tsuen Wan had grown to about 400, with a claimed total membership of 400,000; see *Wah Kiu Yat Po*, February 26, 1979. According to the 1976 by-census, the population of Tsuen Wan New Town was then 448, 710.

If the case of Tsuen Wan is one characterized by 'outsiders' dominating the scene with the 'original inhabitants' totally ignored and subsisting only in the niches, the case of Tuen Mun is one where the leaders of the 'original inhabitants' are actively seeking community-wide leadership both by wooing the 'outsiders' and by granting the necessary concessions to them. As Tuen Mun is only a newly developed area, the newcomers ('outsiders') is still relatively small.[19] Moreover, most of them have moved in only in the last several years, and they lack both organization and established leadership. From a historical point of view, Tuen Mun has been a prosperous seaport in Southern China for several hundred years; hence, the residents there have a more cosmopolitan outlook and more experience in dealing with strangers than in many other places in the New Territories. The policy of the Government to develop Tuen Mun into one of the important industrial centres in Hong Kong means that, like it or not, the 'original inhabitants' there will become an insignificant minority in less than ten years' time. Given all these relevant conditions, what we find in Tuen Mun is that the elites of the 'original inhabitants' have demonstrated dynamic leadership both in defending their own interests and, more importantly, in upgrading themselves into the position of being legitimate leaders of the 'outsiders' too. Needless to say, antagonisms between the leaders of both parties are there, but they assume only a subtle and latent form, and have not prevented either side from cooperating with the other. This accommodative attitude on the part of the rural leaders may be partially explained by their foresight and by their need to seek the help of the newcomers in developing their commercial undertakings. What is more important is that the structural situation in Tuen Mun has allowed the rural leaders a chance to assert themselves, and they have not failed to grasp it. Thus, as previously noted, they opened the door of the Rural Committee to the newcomers, they also participated in their organizational activities and they are willing to lend them their political influence in the defense and promotion of their interests. In short, the enlightened rural leaders in Tuen Mun have not only been able to free themselves from the ascriptive ties to their 'original' fellow villagers but they are also capable of earning their support in their policy of accommodation with the 'outsiders'.

The pattern of relationship between the 'original inhabitants' and the outsiders in Sha Tin is far from clear, but our impression is that it falls somewhere between that of Tsuen Wan and Tuen Mun. Like Tuen Mun, Sha Tin New Town is still in its infancy period, so the number of 'outsiders' is relatively small and the overwhelming majority of them are concentrated in a newly-built housing estate, which is geographically isolated from the villages in which

---

[19] The population of the Tuen Mun New Town in 1976 was 33,070.

the 'original inhabitants' numerical superiority has not yet been threatened.[20] The 'outsiders' in the villages of Sha Tin and in its old market town are engaged mainly in commerce, vegetable and flower growing, and cottage types of industrial production, fields into which the 'original inhabitants' seldom venture. Consequently, there is no urgent need for the 'original inhabitants' to develop ties with the 'outsiders', or vice versa. During the last couple of years, as 'outsiders' have gradually moved in, rural leaders in Sha Tin have still not taken any initiative at legitimizing their leadership positions among them, aside from the making of some verbal claims which did not amount to too much. One explanation of this relative nonaction may be that there is a lack of dynamic and forward-looking leadership in the district, though we are far from certain about this.

Anyhow, within the next decade, we expect to see rural leaders, rural interests, and rural organizations reduced to an immaterial component in the political system of the New Territories. With the resettlement of many 'original inhabitants' in the new towns and in other urban centres, their sentiments of regionalism will gradually peter out, and they will live like their one-time 'outsiders' counterparts in a homogenized political and social environment, while (except for the few who are able to make it in the new political arena) the one-time rural leaders will have to withdraw from playing the political game.

Discussion

In this paper, we are touching upon a very puzzling phenomenon: a supposedly anachronistic colonial administrative system, when assigned the task of development management, has manifested a capability to adapt itself to the new needs, and, judging from the results, it seems to be doing quite well. What is even more surprising, however, is the fact that the adaptation process follows a direction of reducing the extent of popular participation and democratic decision-making in the area under study. In comparison with the village representation system in the past, it is an undeniable fact that the newly-installed District Advisory Board system is less 'democratic', inasmuch as it does not allow for elected representatives of the people and it leaves the ultimate decison-making power in the hands of the Government, which will no longer be encumbered by an elected body claiming to represent local interests.

[20] According to a population survey conducted by the Sha Tin Rural Committee in 1977, there were then 8,134 'original inhabitants' and 6,095 'outsiders' in the villages of the district. In addition, there were 14,229 inhabitants in the newly-built Lek Yuen Housing Estate, who were predominantly 'outsiders'. For detailed information, see *Wah Kiu Yat Po*, May 5, 1977.

In view of the fact that the constitutional structure of urban Hong Kong is one characterized by an administrative apparatus which is not subjected to control or supervision by any elected representatives of the citizens, the old political system of the New Territories, though looking like a misplacement, can be explained by arguing that it is a historical legacy which suits aptly only a bygone political context. Needless to say, the Government would never be willing to extend the application of the electoral principle from the New Territories to urban Hong Kong, for fear that the whole constitutional setup of the Colony would then have to be drastically altered. The policy it has adopted, consequently, is to de-democratize and de-politicize the New Territories, so that once again the political game is under the direction of the Government.

One may query the causes of the adaptability of the political system in the New Territories. In structural terms, we would expect a political structure to display high levels of adaptability (a) when its institutional structure and its policy goals can be transformed with ease by the decision-makers at the centre; (b) when the process of transformation does not encounter insurmountable opposition; (c) when the process of transformation does not entail rapid mobilization of the masses whose interests are conflictual (otherwise the conflict-resolution capability of the system will be insufficient to prevent the occurrence of political instability); and (d) when the government's political legitimacy is maintained throughout the process of transformation. It is not difficult to see that all these conditions obtain in the New Territories to-day. The New Territories Administration, being a component part of the Hong Kong Government, is amenable to restructuration by the centre, though naturally many of the officials so affected may harbour some displeasure at the loss of functions of their department. The Heung Yee Kuk and the Rural Committees, which have only an advisory capacity and are devoid of any executive power, have no statutory or constitutional means to determine their position in the political system, and are hence subject to the manipulation of the Government, which reserves the right to prescribe the rules of the game.

As the nature of development in the New Territories is service- or welfare-oriented, it is generally supported by the people of Hong Kong. Even the 'original inhabitants' and their leaders are, in principle at least, receptive to the development programmes. When they are in opposition, they are mostly concerned with the details of compensation, and these can be conveniently dealt with by administrative means. The selective dispensation of benefits and disincentives to the rural leaders serves to break apart any united front that might be formed among them, consequently, the possibility of the mobilization of the villagers against the Government is minimized.

The Government has thus far abstained from mobilizing the 'outsiders' in the New Territories and using them as a political weapon against any 'original inhabitants' who happen to oppose the development programmes. In the first place, it is not necessary. In the second place, it is the last intention of the Government to instigate confrontations and conflicts. On their part, 'outsiders' are lowly mobilizable because of a dearth of the necessary organization and leadership. Even the rural leaders shy away from mobilizing their constituents as that would put their political career and other material benefits in jeopardy, these being controlled by and in the hands of the Government.

Throughout the process of development, the legitimacy of the Government in the eyes of the Hong Kong citizens has not been diminished; on the contrary, it may even have increased. In addition to the general support rendered to the development programmes by the populace, the Government's actions in dismantling the privileged status of the 'original inhabitants' as a group also draw their applause, even though what the Government is adopting is a politically 'backward' policy.

One last word. As the case study of the New Territories has amply shown, planned social development need not necessarily be accompanied by political development. Under a certain set of conditions, planned social development may indeed be implemented more effectively and smoothly in a de-politicized environment.

Chapter 10

Utilitarianistic Familism:
The Basis of Political Stability*

Siu-kai Lau

To many observers, Hong Kong is a political puzzle. A tiny territory, located at the edge of a colossal communist power which persistently vows to demolish all residual colonialism in the world, and which could take it over at any time, Hong Kong still remains a crown colony of Great Britain. It is even more intriguing to find that in the last several decades not only has Hong Kong been prospering economically but she also has been that rather rare phenomenon in the modern era—a politically stable society. Since the Second World War, only three instances of riotous activities have been reported, none of them was related to attempts to challenge the legitimacy of the colonial government or to drastically change the political status of the Colony. Moreover, popular participation in these violent activities was minimal, and they were greeted with either stern resistance or passive noncooperation by the populace at large.

To grapple with the problem of political stability in Hong Kong, it is not sufficient to attempt only to explain her continual existence as a British colony as many analysts have done, for this would enable us to solve merely a part, and not a very essential part, of the problem. The colonial status of Hong Kong is primarily contingent upon the delicate political relationships between Britain and China together with a host of international factors, but these are all exogenous matters which fail to take into consideration the social organization and political structure of the Colony itself. More specifically they leave out of consideration the typical normative and behavioural

*This paper is based on a survey study on the social and political behaviour of the Chinese residents in Hong Kong carried out by the author in 1976-1977. The research was supported by a grant from the Harvard-Yenching Institute. I am grateful to Drs. Ambrose King, Kuan Hsin-chi and Lau Chong-chor of the Chinese University, Professor Murray Groves and Mr. Henry J. Lethbridge of the University of Hong Kong, for reading and commenting on an earlier and enlarged version of the paper. Some of the suggestions have been incorporated into this paper. Gratitude must also be extended to Ms. Barbara Ward and Dr. Michael Bond for meticulously editing the paper for publication in this book and for alerting me to many possible problems in theoretical exegesis and interpretations. Responsibilities for any errors in the paper, needless to say, lie with the author.

patterns of the Chinese majority which structure their relationships with the colonial regime. An analysis of the internal structural and cultural aspects of Hong Kong society is a necessary prerequisite for understanding the striking political stability of the Colony.

Varieties of Structural-Cultural Explanations

Among the structural-cultural explanations proffered, two are particularly propagated and entertained: the political apathy of the Chinese people,[1] and the political support rendered to the colonial regime by the Chinese elites in Hong Kong.[2]

The view that the Chinese people in Hong Kong are, generally speaking, politically apathetic has been corroborated by some research findings,[3] though so far no study has yet specified the analytic dimensions of the generic concept of political apathy and their distribution in the Chinese populace. A subordinate group which is considered to be politically apathetic will not be expected to challenge the authority and decision-making prerogatives of the dominant group, though, correspondingly, the degree of legitimacy granted to the dominant group will also be low. Be that as it may, a colonial society such as Hong Kong with its apathetic Chinese majority group does exhibit a low level of political activism and, hence, a high level of political stability.

Many factors have been attributed to the prevalent apathetic political attitudes among the Chinese citizens. Among them are: (1) A large portion of the Hong Kong population consists of ex-refugees from China, and the "traumatic experience they have undergone predispose most refugees to

---

[1] See for example, Norman Miners, *The Government and Politics of Hong Kong* (Hong Kong: Oxford University Press, 1975), pp. 29–39; Ambrose Yeo-chi King, *The Political Culture of Kwun Tong: A Chinese Community in Hong Kong* (Social Research Centre, The Chinese University of Hong Kong, 1972); Stan Shively, *Political Orientations in Hong Kong: A Socio-Psychological Approach* (Social Research Centre, The Chinese University of Hong Kong, 1972); and J. Stephen Hoadley, "Hong Kong is the Lifeboat: Notes on Political Culture and Socialization," *Journal of Oriental Studies*, vol. 8, 1970, pp. 206-18.

[2] See, for example, Miners, *op. cit.*, pp. 185-94; Ambrose Yeo-chi King, "Administrative Absorption of Politics in Hong Kong: Emphasis on the Grass Roots Level," *Asian Survey*, vol. XV, no. 5 May 1975, pp. 422-439; Theordore Geiger and Frances M. Geiger, *The Development Progress of Hong Kong and Singapore* (Hong Kong: Macmillan Publishers, Ltd., 1975), pp. 141-144; John Rear, "One Brand of Politics," in Keith Hopkins (ed.), *Hong Kong: The Industrial Colony* (Hong Kong: Oxford University Press, 1972), pp. 55-139; and S. N. G. Davies, "One Brand of Politics Rekindled," *Hong Kong Law Journal*, vol. 7, part 1, 1977, pp. 44-84.

[3] King, *The Political Culture of Kwun Tong* and Hoadley, *op. cit.*

political quietism."[4] (2) Since most of the Chinese citizens are reluctant to live under Communist rule, "for the present apparently most prefer to endure the British devil that they know rather than run the risk that any attempt at political agitation might unintentionally put an end to the colony's separate existence."[5] (3) Hong Kong's phenomenal economic performance and the rising living standards for the majority predispose them toward acceptance of the existing conditions. (4) The administration of the colonial government is efficient and there is a relative compatibility between the political institutions and the existing patterns of political culture.[6] (5) The co-option of potentially disaffected leaders into the government machinery deprives protest movements of leadership and makes mobilization of the mass for political movements extremely difficult. (6) The limited time-span of the colony's existence makes for toleration with the status quo as it is regarded to be only temporary.[7] (7) The survival and continuance of the traditional Chinese attitudes to government, which feature bureaucratic paternalism and passive acquiescence among the public, continue to play a part.[8]

Explaining political stability in Hong Kong by means of the alleged apathy of the Chinese majority is highly appealing in that it provides a short-cut solution to a series of perplexing problems. Nevertheless, it is at once too simplistic and too inadequate to serve as an explanatory schema. Using the term 'apathy' indiscriminately and unconditionally tends to stretch the meaning of the concept so far that it can explain almost everything but it then becomes useless in any specific case; and it fails just because it cannot explain

[4] Miners, *The Government and Politics of Hong Kong*, p. 32.
[5] *Ibid.*, p. 32.
[6] Hoadley, *op. cit.*, pp. 217-8;
[7] Miners, *op. cit.*, p. 34.
[8] It is interesting here to note the Hong Kong government's interpretation of the Chinese conception of politics. In a *Report of the Working Party on Local Administration*, it was phrased in this way: "the traditional Chinese view of the ideal relationship between government and people. . . is analogous to that which should exist between parents and children or between a shepherd and his flock. The actions of both parties should be in strict accordance with a moral code, under which the rulers of a society, who should be men of learning, virtue and ability, must ensure that the community enjoys peace, order and security, leaving individuals free to pursue their affairs without undue governmental interference. In return, the people must impose their full trust and confidence in their rules, and have cause to oppose them only if the regime fails to provide the conditions of peace, order and security to which the community is entitled. Save for such opposition, this traditional concept does not contemplate the direct participation of the population in the organization or processes of government." (Hong Kong: Government Printer, 1966). Though this complacent attitude of the government has weakened a little since 1967, the main thrust of the above statement can still be considered to be the working philosophy of the government.

why some people spontaneously participated in, say, the 1966 Star Ferry incident[9] and the various petition activities[10] in the last several years. My major objection to the adoption of 'political apathy' as the primary, or sole, causal variable to explain political stability in Hong Kong is that it tends to attribute to the Chinese citizens an innate psychological trait which may, upon further analysis, simply be an adaptive device developed, consciously or sub-consciously, in order to negotiate with the wider social and political environment. From this point of view, 'political apathy' is merely a reaction to the social-cultural context, and this context must be analyzed in order to furnish us with more adequate explanations.

An alternative explanation of political stability in Hong Kong focuses on the support to the colonial government rendered by the Chinese elites, parti-cularly prominent among which are those in the commercial and industrial sectors. As Hong Kong is not an independent or democratic state, represen-tative institutions wherein elites with differentiated interests and resource bases vie for political power and influence are largely absent. Nevertheless, elite-group participation in policy-making in the colony is effected through the so-called process of 'administrative absorption of politics.'

> By [the administrative absorption of politics] we mean a process by which the government coopts the political forces, often represented by elite groups, into an administrative-decision-making body, thus achieving some level of elite integration; as a consequence, the governing authority is made legitimate, a loosely integrated political community is established.
>
> . . . [It] is our view that conceptually and empirically the concept of 'synarchy' is the key to understanding the art of government and politics in Hong Kong. 'Synarchy' . . . implies a joint administration shared by both the British rulers and non-British, predominantly Chinese leaders. The kernel of synarchy is a form of elite consensual government; it is a grass-tops approach to the problem of political integration. The British have consciously or unconsciously governed the colony on the synarchical principle by allowing, though limiting, non-British participation in the ruling group.[11]

The Chinese elites thus coopted constitute a solid and cohesive group with interlocking business and kinship relationships among a large portion of their

---

[9] The Star Ferry incident consisted of a series of riots which were provoked by the Star Ferry Company's decision to raise the passenger transport fare, see *Kowloon Disturbances 1966: Report of Commission of Inquiry* (Hong Kong: Government Printer, 1967).

[10] In the last couple of years, groups, largely from the lower sectors of society, sharing some specific common grievances have launched a variety of petition activities, the targets of which have been the government departments concerned. Though no politically significant social or political movements have yet arisen, it can still be said that the under-privileged classes in the colony are becoming more adept at articulating their interests.

[11] King, "The Administrative Absorption of Politics in Hong Kong," pp. 424-5.

[12] S. N. G. Davies, *op. cit.*, pp. 61-9.

members.[12] Cooperation with and cooption of the Chinese elites by the colonial government not only smoothen the operation of the polity, they also confer an aura of legitimacy to the decisions and undertakings of the government. Most importantly, the processes enlist elite support and so serve to maintain political stability.

However, in several ways the 'elite support' theory fails to account sufficiently for the prevalence of political stability in Hong Kong. First, the elite absorption process is never complete. As a matter of fact, the degree of diversity of elites who can gain access to the policy-making realm in the Hong Kong government is rather low.

> . . . All groups do not have equal access to government and officials are highly selective in choosing the groups with which they are willing to hold consultations. This system favours the richer business and employer groups, who are largely represented on advisory committees. Government needs their help, and so must pay attention to their views. Other groups, particularly the trade unions and those speaking for the poorer sections of society, can provide less positive assistance in administration to the bureaucracy and so are more easily ignored. Officials sometimes argue that such groups are not really representative and that if government consulted with them it would give them an exaggerated idea of their own importance. Unions in particular are regarded with suspicion because the majority of them are affiliated to communist or nationalist dominated organizations, and in consequence they have representation on only two advisory bodies . . .[13]

Second, participation in voluntary organizations is still minimal among the Hong Kong citizens. As most of the members in the elite groups are also incumbents of the administrative positions in these organizations, the extremely low social participation rate of the Chinese citizens means that formally these Chinese elites hardly represent the interests of the majority of the people. Generally speaking, the majority of Chinese citizens being unrepresented by any elites, there should always be a possibility of people's being mobilized into action by disgruntled, non-coopted elites. Therefore, the 'elite support' theory of political stability at most posits a situation wherein a close coalition between the government and an extremely small elite group is in

---

[12] S. N. G. Davies, *op. cit.*, pp. 61-9.

[13] Miners, *op. cit.*, pp. 191-2. In 1967, immediately after the Communist-instigated riot was over, the Hong Kong government came to appreciate the communication gap between the rulers and the ruled, and some measures were adopted to consult with the people and solicit their opinion on a variety of public issues. Though nothing substantial has yet been achieved, we can still witness a gradual shift in policy priorities, which will inevitably have some impact on the future political system of Hong Kong. A succinct presentation of recent political changes can be found in an unpublished paper of Dr. Kuan Hsin-chi of the Department of Government and Public Administration, The Chinese University of Hong Kong (1978), which is entitled "Political Stability and Change in Hong Kong."

operation, and there is no guarantee that this coalition is sufficient in itself to ensure political stability in Hong Kong. If, under such a political arrangement, political stability is still maintained, the answer must be sought in the social organization and cultural orientations of the non-elite, with particular emphasis on the social structural factors which hinder their being mobilized into hostile political movements, and their attitudes toward the political system.

Both the 'political apathy' theory and the 'elite support' theory are inadequate precisely because they fail to deal with the problem of the mobilization potential of the subordinate Chinese majority, the analysis of which is contingent upon a cultural and structural study of the social organization of this large group. In this paper, these significant problem-areas will constitute our main themes of enquiry. The arguments are primarily based on data collected in a questionnaire survey of 550 Hong Kong Chinese citizens made in the period December 1976-March 1977.[14]

[14] The sample of respondents was derived from the sample of respondents used in the Biosocial Survey conducted by the Social Research Centre of The Chinese University of Hong Kong (in cooperation with the Australian National University) in 1974. The sampling frame of the Biosocial Survey was a stratified sample with equal probability in the selection of sampling units. The resulting sample was a proportionate stratified random sample with 4,001 sampling units in the form of living quarters. In addition, a supplementary list of 1,600 addresses was also randomly drawn to replace those unsuccessful interviews in order to obtain the required number of 4,001 completed cases. At the completion of the survey, a total of 3,983 households had been successfully interviewed, and they represented cases from both the original sample and the supplementary sample.

These 3,983 completed interview cases constituted the sampling frame of our survey with one modification: cases from one of the census districts had been deleted because these census districts lay outside the urban centres of Hong Kong and Kowloon and the inclusion of them would increase substantially interview costs. A systematic sample of 735 addresses was taken from this modified sampling frame. Students from the Chinese University of Hong Kong were employed as interviewers, some of whom had accumulated considerable experience from previous surveys conducted by the Social Research Centre. A total of 550 interviews was successfully completed, thus obtaining a response rate of 74.8%, which was not at all unsatisfactory given the difficulty of interviewing in Hong Kong.

Among the 550 respondents, most were males (59.5%), married (77.5%), largely located in the lower educational levels and in the low or moderately low income categories. The socio-economic profile of our respondents can be said to be biased toward the lower ends of the social hierarchy in Hong Kong. Nevertheless, as the Chinese people who are low in socio-economic status represent the majority of the Hong Kong population, they are pivotal to the political stability of Hong Kong. We can safely assume that the upper and middle classes in Hong Kong are ardent supporters of the status quo. The same assumption, on the other hand, cannot be made with impunity with regard to those in the lower rungs of the social hierarchy. In fact, it is the silence and resilience of the lower classes which intrigue us the most. The intensive attention to the lower class Chinese which our sample of respondents affords us should be greeted with delight rather than deplored with regret.

Utilitarianistic Familism as the Alternative Explanatory Schema

We have already stated that any inquiry into the basis of political stability in Hong Kong must be based on a meticulous analysis of the normative and behavioural patterns characteristic of the majority of the Chinese people, and the interactional and organizational structure which can be inferred from them. Our research has as its principal goal the construction of an alternative theoretical framework for the study of the problem of political stability in Hong Kong. This new theoretical framework is built upon the key concept of utilitarianistic familism, which is a syndrome of normative and behavioural traits typical of a majority of the Chinese people in Hong Kong. Geared to the investigation of political stability in Hong Kong, the concept of utilitarianistic familism is an ideal-type concept since it abstracts from the mélange of normative and behavioural traits of the majority of the Chinese a relatively coherent set of normative and behavioural tendencies which can be used for explanatory purposes. This coherence, however, is primarily a theoretical construct of the researcher, and may not necessarily exist in the consciousness of the individuals concerned.

Briefly, utilitarianistic familism can be defined as a normative and behavioural tendency of an individual to place his familial interests above the interests of society or any of its component individuals and groups, and to structure his relationships with other individuals and groups in such a fashion that the furtherance of his familial interests is the primary consideration. Moreover, among the familial interests materialistic interests take priority over all other interests.

Utilitarianistic familism differs from the kind of familism characteristic of traditional China. Familism in traditional China was derived from a family system which was multi-functional, more or less self-sufficient, hierarchically structured, and complexly organized.[15] The existence of common familial property and the concentration of the familial members in a certain locality were the key factors for familial cohesion and solidarity. This was made possible in particular by the larger society which was built upon an agricultural system. In a certain sense, traditional familism was normatively and behaviourally functional for social stability and integration in an agrarian society. Utilitarianistic familism can be considered as an adaptation of traditional familism to the industrial, urban and colonial society of Hong Kong

[15] See Francis L. K. Hsu, *Clan, Caste and Club* (Princeton, N. J.: D. Van Nostrand Co., Inc., 1963), p. 72; Liu, Hui-chen Wang, *The Traditional Chinese Clan Rules* (New York, N. Y.: J. J. Augustin Incorporated Publishers, 1959), pp. 1-3; Hu Hsin-chin, *The Common Descent Group in China and. Its Functions* (New York, N. Y.: Viking Fund Inc., 1948); and Olga Lang, *Chinese Family and Society* (Archon Books, 1968, Orig. Yale University Press, 1946), pp. 12-23.

where individuals are more or less alienated from the social and political order, and are uncertain about the future. In urban Hong Kong today virtually none of the organizational and ecological features of the traditional family exist. The typical family in Hong Kong is a small family (a nuclear family plus perhaps a number of relatives) which depends on other social units for the satisfaction of most of its needs, and this dependence will become greater with growing division of labour in the Hong Kong society.[16]

Utilitarianistic familism is, hence, a kind of familism wherein the family (the extent of inclusion of actual members varies) represents the major reference group with which an individual identifies and for whose material well-being he/she strives. Here lies the main difference between utilitarianistic familism and traditional familism, at least in terms of their ideals. Traditional familism, with the scholar-gentry class as its principal propounder (a class which does not exist in Hong Kong), treated the family as an integral part of society, thus both the political and social participation of the familial members were encouraged, as is unmistakably stipulated in the Confucian classics.[17] As a matter of fact, symbolic and cultural rewards from society were deemed of prime importance. Contrariwise, utilitarianistic familism, typically the cultural ethos of the ordinary Chinese (who constitute the overwhelming majority of the Chinese immigrants to Hong Kong), does not value very much the non-material rewards which society can proffer; rather, society is considered to be largely insignificant, and the family is to 'exploit' society for its own utilitarian purposes.

There are several dimensions to this concept of utilitarianistic familism, and each dimension can be further divided into a normative and a behavioural component. These dimensions and components are conceptual categories in an analytic sense, they are not statistical categories as inferred from, for instance, the multivariate statistical technique known as factor analysis. These conceptual categories were constructed before the data were collected in order to structure the process of collection; they are therefore not to be regarded as conclusion derived from the data analysis. Nevertheless, data obtained from the 550 respondents do corroborate the existence of these

---

[16]See, for example, Wong Fai-ming, "Modern Ideology, Industrialization, and Conjugalism: The Hong Kong Case," *International Journal of Sociology of the Family*, vol. 2, September 1972, pp. 139-150; and the same author's "Industrialization and Family Structure in Hong Kong," *Journal of Marriage and the Family*, vol. 37, November 1975, pp. 985-1000.

[17]The conformity of actual values and behaviour to the Confucian stipulations is, of course, not perfect. Liu, *op. cit.*, after an exhaustive content analysis of clan rules in a sample of Chinese genealogies, came to the conclusion that the ideal behavioural patterns demanded by these clan rules fell short of the Confucian prescriptions.

dimensions and components, though with some minor revisions and modi-fications.

Dimension I: Major Normative Orientations

The content of this dimension contains in broad strokes the most salient tenets embedded in the normative orientation of the Hong Kong Chinese. In other words, this may be considered to be the gist or essence underlying the various manifestations of utilitarianistic familism, or the basic scaffolding on which utilitarianistic familism is built.

(1) *Emphasis on materialistic needs and immediate materialistic satisfaction* Materialistic value is the primary criterion for the evaluation of any intrinsic good in the world. Materialistic considerations are involved in most cost-benefit analysis by the individuals and thus influence their behaviour in one way or another. When asked about their criteria for the choice of jobs, only 39.6% of our respondents were *definite* in not using salary as the only criterion for the acceptance of a given job, while a majority of them was at best hesitant. Even *if* they were already well-fed and well-clothed, 58.9% of them still expressed yearnings for more money, and only a minority or 29.6% of them did not cherish such an aspiration and remained content with the satisfaction of their basic needs.

(2) *Short-term time horizon* When asked about whether they had plans for the next two to three years, 67.1% of the respondents gave the reply that they had no plan at all. If the time period of reference was lengthened to 15 to 20 years, the percentage of respondents with no plan in mind jumped to a striking 80.4%.

(3) *Emphasis on social stability.* Social stability loomed large in the mind of the respondents. An overwhelming majority of them, 87.3%, would definitely prefer social stability to economic prosperity. To measure the intensity of this preference for social stability, our respondents were asked another question: whether they would still remain in a society with social stability but without too much social justice. Again, 48.1% of the respondents indicated willingness to remain in that society, and only a minority of them was definite in their unwillingness to stay. In Hong Kong, many people are disposed to preserve social stability at any costs, and this disposition implies that our respondents would withdraw from any activities which they perceived would lead to the disruption of social stability.

Dimension II: Relationship Between the Individual and the Family

Generally speaking, to the respondents, the ideal-typical familial group comprised oneself, one's parents, spouse, siblings, children, some close rela-tives and friends (who are treated as family members). Most of the social interactions were among the core familial members, but these, together with other close relatives, close friends and distant relatives, made up the grouping with which one diffusely identified. For the non-core members, a measure of selectivity, based on utilitarian considerations, in the recruitment process was evident.

(1) *Normative component.* The significance of the family is clearly evident as 85.6% of the respondents rated either 'the family more important' or 'both family and society equally important', as against 13.5% of them who considered 'society more important.' On the other hand, when asked about their felt responsibility to elevate the status of their families, a substantial percentage of them (47.8%) took the rather uninvolved stance of 'having some responsibility'. 30.5% of them shirked all responsibilities whatsoever. Only a minority of them, 19.8%, considered themselves as being responsible for earning status for the family. Hence, contrary to the ideal in traditional China, the status of the family in society is not of much concern to the average Chinese in Hong Kong. Not only is familial prestige as a whole not significant, but prestige earned by someone else in the family also does not arouse any sense of pride within them. When asked whether they felt proud because of other family members' achievements in society, 63.1% of the respondents did not have such feelings. It seems, therefore, that symbolic rewards from society are de-emphasized in the ordinary operations of Hong Kong families.

In addition to its capacity to confer symbolic rewards, the family is also highly instrumental in a material sense. If they were in financial straits, more than half (59.8%) of our respondents would consider approaching their own families initially for assistance. Surprisingly, we find only 3.1% and 1.6%, respectively, of our respondents who would consider approaching social welfare organizations and government departments for help, especially in view of the fact that the welfare functions assumed by the government have increased dramatically in the last decade. This suggests cogently not only the crucial role played by the 'informal welfare system' in the social organization of the Hong Kong Chinese but also how remote are government and society in the psychological horizons of the average Hong Kong person.

(2) *The behavioural component.* The significance of the family is further indicated by the fact that 86.0% of the respondents stated that they spent most of their spare time with their families. Moreover, more than half of the respondents had either received or given at least some amount of financial and other contributions from or to their family members.

Dimension III: Relationship Between the Individual and Family to Other Social Groups

A family in Hong Kong usually prefers to adopt an attitude of avoidance toward other social groups, and, in order to ward them off, the family is even prepared to resort to some degree of self-sacrifice. On the other hand, a certain amount of interaction with other social groups is allowable if utilitarian interests are involved.

(1) *Normative component.* When asked about whether conflict with out-siders (people outside the family) should be avoided as far as possible even if that would incur damage to oneself and one's family, 82.2% of our respon-dents answered in the affirmative. This indicates that even though familial interests are of enormous importance, these still do not justify conflict with outsiders, the results of which may further threaten these interests. Unless the stake at hand is so large that conflict avoidance would mean utter dissolution of familial interests, the family is anxious to shun conflict wherever possible. Furthermore, our respondents not only set appropriate behavioural standards for themselves with regard to conflict with outsiders, they also applied these standards to others. 56.0% of them would not approve of the behaviour of those people who, in safeguarding their own familial interests, engaged in social conflict with others. Social stability, to reiterate, was very much in the mind of our respondents, and they would not countenance socially disruptive activities on the part of others, even though these activities might be justified by familial interests. The finding here seems to imply that to many Hong Kong Chinese, even though everybody is entitled to pursue his own interests, he is also expected to observe certain rules of the game; the consequence of such observance being to ensure an adequate quantity of social stability in society, without which everyone's private interests will be jeopardized.

That a certain amount of interaction with outsiders is allowed provided utilitarian interests are involved can be demonstrated by the answers given to a question, which asked the respondents whether they would still keep a per-son as their friend if that man was deficient in many ways but could help his family solve their problems. Aside from the non-committal answer 'it depends', it is evident that more of our respondents (38.9%) would still prefer to befriend that person, compared to those (22.0%) who would not do so.

On the whole, the ideal relationship between the family and other social groups is one characterized by (a) a minimal level of social conflict, (b) a low level of intimacy, and (c) an emphasis on the utility of the other social groups to the family.

(2) *Behavioural component.* The normative component mentioned in the last section is also largely translated into actual behaviour by our respondents. In the case of participation in voluntary associations, only 19.6% of our respondents had joined voluntary associations of any kind. Even among that 19.6% it is also possible that many, particularly those who joined trade unions under the social pressure of their workmates, were far from being active in

their membership. Among the joiners, those who had joined two voluntary associations or fewer amounted to 89.4%. Among the voluntary associations joined, many were closely connected with familistic relationships (such as clan and locality associations), with the requirements of one's job (e.g., trade unions), or with one's personal needs (e.g., religious associations and recreational associations). Voluntary associations which were primarily society-oriented could claim only meagre membership.

As to the reasons for joining voluntary associations, 55.6% of the respondents claimed that it was to serve their own interests and those of their families, while only 22.2% of them had society or social interests in mind. It seems that the Hong Kong Chinese families shun involvement with other social groups so long as involvement in them does not explicitly gratify their own private interests. However, if such interests can be served through such involvement, interaction with other social groups will be undertaken.

Dimension IV: Relationship Between the Individual/Family and Society

Under this dimension the main issues involved are: what is the proper relationship between oneself/one's family and society? Is 'society' a distant entity which is only remotely anchored in one's mind?

(1) *The normative component.* When asked about the relative importance of one's own family and the society of Hong Kong, 36.0% of the respondents rated their own families as more important, as against 9.6% who put society first. Nevertheless, even though society in the abstract was probably an unfamiliar concept to most of our respondents, Hong Kong society as a real place to make a living in was favourably evaluated: 52.7% of them stated that they would still prefer to stay in Hong Kong even if opportunities arose elsewhere. Yet, at the same time they did not contemplate trying to transform it to suit their own cherished ideals. Dualistic attitudes toward society characterize the Hong Kong Chinese, and it might be that these attitudes are instrumental in enabling them to adapt so successfully to a place such as Hong Kong, where they live but with which they fail to identify.

(2) *The behavioural component.* At the behavioural level, it can be said that the Hong Kong Chinese are cognitively involved in society but attitudinally and affectively detached. Our data indicate that a majority of the respondents paid attention to what happened in Hong Kong, and among them as many as 62.7% even claimed that they paid close attention to local affairs. On the other hand, their interests in society had not been translated into a high level of affective involvement in or identification with society, for 51.6% of them felt no pride at all in the achievements of some of their fellow Hong Kong citizens. Nonetheless, the compartmentalization between cognitive involvement and attitudinal and behavioural involvement can be satisfactorily explained by

the conceptual framework of utilitarianistic familism, since it is pragmatically logical for an individual who wishes to 'exploit' society for the good of his family to be well-informed about society, yet he may not be interested in changing it or concerned about its well-being unless his familial interests are in jeopardy. Cognitive awareness of social happenings serves an instrumental function and the possible conflict between cognitive awareness and an absence of interventional efforts does not necessarily disturb the Hong Kong Chinese psychologically.

Dimension V: Relationship Between the Individual and the Political System

The main issues involved in the relationship between the individual and the political system are: how do the Hong Kong Chinese perceive the political system and what role do they attribute to the government?

(1) *The normative component.* There is a diffuse feeling of political power-lessness among the Hong Kong Chinese: as many as 91.1% of our respondents felt they had no power to change the society of Hong Kong. Furthermore, an even higher percentage of them, 97.6%, maintained that they had no influence whatsoever on the formulation of governmental policy. These findings indicate not only that the sense of political efficacy is low among the Hong Kong Chinese, but also that most of them are not aware of any possible forms of interest articulation or interest aggregation, not to say interest representation, at the governmental level. The government appears to be an invulnerable entity which controls their fate; it is beyond their capability to do anything about it. In this sense traces of the subject political culture, to use the term of Almond and Verba, seem to be apparent, and adaptation rather than active intervention appears to be the guiding principle regulating the relationship between government and people.[18]

The primary role of government in society is largely conceived to be that of maintaining social stability. 57.3% of the respondents regarded the major responsibility of the government as the performance of this duty, in comparison to the 10.5% of them who would put the establishment of a democratic and egalitarian society on the top priority list of governmental responsibilities. That Hong Kong is still in a colonial status with all the

---

[18] Despite their sense of powerlessness, we can still detect a fairly strong desire among the Hong Kong Chinese to exert influence over the government, as can be seen from the fact that 58.5% of the respondents expressed such a desire. The data, however, do not indicate the direction of this coveted influence exertion: it could be in the direction of the commonweal of society, or it could be in the direction of satisfaction of their own familial interests or the minimization of the negative effects of governmental policy on these interests. Taking into consideration the meanings which all our available data convey, the latter possibility seems to be the more plausible.

concomitant political injustices does not bother the majority of the Chinese very much. As long as the government can maintain social stability it will be *tolerated*, and the level of political frustration among the Chinese will be held within controllable limits. However, for the Chinese to be *satisfied with* the government, it seems that more may have to be done, as 50.5% of the respondents declared that they did not consider the government to be good as, aside from the maintenance of social stability, it had done few other things.

The characteristics of the traditional Chinese political culture as depicted by both Lucien W. Pye and Richard H. Solomon turn out to be largely substantiated by the empirical findings here, particularly those connected with what they called the needs of the Chinese for dependency on authority and for political harmony, and the reluctance of the Chinese to question those in authority positions;[19] though, however, they describe the older respondents better than the younger ones.

(2) *The behavioural component.* The relatively passive political attitudes of the Hong Kong Chinese are also directly reflected in the low level of political participation which they display. An overwhelming majority of our respondents, 88.5%, reported that they had not had any discussion of public affairs at all with government officials and social leaders before, thus signifying the wide communication gap between the government and the governed. In the Urban Council elections, among those who were qualified to vote (who constituted less than one quarter of the total adult population), those who actually turned out to do so were still fewer.[20] Among our respondents, only 36.7% of them desired the right to vote in these elections, and, even if they were given the right to vote, only 36.7% gave us the assurance that they would make the effort to go to the ballot box.

Statistical analysis shows that the five dimensions of utilitarianistic familism are fairly closely correlated, while the relationship between the normative and behavioural components in each of the dimensions varies from fairly close to very close. Therefore, the characterization of the normative and behavioural patterns of the Hong Kong Chinese by means of the syndrome of utilitarianistic familism should generally be appropriate, as it seems to be able to capture the main social and political tendencies among our subjects.

[19]See Lucien W. Pye, *The Spirit of Chinese Politics* (Cambridge, Mass.: The M.I.T. Press, 1968), pp. 12-35; and Richard H. Solomon, *Mao's Revolution and the Chinese Political Culture* (Berkeley and L. A., Calif.: University of California Press, 1971), pp. 99-153.

[20]For details, see J. Stephen Hoadley, "Political Participation of Hong Kong Chinese: Patterns and Trends," *Asian Survey*, vol. XIII, no. 6 (June 1973), pp. 604-616.

Utilitarianistic Familism and Political Stability in Hong Kong

If utilitarianistic familism represents the dominant ethos of a majority of the Hong Kong Chinese, it would not fail to generate serious implications for the political stability of Hong Kong. Before delving into a fuller discussion of the relationship between the two phenomena, it is pertinent to repeat that the problem of political stability in Hong Kong is a multi-faceted one, and no single theory can aspire to explain it in full. International power politics, the political apathy of the Chinese people, the power elite in Hong Kong and other factors have often been mentioned as being conducive to political stability in the colony. Undoubtedly all play some part and our purpose is not to categorically reject any of them. Indeed, they are essential background conditions which we have to take into consideration in formulating our own explanatory strategy. Our sole intention in this study is grounded on a key question: Even if political movements that challenge the legitimacy of the existing political structure are rare, why is it that social and political movements with less grandiose goals also occur so infrequently?

Of course it can be argued (and many observers in fact have so argued) that the government has actually managed to satisfy the modest needs and desires of the majority of the people, thus making political action redundant. However, a closer look at the aspirations and needs of the Hong Kong Chinese would convince one that this is really not the fact. The increasing number of petitions to the government by individuals and groups in recent years appear to refute any thesis that the people are highly satisfied. It is our contention here that the resolution of this political enigma necessitates the exploration of the normative and behavioural patterns of the subordinate people in the colony, to infer the type of social organization which tends to follow from such patterns, and lastly, to assess, through educated reasoning, the mobilization potential of the subordinate Chinese. In other words, our main preoccupation is with the endogenous social factors that contribute to political stability in Hong Kong. We feel that the arguments generated from such a fresh approach may both furnish more satisfactory explanations, and, possibly open up new lines of thinking and research. The 'theory' of utilitarianistic familism is not meant to displace all other 'theories', but to refine and supplement them in various ways.

Given the ethos of utilitarianistic familism, what is likely to be the typical social organization of Hong Kong society? Needless to say the social structure of any concrete society can be conceptualized in diverse manners, depending on the basic premises and research purposes of the individual investigator. In this study, our primary riddle is political stability in Hong Kong, and the characterization of the social organization of Hong Kong will be geared to this concern.

In a society where a majority of the people subscribe to the normative and behavioural patterns associated with what we are calling utilitarianistic familism, social and political stability is maintained neither by coercion nor by consensus between the ruling minority and the subordinate majority. Of course, both elements of coercion and consensus can be found in Hong Kong, however, the colony does not fit into either the coercion model or the consensus model. In Hong Kong, a minimal level of coercion and consensus is involved. The amount of political, economic, and military power controlled by the ruling minority is far from sufficient to enable it to exercise the coercive manipulation of individual behaviour and institutionalize extensive political control of the populace. It is more appropriate to say that the political legitimacy enjoyed by the British government in Hong Kong has been granted to it by the majority of the Chinese rather than wrested from them by the threat of the use of force. On the other hand, the legitimacy granted is not the broad-scope, full-scale type of legitimacy which involves active political support. The major precondition for conferring of legitimacy on the government centres around its ability to maintain stability so that individual Chinese can be left undisturbed to pursue materialistic satisfactions both for themselves and for their families. Thus, the major form of political support rendered to the government by the Chinese majority is not active participation in the formulation and implementation of public policies, but only passive acquiescence in the existing political arrangements.

Within a fairly broad range, the Chinese are politically highly tolerant, since their demand for output from government is minimal; and the ability of their families to cater to a variety of their material and psychological needs reduces the extent of politicization of social needs in the colony, with the result that the capability of the government is not excessively taxed. If there is indeed consensus between the dominant and the subordinate, it is that they have agreed upon a narrow range of goals (the necessity for social stability being the most conspicuous), and it is obligatory for both parties to see them accomplished. Other than this, both parties are left relatively free to pursue their own interests. Whether or not these interests are similar, the operating principle is that behaviour contrary to the fulfillment of the common goals should be eschewed voluntarily by both sides, otherwise coercion from one party and/or revolt from the other will ensue. In this way, the very small amount of coercive capacity that is available in Hong Kong is enough to buttress the narrow range of consensus that does exist (as the number of people who do not participate in the consensus is small and can easily be controlled). On the other hand, the narrow range of consensus is sufficient to legitimize the exercise of coercion whenever it is necessary to bring down the dissenters. In short, political integration in Hong Kong is based neither on the granting of full legitimacy to the dominant group by the subordinate group, nor on the congruence in cultural ethos between the two, nor on the submissiveness of the subordinate group before an apparatus of coercion controlled by the dominant group, but is a result mainly of reciprocal goal definition which, implicitly and explicitly, delineate the proper political obligations and rights for the two parties. These mutual definitions touch on but a tiny portion of the total configuration of socio-political behaviour engaged in by the individuals in the colony. In a broad sense, this is political integration in a passive manner; it is neither democratic nor autocratic, but it functions.

The basic socio-political organization of Hong Kong today is a hierarchical structure with a power elite (composed largely of the British colonial officials and nonofficials, and Chinese elites) at the top, and a mass of more or less isolated, but overlapping, familial groups at the bottom, without an intermediate level of politically-oriented organizations mediating between them. On the whole, both the British and the Chinese elites have minimal popular support, and, as a matter of fact, their power and status are not based on mass support or mass mobilization. The interests of the majority of the Chinese people are not represented by the elites at the top, and they suffer from a paucity of institutionalized or personalized avenues through which to make their influence felt at the highest decision-making levels. Thus, at the bottom of the hierarchical structure, there are numerous individual familial groups which, largely preoccupied with the pursuit of their own interests and suspicious of other social groups, are relatively detached from each other. Even though most of the familial groups overlap with others, as they share some of their members (by marriage for example, or because a core member in one familial group can also be a distant member in another), the fact is that they are bounded systems in themselves and cooperative activities among familial groups are difficult to organize. As the rate of social participation of the majority of the Chinese is low (as indicated by our data above), these familial groups are not adequately united and organized by intermediate associations for concerted action in pursuit of common interests.[21] In other

[21] One may of course point to the large number of voluntary associations among the Hong Kong Chinese to refute my statement that most of them do not organize beyond the familial groupings. What I am concerned with here, however, are the politically-oriented organizations which mediate between the elites and the mass, and it is this kind of organization (for example, political parties) which is conspicuously absent in Hong Kong. Regarding those voluntary associations among the Hong Kong Chinese, my suspicion is that there is much overlapping of membership there, so that it is still true that for most of the Hong Kong Chinese, these associations do not play a significant role in their lives. Moreover, many of these voluntary associations function as recreational and mutual-aid organizations, and they seldom come into contact with politics. In fact, because of their

words, the objective interdependencies between individuals fostered by the industrial society of Hong Kong fail to generate the high level of 'organic solidarity' visualized by Emile Durkheim. It follows that this mass of individual familial groups are left in a position in which they are directly exposed to the power elite without being represented or mediated by larger-scale politically-oriented organizations, and there is a dearth of institutionalized norms regulating mass-elite intercourse, if it ever takes place.

Nevertheless, there is no large-scale, deliberate effort on the part of the power elite to manipulate the mass of familial groups. The power elite is satisfied with leaving these groups in a relatively dormant state so as to avoid any possibility of social instability. At the same time, because their vested interests are tied to the maintenance of the status quo, the elite group itself is cohesive and consensual enough to prevent the formation of hostile factions within itself. It is thus able to ward off the danger that such factions might utilize the easy accessibility of the mass familial groups to mobilze them in a power struggle and so trigger off political movements with destabilizing effects. Concurrently, it does not follow from the relative lack of an intermediate level of politically-oriented organizations that the individual members of the mass of familial groups are mobilizable and helplessly subject to whatever influence comes from the top. For the familial groups themselves, which are politically passive, act as powerful social control and socialization agents for their members; any embryonic political activism among them will usually be suppressed. Thus, in one sense, the familial groups themselves are resistant to social or political mobilization, and this is conducive to political stability in itself; in another sense, the relative social isolation of the familial groups and the lack of intermediate level organizations prohibit the mobilization of the Chinese majority on a familial basis, as the inclusion of a large number of individual familial groups into a relatively *long-term organizational structure* which is geared to the pursuit of some political objectives (objectives related to changes in the political system) is too formidable a task for the potential leaders.

This low mobilization potential of the Chinese majority in Hong Kong is a consequence of the operation of utilitarianistic familism, and many issues which might have led to political discontent in other societies are dissipated either through the process of self-restraint in the articulation of political

---

existence, they have taken over many of the functions which are normally performed by the government in advanced societies, and, by serving to lessen the demands made on the government by the populace, they render politics even more remote from the mind of the ordinary Hong Kong Chinese.

demands within the individuals (for example, after they have taken into consideration the effects of their action on social stability), or through the process of 'familization' of politics within the familial groups. What I am calling the 'familization' of politics means that many potential political issues are resolved through social means, making use of the existing social arrangements. A case in point in the welfare needs of the Hong Kong Chinese, which are fulfilled largely by self-help activities among themselves. Consequently, the prevalence of utilitarianistic familism leads to a drastic reduction of the number of politically relevant issues, thus lessening the popular impact on the political sphere.[22] Both the de-politicization of many social or other issues, and their deployment and solution within the familial groups are extremely functional to the maintenance of the colonial regime, as they reduce the need for expanding political participation and representation. Moreover, the lack of organization among the socially isolated familial groups prevents their easy mobilization by demagogues or other interested parties even if they had the intention to do so, and this accounts pretty well for the relative sparseness of issue-oriented social and political movements in the last several decades. If, from the perspective of the top, the political stability of Hong Kong is in large measure due to the administrative absorption of politics, then, from the perspective of the bottom, it is the social (familial) absorption of politics that contributes to the political stability of Hong Kong.

Discussion

Because the sole intention of this paper has been to depict in an ideal-typical way the relationship between utilitarianistic familism and political stability in Hong Kong, many conditional factors and qualifying statements have temporarily been brushed aside. However, now is the time to bring them back into the discussion so that a more realistic assessment of the prospect of political stability in Hong Kong can be made, otherwise readers may be left with too rosy a picture of the political situation in which the long-term stability of Hong Kong is guaranteed by the continual existence of the socio-cultural syndrome we have called utilitarianistic familism.

Utilitarianistic familism is neither an 'absolute' phenomenon nor is it a fixed, unchanging one. On the contrary, it is contingent upon a host of other factors whose configuration more or less affects its content and intensity. Moreover, as these independent factors change—and we have reason to think that they have experienced changes in the last several decades—both the distribution of utilitarianistic familism among the different sectors of the

[22] See Kuan Hsin-chi, *op. cit.*, pp. 13-23.

population and its contribution to the maintenance of political stability will also undergo accompanying changes.

Utilitarianistic familism is a historical-situational occurrence, and many of the phenomena subsumed under this overarching concept can be understood as the adaptation of traditional socio-cultural patterns to a society made up largely of immigrants and to an economy which is dependent on the world outside both for its markets and for the supply of raw material (including food). Because the majority of the immigrants came from the province of Kwangtung the Cantonese imprint is very much in evidence in Hong Kong, and because the large clan system was more in evidence in Kwangtung before the Communist takeover than in northern China. It is not surprising to find that 'familism' can be transplanted so smoothly into the Hong Kong context, with its Cantonese Chinese majority.

The emergence of utilitarianistic familism in Hong Kong can be briefly explained in a sequential manner:

(1) The sudden intrusion of a huge number of refugees and immigrants since 1947 placed serious strains on the Hong Kong society and economy, and, given the small indigenous population (most of whom were also immigrants in the past), assimilation of the immigrant people by the 'locals' was out of the question. Rather, most of the immigrants had to rely on themselves in adjusting to the new environment. In this spontaneous and natural process of adjustment, with all its insecurities and psychological strains, the family system had to play a salient role.

(2) As many of the immigrants came from rural areas they were predominantly traditional in outlook, and, as mentioned before, familism was a major constituent element in this traditional *weltanschauung*. Even those arriving from towns and cities shared much of this traditional orientation.

(3) The fact that the political status of Hong Kong is contingent upon the interplay of power politics on the international scene and the continued presence in this situation of a colonial government have practically debarred the Hong Kong Chinese from any opportunity to exercise political rights and responsibilities. There are substantial limits on the amount of political power the Hong Kong Chinese can exercise, and the residual power which is available is not enough to allow them to determine their fate. The futility of political participation is well understood by most Chinese people, and this is reinforced by the common understanding that the Hong Kong government is also a 'dependent' government, which means that the acquisition of governmental power by the Chinese would do more harm than good. At the same time, the capitalistic economic institutions of the Colony, coupled with the fact that the growing economy is based primarily on international trade seems to be able to whet rising appetites and has managed to focus the Chinese people's

attention and cravings onto the economic realm and encouraged an ethos of materialism and utilitarianism among them.

(4) The laissez-faire policy of the government encourages economic adventures and undertakings by both the Chinese and foreign capitalists. However, for most of the Chinese capitalists, the capital which is necessary for the launching of any economic enterprise has to come from one's family and relatives. The proliferation of small businesses (commercial firms and factories) which are family-owned and under family management testifies to the tremendous importance of the family in the economic development of Hong Kong. Sociologically speaking, the importance of the family in the economic sector reinforces its importance in the social sector.

(5) The laissez-faire policy of the Hong Kong government is also reflected in the outdated social welfare system of the Colony. Even though some overhaul of the system has been evident in the last several years, still social welfare facilities are far from adequate for the increasing welfare needs. In tackling the many needs that are not dealt with by the institutionalized welfare system, the family as an informal welfare system plays an indispensable role. To a large extent, social and economic insecurities have been absorbed by the individual families and familial groups. Along the process, the potential for social disturbance is lessened, while the significance of the family is also substantially enhanced.

These structural and developmental conditions have left their impact on all Chinese in Hong Kong, but most heavily on those in the lower socio-economic strata. The effects of these factors converge to foster utilitarianistic familism among a majority of the Chinese in Hong Kong, and most saliently among the more disadvantaged.

Many of these factors have been changing rather slowly in the last several decades, and utilitarianistic familism, though diminishing gradually, is still the dominant ethos in Hong Kong. However, as most of the former refugees settle down the overriding importance of familism will recede, and there is reason to believe that it is receding. More importantly, the changes in the demographic composition in Hong Kong mean that a growing proportion of the population is already made up of young people who were born in Hong Kong. These young people have not experienced the turmoil which their parents went through and at the same time, through westernized education they have developed wider aspirations both for themselves and for the society as a whole. From the data we have collected, it is very clear that the younger generation is much less utilitarianistically familistic than the older generation. Moreover, the appeals of nationalism and racism will have more effects on them, as can be seen in the 1966 and 1967 riots where the young people played a very significant role, especially in physical aggression against person and property. From the gradual erosion of parental authority and the diminution of social control exercised by the families, together with the continued modernization of Hong Kong which is likely to mean that more and more demands will be directed to the decision-makers in the government, we can expect more and more emotionally-charged aggressive behaviour from the young people unless a stronger sense of identification with the Hong Kong society can be instilled in them and governmental authority is more efficient in gratifying their aspirations.[23]

In view of the fact that there is a number of conspicuous lines of social cleavage in Hong Kong society (for example, allegiance to the Communist regime versus allegiance to the Nationalist regime, the poor versus the rich, the Chinese versus the British), any social issue, if repeatedly unresolved, may be expected to have serious political reverberations. The delicate international position of Hong Kong also means that even a modicum of political instability, if allowed to erupt uncontrolled, will gather momentum speedily and spell the doom of the colony. Under the dominance of utilitarianistic familism, however, there is still a minimum of consensus among the Chinese people as to the major societal goals to be sought and to be respected by all, and the government has been capable and flexible enough so far to contribute to the fulfillment of those goals which fall within its jurisdiction, with the result that these potential social cleavages have remained relatively dormant.[24] The inevitable decline of utilitarianistic familism in the future does not mean that the Hong Kong Chinese can be politically organized, it simply means that some of the more activist and aggressive tendencies in Chinese culture will be more difficult to suppress—and the society is likely to become much less stable.

[23]The inference here is based on the thesis of Lucien W. Pye that "the Confucian tradition, both structurally and ideologically, created forms of authority that gained strength by denying the legitimacy of sentiments of aggression. Therefore, once this system of authority was disrupted, the problem of controlling aggression complicated the process of establishing new forms of authority." See Pye, *op. cit.*, p. 32. The Confucian tradition was realized through the socialization processes in the Chinese families. This thesis is also useful for understanding the sporadic spurts of emotionalism, short-term in duration and largely unorganized, that have occurred among the Chinese youths of Hong Kong identity in the last several decades.

[24]For example, our survey data show that there is no significant difference in the level of utilitarianistic familism between the majority of respondents who were against communism and the minority who were not very much against communism.

Chapter 11

Effects of the Employment of Mothers on Marital Role and Power Differentiation in Hong Kong*

Fai-ming Wong

The dynamics of marital relations can be analyzed in terms of role and power differentiation. In fact, the pattern of role and power allocation between the husband and wife has been a matter of continuing interest among family sociologists throughout the recent decades. Among the early researchers Lumpkin (1933) is known to have applied the concept of role to the study of family relationship and differentiated the husband, wife, and parental roles. Herbst (1952) studied the differentiation of family tasks between the martial partners in terms of the dimensions of activity and decision, and came up with four basic configurations of autonomy, husband dominance, wife dominance, and syncraticity. Likewise, Parsons and Bales (1955) proposed the analysis of family roles along the axes of power and function, by means of which the husband's role is described as superior in power and instrumental in function, whereas the wife's role is also of superior power but with expressive function. This proposed paradigm was empirically tested and confirmed by Zelditch (1955) as a general principle of differentiation of function between the sexes as well as a universal characteristic of the nuclear family.

Blood and Wolfe (1960) analyzed the interplay of husband-wife relations in terms of the dimensions of decision-making power and division of labor which were found to have been greatly determined by their relative resources. Rodman (1967) discussed the importance of cultural factors in affecting the degree of power of husbands and wives as shown in some cross-national data. Mowrer (1969) examined the integration and differentiation of roles in the marriage relationship in terms of the dimensions of power, instrumentalism, expressiveness, and companionship. In addition, Centers, Raven and Rodrigues (1971) re-examined the relative power of husbands and wives using a sample of both sexes and a representative sampling of conjugal decision areas.

*Reprinted from *International Journal of Sociology of the Family*, 7 (July–December 1977): 181–195. The research was part of the Kwun Tong Industrial Community Research Programme (directed by Ambrose King) which was financially supported by the Harvard-Yenching Institute and was conducted during 1971-72 under the auspices of the Social Research Centre, The Chinese University of Hong Kong.

There have been relatively few studies of the systemic relationship of maternal employment and family role differentiation, even though the number of mothers being gainfully employed outside the home has shown a substantial increase and the impact of such a movement upon family relations becomes increasingly more important. Among these studies Hoffman (1960) investigated the effects of the mother's outside employment on the task participation of the marital partners, their routine decision-making, and their power relationship in the family. Buric (1963) proposed to treat maternal employment as a causal variable and study its effects on the transformation of family life particularly in its standard of living, conjugal relationship, family aspirations of social mobility, and family ideology. Other studies were concentrated primarily on the effects of maternal employment upon the adjustment of children (Nye, 1959; Stolz, 1960; Powell, 1961).

Broadly speaking, this study is concerned with the impact of urban industrialization upon the pattern of family role and power differentiation in Hong Kong. Specifically, it aims at detecting the effects of the gainful employment of mothers on the allocation of roles and power between the husband and wife. Maternal employment is here taken as an indicator of the influence of urban industrialization exerted upon the family, and the manner and extent of its impact particularly upon marital task and decision-making participation is to be closely examined. This subject is considered important and timely for study for two reasons. In the first place, there has been an enormous increase in the gainful employment of women since the rise of industrialization after the Second World War. Taking Hong Kong as a whole, female employment has increased as much as 56 per cent with over half a million workers or from 28.4 per cent to 33.7 per cent of the total working population during the 1961-1971 decade (Choi and Chan, 1973: 4), and the employment of married women has risen to a proportion of about 30 per cent among the married labor force in 1971 (Hong Kong Population and Housing Census, 1971: 54). With every likelihood this tendency is expected to continue in the foreseeable future. In the second place, this ever-expanding movement of gainfully employed women is bound to exert a direct and wide-spread impact upon the family and cause it to transform in its structure and functions as well as in its pattern of family relations (Wong, 1972a and 1972b). These situations have therefore heightened research interest in the effects of maternal employment upon the pattern of marital role and power differentiation.

As proposed for the present study, maternal employment is to be treated as an independent variable, which means in operational terms the engagement of mothers in gainful activities inside or outside the home. It is then broken down, for analytical reasons, into three categories: full, partial, and no employment. The dependent variables consist of family task performance, family decision-making, and power relationship between the spouses. Family tasks as a whole are grouped into four areas, each of which is arranged along a continuum of instrumentalism or expressiveness, i.e., from "economic activities" as a highly instrumental (or lowly expressive) area, to "social activities," "child care and control," and lastly "household duties" a lowly instrumental (or highly expressive) area. Each of these task areas is in turn composed of a number of specific household tasks which require the making of decisions about what, when, and how to carry them out as well as the actual performance of these tasks in the daily routine of a family. Furthermore, conjugal or familial power has been generally defined as "the ability to influence or control other persons' behavior. . . " (Misher and Waxler, 1968), or more specifically "measured through the outcome of decision-making, the patterns of tension and conflict management, or the type of prevailing divison of labor" (Safilios-Rothschild, 1970: 540). Family power, according to the latter form of definition, is more specific and operationally oriented, and is here measured in terms of the decision-making about and the performance of household tasks which is as a rule negotiable between the husband and the wife in a nuclear family setting.

These variables are closely interrelated and mutually reinforcing, and may thus be viewed as a system in which change in one variable leads to changes in the other variables (cf. Hoffman, 1960: 27-28). For example, the mother's gainful employment at or out of home may exert some pressure toward the father's increased participation and decision-making in household tasks. The increased involvement of the latter in these tasks may in turn facilitate the former's employment by reducing demands on her conventional home-making role. Similarly, maternal employment is related to husband-wife power relations. It seems likely that employment would increase a woman's power vis-a-vis her husband because of the direct or implied importance of her monetary contribution to the family coffer. On the other hand, a woman who already has high power would be more likely to seek employment because of "greater motivation, greater control over her own decisions, and greater success in obtaining her husband's participation in household tasks."

The major focus of this study, then, is to examine whether or not the mother's employment gives rise to changes in the pattern of the husband-wife participation in performing and making decisions about household tasks as well as in that of their power relations. The specific hypotheses are proposed as follows:

Hypothesis 1. The mother's engagement in gainful employment will function to decrease her participation in overall household tasks.

Hypothesis 2. The mother's employment will affect the pattern of family division of labor such that she will participate more in instrumental tasks and less in expressive tasks.

Hypothesis 3. The mother's engagement in gainful employment will function to decrease her decision-making in overall household tasks.

Hypothesis 4. The mother's employment will affect the pattern of family division of decision-making such that she will decide more about instrumental tasks and less about expressive tasks.

Hypothesis 5. The mother's engagement in gainful employment will function to increase her power vis-a-vis her husband.

Hypothesis 6. The mother's employment will affect the pattern of husband-wife relations such that it will change from an individually autonomous type into a mutually collaborative one.

The assumption behind the first hypothesis is that, because of the occupational demands upon her time and energy, the working mother simply cannot assume a full role at home satisfactorily and therefore has to request the assistance of her husband in undertaking some of the household tasks. This collaboration pattern is necessary in order to maintain the smooth functioning of their family. Likewise, the third hypothesis is based on the assumption that, if the mother's employment gives rise to a decrease in her household task participation and, by implication, an increase in that of her husband, there should be corresponding changes in family decision-making. This is so because most family decisions are rather trivial and are usually made routinely by the person who peforms the task in question, e.g., what will be made for dinner is most likely decided by the person who cooks. Furthermore, it seems likely that the employed mother would be willing to relinquish some of her decision-making power so as to obtain her husband's help with household tasks.

The second and the fourth hypotheses are also closely related. To allow the testing of these hypotheses, the household tasks as a whole are grouped into four task areas under two categories. On the one hand, the areas of economic and social activities are considered more instrumental in nature because they are usually transactions between the family and the outside world and are conventionally performed mainly by the husband, e.g., to earn an income and draw a budget and to initiate organizational and kin activities. On the other, the areas of child care and control and household duties are regarded as more expressive simply because they are undertaken at home and usually by the wife, e.g., to feed and clothe a child and to tend to routine household chores. These four areas of household tasks form a task scale ranging from tasks pertaining to the instrumental role on one end to those connecting with the expressive role on the other end, with mixed role tasks in the middle. Hence, the assumption behind the second hypothesis is that, if the working mother had to relinquish some of her former expressive tasks at home because of occupational commitments, she would now take up a certain portion of the instrumental household duties. Similarly, the fourth hypothesis assumes that once she began to participate in the performance of these tasks, she would tend to share in the decision-making about them.

The fifth hypothesis deals with the power relationship between the husband and wife. Power is here considered as the extent to which one person decides over the other's behaviour, and is therefore measured by the outcome of decision-making over household tasks. The proposition that the mother's engagement in gainful employment will function to increase her power vis-a-vis the husband is based on three assumptions: (a) money is an important basis of economic independence so that the control of money simply means the possession of economic independence, (b) a person has more control over the money she earns than other persons have, and (c) economic independence carries with it deciding power over household activities, and the amount of this power is likely to be roughly proportional to that of economic independence. The reasoning is that, as a result of her employment, the mother gains control of a certain sum of money, thus earning for herself a certain amount of economic independence. This economic independence in turn enables her to obtain some familial power. Moreover, because she is working and earning money, she may gain a new image of her own importance and thus become more assertive. Finally, both the husband and the wife are more likely to accept the legitimacy of the employed woman's claim to power.

The sixth hypothesis is related to the fifth one in that, should a change in the marital power structure have taken place, a new form of relationship would evolve between her and her husband. It is then hypothesized that, once a mother has actively engaged in gainful activities and thereby raised her status in the family, she will no longer be satisfied with her conventional role as belonging to the home and taking care of routine household matters alone, but will ask her husband to join her as a collaborative team in handling these matters.

Sample and Procedure

Sample

The total sample of the study consisted of 637 Chinese families which were drawn separately from three groupings in terms of the mother's occupational involvement. These families lived in a newly developed industrial community called Kwun Tong, which was located on the eastern end of the Kowloon Peninsula, Hong Kong, and had a population of about 450,000 spreading in an area of some 13 square kilometers.

The sampling procedure went through three stages. First, a sample was drawn by the stratified random sampling method from the large sample of another study.[1] As it turned out, this sample did not produce sufficient families with mothers working either full-time or part-time and therefore had to be extended in order to meet the sample requirements. Secondly, the quota sampling method was applied to locate more of the employed women. A quota of families was taken proportionally from each of the ten housing types and areas of the community, and this operation was carried out by using the method of door-to-door checking and occasional shiftings of potential families. However, this process was later found to be too time-consuming and costly, and a supplementary strategy had to be used to make up the size of the sample. Thirdly, a number of manufacturing factories were asked for cooperation, and a simple random sample of their female workers was taken. The final sample included 264 full-time and 165 part-time employed mothers, and 208 housewives.

The mothers under study were mainly middle-age Cantonese—the predominant speech group of Hong Kong, and over 92 per cent of them had lived in the urban environment for more than ten years. Their families represented a lower socio-economic segment of the population. Over half of the fathers had completed only six years of school, with approximately one quarter of them being illiterate or able to read a little and the other quarter having more than six years of formal education. They were usually employed in blue-collar or minor clerical posts of some industrial factories or commercial shops, making an average monthly income of HK$611 (about US$120). The educational level of the mothers was even worse; 90 per cent had not gone to school for more than six years, and the rest were lucky enough to have obtained beyond the elementary level of education. Because of economic reasons most of these women had to work regularly or irregularly in semi-skilled or unskilled jobs, and earned an average income of HK$246 per month to help maintain a decent family living condition. These families were chiefly of a nuclear type (over 75 per cent), with an average size of 6.45 persons. They were located mostly in the small housing units of those newly-built public resettlement blocks or some being tenants of the small private apartments, both in any case representing a crowded, substandard housing condition.

Measures

Data reported here were gathered through a structured interview schedule

[1] This was a representative random sample drawn from the total population of Kwun Tong and originally used for the Life Quality Study which was part of the Kwun Tong Industrial Community Research Programme. The sample was taken in May 1971.

which was administered during an interview with the mothers. The interview schedule was composed of two parts. The first part aimed at collecting information about their family background as well as their working conditions. The second part consisted of thirty-four paired questions which were asked in each case as to which family member performed a particular household task and which family member decided about that task. In cases where more than one family member was reported to have handled a certain task, only the major member, e.g., either the husband or the wife or both, was recorded. Fortunately there was only a small fraction of these cases, and they therefore did not affect the bulk of the data in a significant way. Furthermore, these household tasks were grouped under four task areas, each including several related and homogeneous items.

In order to enable the testing of hypotheses, a summarizing method was required for treating the collected data, and operational indices were hence constructed respectively for the independent and the dependent variables as follows:

Maternal employment. This variable was measured by five items: work status, source of employment, work hours, work shift, and location of work. This way of measuring it was considered as more adequate than that of basing it merely on the amount of working time. It took into account several essential aspects of the mother's employment, e.g., flexibility in work pattern, amount of work involvement, effect of work schedule, and physical presence at home, which would all create psychological and physical strains upon her homemaking role. For example, a working mother who was employed by others and worked overtime, at night shift, and in the factory would have more disruptive effect upon her household life than one who was self-employed and worked part-time at flexible shift, and at home, and of course much more so than a housewife. Thus, each of the five components of maternal employment was given several categories with corresponding weightings, and the total scale score of this variable was computed. After that, this score was, for analytical purpose, arbitrarily cut into three portions which were in turn conceptually defined as three types of employment: full, partial and no employment.

Task performance. The task performance scores were computed in four steps. First, the mothers were questioned as to who performed a particular task and their responses were recorded on a five-point descending scale from "wife always," "wife more than husband," "wife and husband equally," "husband more than wife," to "husband always."[2] Each point on this scale

---

[2] There were also other members on the response list like son/daughter, other relatives, neighbor/friend, and master/servant. This portion of the data was not included for analysis because it was too small to make any significant difference.

was then given a weighted numeral, and a total score was derived by summing up the numbers of all items in each task area. Furthermore, the total score was treated in two ways: one was to find out the mean task performance score so as to specify and differentiate the role responsibility of a certain task area between the marital partners, and the other was to arrive at the total score of each respondent in a task area in order to classify her into a certain grouping for analytical reasons. Finally, the overall task performance score representing the total scores of all the task areas was obtained to facilitate analysis at the most comprehensive level.

Task performance covered four task areas: economic activities, social activities, child care and control, and household duties. Economic activities area was operationally defined as including such specific tasks as earning, budgeting, and purchasing of household items ranging from more valuable ones like an apartment or a car to less valuable ones like a televison set or radio or an electric fan. The components of the social activities area included various participations in occupational, religious and welfare organizations; forms of interaction among kins like mutual visits, exchange of gifts, and financial assistance; kinds of family celebration like birthday parties, social festival activities, and wedding feasts; and social entertainment events like dining out, going to movies, and attending functional feasts. The area of child care and control consisted of physical care like feeding, clothing and consulting doctor; behavioral controls like doing school work, asking for pocket money, and general discipline; and career controls like selecting school, deciding about the amount of education, and helping to choose occupation. The last task area was household duties which covered such routine household chores as grocery shopping, cooking, dish-washing, clothes washing, ironing, mending, house cleaning, decorating and maintaining.

Task decision-making. Whereas the measure of task performance was based on responses to the performing questions, the measurement of task decision-making included those to the deciding questions. Likewise, the questions were asked as to which family member decided about each of the household items of the four task areas, and responses to these questions were processed by the same tabulating, weighting and score-computing procedures. Thus, the task decision-making scores were used to indicate the household decision-making roles of the marital partners.

Power relationship. The measurement of the power relationship between husband and wife was based on the mother's responses to both the performing and deciding questions. Power was operationalized to mean the extent to which one marital partner decided over the other partner's behaviour. It was an entity being sought for consciously or subconsciously by the couples through their participation in doing and deciding about routine household tasks. The measuring procedure, as shown in Table 1, was first to use each pair of questions as the coding unit, then assign to each unit a numerical weight, and later treat these units separately or in combination for analysis. A typology of marital power relationships was thus derived by grouping these units in various forms.

Table 1

Scoring and classifying system for marital power measure

Mother's Response	Weight	Type of Power
Wife decides, husband performs	3 ⎫	
Wife decides, both perform	2 ⎬	Wife dominance
Both decide, husband performs	1 ⎭	
Wife decides, wife performs	0	Wife autonomy
Both decide, both perform	0	Equalitarianism
Husband decides, husband performs	0	Husband autonomy
Both decide, wife performs	−1 ⎫	
Husband decides, both perform	−2 ⎬	Husband dominance
Husband decides, wife performs	−3 ⎭	

Findings and Implications

Before testing the hypotheses about the relationships between maternal employment and patterns of marital role and power differentiation, it is appropriate to first ask this question "what makes the mothers engage in gainful employment?" The answer is simple: they work because of economic necessity. The mother's employment was found to be negatively related to her husband's income ($t = 3.38$, $p < .001$), i.e., those mothers who were more engaged in gainful employment also happened to have been married to men who earned a smaller income. There were three facilitating factors: (1) the fully employed mothers had fewer children, e.g., with a mean number of 3.37 as compared to 4.08 for the partially employed and 4.22 for the housewives ($G = .26$, $Z = 4.88$, $p < .001$); (2) their youngest child was somewhat older, with a mean age of 7.49, in contrast to 5.93 of that of the housewives ($t = 2.22$, $p < .02$); (3) they were more likely to have their parents stay with them as compared with the partially employed or housewives ($x^2 = 8.87$, $p < .002$). Thus, with fewer and more mature children in the family and with their parents' help in child care and other household duties, the working mother had fewer worries about the fulfillment of their home-making role and was therefore more free to engage in gainful employment.

Hypothesis 1—Overall Task Performance

The relationship between the mother's employment and her household task performance was measured, and significance tests were made for the overall task performance as well as for each of the four task areas. The findings are presented in Table 2.

Table 2

Mother's employment status and household task performance

Task Performance Area	Direction of Relationship	G-Scores	Z-Scores	p Less Than
Overall task areas	FE < PE < NE*	.18	3.07	.002
Economic activities	FE > PE > NE	.11	2.24	.02
Social activities	FE > PE > NE	—	—	—**
Child care and control	FE < PE < NE	.31	5.81	.001
Household duties	FE < PE < NE	.30	5.15	.001

Note: N = 634. This includes only families which receive no or insignificant assistance in household task performance from servants or outside relatives.

*FE = fully employed; PE = partially employed; NE = not employed.

**In all tables G-scores, Z-scores and p values are not reported if p exceeds .05.

As shown in the top line of Table 2, the finding is both in the predicted direction and highly statistically significant, thus confirming the proposition that the working mother will undergo a decrease in her participation in overall household tasks and, by implication, a comparable increase in her husband's household participation. A brief review of the detailed data shows that the bulk of the total household tasks is undertaken either by "husband and wife equally," with 57.1 per cent for mothers engaging in full employment, 43.8 per cent for those with partial employment and 43.5 per cent for the housewives, or by "wife more than husband," with 33 per cent, 47.8 per cent and 45.4 per cent for the three groupings respectively. Hence, by and large, the fully employed mothers are very much relieved from household duties by sharing them with their husbands, whereas the partially employed and the housewives have to assume a major role in household activities. Furthermore, the image of the woman playing the home-making role all by herself is seldom true not only among the fully employed women (5.9 per cent), but also among the partially employed (6.3 per cent) and the housewives (8.7 per cent). Lastly, the husband as a rule is ready to help in household duties, but they do so only up to the point of sharing them with their wives, and in no cases are they found taking over the home-making role alone.

Hypothesis 2—Performance in Task Areas

Referring to the rest of Table 2, it is seen that, except for the area of social activities, all results are in the predicted direction and bear high statistical significance. Thus, the first half of the hypothesis that the employed mother will participate more in instrumental tasks is only partially confirmed, whereas its second half that can be offered for these slightly incoherent findings is One explanation that can be offered for these slightly incoherent findings is that it is difficult, if not impossible, to locate a clear demarcation line between instrumental and expressive tasks, and that consequently the area of social activities may include a mixture of both role activities. After all, the negative finding in this area is too small to be statistically significant. In short, the hypothesis as a whole can be claimed as confirmed, as the mother's employment exerts a clear-cut effect upon the direction in which she will participate in household tasks, i.e., more in instrumental tasks and less in expressive ones.

Hypothesis 3—Overall Task Decision-Making

Likewise, the relationship between the mother's employment and her decision-making over household tasks was examined, and significance tests were made both for the overall task decision-making and for each of the four task areas. The results are given in Table 3.

Table 3

Mother's employment status and household task decision-making

Task Decision-Making Area	Direction of Relationship	G-Scores	Z-Scores	p Less Than
Overall task areas	FE < PE < NE*	.17	2.89	.002
Economic activities	FE > PE > NE	—	—	—**
Social activities	FE > PE > NE	—	—	—
Child care and control	FE < PE < NE	.22	4.44	.001
Household duties	FE < PE < NE	.26	4.57	.001

Note: N = 634. This includes only families which receive no or only insignificant assistance in household task decision-making from servants or outside relatives.
*FE = fully employed; PE = partially employed; NE = not employed.
**In all tables G-scores, Z-scores and p values are not reported if p exceeds .05.

Looking across the top line of Table 3, it is clear that the finding is not only in the predicted direction but also highly statistically significant. Thus, the hypothesis that the mother's employment will function to decrease her decision-making about overall household tasks is confirmed. There are several corresponding discoveries in the data as in those of overall task performance. First, the fully employed mothers (58.6 per cent) tend to share their decision-making about overall household tasks with their husbands, as compared with 44.6 per cent of the partially employed and 43.9 per cent of the housewives. Secondly, the partially employed women (46 per cent) and the housewives (44 per cent) usually play a more important role in deciding about household matters than the fully employed mothers (32.5 per cent). Thirdly, few women are allowed to take charge of all decisions concerning household affairs. Finally, the traditional conception of the father as an all-powerful autocrat of the household does not exist even in one single case.

Hypothesis 4—Decision-Making in Task Areas

As seen in Table 3, only the results in the areas of child care and control and household duties come out as predicted and with high statistical significance, whereas those in the areas of economic activities and social activities are, though in the predicted direction, too small to be significant. Hence, the hypothesis that the mother's employment will enable her to decide more about instrumental tasks and less about expressive tasks is only true in its latter part. An examination of the data shows that, even though the fully employed mothers do not make too many more decisions about social and economic activities than the partially employed and the housewives, they in fact share the making of such decisions with their husbands much more frequently than the other two groups. So this becomes a collaborative decision-making pattern between the working mother and her husband.

Hypothesis 5—Marital Power Differentiation

This hypothesis is tested against the collected data, and, as shown in Table 4, the result is both in the predicted direction and statistically significant.

Table 4

Maternal employment and marital power differentiation

Type of Power Relations	Maternal Employment			Total Cases
	Full	Partial	None	
Mother-dominance	13	22	18	53
Equalitarianism	106	76	71	253
Father-dominance	13	24	22	59
Total cases	132	122	111	365

$x^2 = 11.97$, df = 4, $p < .02$

Note: The number of cases here includes only those who expressed a clear-out power relationship between the marital couples.

It is therefore appropriate to accept the postulate that a mother's employment will function to increase her power vis-a-vis her husband. A further look at the data shows that, while the majority of the studied mothers have begun to enjoy a relatively more equal status with the husband,[3] most of them, or 80 per cent, come from the fully employed group, as compared to 62 per cent of the partially employed and 64 per cent of the housewives. In addition, it is reported that dominance by either the husband or the wife is much less accepted among the first group than among the other two groups.

Hypothesis 6—Marital Relationship

Hypothesis 6 seeks to examine another aspect of the marital power structure—change in marital relationship, and to relate it to the occupational involvement of the mother. The result appears in Table 5.

Table 5

Maternal employment and marital relationship

Type of Marital Relationship	Maternal Employment			Total Cases
	Full	Partial	None	
Mutual collaboration	106	76	71	253
Individual autonomy	72	103	95	270
Individual dominance	26	46	40	112
Total cases	204	225	206	635

$x^2 = 18.93$, df = 4, p. $<.001$.

Note: "Individual autonomy" includes both the categories of "husband-autonomy" and "wife-autonomy," and "individual dominance" those of "husband-dominance" and "wife-dominance."

As found in Table 5, the finding is again in the predicted direction and bears strong statistical significance. Hypothesis 6 is therefore confirmed, thus upholding the proposition that the mother's employment leads to a change in the pattern of marital relationship from an individually autonomous or dominant type to a mutually collaborative one. This further implies that, with the participation of women in the occupational world, the traditional

[3]This finding is consistent with those of other comparable studies on the Chinese family structure: Fai-ming Wong, "Modern ideology, industrialization, and conjugalism: the Hong Kong case," *International Journal of Sociology of the Family* 2 (September 1972): 139-150; "The impact of social and family change upon social service in Hong Kong," *Journal of the Hong Kong Council of Social Service* 40 (Spring 1972): 11-18; Olga Lang, Chinese Family and Society, Anchor Books, reprinted 1968, pp. 203-218.

husband-dominant family has rapidly decreased in importance and practice, and the conventional home-making role of the mother has greatly diminished and is increasingly shared by other members of the family, particularly her husband. Thus, the working mother is seen to have moved out of her past institutional role and into a new role which allows her to actively participate in economic activities on the one hand and collaborate with her husband in routine household tasks on the other.[4]

Summary and Conclusions

This study was concerned generally with the systemic relationship of urban industrialization and the family system, and attempted to examine specifically the effects of the mother's gainful employment on the patterns of marital role and power differentiation among the lower-income Chinese families in Hong Kong. Maternal employment was then used as an independent variable, whereas the allocation of roles and power between the husband and wife formed the dependent variables. Marital role was analyzed in terms of their performance of and decision-making about the routine household tasks which were grouped into task areas and arranged along a scale of instrumentalism or expressiveness. Conjugal power was defined as the ability of one spouse to influence or control the behavior of the other spouse and measured through the outcome of the interplay of these two dimensions of household task participation. The general hypothesis was that the engagement of mothers in gainful employment will tend to affect the patterns of marital role participation and their power relationship.

Data were collected from a representative sample of 637 families who lived in the new industrial town of Kwun Tong, Hong Kong, and came from a relatively lower socio-economic sector of the population. These families represented three separate groupings which were categorized in terms of the extent of economic involvement of the mothers, i.e., full, partial and no involvement, and only these mothers were interviewed with a structured schedule. To facilitate the analysis, several specific hypotheses were formulated and various operational measures were constructed including the indices of maternal employment, task performance, task decision-making, and power relationship.

The findings were summarized as follows:

(1) The employed mothers as a rule worked because of economic reasons. Their engagement in gainful employment was faciliated by the fact that they

[4]These are what Burgess and Locke would have described as symptoms of change toward the companionship type of family. See Ernest W. Burgess, Harvey J. Locke, and Mary M. Thomes, *The Family,* New York: American Book, 1963, 3rd edition, pp. 3-5.

had fewer and older children and that they could rely on their parents' assistance in household duties.

(2) Working mothers generally participated less in the performance of overall household tasks, and, in particular, more in instrumental tasks and less in expressive tasks, as compared with the housewives.

(3) Working mothers generally made fewer decisions about overall household matters, and particularly more about instrumental matters and less about expressive matters, as compared with the housewives.

(4) Working mothers were found to have practised relatively more equalitarianism and less dominance by either partner than the housewives. Their relationship with the husband has shifted from one of individual autonomy or dominance to that of mutual collaboration.

It may thus be concluded that a mother's employment leads to her decrease in household task performance and decision-making and a corresponding increase of her husband in assuming some of the routine household duties and making decisions about them. Her employment also enables her to enjoy a relatively more equal status with her husband and maintain a collaborative type of relationship with him in place of that of individual autonomy or dominance.

References

Blalock, Hubert M. (1960)
   Social Statistics. New York: McGraw-Hill.
Blood, Robert O. Jr. and Donald M. Wolfe (1960)
   Husbands and Wives: The Dynamics of Married Living. Glencoe, Ill.: The Free Press.
Buric, Olivera (1963)
   "The impact of maternal employment upon the family," *Current Sociology* 12 (1): 82-92.
Centers, Richard, Bertram H. Raven, and Aroldo Rodrigues (1971)
   "Conjugal power structure: a re-examination," *American Sociological Review*. 36 (April): 264-278.
Choi, C. Y. and K. C. Chan (1973)
   The Impact of Industrialization on Fertility in Hong Kong: A Demographic, Social and Economic Analysis. Hong Kong: Social Research Centre, The Chinese University of Hong Kong.
Herbst, P. G. (1952)
   "The measurement of family relationships," *Human Relations* 5: 3-35.
Hoffman, Lois Wladis (1960)
   "Effects of the employment of mothers on parental power relations and

the division of household tasks," *Marriage and Family Living* 22 (February): 27-35.

Hong Kong Government (1972)
Hong Kong Population and Housing Census: 1971 Main Report. Hong Kong: Census and Statistics Department.

Lumpkin, Katherine D. (1933)
The Family: A Study of Member Roles. Chapel Hill: University of North Carolina Press.

Misher, Elliot G. and Nancy E. Waxler (1968)
Interaction in Families. New York: John Wiley and Sons.

Mowrer, Ermest R. (1969)
"The differentiation of husband and wife roles," *Journal of Marriage and the Family* 31 (August): 534-540.

Nye, F. Ivan (1959)
"Employment status of mothers and adjustment of adolescent children," *Marriage and Family Living* 21 (August): 240-244.

Parsons, Talcott and Robert F. Bales (1955)
Family, Socialization and Interaction Process. Glencoe: The Free Press.

Powell, Kathryn Summers (1961)
"Maternal employment in relation to family life," *Marriage and Family Living* 23 (November): 350-355.

Rodman, Hyman (1967)
"Marital power in France, Greece, Yugoslavia, and the United States: a cross-national discussion," *Journal of Marriage and the Family* 29 (May): 320-324.

Safilios-Rothschild, Constantina (1970)
"The study of family power structure: a review 1960-1969," *Journal of Marriage and the Family* 32 (November): 539-552.

Stolz, Lois M. (1960)
"Effects of maternal employment on children: evidence from research," *Child Development* 31: 749-782.

Wong, Fai-ming (1972a)
Maternal Employment and Family Task-Power Differentiation among Lower Income Chinese Families. Hong Kong: Social Research Centre, The Chinese University of Hong Kong.
——————(1972b)
"Modern ideology, industrialization, and conjugalism: the Hong Kong case," *International Journal of Sociology of the Family* 2 (September): 139-150.

Zelditch, Jr., Morris (1955)
"Role differentiation in the nuclear family: A comparative study," Talcott

Parsons and Robert F. Bales, eds., *Family, Socialization and Interaction Process*, pp. 307-351. Glencoe: The Free Press.

Chapter 12

Social Factors Contributing to Fertility Decline[1]

Pedro Pak-tao Ng

After the Second World War and especially during the last two decades or so, Hong Kong has emerged rapidly as an industrial metropolis and an important centre for international trade. Her population has more than doubled from approximately two million in 1951 to over four million in 1972. About 80 per cent of this population lives in urban areas of roughly 20 square miles, despite a total land area of nearly 400 square miles. The result is a population density of more than 200,000 per square mile which is certainly among the highest in the world. In some commercial-residential districts and many of the public housing estates, the spot density is even several times higher. A population density of this magnitude is bound to have grave implications for housing, education, health, welfare, and other social services. This is especially true in a place that is deficient in inhabitable land and natural resources, where employment is highly competitive and the health of the economy is largely dependent on the fluctuations of the international market. Although a great deal has been achieved over the last two decades in such areas as public housing and the development of new towns to decentralize part of the population, the "population pressure" has not dissipated.

During this period the importance of and need for limiting population growth began to receive more public attention and discussion which came to a peak at about the time of World Population Year 1974 many of whose local activities were sponsored by the Family Planning Association of Hong Kong.

[1] This is a revised version of the author's article "Family Planning, Fertility Decline, and Family Size Preference in Hong Kong: Some General Observations" published in *Internationales Asienforum*, No. 1/2, 1980. Part of the data used in this paper comes from the People of Kwun Tong project (data collected in 1973-74) and the Survey on the Impact of Industrialization on Fertility in Hong Kong (data collected in 1972). Both studies were conducted by the Social Research Centre of The Chinese University of Hong Kong. The second study was also jointly carried with the Family Planning Association of Hong Kong. Both studies were supported with funds from the Asia Foundation. The author is grateful to Miss Hsu Suet-ming, Research Assistant at the Social Research Centre, for her assistance in compiling some of the data presented in this paper.

However, there is to date no official population policy on the part of the Hong Kong Government other than developing the new towns and tightening up immigration control with respect to migrants from mainland China.[2] The task of promoting the limitation of family size in an organized manner is left almost entirely to the Family Planning Association of Hong Kong which is essentially a private organization although it receives financial support from the Government.

This paper is about family planning in Hong Kong. It will first describe some characteristics and achievements of family planning in Hong Kong and its contribution, along with changing social and economic conditions, to the recent fertility decline in Hong Kong. It will then review some data showing the family size preferences of some married women and students in order to demonstrate the emergence of a small family norm in Hong Kong. The essence of these general observations is to suggest that the future prospect of fertility control in Hong Kong is rather favourable.

The data used in this paper come from a variety of sources. They include Government censuses, statistics compiled by the Family Planning Association of Hong Kong, and several survey studies undertaken by the Social Research Centre of The Chinese University of Hong Kong.

Family Planning and Fertility Decline in Hong Kong

The first organized effort towards promoting birth control in Hong Kong started in 1936 with the founding of the Hong Kong Eugenics League, predecessor of the Family Planning Association of Hong Kong. Family planning activities did not, however, begin to "take off" until the mid-fifties, when the Family Planning Association of Hong Kong, instituted in 1950, rapidly expanded its services and acquired a good number of clinics with Government subventions. Beginning from 1965, the recruitment of clients or persuasion of mothers to adopt family planning concentrated in the Maternal and Child Health centres and many hospitals, a method which later developed into the Association's post-partum programme. In the early sixties, the Association started its information programme aimed at motivating the public to learn about contraception. This programme has been gradually intensified and diversified, utilizing a variety of communication channels. A separate Information, Education, and Communication Department was formed in 1976.

Over the last two decades, a change in the theme of family planning

---

[2]Migration from China was an important factor increasing the population of Hong Kong following the change of government in China in 1949. Such migration has continued, though to a much reduced extent, throughout the years since (except for an influx in 1962).

communication, as expressed, for example, in the Association's posters, reflects more or less the change in the general notion of family planning in this period. The early posters typically showed the woes and difficulties brought about by a large family and on the whole tended to arouse a pathetic feeling. Later posters, especially those of the last few years, were much more "positive" and "lively" as they mostly appealed to a desire for planned and small families. The accent turned to the happiness that such families are likely to bring. To many people, family planning used to mean at best preventing a larger family after the fact of many births. According to the Family Planning Association's records, the highest number of children ever borne for acceptance of contraception among its recruited clients was six or above in 1961.[3] This is basically the same as reported by Richard and Margaret Coughlin in a study of 300 women applicants to the Family Planning Association's central clinic in 1958-59. They reported that about 52 per cent of these women had four or more children already.[4]

The intensification of the Family Planning Association's activities in the sixties included the introduction of the IUD (intra-uterinal device) in 1964-65 and the oral pill in 1968. These two methods of contraception (now particularly the pill), together with sterilization which is more commonly adopted by older mothers, have been the main methods accepted by women. Since 1965 the characteristics of acceptors of contraception recruited by the Family Planning Association in terms of age and number of children ever borne showed a notable change. The proportion of younger mothers (under 25 years of age) increased from 18 per cent in 1965 to 26 per cent in 1969, and the proportion of acceptors with two children or fewer increased from 29 per cent in 1965 to 62 per cent in 1969.[5] Thus, *family planning was attracting more and more younger mother at an increasingly earlier stage in their childbearing experience.* Indeed, some of the findings from two surveys confirm this trend. Robert Mitchell's Urban Family Life Survey was carried out in 1967 by the then Social Survey Research Centre of The Chinese University of Hong Kong and the Survey on the Impact of Industrialization on Fertility in Hong Kong (referred to later in this paper as the Fertility Survey) was undertaken jointly by the Social

[3] Family Planning Association of Hong Kong, *Twentieth Annual Report, 1970-1971,* p. 26.

[4] Richard J. Coughlin and Margaret M. Coughlin, "Fertility and Birth Control Among Low Income Chinese Families in Hong Kong," *Marriage and Family Living, 25* (May 1963), 171-177.

[5] K. C. Chan, "The Influence of the Family Planning Programme on Hong Kong's Fertility Decline." (A paper prepared for the World Population Year Programme, April-May 1974. Mr. Chan is Statistics and Evaluation Officer of the Family Planning Association of Hong Kong.)

Research Centre of The Chinese University of Hong Kong and the Family Planning Association of Hong Kong in 1972. This research showed that the practice of contraception has tended to start at earlier pregnancies, especially among younger mothers. Thus, for instance, the model starting point for contraception among mothers under 30 years of age was after the second pregnancy in 1967 but was after the first in 1972. Similarly, 58 per cent of mothers 30 to 34 years of age in 1967 reported starting to practice contraception after the fourth pregnancy, but in 1972 48 per cent of mothers of the same age group reported that they started such practice after the first or second pregnancy.[6] According to the Fertility Survey of 1972, 65 per cent of the 2,270 women of reproductive age studied had used contraception sometime in the past. The proportion of ever-users rose to three-quarters or more among those in the 30-39 age group as contrasted with 47 per cent among those aged 45-49. The findings also showed an earlier practice of contraception among the younger women. Of those under 30 years of age, for instance, about 11 per cent started to practise contraception *before* the first pregnancy and about 45 per cent *after* it.[7] Therefore, it would be reasonable to predict that the likelihood of Hong Kong's married women to have used contraception relatively early in their reproductive cycle will become increasingly great in the years to come. It would also be plausible to infer that the awareness of the need to plan and space births is on the rise.

What effect would these changes have on fertility in Hong Kong? The empirical evidence just cited indicate that the past decade (roughly since the mid-sixties) has witnessed more married young women taking to family planning at an early stage in their married life. That decade has also witnessed a rather phenomenal decline in the birth rates of Hong Kong, both overall and age-specific (see Tables 1 and 2). The decline in the crude birth rate during the early sixties, i.e., 1961-65, was predominantly a result of changes in the age structure of the population brought about by the last war. Birth rates declined during and just after the war years, thus leading to a relatively low proportion of females in the early childbearing ages about twenty years later. However, as Freedman and his associates have pointed out, almost all of the decline in the crude birth rate in the years after 1965 was due to a true decline in fertility.[8] Similarly, a recent United Nations monograph on Hong Kong's

---

[6]Quoted in K. C. Chan, *op. cit.* See also C. Y. Choi and K. C. Chan, "The Impact of Industrialization on Fertility in Hong Kong: A Demographic, Social, and Economic Analysis" (Working paper of the Social Research Centre, The Chinese University of Hong Kong, September 1973), p. 108.

[7]C. Y. Choi and K. C. Chan, *op. cit.*, p. 108.

[8]Freedman and his associates prepared a series of three reports on fertility trends in Hong Kong using estimates prepared under the joint auspices of the Hong Kong Family

Table 1

Crude birth rate, 1961-1978

Year	Crude birth rate (per 1,000 population)
1961	35.0
1962	34.0
1963	33.5
1964	30.7
1965	28.1
1966	25.3
1967	23.7
1968	21.7
1969	21.4
1970	20.0
1971	19.7
1972	19.5
1973	19.5
1974	19.3
1975	18.2
1976	17.7
1977	17.7
1978	17.5

Sources: Rates for 1961 to 1971 were taken from United Nations, *The Demographic Situation in Hong Kong* (ESCAP Country Monograph Series No. 1, 1974), table 119. Rates for 1972 to 1978 were taken from Census and Statistics Department of Hong Kong, *Hong Kong Monthly Digest of Statistics* (January 1979), table 15.1.

Planning Association and the University of Michigan Population Studies Center: Ronald Freedman and A. L. Adlakha, "Recent Fertility Declines in Hong Kong: the Role of the Changing Age Structure," *Population Studies* 22(2) (July 1968), 181-198; Ronald Freedman, D. N. Namboothiri, A. L. Adlakha, and K. C. Chan, "Hong Kong: The Continuing Fertility Decline, 1967," *Studies in Family Planning*, No. 44 (August 1969), 8-15; and *Idem*, "Hong Kong's Fertility Decline, 1961-68," *Population Index* 36(1) (January-March 1970), 3-18.

Table 2

Age-specific birth rates for selected years from 1961 to 1978

Year	Births per 1,000 women aged						
	15-19	20-24	25-29	30-34	35-39	40-44	45-49
1961	47	238	313	231	139	57	9
1965	41	252	318	211	122	39	3
1966	29	213	291	203	111	42	3
1967	29	178	268	201	123	40	6
1968	27	158	234	170	102	36	2
1970	18.2	155.1	233.1	168.6	87.0	30.9	4.7
1971	17.0	145.6	243.8	162.5	83.6	28.4	3.6
1972	17.4	139.3	248.0	145.8	77.4	25.8	3.2
1973	17.9	132.5	243.3	141.8	72.4	23.5	3.2
1974	18.8	133.3	219.2	137.4	65.7	21.1	2.5
1975	17.8	121.5	198.6	126.0	54.5	18.3	2.4
1976	17.4	109.7	192.1	119.6	48.9	14.6	1.5
1977	17.4	105.1	185.6	115.3	45.6	12.9	1.1
1978	15.3	98.9	178.6	113.0	43.6	11.3	1.1

Sources: Rates for 1961 and 1965-68 were taken from Ronald Freedman et al., "Hong Kong's Fertility Decline, 1961-68," Population Index 36(1) (January-March 1970), 3-18. Rates for 1970 and 1971 were taken from United Nations, op. cit., table 120 which computed them from the vital statistics compiled by the Census and Statistics Department of Hong Kong. Rates for 1972 to 1978 were supplied by the Census and Statistics Department of Hong Kong.

population reports that "for the period 1965-1971, . . . some 90 per cent of the decline in the birth rate was the result of decline in age-specific birth rates."[9] The crude birth rate began to fall below 20 per thousand in 1971 and is currently about 18 per thousand, which is drastically below the near-40 per thousand level of the fifties. Further, as shown in Table 2, age-specific birth rates have reduced substantially almost throughout the childbearing ages. It should be noted that between the years 1965 and 1968 fertility decline was particularly substantial in the younger childbearing ages. Thus, the birth rates for the 20-24 and the 15-19 age groups dropped 37 per cent and 34 per cent respectively. The corresponding figure for the 25-29 age group is 26 per cent.

Declines for the older age groups are relatively much smaller. However, as pointed out by Freedman and his associates, a more rapid decline in fertility among the younger age groups is likely to lead to a greater and probably more permanent decline in overall fertility.[10] This is an important factor that partly accounts for the fact that the crude birth rate continued to remain low after it fall below 20 per thousand in 1971 even though a large proportion of the female population toward the bottom of the population pyramid in 1961 have begun to enter childbearing age in the seventies.

Why has fertility declined in Hong Kong? The findings concerning the practice of contraception and the activities of the family planning programme (e.g., operation of family planning clinics, the post-partum programme, introduction of the IUD and the pill in the mid-sixties, and the expansion of information, education and communication activities in the 1970s) during this recent period of fertility decline tend to suggest that the family planning programme has probably played an important role. It would be difficult indeed to determine just how much of the fertility decline was actually due to the family planning programme of the Family Planning Association of Hong Kong and how much is attributable to changing social and economic conditions in Hong Kong. It would be correct, however, to say that both sets of factors have brought about the fertility decline.

The rapid industrialization of Hong Kong during the last decade or two has been accompanied by a rapid expansion of education, first at the primary level and then at the secondary level. From the censuses of 1961 and 1971 we know that the proportion of persons with a secondary school education or above among the economically active population increased from 27 per cent in 1961 to 33 per cent in 1971. Since 1971 education has been free in

[9]United Nations Economic and Social Commission for Asia and the Pacific, *The Demographic Situation in Hong Kong* (ESCAP Country Monograph Series No. 1, 1974), p. 94.
[10]Ronald Freedman *et al.*, "Hong Kong's Fertility Decline, 1961-68," *Population Index* 36(1) (January-March 1970), p. 4.

Government primary schools and the school attendance rate among primary school age (6 to 11) children has reached 92 per cent in 1978.[11] Efforts are now under way to provide at least up to three years of secondary schooling to as many youths as possible. It is only logical to expect, therefore, a continual rise in the general level of educational attainment in the population.

The social and economic consequences of a rising educational level are of course many, including, for instance, rising and more diversified expectations of life, increasing employment of women in a wider variety of occupations in a society that is undergoing industrialization and modernization, greater exposure to and hence acquaintance with contraceptive knowledge, greater desire for upward social mobility, and probably a higher degree fo awareness of and inclination towards planning and achievement. All these tend to favour and encourage a motivation to limit family size. That higher educational attainment is closely associated with smaller family size and greater use of contraception is already well documented in a great number of studies concerned with fertility.[12] In the case of Hong Kong it was found, both in the Fertility Survey cited above and in the People of Kwun Tong Survey,[13] that *even after controlling for age the better educated mothers clearly tended to have fewer children*. Indeed, the data from these surveys indicate that for women aged 25-34, for example, those with a post-secondary education had an average of roughly 1.8 children while those without any schooling had over three on the average.[14]

[11]Calculated from figures given in the Director of Education's Annual Summary of 1977-78, p. 32.

[12]The following are just a few example: Robert O. Blood, Jr. and Donald M. Wolfe, *Husbands and Wives: The Dynamics of Married Living* (New York: The Free Press, 1960), pp. 130-131; Bom Mo Chung, James A. Palmore, Sang Joo Lee, and Sung Jin Lee, *Psychological Perspectives: Family Planning in Korea* (Seoul: Korean Institute for Research in the Behavioural Sciences, 1972), pp. 181-186; The Chinese Center for International Training in Family Planning, *Population and Family Planning in Charts, Taiwan Area, Republic of China*, 6th edition (Taichung, 1975), p. 23; Ann Cartwright, *How Many Children?* (London: Routledge and Kegan Paul, 1976), chapter 10; and Charles B. Nam and Susan O. Gustavus, *Population: The Dynamics of Demographic Change* (Boston: Houghton Mifflin, 1976), pp. 118-121.

[13]The People of Kwun Tong Survey, carried out by the Social Research Centre of The Chinese University of Hong Kong in 1973, aimed at studying the relationships between socioeconomic characteristics of the family and family structure on the one hand and fertility and family planning behaviour on the other. Kwun Tong is a relatively new industrial-residential town of Hong Kong, with a population of approximately half a million. Included in the survey were a total of 818 families. In two-thirds of these, both husband and wife were interviewed; in the majority of the rest the wife was the respondent. Like the Fertility Survey of 1972, the People of Kwun Tong Survey was supported with funds from the Asia Foundation.

[14]See C. Y. Choi and K. C. Chan, *op. cit.*, pp. 87-88, and Pedro Ng (with the colla-

In the context of modern industrial Hong Kong, better education is probably associated with a change, subtle and complex as it may be, in people's attitudes towards traditional Chinese values concerning the family, including such themes as the centrality of patrilineage and the associated strong preference for boys as male heirs, the submissive role of women vis-a-vis men and of children in relation to parents, and the large family *ideal*.[15] It is not unlikely, therefore, that children and having children are viewed not so much with an eye to their possible contribution to the social prestige of the family or to the security of the parents in their old age as with a concern over what the family can afford or provide in terms of the quality of life that would be available to their children. Indications of this pattern are found in the People of Kwun Tong Survey. When asked what they thought was the primary advantage of having children, only less than one-tenth of the eight hundred odd parents interviewed mentioned "perpetuation of the family line" and a similar proportion mentioned "security in old age." By contrast, almost two-thirds of them mentioned "emotional satisfaction" or "fun to the family." Moreover, emotional strain and financial burden were the most often cited disadvantages of having children. This suggests a very practical and realistic approach to assessing the value and cost of children.

Another aspect of the family pattern brought about by rising educational levels and other influences of industrialization is that inter-spouse relationships in the average Hong Kong family have by and large become more equalitarian although the husband is still relatively dominant. This statement is borne out

---

boration of Chung Ching-ngor and Davy Leung), *The Family and Family Planning in Kwun Tong: An Overview of Findings* (Social Research Centre, The Chinese University of Hong Kong, 1976), pp. 91-92.

[15] For a concise statement of the essence of traditional Chinese familistic values, see Yih-yuan Li and Kuo-shu Yang (eds.), *The Character of the Chinese: An Interdisciplinary Approach*, Institute of Ethnology, Academia Sinica, Monograph Series B, No. 4 (Taipei, 1973), pp. 134-138 (significance of familism for perpetuation of the virtues and ideals of ancestors); 142-144 (having children seen as fulfilling the basic requirements of filial piety); and 204-205 (traditional Chinese society is clearly patriarchal and patrilineal, as indicated in folk stories and traditional popular novels). For a statement of the relationship between education and modernity, see Alex Inkeles, "The Modernization of Man," in *Modernization: The Dynamics of Growth*, ed. by Myron Weiner (New York: Basic Books, 1966), pp. 138-150. Empirical evidence showing that increased educational attainment is associated with "modern" attitudes (e.g., newly-weds should not live with their parents; parents should not interfere in the affairs of married children) among the young adults (age 15-29) in Hong Kong is found in, for example, David C. Chaney and David B. L. Podmore, *Young Adults in Hong Kong: Attitudes in a Modernizing Society* (Hong Kong: Centre of Asian Studies, University of Hong Kong, 1973), pp. 96-98.

by a number of studies of the Hong Kong family.[16] In the People of Kwun Tong Survey, it was found that the better educated couples tended to engage more frequently in discussion of birth control than the less educated ones, and that those couples who had experienced some or many such discussions were considerably more likely to have been users of contraception sometime in the past than those who had little or none.[17]

One of the likely factors that have brought about more equalitarian husband-wife relations is the expansion of female economic opportunities which is certainly closely associated with rising educational levels but which also tends to affect family structure and fertility motivation independently of education. With the continued growth of the Hong Kong economy in the last couple of decades, employment opportunities in both the manufacturing and service sectors have expanded and diversified. Relatively new industries, such as electronics and toy-making, along with the traditional textile and garment industries are all employing large numbers of female workers. At the same time, the expansion of Hong Kong's international trade has rapidly given rise to the expansion of all sorts of opportunities for clerical and service occupations for the more educated females. The censuses of 1961 and 1971 showed that, on the whole, female employment rates rose substantially for the younger age groups. In the 20-24 age group, for example, the employment rate was 51 per cent in 1961; in 1971 it was almost 70 per cent.[18] For many of the younger and married females, the increased occupational opportunities, coupled with expanding educational opportunities, are most likely to lead them to orient themselves towards some sort of occupational career and to remain unmarried for some more time than would otherwise be the case. Indeed, data from the censuses show that there has been a substantial decline in the proportion of married females under 25 years of age, thus indicating a tendency to postpone marriage (see Table 3). *For married females, the increased employment opportunities may have encouraged a desire to delay*

---

[16] See, for example, Lawrence K. Hong, "The Chinese Family in a Modern Industrial Setting: Its Structure and Functions" (Unpublished Ph.D. dissertation, University of Notre Dame, 1970); and F. M. Wong, "Maternal Employment and Family Task-Power Differentiation among Lower Income Chinese Families" (Occasional paper of the Social Research Centre, The Chinese University of Hong Kong, 1972).

[17] In the People of Kwun Tong Survey, it was found that 70 per cent of the wives who were secondary school educated or above had discussed birth control with their husbands "sometimes" or "often," as compared with 46 per cent among those wives without any schooling. Of those wives who had often discussed birth control with their husbands, 87 per cent had used contraception sometime in the past; the corresponding figures for those who had "seldom" and "never" discussed birth control with their husband were 51 per cent and 26 per cent respectively.

[18] United Nations, *op. cit.*, table 52.

Table 3

Percentage of female population married,
under 30 years of age for selected years

Age	Year			
	1961	1966	1971	1976
15-19	6.4	4.7	2.9	3.9
20-24	51.0	42.7	32.3	31.5
25-29	83.4	85.2	79.5	74.0

Sources: Reports on the 1961 census, the 1966 By-Census, the 1971 census, and the
1976 By-Census.

child-births or not to have too many children. Thus, both in the Fertility
Survey and in the People of Kwun Tong Survey, it was found that family size
and employment of mother are negatively associated. That is, those mothers
who worked full-time, as compared with those who worked only part-time or
who did not work at all, either at the time of the survey or even before
marriage, tended to have on the average significantly fewer children.[19]
Naturally, the causality of the relationship between fertility and work can be
either that some women work because they have fewer children or that some
women have fewer children because they work. In the latter case, a more
conscious effort to control and space births would be called for.

From the above discussion it seems reasonable to argue that *the social and
economic conditions of Hong Kong in the last couple of decades have been
such that there is now in the population a greater demand for limiting family
size than ever before.* It is, in a sense, "timely" that family planning technology and the family planning programme in Hong Kong developed actively
also during this period. The activities of the Family Planning Association of
Hong Kong, augmented by the diffusion effort of these activities, have, as
Freedman argues, met a good part of the demand for birth control. Freedman
also argues that the Association may have helped to define and to increase that
demand.[20] Given the continuing pattern of Hong Kong's social and economic
conditions and given that the Family Planning Association will continue to
expand its educational as well as clinical services, then the latter argument
seems plausible indeed.

Having seen that the recent fertility decline in Hong Kong is largely the

[19]C. Y. Choi and K. C. Chan, *op. cit.*, p. 84; and Pedro Ng, *op. cit.*, p. 96.
[20]Ronald Freedman *et al.*, "Hong Kong's Fertility Decline, 1961-68," p. 12.

result of both the development of the family planning programme and changes in social and economic conditions, let us now turn to an examination of some data on family size preference which may shed some light on the future prospects of fertility control in Hong Kong.

Family Size Preference in Hong Kong

From census information and the findings of the surveys cited earlier, we know that in Hong Kong the present average number of children a married couple have living with them is around 3.5. This number would be different if we were looking at different sections of the population. In the resettlement estates, for example, which are the older types of public housing generally accommodating families of lower socioeconomic status, the average family size would be around five. In spring 1975 a group of 224 first year under-graduates at The Chinese University of Hong Kong were asked to answer a questionnaire concerning family life and family size. The average size of the families from which these students came was found to be just a little over five. Their families were earning a median income of approximately HK$2,100 (US$420) a month which by Hong Kong standards was roughly upper-lower class. More than half of their fathers and about 80 per cent of their mothers had no more than a primary school education.

There is a good amount of empirical evidence to show that almost irrespec-tive of the actual family size, both the parents' generation and the younger generation such as these students demonstrate a remarkable convergence in family size preference. Such convergence is especially well-defined among the youths and suggests *a norm for the "ideal" family of two to three children.*

In the People of Kwun Tong Survey, the mothers were asked how many children they would like to have if they had the choice to start all over again. In responding to this question they were reminded to take all their previous life experiences into consideration. The results are presented in Table 4 which also lists the average actual family size of each age group and the percentage in each age group preferring two children. It can be seen that while the average actual family size varies from 1.39 to 5.14 across the span of the age groups, there is considerably less variation in the average preferred family size, i.e., from 2.74 to 3.41. It should be noted that while the mothers under 30 years of age tend to prefer rather more children than they already have (many of them have two children or fewer), the mothers aged 30 and older all tend to prefer a family size smaller than the ones they have; this is especially true of the older mothers. It should also be noted that *the percentage of mothers preferring two children increases substantially among the younger mothers.* Thus, close to 40 per cent of the mothers under 30 think that two children

Table 4

Actual and preferred family size (number of children) by mother's age

Mother's age	Mean actual family size (A)	Mean preferred family size (B)	Difference (B)−(A)	Modal preferred family size	% preferring two children	Base N
Under 25	1.39	2.74	1.35	2	40.4%	(47)
25–29	2.32	2.85	0.53	2	37.9%	(87)
30–34	3.49	3.12	−0.37	3	29.0%	(93)
35–39	4.22	3.23	−0.99	4	28.3%	(145)
40–44	5.05	3.53	−1.52	4	17.3%	(162)
45 or older	5.14	3.41	−1.73	4	16.3%	(215)

Source: People of Kwun Tong Survey (1973–74), Social Research Centre, The Chinese University of Hong Kong.

would be ideal if they could start all over again.

It is quite clear from the overall pattern that the younger women are much more likely to favour a small family. This has a special significance when one takes into account that the survey was made in Kwun Tong, an industrial town that contains a very high proportion of families (about 80 per cent) living in public housing estates which for the most part belong to the lower end of the socioeconomic scale in Hong Kong. It suggests that, assuming a fairly typical preference for small families among the upper social strata, there is probably not much class difference in the notion of what an "ideal" family size ought to be. This, indeed, is also suggested by findings on "desired" family size of the Fertility Survey which used a more comprehensive Hong Kong-wide sample. In that survey, it was found that although younger mothers desired smaller families than older mothers, there was no significant difference in the average desired family size among mothers living in the various types of housing after controlling for age.[21] In Hong Kong the type of housing is a rough indicator of socioeconomic status: families living in private housing generally belong to the middle and upper social strata while those in resettlement estates and low-cost housing are typically of the lower strata. Thus, *the desired family size is more a function of one's age than of one's social class*.

The data in Table 4 can be analyzed in greater detail by taking into consideration the variation in preferred family size according to both actual family size and mother's age. We notice certain interesting patterns of how the preferred family size is "affected" by the actual family size. Table 5 shows, for each age group, the percentage of mothers preferring the same family size as the actual family size among those with a particular actual family size. We see that, on the whole, the likelihood for mothers to prefer the same family size as their actual family size is highest when the actual family size is three and second highest when the actual family size is two. In other words, it appears that *women tend to be most contented with their fertility performance when they actually have two or three children*.

Furthermore, from the same data but not directly shown in Table 5, we found that (a) when the actual family size reaches five or more, the overall tendency is overwhelmingly towards preferring fewer children, and that (b) when the actual family size is two or smaller, the majority tend to prefer two children, almost irrespective of the mother's age.

From the above analysis of family size preferences of women in the People of Kwun Tong Survey, we may make the following observations: (1) Younger mothers tend to prefer a smaller family size than do older mothers, but the

[21] C. Y. Choi and K. C. Chan, *op. cit.*, p. 92.

Table.5

Percentage of mothers preferring same family size (number of children) as actual family size by actual family size and age

Mother's age	Actual family size							
	0	1	2	3	4	5	6	7+
Under 25	0.0 (9)*	5.6 (18)	30.8 (13)	40.0 (5)	0.0 (1)		0.0 (1)	0.0 (1)
25-29	0.0 (6)	13.3 (15)	50.0 (34)	60.0 (15)	40.0 (10)	16.7 (6)		0.0 (1)
30-34	0.0 (2)	0.0 (2)	61.5 (13)	41.4 (29)	48.0 (25)	15.4 (13)	0.0 (4)	0.0 (5)
35-39	0.0 (2)	50.0 (2)	71.4 (21)	72.0 (25)	69.4 (36)	21.7 (23)	19.0 (21)	0.0 (15)
40-44	0.0 (3)	0.0 (2)	60.0 (10)	72.2 (18)	57.1 (35)	20.6 (34)	14.3 (28)	0.0 (32)
45 or older	0.0 (3)	14.3 (7)	70.6 (17)	80.0 (20)	64.5 (31)	12.5 (40)	6.7 (30)	0.0 (67)

Source: People of Kwun Tong Survey (1973-74), Social Research Centre, The Chinese University of Hong Kong.
*Base number for percentage.

difference is not as great as that between the actual numbers of children they have. (2) The higher the number of children is above two the more likely a mother is to prefer two or three children. (3) While more of the younger mothers prefer two children, mothers of all age groups who actually have two children tend to prefer two children also.

To gain some idea of how the younger generation of these Kwun Tong mothers thought about family size, their children between the ages of 17 and 21, if any, were asked how many children of their own they would want in the future. We obtained replies from a total of 116 such young people from 90 families. Only 76 of them, however, indicated a distinct family size preference. About half of these respondents preferred two children, and another 30 per cent preferred three. Thus, the family size preference of these young people parallels closely that of their parents.

In the survey of 224 first year university students mentioned before, the question was also asked as to how many children they would like to have in the future. As it turned out, 58 per cent of them preferred two children and 28 per cent preferred three. No one preferred more than four. In fact, this pattern remains basically the same regardless of the size of their family of orientation, as shown in Table 6. When asked what number of children would make a family too large, 36 per cent of the students said four and 41 per cent said five, thus resembling the pattern of the Kwun Tong mothers, almost none of whom preferred to have more than five children if they had the chance to start all over again.

Table 6

Students' family size preference by size of family of orientation

Preferred family size	Size of family of orientation				All
	1-2	3-4	5-6	7+	
1	4.4%	1.5%	5.6%	9.1%	4.9%
2	56.5	61.2	57.8	54.5	58.0
3	21.7	29.8	32.2	20.5	28.2
4	17.4	7.5	4.4	15.9	8.9
Total	100.0%	100.0%	100.0%	100.0%	100.0%
(N)	(23)	(67)	(90)	(44)	(224)

Source: A survey on students' fertility socialization (1975), Social Research Centre, The Chinese University of Hong Kong.

These data on family size preference, limited in representativeness as they may be, do suggest a consistent phenomenon. Both married women with actual childbearing and child-raising experience and the younger generation who are soon to establish their own families tend to favour a small family of two to three children. We have seen that this tendency is particularly strong among the younger generation. While the family size preference of the married women is influenced by the number of children they actually have, that of the young people is not influenced by the number of their siblings. Of course, the meaning of family size preference is different for the two categories of persons. In the case of the young people, the preference is purely anticipatory and essentially tentative. It is subject to change and may well not agree with their actual family size in the future. However, the fact that their preference has converged so highly towards the two- or three-child family does reflect that the desirability of a small family is widely shared among the young people of today. In the case of the mothers, by contrast, the preferred family size is very much a result of more or less assessing what the actual family size has meant in the light of past and present life experiences. The emergence of a marked preference for two or three children cannot but suggest that social conditions in Hong Kong and the considerable publicity given to family planning in recent years have indeed crystallized a desire for small families, even if only as an ideal.

Conclusion and Discussion

In this paper I have tried to portray the significance of family planning in Hong Kong with special reference to the following three points: (a) family planning as an organized programme to facilitate limiting family size is a relatively recent phenomenon in Hong Kong; (b) fertility in Hong Kong has declined markedly since the mid-sixties and has remained at a low level as a result of changing social and economic conditions favouring a desire for smaller families on the one hand and the expansion of family planning activities and services on the other; and (c) on the individual level, there is now in Hong Kong a marked tendency for both the parental generation and the younger generation to prefer a small family of two to three children.

The sixties in Hong Kong was a decade of rapid expansion in education. The youth of that decade, and of the years that followed, have been direct beneficiaries of that expansion. They would therefore be expected to grow up to be a generation of supporters of small families. The evidence we have suggests that this is in fact the case. Indeed, *it is not just small families that the younger generation have now widely accepted, but also relatively late marriage and child spacing.* Thus, for example, the two hundred odd university students cited before showed a modal preference for males to marry at the age of 28 and females at 25. The first child, more than 40 per cent of them thought, should not be born until two years after marriage and the second child another two years after that. Another 22 per cent thought that the second child should come three years after the first.

It would be difficult, of course, to execute a study which follows a cohort of present-day young people until they marry and have children, in order to see whether their future fertility behaviour is consistent with their preferences and attitudes now. Naturally, all kinds of intervening factors are likely to operate and lead to deviations of actual behaviour from values and norms. However, juding from the fact that more younger married couples are taking to birth control before the first childbirth and that the concept of family planning is increasingly gaining acceptance, it would be reasonable to suppose that the future fertility behaviour of our present-day young people in Hong Kong will be in line with their current overwhelming support of the two- or three-child family.

This is not to say, however, that promoters of family planning in Hong Kong can afford to be complacent. The task of educating and motivating the public must continue. That task is in many ways benefiting from the social environment of an industrializing and modernizing Hong Kong which is, as we have seen, conducive towards encouraging small families. In fact, as is well known, the Family Planning Association of Hong Kong has been giving increasing emphasis to educational and motivational work in various forms and through various channels, and much of this is directed at the younger age groups in the population. Hong Kong being such a large metropolis, however, the work of the Family Planning Association alone will not be sufficient. It has been suggested more than once (and especially during World Population Year, 1974) that much more population-related material and certain forms of family planning knowledge ought to be incorporated into the school curriculum. Up to the present little progress has been made in this direction, but it must be stressed that teaching both men and women about family planning should take a more deliberate and systematic form. This could best be done by making it a part of formal (school) education.

Judging from the fairly wide acceptance of contraception, the increased use of contraception for child spacing rather than for preventing an already large family from getting larger, and the emergence of a norm of two or three children as the ideal family size, it may be said that the family planning programme in Hong Kong has achieved a sizeable success. On the whole, there has been little or no significant cultural resistance to contraception, although the large family ideal used to be a core value of traditional Chinese familism. Yet difficulties are still present, such as the relatively low rate of contraception acceptance among certain dialect-ethnic groups (e.g., those of Chiu Chow origin) and the fishermen. Preference for boys still persists to some extent, even among the better educated. Thus, for example, nearly two-thirds of the undergraduates studied in one of the cited surveys indicated that if the first two children turned out to be girls they would want a third child, hoping that it would be a boy. The same study also revealed that the students' knowledge of contraceptive methods was limited. There is certainly plenty of room for more active educational work on the part of the Family Planning Association. At the same time, there is also an increasingly strong case for encouraging a more active and direct role on the part of the Hong Kong Government in helping to promote family planning.

Chapter 13

Chinese and Western Health Care Systems:
Professional Stratification in a Modernizing Society*

Rance P. L. Lee

The process of modernization has been so pervasive in recent centuries that it can be taken as part of the universal human experience. Societies in the course of modernization characteristically change at an accelerated rate from a technologically simple, structurally less differentiated and sacred- or traditionally-oriented pattern of beliefs and social action toward a technologically complex, structurally more differentiated and secular- or rational-utilitarian-oriented pattern. Many Western nations have been undergoing this complex process for several centuries. Because of the impressive socioeconomic and political successes of these Western nations, most countries in Africa, Asia and Latin America have also begun to struggle for modernity in recent decades. For many of these "newcomers" modernization in effect means Westernization, though some countries look to modernized countries of socialist persuasion for models.

The process of modernization usually involves importing technological, social-organizational and ideological systems from advanced nations. The introduction of foreign products, however, cannot displace the existing indigenous elements within a relatively short period of time. Nor can such elements be introduced in an isolated way without interacting with other elements in the host culture. The consequence is the coexistence of two sociocultural systems in a modernizing society—the traditional and the modern sectors.

In the modern sector, we usually find an increasingly large number of professional roles whose occupants have received "a prolonged specialized training in a body of abstract knowledge" and have developed "a collectivity

*This is a revised version of the paper entitled "Health Services System in Hong Kong: Professional Stratification in a Modernizing Society," published in *Inquiry*, Supplement to Volume XII, June 1975, pp. 51-62. Data were drawn from the author's Health Systems Study, which was carried out under the auspices of the Social Research Centre, The Chinese University of Hong Kong, and was financed by the Harvard-Yenching Institute, the Lotteries Fund of the Hong Kong Government and The Chinese University of Hong Kong. The author wishes to acknowledge the comments and suggestions of Ray H. Elling, Ambrose King, and S. L. Wong.

or service orientation."[1] Although professionals are more and more numerous and important in the modern sector, their counterparts (such as the medical healers and religious "specialists") have existed in the pre-modern or traditional sector for a long time before the modern sector was imported. Hence we may postulate that in a modernizing society, there coexist two distinct and specialized occupational roles, one in the traditional sector and another in the modern sector, each of which claims to have a legitimate right to perform similar functions for the society. The coexistence of these two professions represents alternative responses to particular social needs.

Although the traditional and the modern professions coexist, they tend to obtain different amounts of social, political and economic resources from the society. There emerges a *stratificational order* between the two "professions." In the very early stage of modernization, the traditional profession may retain a higher stratificational position. The process of modernization, however, leads to a reversal of the stratified ranking between the two professions. Compared with the traditional profession, the modern profession commands higher prestige in the social order, greater power in the political realm and more wealth in the economic order.

The stratificational ranking of the modern profession is higher than that of the traditional profession because it is able to acquire greater support from salient segments of the society. Its specialized knowledge is legitimized by the dominant social values and academic authority in the modernizing society; and its members are delegated by the political authority to have a greater, or the sole responsibility for providing and controlling certain services.[2]

However, the traditional profession is not entirely passive. In order to struggle for survival and to compete for more socioeconomic and political resources, the traditional profession may strive for a rationalistic revivalism; i.e., an improvement in its stratificational ranking by rationalizing (in Weber's sense)[3] its technical knowledge and social organization.

---

[1]Goode has argued that other characteristics of a profession can be derived from these two "core" characteristics. See: William J. Goode, "Encroachment, Charlatanism, and the Emerging Profession: Psychology, Medicine, and Sociology," *American Sociological Review* 25:902-914 (1960).

[2]Barber has postulated that the greater the amount of knowledge and/or responsibility required for performance in a given social role, the higher the stratificational position of the incumbent of that position. See: Bernard Barber, *Social Stratification: A Comparative Analysis of Structure and Process* (New York: Harcourt, Brace & World, Inc., 1957), pp. 24-30.

[3]Rationalization refers to "the methodical attainment of a definitely given and practical end by means of an increasingly precise calculation of adequate means." See: H. H. Gerth and C. Wright Mills (eds.), *From Max Weber: Essays in Sociology* (Fair Lawn, N. J.: Oxford University Press, 1958), p. 293.

The major objective of this paper is to elaborate and illustrate these general statements concerning the dynamic process of interaction between the traditional and modern "professional" groups in a modernizing society by analyzing the structure and functioning of the health services system in Hong Kong. I shall begin with a brief description of some features of Hong Kong as a modernizing society, and then discuss (1) the extent to which the traditional and the modern medical professions coexist, (2) the stratificational order between the two medical professions, (3) the differential social support of the two professions, and (4) the revival of traditional medicine.

Hong Kong: A Modernizing Society

Hong Kong is situated on the southern coast of mainland China. It became a colony under the British Crown in 1842, and presently has a total land area of about 1,052 square kilometres. Ever since the establishment of the People's Republic of China on the mainland in 1949, Hong Kong has been undergoing rapid demographic, social and economic transformations.[4]

Primarily because of the great influx of refugees from China, Hong Kong's population has grown from an estimated 600,000 in 1945 to 3.95 million in 1971, an increase of nearly seven fold over one quarter of a century. It was estimated that by the end of June 1979, the total population was 4.9 million. A very great majority of the local residents are Chinese. According to the March 1971 census, about 98.3 per cent of the total population can be classified as Chinese in place of origin.

Concomitant to population growth is the rapid modernization of Hong Kong's technological and institutional systems. For example, the proportion of working population engaged in manufacturing has increased from less than 10 per cent in 1948 to about 44 per cent in 1978. From 1964 to 1976, electricity consumption rose from 2,072- to 8,342-million kilowatt-hours, and gas consumption from 4,527- to 18,479-thousand therms. The number of private motor cars increased from about 51 thousand in 1964 to 114 thousand in 1976. Government expenditure rose from HK$1,381 million in 1963/64 to HK$6,585 million in 1975/76; more specifically, the per capita government expenditure during this period increased from HK$404 to HK$1,498.[5] More-

---

[4] See: *Hong Kong Social and Economic Trends 1968-72* and *Hong Kong Statistics 1947-67*, published by Census and Statistics Department, Hong Kong Government. For some discussions, see: David Podmore, "The Population of Hong Kong," pp. 21-54; and E. E. Phelps Brown, "The Hong Kong Economy: Achievement and Prospects," pp. 1-20 in Keith Hopkins (eds.), *Hong Kong: The Industrial Colony* (London: Oxford University Press, 1971). Also see: T. B. Lin, Rance P. L. Lee, and U. E. Simonis (eds.), *Hong Kong: Economic, Social & Political Studies in Development* (N. Y.: M. E. Sharpe, 1979).

[5] H.C.Y. Ho, *The Fiscal System of Hong Kong* (London: Croom Helm, 1979), pp. 27-29.

over, according to the census in 1961 and in 1971, the proportion of population (age 5 and over) with primary school education or above was expanded from 69.1 per cent to 75.2 per cent over the ten years. Of no less importance has been the rapid increase in enrolment at the post-secondary level of education: from 1964 to 1978, the total number of full-time students rose from about 7 thousand to 23 thousand.

Within the last three decades, Hong Kong has become one of the greatest commercial-industrial centres in Asia. As of 1978, the G.N.P. per capita was HK$13,826 (about US$2,904), which was third only to Japan (US$8,324) and Singapore (US$3,205) in the entire Far East region. Furthermore, Hong Kong is probably the third city in the world next only to London and New York in terms of the number of foreign banking and quasi-banking institutions.

As regards to the state of health, Hong Kong has caught up with many developed countries. Over the last several decades, there have been downward trends in the incidence of various kinds of infectious diseases including, for instance, typhoid, bacillary dysentery, tuberculosis, chickenpox, diphtheria and whooping cough. Infectious diseases have been replaced by chronic illnesses, such as malignant neoplasms and heart diseases, as major causes of death. Infant and maternal mortality rates have also been substantially reduced.[6] For instance, the crude death rate dropped from 10.2 per thousand in 1951 to 5 per thousand in 1978, and the infant mortality rate decreased from 55.5 per thousand live births in 1959 to about 12 per thousand in 1978. The life expectation at birth is at present 70 for men and 77 for women. These changes in the state of health might be partly due to social and economic progress. But one supposes that the advancement in medical technology has been an important contribution to the improved health status. A striking phenomenon in the modernizing society of Hong Kong is the increased utilization and expansion of medical science and technology developed in "advanced" nations. The government expenditure on the medical and health services increased from HK$15.6-million (about 6.2 per cent of the total expenditure) in 1950/51 to HK$666-million (about 10 per cent of the total expenditure) in 1976/77.[7]

Professional Coexistence

The medical care systems in Hong Kong are pluralistic, comprising a variety of traditional Chinese and modern Western health services. In the modern

[6]For statistics, see: R. K. Bowman, F. I. Forbes, and J.D.F. Lockart, "Trends in Notifiable Infectious Diseases in Hong Kong Island 1961-1965," *Far East Medical Journal* 6:223-229 (August 1970); and M. J. Colbourne, "Mortality Trends in Hong Kong," *Journal of The Society of Community Medicine, Hong Kong Branch* 8:18-42 (1976).

[7]For some discussions, see Ho, *op. cit.*, pp. 72-76.

Western medical sector, there were 3,742 doctors at the end of 1976, the doctor-population ratio being 1 to 1,190. Of these, 3,127 were registered in the Medical Council of Hong Kong. 210 were provisionally registered (i.e., new graduates from medical school, working as interns for one-year), 116 were unregistrable doctors being engaged in university teaching or government services, and 289 were unregisterable doctors practising in charity clinics exempted from registration. (In addition to these legal doctors, there might be a thousand or so practitioners who illegally practised modern medicine in Hong Kong.) In 1976, there were also 27 government hospitals (including 15 in prisons), 21 government-assisted hospitals and 11 private hospitals. These modern medical hospitals provided a total of 18,706 beds; the bed-population ratio was 4.3 per thousand. Moreover, the government had established 51 out-patient clinics and 23 polyclinics and specialist clinics, whereas in the private sector there were a total of 414 out-patient registered under the Medical Clinics Ordinance. (In this paper I shall focus on modern-trained physicians, the most dominant profession in the realm of modern medical services.)

Chinese medical services can be classified into three types:

1. The classical or great tradition of medicine, which is based on the cosmo-logical conception of Yin-Yang and Five Elements and has been developed and accumulated for over 3,000 years;
2. The folk-empirical traditions of medicine, which are shared and practised by indigenous populations in various localities of China;[8] and
3. The religious-medical practices, which are based on the belief in super-natural determination of illness and on the application of magical pro-cedures to the treatment of diseases.[9]

[8]See: Chung Yung, *Folk Medicine* (Hong Kong: Tak Lee Book Co., 1972); Gerald Choa, "Some Ideas Concerning Food and Diet Among Hong Kong Chinese: The Con-stitution and Food Therapy," *Brochure of the Hong Kong Branch of the Roayl Asiatic Society* (October 1966); E. N. Anderson, *The Floating World of Castle Peak Bay* (Washington, D. C.: American Anthropological Association, 1970); and Y. Chung, *Food Therapy* (Hong Kong: Tak Lee Book Co., 1973), Volumes 1-4.

[9]See: Francis L. K. Hsu, "A Cholera Epidemic in a Chinese Town," in Benjamin D. Paul (ed.), *Health, Culture, and Community* (New York: Russel Sage Foundation, 1955), pp. 135-154; and Katherine Gould, Martin, "Ong-la-Kong: The Plague God as Modern Physician," presented to the Conference on the Comparative Study of Tradi-tional and Modern Medicine in Chinese Societies, Seattle, Washington, February 4-6, 1974. Hsu's study was conducted in a south-western town on mainland China in 1942, while Martin's field work was carried out in Taiwan in 1972-1973. John Myers is presently exploring the structure and functioning of religious-medical practices in urban Hong Kong For some of his findings, see: John Myers (in collaboration with Davy H. K. Leung), "An Urban Chinese Spirit-medium Cult," Social Research Centre, The Chinese University of Hong Kong (1974).

The classical tradition has dominated Chinese medicine and will, therefore, receive the most attention here.

The classical tradition of Chinese medicine emerged in China in about 800 B.C. and increasingly dominated the entire sector of medical and health care. It was well documented by medical scholars and supported by governing regimes throughout the history of China. *The Classic of Internal Medicine* (Nei Ching), *Treatise of Fevers* (Shang-han Lun), *General Compendium of Materia Medica* (Pen-Ts'ao Kang-mu) and *The Pulse Classic* (Mo-Ching) represent some of the major literature in classical medicine. Each of these documents typically consists of an abstract theoretical framework and a detailed classification of diseases and medicaments.[10] The classical tradition was not formulated through the use of scientific procedures, but was based on naturalistic and rationalistic principles.[11] It was a product of conceptualization (primarily in terms of Yin-Yang and Five Elements) and empirical observations for several thousands of years.

Practitioners of the classical tradition of medicine have played the most distinctive role in the history of Chinese medical care. They strongly claim to be service-oriented. A central ethic of this specialized occupational group is to care for people. Moreover, in order to become practitioners, they normally have to spend several years, usually through apprenticeship, studying the literature and learning clinical experience. These practitioners, therefore, possess at least two core attributes of a profession—namely, a collectivity orientation and prolonged specialized training in a body of abstract knowledge. In traditional China, they commanded the most legitimate right to practise medicine, and gained a great deal of support from political authorities.

Within the profession of Chinese medicine in Hong Kong, there are three special types of practitioners: (1) herbalists, specializing in the use of herbs for internal medical care; (2) acupuncturists, treating illness by inserting needles into certain points of the body; and (3) bonesetters, specializing in the treatment of sprains and contusions. According to a survey conducted in 1969 by the then Chinese Medical Association[12] in cooperation with the government's Census and Statistics Department, there were then 4,506 Chinese

---

[10]For more discussion on the historical development of medical theories and practices in China, see: Stephan Palos, *The Chinese Art of Healing* (New York: Herder & Herder, 1971); and Pierre Huard and Ming Wong, *Chinese Medicine* (New York: McGraw-Hill, 1968).

[11]For a fuller discussion on this point, see: Ralph C. Croizier, *Traditional Medicine in Modern China: Science, Nationalism and the Tensions of Cultural Change* (Cambridge: Harvard University Press, 1968), pp. 14-19.

[12]This is an association of modern-trained physicians. Its name has been changed to "Hong Kong Medical Association."

medical practitioners of various kinds. It was estimated that in the same year there were a total of 2,317 modern-trained doctors.[13] Thus there were more Chinese than modern-trained medical practitioners in Hong Kong. A great majority of the Chinese medical practitioners are herbalists (about 70 per cent), followed by bonesetters (about 20 per cent) and acupuncturists (about 10 per cent).

These statistics indicate that both the profession of modern medicine (i.e., modern-trained physicians) and the profession of Chinese medicine (i.e., the practitioners in the classical tradition of Chinese medicine) coexist in the modernizing society of Hong Kong. Instead of coexisting in a coordinated fashion, however, these two systems of professional services are competitive on an unequal basis.

Professional Inequality

Although the role of government in the provision and subvention of medical and health care services has been increasingly important, the centre of gravity of medical care in Hong Kong remains in private practice. Unlike Britain, there is no national health scheme in Hong Kong, although the government has been financing a comprehensive School Medical Service for a small fraction of the student population.[14] The government employs about one-fourth of all the modern-trained physicians, but none of the Chinese medical practitioners. In other words, all the Chinese medical practitioners and three-fourths of the modern-trained doctors are in private practice. Furthermore, over 60 per cent of the general hospitals beds in Hong Kong are provided by nongovernmental hospitals.[15] The medical and health sector in Hong Kong can thus be characterized as *pluralistic* and predominantly *entrepreneurial*. The emphasis of the entire private sector is on the "individual, fee-for-service" mode of compensation and "free choice" of medical practitioners.

In such a pluralistic health context, modern-trained physicians are relatively more predominant than are Chinese medical practitioners. Although both

[13] See the brochure, "Hong Kong's Medical & Health Services," issued by Hong Kong Information Services (July 1970).

[14] It was reported by the School Medical Service Board that a total of 70,758 students took part in the scheme during the academic year 1972-1973, constituting less than 10 per cent of those eligible. These students were attended by 181 modern-trained doctors in private practice. In 1978, the number of students participating in the scheme increased to about 110 thousand, while the number of doctors in the scheme were over two hundred.

[15] *Report of the Medical Development by the Advisory Committee 1973*, published by Hong Kong Government (1973).

professions claim to perform the same functions for the society (i.e., the maintenance of health and the treatment of diseases), there exists a stratificational order between them. The profession of modern medicine is superior to that of Chinese medicine in the major dimensions of social stratification: power, prestige and wealth.

Power

The profession of modern medicine has obtained greater control not only over the social organization of medical care in Hong Kong but also over the technical content of medical work.[16] The Medical Council of Hong Kong, established by the government, plays the most crucial role in the legitimation and supervision of medical practice. The council, chaired by the director of the government's Department of Medical and Health Services, consists of representatives from the armed forces, government health services, university medical school and two major medical professional associations in Hong Kong.[17]

The council has been granted a mandate by the government to register medical practitioners and to regulate their medical practices through the setting of minimum and uniform standards. Only physicians holding a diploma granted by the Hong Kong University or some other diploma recognized by the General Medical Council of the United Kingdom are registerable with the council, and are then recognized by law as qualified medical doctors. Chinese medical practitioners are, therefore, excluded by the council and are not recognized by the legal authority as duly qualified. They are deprived of certain privileges which are granted to registered modern-trained doctors. For instance, Chinese medical practitioners are not permitted to issue death certificates and have no access to hospital beds for their patients.

In the formulation of policies dealing with medicine and health, the government normally consults with representatives from the two major medical professional associations, the Hong Kong Medical Association and the Hong Kong Branch of the British Medical Association. Both associations are oriented to modern medicine. In fact, the government rarely seeks any advice from Chinese medical practitioners, and there is no Chinese medical practitioner working in the government's Department of Medical and Health

---

[16] For a detailed discussion on professional control over social and technical terms of work, see: Eliot Freidson, *Profession of Medicine* (New York: Dodd, Mead, 1972); and also by Freidson, *Professional Dominance: The Social Structure of Medical Care* (Chicago: Aldine, 1970).

[17] See: Harry S. Y. Fang, (ed.), *Medical Directory of Hong Kong*, published by The Federation of Medical Societies of Hong Kong (1970).

Services. All doctors in public service are trained in modern medicine. Thus it is not surprising to see that though the government has provided and subvented an increasing volume of different kinds of medical and health programme, none of them is involved with Chinese medicine.

With regard to the future development of health care services, the governor appointed a Medical Development Advisory Committee early in 1973 to make recommendations appropriate for the next 10 years. Four of the 11 committee members were modern-trained doctors, and none were Chinese medical practitioners. The plans recommended by the committee are primarily concerned with the provision of hospital beds and the increased supply of doctors and nurses in modern medicine.[18] There has been no discussion about the development of Chinese medicine. Quite evidently, the social organization of medical care in Hong Kong has been under the influence of the modern medical profession, rather than the Chinese medical one.

The profession of modern medicine also has a greater degree of technical autonomy than the profession of Chinese medicine. As suggested by the previous discussion concerning the structure and functioning of the Medical Council of Hong Kong, the modern medical profession has acquired an officially approved monopoly on the right to determine how and by whom the work of healing should be done and evaluated. Members of the profession are free to practise with very few formal constraints that are not made by their own professional colleagues. Relative to the profession of modern medicine, Chinese medical practitioners have a lower degree of technical autonomy. Their practices are constrained by the legal authority in many ways. For example, Chinese medical practitioners are not permitted to practise surgery, to undertake the treatment of eye diseases, to possess antibiotics and dangerous drugs, or to make use of certain modern medical technology such as X-ray and inoculation.

In addition to the technical constraints imposed by "outsiders," the Chinese medical practitioner is also prohibited by law from using any name or title which may induce anyone to believe that he is qualified to practise according to modern scientific methods. These legal constraints serve to prevent traditional practitioners from misusing modern techniques, but also serve to protect the economic interest and medical dominance of the modern medical profession.

In sum, the profession of modern medicine has obtained a greater degree of political power and, thereby, control over the social organization of health care services and the technical content of medical work.

---

[18] *Report of the Medical Development by the Advisory Committee 1973.*

Prestige

Status honours are not evenly distributed between the two professions. The profession of Chinese medicine carries a high prestige in traditional China, but its prestige has been declining in the modernizing society of Hong Kong. It is the profession of modern medicine, rather than that of Chinese medicine, which is greatly respected and honoured by most segments of the local population. The uneven distribution of status honours can be reflected by the ways in which the technical competency of the two professions are evaluated and by the extent to which the services of the two professions are utilized. To shed light on these points, I will use part of the empirical data my colleagues and I gathered in 1971-1972 about medical organizations and health behaviour in the district of Kwun Tong, Hong Kong.

The district of Kwun Tong is located on the east coast of the Kowloon Peninsula of Hong Kong, covering about 32 hundred acres. Over the last two decades, it has developed into one of the largest industrial and residential satellite towns in Hong Kong. There were about 2,000 industrial enterprises and about 500,000 Chinese residents in this area in 1971-1972. Most people reside in public housing of various kinds. About 14 per cent live in private apartments and tenement buildings. Residents are largely in middle- or lower-income groups.[19] Kwun Tong is by no means a self-contained community. The social, economic and political life in the community is to a large extent connected with, and thus in many ways similar to, the Hong Kong society as a whole.[20]

We undertook three health surveys in Kwun Tong in 1971-1972. The first was a complete enumeration of the medical and health care units in various subdistricts of Kwun Tong. The second survey focused on the organizational structures.[21] The third studied a random sample of 702 household heads for the purpose of understanding their health concepts and utilization. The data collected in these three surveys will be used in the following discussions.[22]

---

[19] For a more comprehensive description of the Kwun Tong community, see: Y. K. Chan, "The Rise and Growth of Kwun Tong: A Study of Planned Urban Development," Social Research Centre, The Chinese University of Hong Kong (August 1973).

[20] Ambrose King, "A Theoretical and Operational Definition of Community: The Case of Kwun Tong," Social Research Centre, The Chinese University of Hong Kong (1973).

[21] These two specific types of surveys were chosen for the study on the basis of the consideration that both of them would include the majority of medical practitioners and that their services are most widely utilized by the public.

[22] For a comprehensive description of the research procedures and statistical findings of the three health surveys, see the following research reports and papers by my colleagues and me published by the Social Research Centre, The Chinese University of Hong Kong in 1972. They are: "Spatial Distributions of Modern Western and Traditional Chinese Medical Practitioners in an Industrializing Chinese Town," "Study of Health

I believe the survey findings can be reasonably generalized to apply to the Colony as a whole.

There were a total of 174 Chinese and 101 modern health care units in the entire district of Kwun Tong in 1971-1972. The distribution of both types of services showed a correlation coefficient of .55, indicating that the larger the number of Chinese services in a particular area, the larger the number of modern services.

Both the distribution of Chinese medical services and that of modern services are greatly dependent upon the socioeconomic status of particular subdistricts. The correlation coefficient between the distribution of Chinese medical services and socioeconomic status was .54, while that between modern medical services and socioeconomic status was .68. Hence the higher the socioeconomic status of a particular area, the more Chinese as well as modern medical services are available.[23]

Comparing the two correlation coefficients, we observe that modern-trained doctors are more likely than Chinese medical practitioners to concentrate in economically wealthier areas. To avoid competition, Chinese practitioners have to move into poorer areas, and cannot afford to be as selective as modern-trained doctors.

According to our survey sample of 702 adults in Kwun Tong, most people (67 per cent) perceive that modern-trained doctors are in general more competent technically than Chinese practitioners. However, our sample did have different evaluations of different aspects of medical practice. Most people (84 per cent) believe that modern medicine is more effective than Chinese medicine in the *prevention* of infectious diseases. With regard to tonic care, i.e., the promotion and maintenance of good health, most people believe in Chinese herbs (70 per cent) rather than modern drugs (12 per cent).

For the treatment of illnesses, a greater number of people are more confident in modern medicine (65 per cent) than in Chinese medicine (10 per cent). About 60 to 80 per cent suggest that in the treatment of most diseases (1) modern medical care works faster than Chinese medicine, but (2) Chinese

Systems in Kwun Tong: Health Attitudes and Behavior of Chinese Residents," and "Study of Health Systems in Kwun Tong: Organizations and Attitudes of the Western-trained and the Traditional Chinese Personnel in an Industrial Community of Hong Kong."

[23]The socioeconomic status of a subdistrict is measured in terms of the quality of residential housing. For a fuller discussion and more elaborate analysis of the relationships between socioeconomic status and distribution of various types of health services in Kwun Tong, see: Rance P. L. Lee, "Population, Housing and the Availability of Medical and Health Services in an Industrializing Chinese Community," *Journal of The Chinese University of Hong Kong* 1:191-208 (1973).

herbs are less likely to produce side effects, and (3) modern medicine is good for the treatment of "symptoms" while Chinese medicine is more effective in the "curing" of disease.

The evaluation of the effectiveness of medical treatment may be dependent upon the specific types of diseases in question. Respondents were given a list of illnesses and were asked to make comparisons between the two medical approaches. The responses are presented in Table 1. The data suggest that most people prefer modern services for the treatment of most diseases, especially tuberculosis and fever. Opinions are evenly split with respect to measles. Chinese medicine is considered more effective in dealing with rheumatism, sprains and fractures.

Table 1

Comparison by sample population* of the effectiveness of modern
and Chinese medical treatment for specific diagnoses, 1971-1972

Diagnosis	Modern treatment better (%)	Chinese treatment better (%)	Treatments about the same (%)
Tuberculosis	91.2	1.4	7.4
Fever	90.5	5.7	3.8
Heart diseases	84.9	0.9	14.2
Stomach ache	84.3	3.4	12.3
Mental illness	84.0	0.4	15.5
Skin diseases	83.6	6.6	10.4
Throbbing and diarrhea	78.3	13.4	8.3
Whopping cough	76.9	14.0	9.1
Dysmenorrhea	65.0	17.5	17.4
Anemia	55.0	29.1	16.0
Measles	47.9	47.0	9.1
Rheumatism	24.2	54.1	21.7
Sprains and fractures	8.2	86.5	5.3

* N = 702.

All these findings suggest that in general the lay population of Kwun Tong district is more trustful of modern medical care than Chinese medical care. Nevertheless, Chinese medicine is more trusted in some ways such as for tonic care, for the occurrence of fewer side effects from treatment, for the curing of diseases (but not treatment of symptoms), and for treatment of certain illnesses such as measles, rheumatism, sprains and fractures.

Then to what extent are the two types of professional services utilized by the population? Among the various types of modern services, private physicians are most often visited by people (70 per cent). Among the three major kinds of Chinese services, herbalists are most often consulted (36 per cent), while acupuncturists have been visited by a very small fraction of the population (2 per cent).

Concerning the relative utilization of Chinese versus modern services, we noted the following:

1. Among those respondents who sought some help for illness during the past three years, 83 per cent reported that they visited modern-trained doctors while 11 per cent consulted Chinese practitioners.

2. Among those whose parents used health serbices during the last three years, 68 per cent reported that their parents visited the modern-trained doctors, while 20 per cent sought out Chinese practitioners.

3. Among those whose children used health services during the past three years, 92 per cent reported that their children were seen by modern-trained doctors, while 5 per cent received Chinese services.

These findings indicate that modern medical services are more widely utilized by the people than Chinese medical services. Moreover, it seems that the younger the generation, the more extensive the use of modern medical care compared to the use of Chinese services.

Table 2 presents data showing the process of seeking medical help. In the initial stage, people are more likely to be self-medicated (58 per cent) rather than seeking help from modern-trained doctors (38 per cent) or Chinese medical practitioners (4 per cent). When this first move does not work, most of those who initially relied on self-medication or Chinese medical practitioners shift to the use of modern-trained doctors, while most of those who consulted the modern-trained doctors in the initial stage continue to use them.

Table 2

Process of seeking medical treatment in initial and later stages of illness
from self-medication, modern medicine and Chinese medicine,1971-1972

Later stage	Initial stage		
	Self-medicated (%)	Modern medicine (%)	Chinese medicine (%)
Self-medicated	14.5	8.1	4.0
Modern medicine	76.7	79.3	52.0
Chinese medicine	8.8	12.6	44.0
(N)	(407)	(270)	(25)

I have presented some findings about the evaluation of medical efficacy and the utilization of services by the lay population. How are the two types of professional services evaluated and utilized by medical professionals themselves? According to the survey of medical practitioners (174 Chinese medical practitioners and 101 modern-trained doctors) in Kwun Tong, most modern-trained physicians (84 per cent) believe that their own colleagues are medically more competent than those in Chinese medicine, while most Chinese practitioners (73 per cent) feel that there is no significant difference in competence between the two groups.

How are the two kinds of services utilized by practitioners? Over three-fourths of the modern-trained doctors interviewed have referred patients to their own professional colleagues, while less than one-fourth of the interviewed Chinese practitioners have done so. Unlike the modern physicians, the network of patient referrals among Chinese practitioners is rather weak. Do Chinese and modern-trained medical practitioners refer patients to each other? Over one-half of the Chinese practitioners have referred patients to modern-trained doctors, especially those working in hospitals. The referral of patients from modern doctors to Chinese practitioners is a rarity: only two per cent of the modern-trained doctors have done so. Apparently there exists an asymmetric process of patient referral between modern-trained and Chinese practitioners.

In sum, we have seen that the services of the profession of modern medicine are more favourably evaluated and more extensively utilized by both the lay population and the medical professionals themselves. This pattern of differential evaluation and utilization suggests that the two professions of medicine command different degrees of honour and respect in the modernizing society of Hong Kong. In terms of social prestige, the profession of modern medicine is superior to that of Chinese medicine.

Wealth

The profession of modern medicine is economically much better off than the profession of Chinese medicine. There are no statistical data to show the actual income, but from the survey of medical practitioners in Kwun Tong, it was found that 58 per cent of modern-trained doctors felt that they earned more income than Chinese medical practitioners while only 5 per cent felt that Chinese medical practitioners earned more. Eighty-seven per cent of the Chinese practitioners felt that modern-trained doctors made more money, while none of them felt that modern-trained doctors made less.

Moreover, it is worth observing that on the average the total number of service hours provided by modern-trained doctors is about 31 per week while Chinese practitioners provide about 37. However, the average number of patient contacts for each modern-trained doctor is about 244 per week, while Chinese practitioners see only about 100 patients a week. Hence, as compared to the profession of Chinese medicine, the profession of modern medicine provides a smaller number of service hours but has a larger number of patient contacts.

Another indicator of the uneven distribution of wealth between the two professions is the financial support from government. The government has subvented an increasing volume of different kinds of medical and health programmes, but none of them is involved with Chinese medicine. All the government-subvented medical projects are modern oriented.

All these findings indicate that, compared to the profession of Chinese medicine, the profession of modern medicine commands more economic resources.

Differential Support

We have seen that modern medicine is superior to Chinese medicine in all the major dimensions of stratification: namely, power, prestige and wealth. Why is this so?

The stratification between the two medical professions may be due to differential support from the community. The establishment and functioning of a profession have to be legitimized by the society. What the profession does must be considered necessary and desirable. A profession would enjoy a high degree of legitimacy if its knowledge and role-performance are (a) congruent with the dominant values of the society, (b) conferred by the academic authority such as the university, and (c) supported by political authority such as government.

Scientific principles are originally secular and utilitarian in nature. The application of scientific principles has been so powerful and successful in solving many problems that science has gradually become a dominating "sacred" value in most, if not all, modernizing and modernized societies. Anything connected with science would, therefore, be accepted with little resistance.

The "good results" of modern medicine may be an important source of its dominance over Chinese medicine in Hong Kong. That dominance may also result from modern medicine's association with science. It has been widely perceived by the local population that the knowledge and skills of modern medicine were developed through the use of scientific procedures, while Chinese medicine is unscientific and is, therefore, less reliable. Being supported and justified by the dominant value of science, the profession of modern medicine enjoys a higher degree of legitimacy than the profession of Chinese medicine in Hong Kong.

The educational authority in Hong Kong also contributes to the legitimation of modern medicine, rather than that of Chinese medicine. Hong Kong has only one university medical school which produces about 150 graduates each year.[24] The training programme concentrate entirely on modern medical science, giving no attention to Chinese medicine. If one wished to learn Chinese medicine, one might do it either by becoming a disciple of Chinese medical practitioner or by enrolling in one of the 30 or so training schools in Chinese medicine. Up to the present, there is no way for any person to receive a university diploma in Chinese medicine. With its academic authority and prestigious position in society, the university has affirmed the technical competence of modern medicine but not that of traditional Chinese medicine.

With its political and financial resources, the government has been playing a major role in the modernization of medical services in Hong Kong. Its efforts, however, have led to a "partial" rather than "total" modernization in medicine. Because of its colonial policy of minimizing interference with local customs, the government has been tolerant, although not supportive, of Chinese medical practice. The Medical Ordinance in Hong Kong primarily regulates modern medical practice. The government set up no standard examination or licensing procedures for qualifying practitioners in Chinese medicine. In fact, anyone can practise Chinese medicine without any interference from the legal authority. What is required is a payment for commercial registration. It should, however, be noted that the government's tolerance of Chinese medical practice is not unconditional. As mentioned earlier, a Chinese medical practitioner is subject to certain social and technical constraints..

In short, as compared to the profession of Chinese medicine, the profession of modern medicine is more closely associated with the dominant value of science, and receives greater support from both the academic and political authorities. As a result, the profession of modern medicine has obtained a higher degree of legitimacy and hence a higher stratificational ranking than its counterpart.

Professional Revivalism

The Chinese medicine profession is not entirely passive. A revivalistic movement has recently emerged in Hong Kong. An increasing number of medical elites have publicly advocated the improvement of the social organization and technical content of Chinese medical practice. These elites include

[24] Another university medical school has been planned and will begin admitting students in 1981. This school will also provide training only in modern Western medicine.

not only leaders of some major professional associations in Chinese medicine, but also some university faculty members and modern-trained doctors.

The most serious problems faced by Chinese medicine in Hong Kong today is the lack of minimum and uniform control·over education, licensing and practice. Some practitioners may be well-qualified, while others may be quacks. The public is much less certain about the possible results of seeking help from a Chinese practitioner than from a modern-trained doctor. In view of such a serious problem, revivalists have strongly argued for minimum and uniform standards for training and practice. It is also asserted that the university should establish a Chinese medical school so that medical knowledge can be systematically researched and taught in classrooms with standard textbooks. With its rich amount of financial and technological resources and with its great variety of patients and disease patterns, the hospital should include the Chinese medical practice in its research and service programmes. The government and voluntary agencies are urged to provide accessible, low-cost, high-quality Chinese medical services to the public. These advocations indicate the concern of the revivalistic movement with the rationalization and greater general acceptance of Chinese medical care.

In regard to the technical content of work, many revivalists have argued for the use of scientific methods. Traditional treatments should be reexamined and refined through the use of scientific experiment. In fact, academic staff members of the University of Hong Kong, mainly from the Preclinical Departments of the Medical Faculty and from the Department of Chemistry, have been actively engaged in research on the pharmacological actions and other activities of various herbal medicines, and on different aspects of acupuncture.[25] A research team comprising modern-trained doctors and biochemists have been testing the use of acupuncture for the treatment of drug addiction. Under the initiation and direction of a modern-trained physician, a Chinese Medical Research Centre has been established in the community, for the purpose of conducting scientific studies on acupuncture and herbal medicines. A significant event is the formation of the Chinese Medicinal Material Research Centre at The Chinese University of Hong Kong. Its aim is to extract bioactive components from Chinese medicinal herbs by interdisciplinary research. Its staff include chemists, biologists, biochemists, behavioural scientists, and library specialists.

Two of the major barriers against the use of Chinese medicine in Hong Kong today are the rising costs of medicinal herbs and the amount of time and effort required for preparing medical herbs and roots for consumption.

[25]C. W. Ogle, "Research on Chinese Traditional Medicine in Hong Kong and the Role of the University Academic," *Interflow* (Newspaper of the University of Hong Kong), September 1979, p. 2.

Revivalists have asserted that Chinese medical herbs should be transformed into patent medicines by means of scientific procedures of extraction. In recent years, a great variety of Chinese patent medicines have become available in the local market. Most of these patent medicines are imported from the People's Republic of China, and have been increasingly utilized by the local population. These patent medicines include, for example, those used in treating schistosomiasis, tumor, meningitis and snake bite, and in curing septic shock resulting from toxic dysentery.[26]

Apparently the revivalists are pushing toward an increased rationalization of not only the social organization of medical services, but also the technical content of medical work. The emergence of the revivalistic movement may be a reaction to the state of "relative deprivation" of Chinese medicine. Being confronted with the rising status of modern medicine, the profession of Chinese medicine has to struggle for existence. In order to survive and to compete for more social-political and economic resources, the profession of Chinese medicine considers it not only a matter of desirability but also of necessity to rationalize its social organization as well as its technical content.

In this paper, I have focused on the "internal" sources of change affecting Chinese medicine in Hong Kong. However, it should be recognized that powerful "external" factors, especially the revival of traditional medicine in the People's Republic of China, coupled with internal anxiety over class disparities, may expedite the emergence of the revivalistic movement in Hong Kong.

Summary

A characteristic of modernizing societies is the coexistence of modern and traditional professions that claim to perform the same functions for the society. As a result of differential support by the dominant social values, and by the academic and the political authorities, the modern profession occupies a higher stratificational ranking than the traditional profession. In order to struggle for survival and to compete for more social-political and economic resources, the traditional profession advocates a rational revival, i.e., a rationalization of its social organization and technical content.

In this paper, I have illustrated these generalized statements by analyzing and comparing the profession of modern medicine with that of Chinese

[26] See the bulletin, *Chinese Patent Medicine*, published by Chinese Patent Medicine and Medicated Liquor Exhibition in Hong Kong (June 1972). For a brief report on the development of the pharmaceutical industry in China, see: The Revolutionary Committee of the Chinese Academy of Medical Science, "Developing China's Medical Science Independently and Self-Reliantly," *Peking Review* 13:24-30 (January 1970).

medicine in the modernizing society of Hong Kong. These two types of professional services are coexisting in the pluralistic health context of Hong Kong, but the former enjoys greater power, higher prestige and more economic resources. The state of modern medical dominance may be due to its connection with the dominant social value of science and to its support by the university and the government in Hong Kong. In recent years, however, there has emerged a revivalistic movement in the realm of Chinese medical care.

Chapter 14

Traditional Chinese Religious Practices in an Urban-Industrial Setting: The Example of Kwun Tong*

John T. Myers

Simply stated this paper is about Chinese traditional religion, the forms that it assumes and the roles that it plays in a contemporary urban-industrial community with an almost exclusively Chinese population—Kwun Tong. More specifically we set out to accomplish two major tasks. The first is to assess the vitality of traditional religion in Kwun Tong with particular attention to the extent and intensity of its practice. The second is to show from a basically Durkheimian point of view how the religious situation reflects important social characteristics of Kwun Tong as a contemporary urban community.

Procedurely, we shall begin by reviewing current scholarly opinion on the interrelationship between the urban environment and religion. This will be followed by sections devoted to three key aspects of traditional religion: the cult of ancestors, the worship of deities, and the erection of temples. The data for these sections are derived from a survey conducted by the Social Research Centre of The Chinese University of Hong Kong and the writer's field notes gathered during a year's residence in and numerous subsequent visits to the Kwun Tong district. In the final section we shall attempt to show how traditional religion both in its weaknesses and strengths mirrors important social realities in the urban community.

The Urban Setting and Religion

"Whenever . . . we trace back the characteristic urban form to its beginnings we arrive not at a settlement that is dominated by commerce, a primordial market, or one that is formed on a citadel, an archetypical fortress,

*This is a revised version of the paper published in *Internationales Asien Forum* (Munich), No. 3/4, 1976, pp. 355-377. The field work for this paper was conducted as part of the Kwun Tong Industrial Research Programme, coordinated by Dr. Ambrose Y. C. King and financially supported by the Harvard-Yenching Institute and The Chinese University of Hong Kong. The study was under the auspices of the Social Research Centre, The Chinese University of Hong Kong.

but rather on a ceremonial complex for religious expressions," Wheatley's (1971, p. 225) foregoing suggestion that man's earliest urban centres may have been sacred in origin is in sharp contrast to Cox's (1965, p. 17) assessment of religion's place in the contemporary city. "This is the age of the secular city, through supersonic travel and instantaneous communication its ethos is spreading into every corner of the globe. The world looks less and less to religious rules and rituals for its morality or its meaning." By juxtaposing the preceding quotations we do not signal our acquiescence to a unilineal point of view which would assert that there is an inevitable progression from "sacred" to "secular" city, nor that ancient cities were inherently sacred and contemporary ones secular. Our intent is merely to highlight the commonly held notion that the role, and even the importance, of religion in the urban milieu tends to become more "restricted" rather than "pervasive".

Man's initial transition from rural to urban dweller may have had an immediate effect opposite to the above causing his religion to become more "pervasive" than previously. De Coulanges (1956, pp. 126-127) avers that the move toward urban life entailed a broadening of religion's social nexus and, as a consequence, the content of its ideology, the scope of its ritual, and the composition of its localized groups. He argues that prior to the appearance of the city, man's religious behaviour was centred on the family hearth around which gathered only the tightly-knit rural based kinship unit. The wider social and political order of the city, however, demanded that the structural boundaries of the religious group be widened to include the total urban population as its basic unit of composition and of focus. This was in part accomplished through the establishment of a city hearth dedicated to the supernatural protectors of the urban community. The dominant socio-political position of the urban elite was often symbolized through the conferral of ritual office and legitimized through appropriate ideology. Sjoberg (1960) asserts that the entente between the urban community and religion was essentially maintained over a long period of time in a type of setting that he has labelled the "pre-industrial city". In such a setting, "religion . . . pervades all facets of urban life, and religious ceremonies are crucial in integrating the individual into his community" (Sjoberg, 1960, p. 256).

The erosion of religion's "pervasive" role especially in Western urban regions is attributed by Parsons (1971, pp. 71-85) to the influence of two possibly related developments. The first was a movement toward separation of the political order from explicit attachment to any one specific religious organization. This process began with the Reformation and was hastened by the Democratic Revolutions of the 18th and 19th centuries. The second major happening was the Industrial Revolution which had a much more direct import on the relationship between religion and the smaller structural units of society including the central component of most social systems, the family. Role sets became fragmented both inside and outside of the family as many services previously provided or tasks accomplished by a relatively small number of tightly-knit institutions became the almost exclusive preserve of a large number of specialized ones. Religion in such a setting tended to become the domain of a variety of well-defined structurally independent institutions of the wider society. Thus separated from previous imbededness in other institutions religion became a variable category expressable through conscious membership in a specialized structural unit devoted primarily, if not exclusively, to mediating man's relationship with the supernatural. Religion no longer needed be in form or practice an inheritance derived simply through birth into a particular family, geographical region, or cultural tradition.

In Kwun Tong we have the opportunity to observe the consequences of rapid transition to an urban-industrial environment on the religious behaviour of people largely socialized in a religious tradition that seem better adopted to the rural-agricultural and the pre-industrial settings. Yang (1961) implies Chinese traditional religion's correlation with pre-industrial social forms when he posits that its structure is "diffuse" whereas that of Western religion is "institutional". Listing the distinctive features of each structural type he states, "we can discern two structural forms of religion. One is 'institutional' religion which has a system of theology, rituals, and organization of its own, independent of other secular social institutions. It is a social institution by itself, having its own basic concepts and its own structural system. The other is 'diffused' religion, with its theology, rituals, and organization intimately merged with the concepts, and structures of secular institutions and other aspects of the social order" (Yang, 1961, p. 20). As defined by Yang the "diffuse" type of religion because it is interwoven with the key institutions of a society would also be amenable to being categorized as "pervasive". Also by definition a "diffuse" religion's form and vitality is predicated on that of the secular institutions with which it is interwoven. It would seem logical therefore to assume that in a situation where the secular institutions weaken or cease to exist religious tradition will undergo similar fates. Yang (1961, p. 374) implies the above conclusion when he notes that ancestor worship, a key component of Chinese "diffuse" religion is doomed to debility and eventual extinction in the urban setting which necessarily deprives it of its fundamental institutional base, the wider family unit.

Kwun Tong as an urban-industrial community offers an appropriate site for examining whether the Chinese religious system automatically mirrors the strengths and weaknesses of the institutions with which it has been customarily associated or whether it admits of sufficient flexibility to form a persistent alliance with the newer institutions geared to the demands of an urban-industrial population.

Traditional Religion in Kwun Tong

Despite the obvious existence of numerous variations arising from regional and social class differences we shall join with Freedman (1974, p. 20) in positing that one can speak without undue abstraction or distortion about a single Chinese religious system. Because a fair number of highly readable and readily available works already exist outlining the essential features of that system, e.g. Hsu (1952), Smith (1968), Thompson (1969), and Yang (1961), we shall not dwell in this paper on the details of its composition. What we shall do instead is concentrate on the expression and vitality in Kwun Tong of three of its key practices; the cult of ancestors, the worship of deities, and the erection of temples.

The Cult of Ancestors

While scholars debate the finer details of its elaboration none would take issue with the assertion that ancestor worship is an integral component of Chinese traditional religion. Structurally rooted in the extended family and the patrilineal kinship group it is based on the following three assumptions listed by Hsu (1972, pp. 235-236), "First, all living persons owe their fortunes and misfortunes to the ancestors . . . the second . . . is that all departed ancestors like other gods and spirits have needs that are not different from those of the living . . . the third is that the ancestors continue, as in life, to assist their relatives in the world just as their living descendants can lend a hand to them".

Our concern shall be with discovering the extent to which ancestral worship is still practised by Kwun Tong's residents and its current relationship to secular institutions in that urban setting. Before proceeding, however, we must make clear that we disagree with those who imply that ancestor worship is a form of personal religious identification in the same sense as are "Protestantism" and "Catholicism". Our contention is that survey studies which require respondents to identify themselves exclusively as ancestor worshipper, Buddhists, or members of a Christian denomination, e.g. Mitchell (1974), ignores a key characteristic of Chinese traditional religion, one which Hsu (1972, p. 242) refers to as its "inclusiveness". Unlike in Western "exclusive" religion there is no contradiction attendant on a Chinese person doing ancestral practices along with those associated with one or several other traditions. With the above in mind our attention is directed to whether or not people participate in rites associated with the ancestral cult rather than on the frequency with which they identify themselves exclusively as ancestor worshippers.

The primary source of statistical data on the ancestral cult is a survey recently conducted of 818 representative Kwun Tong households, i.e., the People of Kwun Tong Survey (Ng, 1975). Of special interest to us are two questions which pertain directly to ancestor worship as practised in the households surveyed. The first simply asks whether the husband and/or the wife take an active role in ceremonies associated with the ancestral cult. The data show that one half of the households contain husbands (55.3%) and wives (59.4%) who profess to be active participants in ancestral rites. A second question did not inquire which specific individuals were engaged in worship but simply asked whether or not there was an ancestral shrine present in the home. Ancestral shrines are found in 522 homes (63.8%) including 18 in which neither husband nor wife is an active devotee of the cult. This makes sense if one realizes that some households contain older relatives, usually a grandparent, who continue the rites even though other family members have ceased active participation. The writer knows of several instances in which a grandmother maintains a consistent devote to ancestors despite the fact that all of her children and grandchildren have joined a Christian church.

Examination of typical ancestral shrines in urban homes reveals that most were wooden shelves painted red which can be conveniently attached to the wall or placed on top of a tall piece of furniture. On each end of the altar there is inevitably a red electric lamp shaped like a burning candle. The lamps are turned on in the evening and their distinctive red glow emanating from a multi-storey residential building's windows allow one to make a reasonably accurate count of the number of living units with shrines by tallying the glows from a vantage point on the street. Altars of similar style abound in Kwun Tong commercial establishments. One finds them in such traditional enterprises as tea houses and rice shops as well as in undertakings that are distinctive products of the industrial age such as auto-repair shops and small factories. Ordinarily those found on commercial premises differ from ones in the home in that the former bear in a most prominent position a portrait of a patron deity whereas the latter do not. The altar in the home although it may also be the repository of a deity's statue or portrait usually gives its most central position to a red tablet dedicated to the family's ancestors.

To one familiar with the elaborateness of ancestral tablets found in rural halls or temples, cf. Baker (1968, pp. 105-109), those on urban family altars would appear quite simple. Most often there is only a single tablet inscribed with a general commemoration of all of the family's ancestors. The most common elaboration is a photograph of a recently deceased family member, usually a grandparent. It is rare to find a photograph or any explicit notation of a person who had not been a member of the immediate household. The rites conducted at most such single family dwellings are seldom elaborate. On special feast days or on the death day of a specific ancestor food will be offered, prayers recited, and incense sticks burned. Incense sticks are burned daily at a few shrines but given the crowded conditions of most Kwun Tong households it is not surprising to learn that in several families known to the writer this practice has become a source of household tension with less devout family members objecting to the smell and the smoke created by the incense.

For our purpose there are two facts about the cult of ancestors in Kwun Tong which are worthy of special note. The first is the fact that almost invariably where still operative the cult of ancestors is rooted in and focused on the small household unit, the nuclear family. Seldom has the writer heard an informant mention that he had joined the rites offered for the welfare of the wider descent group since taking up residence in Kwun Tong. The traditional site for the ceremonies has been the village ancestral hall and/ or the large dwellings that housed the more well-to-do rural extended family units. Kwun Tong, however, is almost exclusively a community of multi-storeyed housing blocks with individual living units barely large enough to accommodate families with several children. Ancestral worship where it persists has therefore altered its diffuse structural forms from the wider kinship unit to the compressed nuclear family. Yang (1961, p. 376) contends that the nuclear family alone is not an adequate base for the long-term vitality of the ancestral cult. "While ancestral worship was a vital factor in the solidarity of the traditional consanguinary family, it performed little function for the small conjugal family, which was becoming increasingly common in the urban centers. It is the rural areas where the traditional family has remained the basic unit of social life, that the ancestral cult has retained its vitality."

The second fact is that in many cases there is a lack of family unity even at the nuclear level in the practice of the ancestral cult. We have already noted that there are instances in which only the wife or a grandparent carry on the traditional rites. As we shall note in greater detail below, only about 50% of the children in households where the ancestral rites are practised join in the ceremonies.

The Worship of Deities

The Chinese pantheon consists of an almost innumerable variety of supernatural personages ranging from historical figures deified after death to gods who were from the beginning mythological. Whereas the ancestral cult was rooted in the descent group one can argue that the pantheon in its essential features reflects the political structure of imperial China (Wolf, 1974, pp. 137-145). Serving the political order was not its only role, however, the pantheon also provided gods who could act as protectors and/or advocates for the devout. Two of the gods had an especially prominent place in the traditional household.

The first was Tsao-shen, the Kitchen God, who was charged with overseeing the family's deportment during the year. His image was ordinarily placed near the stove. Each year on the 24th day of the 12th Moon, approximately one week before the Lunar New Year, his image was burned so that he could make his annual report to the Ruler of the Heaven, the Jade Emperor. The second deity was Tu-ti, the Earth God, who was charged with protecting the local region from illness and calamity while also overseeing the population's social deportment. When his shrine is found in the household it is seldom elaborate consisting usually of an incense can on the floor near the doorway or threshold and occasionally a red tablet commemorating the deity.

Because the above two deities and their shrines were common fixtures in the traditional home we propose that their presence or absence in Kwun Tong dwellings is a reliable indicator of the general degree of popularity enjoyed by the cult of the deities in the urban community itself. From the People of Kwun Tong Survey (Ng, 1975), the shrines devoted to the Earth God and to the Kitchen God are present in 494 (60%) and 362 (44%) of the 818 surveyed households, respectively. It is quite clear that Tu-ti whom Werner (1961, p. 527) identifies as a rural, agricultural deity is also popular with residents of Kwun Tong, an urban-industrial community. His shrine is present in almost as many households as are shrines devoted to the ancestors, i.e., Tu-ti = 494, Ancestral Shrine = 522. Tu-ti's greater popularity than Tsao-shen (362 households) may be attributable to both ideological and practical considerations. If, on the ideological level, as Wolf (1974, p. 136) has suggested, we recognize that Tu-ti is more correctly considered a protector of locality rather than simply the guarantor of agricultural prosperity then he can serve this role equally well whether the locale is rural or urban, and, whether the territorial unit be of wide expanse or the crowded quarters of a resettlement estate family. Tu-ti as overseer of the residents' social deportment can also, if necessary, subsume the role of the kitchen god. On the more practical level mitigating against the wider presence of shrines to Tsao-shen is the simple fact that his shrine is not as readily adaptable to the small living units of Kwun Tong dwellers as is that of Tu-ti. Many residents, especially those in older housing estates, just do not have sufficient space within their dwelling units to set aside a place to be used exclusively for cooking. It is common for them to use the passage-way outside of their homes for the preparation of meals. It may indeed seem quite inappropriate to place the Kitchen God's image outside of the home. Tu-ti's shrine, however, since it can simply consist of an incense holder and a tablet placed on the outside threshold is less problematic.

Although shrines to deities are found in well over half of the surveyed households that fact alone, as was also true of the presence of ancestral shrines, provides insufficient grounds for positing that their cult is actively pursued by all members of the households concerned. The lack of family unity in religious matters is quite evident when one looks at the degree to which traditional practices have been adopted by the younger generation in Kwun Tong, the generation born and/or socialized in the urban-industrial setting. The data indicate that the traditional rites are actively pursued by only 24.2% of the children in surveyed households. Even if the 29 households without children are subtracted from the adult total one finds that less than half of the children with at least one parent (457 = one parent) who is active in the ancestral cult and worship of deities follows the example of that parent in religious matters.

The Erection of Temples and Their Cults

Although the essential rites of Chinese traditional religion can easily be carried out in the privacy of the home there is a public dimension expressed in the erection of temples dedicated to favourite local or national deities. In the rural setting such structures were often intimately associated with the host community providing space for worship and the holding of elaborate festivals on the feast day of the patron deity. If the community happens to be an important one for an extended region its temple and deity could serve as a focus of religious devotion for inhabitants of smaller, neighbouring communities, cf. Feuchtwang (1974, pp. 275-276).

One will search in vain for such a temple in Kwun Tong. The district lacks a specific temple associated with itself as a bounded locality or even with any of its sub-units. Residents of Kwun Tong who are wont to frequent temples indicate that they simply worship at those whose deities are judged most efficacious for their present needs. The most popular one is the recently re-modelled (1973) Wong Tai Sin Temple located in an adjacent district that bears the deity's name. The availability of relatively cheap transport also allows for many residents to journey on feast-days or weekends to popular temples in the New Territories or on one of the Colony's outlying islands. Kwun Tong, however, is not without temples. According to the latest un-official estimates there are approximately 40 structures that can be classified as temples in the district. The reason for our offering only an approximation of the number of temples will be clear after we discuss their legal status vis-à-vis the laws of the Colony.

The legal status of temples in Hong Kong is explicitly determined by their conformity or non-conformity to the Chinese Temples Ordinance (Hong Kong Government, 1964, Ch. 153) enacted in 1928 and periodically revised in subsequent years. According to that legislation all temples, monasteries, nunneries, and places where Chinese gods are worshipped and money is collected from the public for such purposes should be registered with the Chinese Temples Committee of the Government's Home Affairs Office and their financial expenditures should be overseen by that same Committee. In some instances the Committee itself actually takes direct responsibility for managing the temples. The expressed purpose of the Ordinance is "to suppress and prevent abuses in the management of Chinese temples and in the administration of the funds of Chinese temples"(Hong Kong Government, 1964, Ch. 153). In Kwun Tong of the approximately 40 temples in existence, only two conform to the Ordinance and are thus considered "legal".

Both of the district's legal temples are dedicated to the Goddess of the Sea—Tin Hau and both are located well outside of the built-up urban area in the vicinity of Lyemun Village. One temple is situated inside of the village itself. It is registered with the Chinese Temples Committee but is administered directly by a committee of local villagers. The other is located outside of the village proper on the near-by seashore. It is under the management of the Chinese Temples Committee. Except for one day a year, the feast day of the Goddess in early summer, the temples attract very little attention from Kwun Tong's urban residents.

Unlike the pair of Tin Hau temples the great majority of the remaining structures were erected by urban dwellers from the "new town". Numbering over three dozen they are considered "illegal" mainly because they are situated on Crown Land belonging to the Government. Several of them have tried to register with the Temples Committee but have been unsuccessful because their sponsors were unable to obtain leases for the land occupied by the temples. Failure to obtain leases and registration has in no way deterred local supporters from constructing sometimes elaborate structures on large tracts of land. The "illegal" temples which are invariably located on hillsides near large housing estates fall into two further categories which define their unofficial relationship with the local authorities. The first is the "illegal-tolerated" temple and the second is the "illegal-untolerated" temple. The above classifications date from the late 1960s when the Government became concerned about the proliferation of "squatter" temples erected on public land near crowded public housing estates. It was then recognized that some served a rather sizeable clientele and seemed to be meeting the religious needs of estate residents while others were make-shift structures used infrequently by worshippers. It was decided that those in the former category could be "tolerated" as long as the land on which they stood was not required for other purposes while those in the latter category were to be torn down by the Squatter Control Sub-office of the Housing Department.

At the time of our most recent inquiry, 1976, there were approximately

20 "illegal-untolerated" temples in the district. These were more often than not make-shift structures of tin and wood which were frequented by only a few worshippers. Many are facilities used by individual religious specialists to dispense sacred medicine and amulets to petitioners. The structures are from time to time torn down by the Housing Department but like a phoenix they appear again after a several day interval.

The second unofficial type of temple, the "illegal-tolerated", is of more importance to us because it usually commands a sizeable clientele and tends to be associated with specific dialect groups in the local community. There are presently 18 temples in Kwun Tong designated as "illegal-tolerated" structures. Two of the largest, i.e. Taih Sing Temple in Sau Mau Ping and Taih Wong Yeh Temple in the Tsui Ping Road Estate, claim to have over 1,000 devotees each. In addition to their being located on hillsides another important geographical characteristic of these temples is their proximity to resettlement estates, the housing units generally peopled by former urban squatters, cf. Table 1. Their location suggests that their clientele is drawn largely from the near-by estates.

Table 1

Location of illegal-tolerated temples

Nearest Residential Complex	N of Temples
Yau Tong Resettlement Estate	2
Lam Tin Resettlement Estate	3
Sau Mau Ping Resettlement Estate	6
Tsui Ping Road Resettlement Estate	4
Jordan Valley Resettlement Estate	1
Ngau Tau Kok Resettlement Estate	2
Total	18

Another characteristic worthy of note about the "tolerated" temples and their devotees is that in the overwhelming majority of cases the temples are associated almost exclusively with natives of non-Cantonese speaking regions of Kwangtung Province. Of the 18 "tolerated" temples 14 are administered and supported by natives of the Chiu-chow counties of eastern Kwangtung Province, 2 by residents of the Hoi Luk Fung region which is adjacent to the western edge of the Chiu-chow counties, and of the remaining 2, only 1 is administered and frequented by Cantonese. The dominant role that Chiu-chow and Hoi Luk Fung natives play in these temples is even more striking when one realizes that they constitute hardly more than a quarter of the district's total population.

We suggest that there are two major factors which account for the tendency of Chiu-chow and Hoi Luk Fung natives to erect their own temples. The first is the existence of a marked regional variation in religious practice between Chiu-chow/Hoi Luk Fung natives and their Cantonese neighbors. The former have a custom of communicatng with the deities through the services of a male spirit-medium known as "Ki-tong". Although the latter do have mediums they are invariably females who specialize in contacting spirits of the deceased rather than possession by deities, cf. Potter (1974), Chiu-chow and Hoi Luk Fung people claim that the temples erected prior to their arrival in Hong Kong which are dominated by Cantonese don't welcome the services of "Ki-tongs". The "illegal-tolerated" temples as well as most of the "Untolerated" ones offer as their primary attraction curing ceremonies conducted by resident mediums. One of the largest and most popular of the "illegal-tolerated temples in Kwun Tong, the "Taih Wong Yeh Miu" in the Tsui Ping Road Estate, was the subject of intensive study by this writer (Myers and Leung, 1974). Taih Wong Yeh which is a Chiu-chow enterprise boasts three official "Ki-tongs" who while possessed by patron deities administer amulets, dispense medicinal herbs, perform exorcism, and predict the future for petitioners. Unlike their rural counterparts in sections of Taiwan, cf. Jordan (1972, pp. 68-69), the urban mediums of Kwun Tong do not conduct ceremonies on demand. Because the mediums hold daytime jobs possession ceremonies except on holidays held each evening at 10 p.m.

The second factor is that shared religious symbols after a minority linguistic group the justification for establishing a place where the native dialect may be spoken freely and where group solidarity can be heightened as well as demonstrated. Taih Wong Yeh is widely recognized in the estate by Cantonese and Chiu-chow as a Chiu-chow undertaking. Members of the temple committee, the spirit-mediums, the over 150 special devotees known as Tang Shang—altar tenders, and the great majority of worshippers are Chiu-chow. Although Cantonese are not explicitly excluded from seeking the medium's assistance their unfamiliarity with the possession ceremony and the Chiu-chow dialect serves as a natural deterrent, cf. Myers and Leung (1974, pp. 31-33). A much more pointed indication of the temple's exclusivity is found in a recent brochure soliciting donations for the construction of a "Hall of One Hundred Surnames" where the tablets of ancestors can be placed. It is explicitly stated that the places in the Hall are reserved for the tablets of "Fellow-Countymen" and their ancestors, i.e. "Fellow Chiu-chow".

The theme of linguistic group solidarity is but thinly veiled in the two most prominent and conspicuously celebrated festivals in the Kwun Tong district. The first is the feast day of the mythological "Great Sage Equal to Heaven" commonly known as Monkey, cf. Wu (1942). On that day which occurs in mid-summer the large "tolerated" temple dedicated to Monkey in the Sau Mau Ping Resettlement Estate sponsors a three day celebration in his honour. A public playground near the temple becomes the site for a large bamboo pavilion in which a Chiu-chow opera is performed. Chiu-chow spirit-mediums from throughout Kowloon hold numerous possession cere-monies and some of the more experienced perform feats such as walking on sword ladders and various types of self-flagellation. The festival attracts by conservative estimate 10,000 people a day and the great majority of whom are Chiu-chow. The second festival celebrated with great public display is the "Hungry Ghosts Festival"—"Yue Lam" which occurs during the Seventh Lunar month. In 1975 there were 13 requests to the local authorities for permission to use public land for "Yue Lam" activities. Invariably the cele-bration calls for the erection of opera pavilions, the holding of spirit possession performances, and the recitation of prayers for the dead. In each instance the promoters, the organizers, and the chief participants were Chiu-chow. It is evident that the festivals serve not only as a symbol of religious devotion but also as an instrument for promoting and expressing Chiu-chow solidarity.

Even our brief discussion of temples in Kwun Tong reveals an important characteristic of the district's social landscape, the importance placed by a sizeable portion of the residents on linguistic identity as basis for the formation of sub-groups. The Chiu-chow in particular have employed that principle in the establishment of specialized associations aimed ultimately at strengthening and/or protecting their niche in the local community. Kwun Tong boasts a sizeable array of Chiu-chow organizations ranging from rice-merchants associations to fraternal societies. The temples and festivals of Kwun Tong testify to a subtle but significant broadening of the institutional base of traditional religion for a sector of Kwun Tong's population. For many Chiu-chow and Hoi Luk Fung natives the host institution is no longer simply the family. It now includes that characteristically urban institution the minority speech group, or less correctly in this instance, the ethnic group.

Conclusion

In this chapter we have touched lightly on only one dimension of the religious situation in Kwun Tong, Chinese traditional religion. A more com-plete treatment must take into account the residents who have become Christians as well as others who profess no religious involvement whatsoever. However, precisely because of this study's limited scope it has been able to bring into sharper relief the role and, perhaps even the essential fate of a "diffuse" religious system in a population's adjustment to an urban-industrial environment.

Kwun Tong conforms neither to Sjoberg's (1960) stereotype of the "scared" pre-industrial city nor Cox's (1965) notion of the "secular" modern urban-industrial metropolis. We suggest rather that it is a community in which a religious system that was formerly "pervasive" throughout the few institutions of a solidified pre-industrial society is undergoing the process of "restriction" to a limited selection of the compressed institutions of a fragmented industrial society. Ancestral worship where practised has been pressed into the service of and effectively restricted to the nuclear family. The cult of deities is invoked almost exclusively on behalf of the individual and his household. Temples erected in the district are devoted to the promotion of solidarity among minority sub-groups rather than to serve the wider community. The most formidable challenge facing Chinese traditional religion is the spirit of individualism fostered by the erosion of particularistic values. As we have seen with respect to ancestral worship and the cult of the deities, family loyalty, regional customs and cultural identity are no longer viewed, especially by the younger generation of Kwun Tong residents, as sufficient cause for pursuing traditional rites. The future vitality or debility of the religious system may rest in its ability to perform a useful role for the ultimate structural unit of a fragmented society, the individual.

Bibliography

Baker, Hugh (1968) *A Chinese Lineage Village: Sheung Shui*. Stanford, Calif.

de Coulanges, Fustel (1956) *The Ancient City*. New York.

Cox, Harvey (1965) *The Secular City*. New York.

Feuchtwang, Stephen (1974) "City Temples in Taipei Under Three Regimes," in *The Chinese City Between Two Worlds*. edited by Mark Elvin and G. William Skinner. Stanford, Calif.

Freedman, Maurice (1974) "On the Sociological Study of Chinese Religion," in *Religion and Ritual in Chinese Society*, edited by Arthur Wolf. Stanford, Calif.

Herberg, Will (1955) *Protestant—Catholic—Jew*. New York.

Hong Kong Government (1964) *The Laws of Hong Kong*. Hong Kong.

Hsu, Francis L. K. (1952) *Religion Science and Human Crisis*. London.

———— (1972) *Americans and Chinese*. New York.

Jordan, David (1972) *Gods, Ghosts and Ancestors*. Berkeley, Calif.

Mitchell, Robert (1974) "Religion Among Urban Chinese and Non-Chinese in Southeast Asian Countries," *Social Compass*, Vol. 21, pp. 25-44.

Social Life and Development in Hong Kong

Myers, John and Davy Leung (1974) *A Chinese Spirit-Medium Temple in Kwun Tong: A Preliminary Report.* Hong Kong.

Ng, Pedro (1975) *The People of Kwun Tong Survey—Data Book.* Hong Kong.

Parsons, Talcott (1971) *The System of Modern Societies.* Englewood Cliffs, N. J.

Potter, Jack (1974) "Cantonese Shamanism," in *Religion and Ritual in Chinese Society*, edited by Arthur Wolf. Stanford, Calif.

Sjoberg, Golden (1960) *The Pre-Industrial City.* New York.

Smith, D. Howard (1968) *Chinese Religions.* New York.

Thompson, Laurence (1969) *Chinese Religion.* Belmont, Calif.

Werner, E.T.C. (1961) *A Dictionary of Chinese Mythology.* New York.

Wheatley, Paul (1971) *The Pivot of Four Corners.* Chicago.

Wolf, Arthur (1974) "God, Ghosts and Ancestors," in *Religion and Ritual in Chinese Society*, edited by Arthur Wolf. Stanford, Calif.

Wu Cheng-en (1942) *Monkey.* Trans. by Arthur Waley. London.

Yang, C. K. (1961) *Religion in Chinese Society.* The Regents of the University of California, Calif.

Chapter 15

Face Saving in Chinese Culture:
A Discussion and Experimental Study of Hong Kong Students*

Michael H. Bond and Peter W. H. Lee

人要臉，樹要皮——"A man needs face like a tree needs its bark." There are many such expressions about face in Chinese folk wisdom which underscore its importance in the subjective culture[1] of the Chinese. In a seminal paper Hu[2] collected many of these sayings, grouping them into one of two categories. According to her analysis there are two basic categories of face in Chinese culture, *lien* 臉 and *mien-tzu* 面子. *Mien-tzu* "stands for the kind of prestige that is emphasized in this country (America): a reputation achieved through getting on in life, through success and ostentation" (p. 45). *Lien*, on the other hand, "represents the confidence of society in the integrity of ego's moral character, the loss of which makes it impossible for him to function properly within the community" (p. 45). This linguistic difference reflects the difference in the conditions under which the two types of face are gained and lost.

In a recent article King and Myers[3] have argued that the *mien-tzu* of Hu's paper corresponds to social/positional face, obtaining of which requires visible success in meeting well-established social guidelines. As such *mien-tzu* can only be won or lost when an audience exists to bestow or deny one face. Hu's *lien*, however, is a moral face whose dictates are typically internalized. As such, *lien* can be lost and a sense of guilt produced in the absence of an audience to witness the transgression. *Mien-tzu* and *lien* thus differ in the conditions necessary for their loss, the former requiring an audience, the latter not.

*This research was supported by a grant to the first author from the Institute of Social Sciences and the Humanities of The Chinese University of Hong Kong. Institutional assistance was provided by the University's Social Research Centre. The authors wish to thank David Ho, Richard Lyczak, and Rance Lee for their wise counsel in the planning stages of this project.

[1] H. C. Triandis, *The analysis of subjective culture*. New York: Wiley, 1972.

[2] H. C. Hu, The Chinese concept of "face". *American Anthropologist*, 1944, *46*, 45-64.

[3] A. Y. C. King and J. T. Myers, Shame as an incomplete conception of Chinese culture: a study of face. Social Research Centre, The Chinese University of Hong Kong, 1977.

Western analyses of face do not distinguish between these two aspects of face, although the distinction can be easily accommodated. The classic discussion in Western social science is that of Goffman.[4] He defined the term "face" as "the positive social value a person effectively claims for himself by the line others assume he has taken during a particular contact" (p. 213). Goffman argues that in any social contact each person communicates his view of the situation, of the other participants, and most importantly, of himself through his verbal and non-verbal acts. This line a person communicates about himself in the face he claims in this particular interaction.

Contacts flow smoothly as long as everybody's claim to face is supported by the events that occur during the contact. As Goffman puts it, "A person may be said to 'have', or 'be in', or 'maintain' face when the line he effectively takes presents an image of him that is internally consistent, that is supported by judgements and evidence conveyed by other participants, and that is confirmed by evidence conveyed through impersonal agencies in the situation" (p. 214). Sometimes, however, events or people conspire to invalidate a person's claim to face. The interaction then breaks down, as all parties to the contact become uncomfortable, flustered, and nervous. The person whose face has been lost will, in addition, feel ashamed and embarrassed. At this point the terms of the interaction need to be reconstructed before the contact can again proceed smoothly.[5]

Using Goffman's analysis, a number of recent studies have explored the state of embarrassment and its effects on the subsequent behaviour of the embarrassed person.[6] The standard technique for producing embarrassment experimentally involves putting the subject into a position where he loses face. So, for example, Apsler induced people to perform foolish tasks in front

[4] E. Goffman, On face-work. *Psychiatry*, 1955, *18*, 213-231.

[5] E. Goffman, Embarrassment and social organization. *American Journal of Sociology*, 1956, *62*, 264-271.

[6] R. Apsler, Effects of embarrassment on behaviour toward others. *Journal of Personality and Social Psychology*, 1975, *32*, 145-153.

B. Berk, Face-saving at the singles dance. *Social Problems*, 1977, *24*, 530-545.

B. R. Brown, The effects of need to maintain face on interpersonal bargaining. *Journal of Experimental Social Psychology*, 1968, *4*, 107-122.

B. R. Brown, Face-saving following experimentally induced embarrassment. *Journal of Experimental Social Psychology*, 1970, *6*, 255-271.

B. R. Brown and H. Garland, The effects of incompetency, audience acquaintanceship, and anticipated evaluative feedback on face-saving behavior. *Journal of Experimental Social Psychology*, 1971, *7*, 490-502.

H. Garland and B. R. Brown, Face-saving as affected by subjects' sex, audiences' sex and audience expertise. *Sociometry*, 1972, *35*, 280-289.

A. Modigliani, Embarrassment, face-work, and eye contact. *Journal of Personality and Social Psychology*, 1971, *17*, 15-24.

of an audience, thus making their implicit claim to face as mature and sophisticated undergraduates untenable. Under these and other threats to face, embarrassed people engage in a wide variety of behaviours in order to restore face.

The experimental work on face in the West has not been concerned with an actor's *lien*, as it is difficult and often unethical to manipulate this aspect of a person's self-concept. Rather, the experimental work has dealt with an actor's *mien-tzu* by bringing into doubt the actor's implicit claim to such amoral features of social/positional performance as poise, competence, or maturity.

The question of face-saving also remains relatively unexplored. There have been no experiments exploring when actors behave in such a way as to prevent damage to another's face from occurring. The study reported in this paper is a first step towards filling this gap.

Since a loss of face creates embarrassment and disrupts the smooth flow of the interaction, it is in the interests of all parties to avoid such an episode. In addition, Goffman[7] has argued that, "Since the individual dislikes to feel or appear embarrassed, tactful persons will avoid placing him in this position" (p. 268). In effect the individual who causes another to lose face, may himself lose face if the situation did not justify his compromising the other person. Having inappropriately embarrassed someone, he can no longer support a social identity as a kind or considerate person. Finally, Ho[8] has observed that causing another to lose face is typically construed as an aggressive act by the person whose face has been discredited. So, to avoid conflict it is prudent to sidestep any behaviour which could lead to another's loss of face. From many points of view, then, a reciprocal conspiracy of face-saving is a mutually beneficial regulator in social interaction.

Protecting another from losing face is an act of consideration, occasionally with some cost to the actor. In some cases one must put loyalty to the vulnerable person ahead of one's view of truth or correctness. In a public setting one may run the risk of being regarded an "uncritical" or "unobjective", in effect suffering a loss to one's own face in the act of protecting another's.

One positive result for the actor who saves another's face, however, is a sense of grateful obligation on the part of the recipient. As one Chinese expression puts the matter: 山水有相逢. Loosely translated the proverb warns that, "At different times and in different places, we will meet again." The implication of the remark, of course, is that we should therefore take

---

[7] Refer to Footnote 5.

[8] D. Y. F. Ho, Face, social expectations, and conflict avoidance. Paper presented at the First International Conference of the International Association for Cross-Cultural Psychology, Hong Kong, 1972.

care to assist one another for we ourselves may later be vulnerable. Conversely, when we assist another by saving his face, there will be future occasions for the recipient to express his gratitude.

In what kinds of society should one expect to see a greater emphasis on face-saving? As the above proverb suggests, being known to one another rather than being anonymous will increase the incidence of prosocial behaviour. Considerable experimental evidence indicates this to be the case.[9] Any society whose membership is geographically stable and whose numbers are relatively small should therefore have a stronger code of behaviour about face-saving, as anonymity will be unusual in such a society.

In addition, the act of saving another's face promotes cohesiveness among group members who help one another in this way. This is particularly true when outsiders are present to witness the potential loss of face. A high value should then be placed on face-saving behaviour in any society where members achieve their identity more through group participation than through individual activities. Face-saving protects group integrity and will therefore be a valued behaviour.

It is not surprising therefore that we have an elaborated social wisdom about face-saving in static societies focussed around group life but much less emphasis on face-saving in mobile societies focussed on individuals. This is not to assert, as have Agassi and Jarvie,[10] that matters of face are pre-eminently an Oriental, rather than a Western concern. The authors agree with Ho[11] that an understanding of face is of universal importance in conceptualizing human behaviour. As Ho has written, "Anyone who does not wish to declare his social bankruptcy must show a regard for face. He must claim for himself, and must extend to others, some degree of compliance, respect, and deference in order to maintain a minimum level of effective social functioning. While it is true that the conceptualization of what constitutes face and the rules governing face behaviour vary considerably across cultures, the concern for face is invariant." (pp. 26-27)

Across all cultures, then, everyone must be careful when criticizing others. Regardless of how strongly the demands of the situation legitimize such criticism, there is always the risk of causing the other to lose face, for criticism involves comparing a person's performance against socially defined standards and finding the performance deficient. Should the person being criticized

---

[9]M. H. Bond and D. G. Dutton, The effect of interaction anticipation and experience as a victim on aggressive behavior. *Journal of Personality*, 1975, *43*, 515-527.

[10]J. Agassi and I. C. Jarvie, A study in westernization. In I. C. Jarvie and J. Agassi (eds.), *Hong Kong: a society in transition*. London: Routledge and Kegan Paul, 1969.

[11]D. Y. F. Ho, On the concept of face. *American Journal of Sociology*, 1975, *81*, 867-884.

regard adequate performance in this area as a part of his or her public identity, his or her face thereby becomes threatened.

Here we can see the judge's dilemma of whether he should serve truth or serve the performer in making his evaluations. Obviously, people must develop some sophistication in judging when and how to criticize the performance of others and yet still protect the face of those being criticized. This dilemma is particularly acute when the actor lives in an authoritarian society and evaluates the performance of a superior, for, as Stover[12] has argued, criticism in this context has implications beyond the face of the superior. The act of a subordinate criticizing a superior threatens the social order, undermining the authoritarian structuring of the society. Under these circumstances the truth of the criticism may be considered less significant than the revolutionary implications of a subordinate's questioning the performance of a superior.

When such criticism is perceived as necessary in such a society, one would except to see the criticism hedged with numerous qualifiers. Thus, for example, the critical comments might be preceded by numerous references to the virtues and skills of the superior in his performance. The subordinate might also deprecate his own abilities, clearly disqualifying himself as a competant critic or as an aspirant for the superior's position. Finally, the content of the criticism would probably be stated indirectly and with many linguistic modifiers. The social ordering thus preserved, the interactants could switch their attention to the content of the subordinate's criticism.

This degree of concern about maintaining order is one relevant way in which societies differ from one another. It is in fact one of the central dimensions along which Hsu[13] has compared Chinese and American cultures. Stover[14] has underscored the importance of structural harmony within Chinese society by emphasizing the importance of *Li* 禮 as one of the Five Virtues. He defines *Li* as, "Right conduct in maintaining one's place in a hierarchical order . . . " (p. 246). The psychological reality of this concern for maintaining order is reflected in research showing relatively higher levels of variables related to this construct (e.g., authoritarianism, social orientation, etc.) in Chinese society.[15] As a common Chinese expression underscores the issue, "Seniors and juniors have their ranking" (長幼有序).

[12] L. E. Stover, *The cultural ecology of Chinese civilization*. New York: New American Library, 1974, Ch. 16.

[13] F. L. K. Hsu, *Americans and Chinese: two ways of life*. New York: Abelard-Schuman, 1953.

[14] Refer to Footnote 12.

[15] C. H. Huang, A study of the personal preferences of Chinese university students by Edwards' Personal Preference Schedule. *Psychology and Education*, 1967, *1*, 52-67.

R. D. Meade and J. O. Whittaker, A cross-cultural study of authoritarianism. *Journal of Social Psychology*, 1967, *72*, 3-7.

If the argument made here is correct, we would expect a more extensive code concerning face, a heightened reluctance to criticize, especially superiors, greater social rewards accorded those skilled at preserving others' faces, and vaguer, more indirect language being used in any criticism of another's performances between any two societies differing in thier concern about order-maintenance. So, although the concern for face may be universal, as Ho[16] has argued, the extent of that concern probably differs from culture to culture in response to this societal variable.

The above hypotheses require cross-cultural studies for their validation. One starting point is to develop a methodology for observing face-saving behaviour. Such is the aim of the experiment recorded here which uses conventional wisdom about face to suggest testable hypotheses about when criticism of others is avoided on the one hand or disinhibited on the other. Hopefully, comparative studies will be done in other cultures using this paradigm.

The ideal situation for criticizing is to allow the persons criticizing to make their comments under the guarantee that the person being evaluated will not see the evaluations. This procedure eliminates the possibility of ingratiation tactics[17] by the judge and prevents embarrassment to the performer. Less ideal is to communicate your criticism to the performer anonymously. Here the performer's face is in jeopardy, but the judge cannot be identified and therefore need not face the consequences of embarrassing the other. A more awkward situation is one where the critic must convey his criticism to the performer in person. Here the judge must witness the embarrassment of the performer and face possible retaliation. The situation becomes even more complicated if others are present when the judge gives his evaluation to the performer. For, here the damage to face is spread more widely, affecting the performer's relationship with others in addition to the judge. Again, retaliation is possible.

The net result of these considerations should be a decrease in critical behaviour by the judges as we move through these four situations. The present experiment attempted to test this prediction by using a situation where judges assessed another's impromptu speech under one of these four conditions.

P. N. Singh, S. C. Huang, and G. C. Thompson, A comparative study of selected attitudes, values and personality characteristics of American, Chinese, and Indian students. *Journal of Social Psychology*, 1962, 57, 123-132.

K. S. Yang, Social orientation and individual modernity among Chinese students in Taiwan. Unpublished manuscript, National Taiwan University, 1979.

[16]Refer to Footnote 11.

[17]E. E. Jones, *Ingratiation: a social psychological analysis*. New York: Appleton-Century-Crofts, 1964.

Method

Subjects

55 female and 45 male undergraduates at the Chinese University participated in the study as partial fulfillment of the requirements for Introductory
Psychology.

Procedure

Contact with subjects throughout the experiment was made by the second
author using the participants' native language, Cantonese. Stimulus materials
were also written in Chinese.

Subjects were recruited in same-sex groups of five persons. As they signed
up, the experimenter asked the students not to join groups where their friends
were already members.

As subjects arrived for the experiment, they sat outside two experimental
rooms. On the doors to these rooms, the experimenter had placed large signs
in Chinese saying "The Chinese University Exploration of Student Public
Speaking".

When all five subjects had arrived for any session, the experimenter escorted
them into Room 1, a moderate-size room empty except for some chairs at
one end and a covered table with chairs in the middle. He explained to them
that the Psychology Department was starting a programme on public speaking.
As a first step students such as themselves were being asked to assess impromptu speeches given by their fellow students. Thus, one of them would
be selected to deliver such a speech, the others to listen and assess. At this
point the experimenter checked to ensure that none of the participants were
friends, as this might "destroy objectivity".

One subject was then chosen by drawing lots to give a three-minute talk on
"The difference between high-school and university life". While the speaker
was planning his presentation, the experimenter took the remaining subjects
to the adjoining Room 2 and asked them to sit at pre-arranged desks.

These four desks all faced a one-way mirror and loudspeaker which connected Rooms 1 and 2. The desks were separated by partitions so that the
judges of the speech could not see one another or what they would later be
writing. The experimenter stood before the curtains drawn across the mirror
to supervise the giving of instructions. On the table in front of all judges lay a
booklet with an identical cover page which read "Chinese University Exploration of Student Public Speaking". Students turned the page and read an
explanation of the study which was similar to the verbal presentation made
earlier by the experimenter. The instructions underscored that they were to
focus on both the strengths and the weaknesses of the speaker. This double

focus was included to counteract too critical a set and provide some latitude of response for the judges.

After checking to ensure all the listeners understood their job, the experimenter asked them to read the next page which contained the experimental manipulations. There were four conditions, one of which had been randomly assigned to each desk before each session began, using a procedure which separated the third and fourth conditions. This design assured that experimental condition was not confounded with viewing position.

The judges in the speaker uninformed condition (condition one) read that their comments and ratings would be seen only by the experimenter. The experimenter would not discuss the evaluation with the speaker and would allow the judge to leave the experiment well before the speaker. In this condition, as in all others, it was noted that the experimenter himself would not read the evaluations until after both judge and speaker had left.

In the informed anonymous condition (condition two), judges read that the speakers would be shown their evaluations by the experimenter. However, it was made clear that the judges would leave the experiment well before the speaker and that the experimenter would leave the room while the speaker was reading the evaluations. This latter precaution was necessary to prevent judges from saving the speaker's face in front of the experimenter.

In the informed face-to-face condition (condition three), the judges were told that they would be taken to the adjoining room so that they could read their comments and their ratings to the speaker privately. It was made clear that the experimenter would leave the room during this report and would not discuss the judge's evaluation with the speaker at any time. Again, these assurances were necessary to stop the judges from saving the speaker's face in front of the experimenter.

Finally, in the informed-audience condition (condition four) the judges were informed that they would read their comments and ratings to the speaker in the presence of the next group of five subjects. As before, the experimenter would not be present nor would he discuss the evaluations with the speaker.

All judges were asked to re-read their instructions. If they had any problems, they were to raise their hands so that the experimenter could come over and clarify any confusions quietly. This procedure effectively prevented the subjects' learning that they had different instructions.

At this stage the experimenter checked to ensure that the speaker was ready. He then turned off the lights, opened the curtains in front of the one-way mirror and knocked on the glass, signalling the speaker to begin. Three minutes later, the experimenter again signalled the speaker to stop, closed the curtains, and turned on the lights.

The instructions on the next page of the booklet asked the judges to spend three minutes writing down the strong and the weak points of each speaker's presentation. Judges were asked to recall how their comments would be used.

A short period of time was given to allow maximum opportunity for face-saving to occur. In a longer period judges might have felt compelled to included everything they had noticed rather than being more selective.

Three minutes later the experimenter had the judges stop and proceed to the ratings of the speaker and the speech. These were Likert-type scales, six for the speech, seven for the speaker, and one for an overall rating. Each scale had seven points, each point with its associated verbal label. So, for example, judges were to check whether the speech was extremely fluent, fluent, mildly fluent, neither fluent nor halting, mildly halting, halting, extremely halting. All points on the scale were labelled, because judges in the informed-face-to-face and audience conditons knew they would be required to read their ratings later. All judges were reminded in their booklets of how their ratings would be used prior to filling out the scales.

After completing the ratings judges were asked in the booklet to write down their general reactions to the task of evaluating the speaker. It was indicated that these comments were for the experimenter only.

The final page consisted of five seven-point scales measuring the judges' reactions to their experience of evaluating a fellow student. The first three tapped perceived difficulty of the task, how carefree vs cautious the judge felt while evaluating, and how concerned he was about the speaker's possible reactions. The final two items mentioned the concept of "face" explicitly, the first scale asking judges how much they worried about the speaker's face when evaluating, the final scale asking judges how much they were concerned about their own face.

When all judges had finished writing, the experimenter asked judges in conditions one and two to leave the room with him. He then thanked and dismissed these subjects separately. Judges in conditions three and four remained, but their positions had initially been separated in the random design to avoid any discussion during the experimenter's absence.

He returned to the judges in conditions three and four about five minutes later. The experimenter took the judge in condition three to Room 1 where the judge read his comments and ratings to the speaker.

Meanwhile the experimenter returned to Room 2 and remarked to the judge in condition four that the next group of students had not yet arrived. Therefore, instead of reading his evaluations to the speaker in front of this audience, the judge would have to give his reactions to the speaker alone.

When the judge in condition three finished reading his other comments to the speaker, he was taken from Room 2 by the experimenter, thanked, and dismissed. The judge in condition four then followed the same procedure.

This process of dismissing the judges was designed to make it appear as if all were in the same experimental conditions and to prevent the opportunity to discover any difference concerning the experimental instructions.

All subjects were debriefed by mail following the experiment and given an opportunity to discuss the study and their reactions with the experimenters.

Content Analysis of Comments

The first dependent measure taken was the judges' written comments about the speaker and the speech. Careful inspection of the protocols revealed a variety of types of comment made. To minimize the number of assumptions used in scoring, all types of comment were treated equally whether they referred to the speech, the speaker or the speaker's behaviour. Each comment was given a score of plus or minus four depending on whether it was a positive or a negative remark.

Any qualification of the statements made, however, was taken into account. Thus, an exaggeration in a comment such as, "The speaker continually figgeted." increased the value of the comment by a half, in this case from minus four to minus six. Similarly a qualification such as, "The speaker was fairly poised", reduced the value by a half, in this case from plus four to plus two.

One category worth nothing separately was the situational reference. This was defined as any reference to the speaker's situation in giving the speech such as, "Despite the short time for preparation . . . . " Such situational references were scored as either qualifications of a negative remark or as accentuations of a positive remark, again changing the value of the associated remark by one half.

The experimenters then practised scoring together until reasonable consensus was achieved. Finally each experimenter independently scored the protocols of all 80 subjects, the first author scoring the English translations, the second author scoring the Chinese originals.

Results

Treatment of Data

One problem in analyzing the data was that the level of competence in public speaking varied widely across the 20 speakers. Thus, there were some speakers who were unanimously rated in very negative terms by their four judges; some speakers who were rated positively. Such differences among speakers have the effect of seriously inflating the within cell variance relative to differences between the four conditons.

To eliminate speaker variance, therefore, the average level of speaker competence was equated in the following way. For any given measure, the four scores for any one speaker were added together and averaged. Deviations from that average were then calculated for each judge. 2 X 4 analyses of variance were performed on the deviations. This procedure had the effect of preserving the differences between conditions without adding speaker variance to the within cell variance which already existed due to differences among the judges in any cell. Such a procedure meant, however, that differences in overall level of criticism between males and females could not be detected. This question was not, however, of major interest.

Analysis of the Rating Scales

There were 14 scales used, seven to evaluate the speaker and six for the speech plus a final overall rating. The 13 specific scales each had a mid-point designated an "neither X nor Y" depending on which attribute was being assessed. A check at this mid-point communicated neither praise nor criticism. In calculating the impact of the rating, therefore, only deviations from this mid-point was scored. These deviations ranged from 1 to 3 and were scored as plus or minus depending on whether the positive or negative side of the attribute was chosen.

The overall impact of the ratings was of greater interest than differences on any of the particular 13 dimensions rated. Consequently, summed deviations were taken from each judge across the 13 scales to yield a total score from the ratings.

An analysis of variance on these total ratings yielded a significant effect across experimental conditons $F(3, 72) = 4.14, p < .01$ with an insignificant interaction $F(3, 72) = 2.54$, ns.

The linear component of the effect across conditions was also significant $F(1, 72) = 11.2, p < .005$. A Duncan's test on the differences among the means showed the speaker uninformed condition as generating more negative ratings than the informed audience condition ($p < .005$).

These differences across conditions could have resulted in one, perhaps two, ways. On the one hand judges could have made more negative than positive ratings. On the other hand, those ratings which showed some deviation could have been made at a more extreme level. Either or both events could have affected the total ratings. These possibilities are examined below.

Number of negative minus positive ratings

The effect across conditions was significant $F(3, 72) = 4.21, p < .01$; the interaction was not $F(3, 72) = 2.07$, ns. A Duncan's analysis of the difference across conditions showed the speaker uninformed conditions as yielding more negative ratings than the informed anonymous ($p < .005$), informed face-to-face ($p < .05$) and informed audience ($p < .005$) conditions. The linear component of this main effect was also significant $F(1,72) = 11.46, p < .005$.

Amount of criticism per deviation

The analysis of this variable also showed a significant difference across conditions $F(3,72) = 4.76, p < .001$ and an insignificant interaction $F(3,72) = 2.56$, ns. A Duncan's test of the main effect showed both the speaker uninformed and informed anonymous conditions as producing higher average levels of criticism than the informed audience condition (p's $< .001$ and $< .05$ respectively). Again the linear component of the effect across conditions was significant $F(1,72) = 13.76, p < .001$.

Table 1

Average total score on 13 rating scales divided by
number of deviations from zero

	Speaker Uninformed	Informed Anonymous	Informed Face-to-face	Informed Audience	
Male Judges	0.2	0.1	0.0	0.5	0.2
Female Judges	−0.3	0.1	0.4	0.5	0.2
	−0.1	0.1	0.2	0.5	

The overall rating

The effect across experimental conditions on this single rating scale was not significant $F(3, 72) = 2.41$, ns. although the linear component across experimental conditions was $F(1, 72) = 5.49, p < .025$. The pattern of cell means was similar to that of the total derived from the 13 scales, correlating .74.

Analysis of the Unstructured Comments

The inter-judge reliability for the criticism scores derived from the unstructured comments was .98.

Total score

An analysis of variance on these scores yielded an $F(3, 72)$ of 2.40 (ns) across conditions and an interaction $F(3, 72)$ of 1.64 (ns). The linear component of the difference across conditions was significant, however, $F(1, 72) = 4.38, p < .05$.

Number of negative minus positive statements

The inter-judge reliability for the number of statements made by the judges was .98. The few discrepancies were resolved by a decision of the senior author.

The analysis of variance showed no effect across experimental conditions $F(3, 72) < 1$ and no interaction $F(3, 72) = 1.49$, ns. The linear component of the difference across conditions was not significant $F(1, 72) = 1.58$, ns.

Amount of criticism per statement

The effect across conditions for this variable was significant $F(3, 72) = 2.77, p < .05$; the interaction was not $F(3, 72) < 1$, ns. A Duncan's analysis of the main effect again showed the subject uninformed condition yielding more criticism per statement than the informed audience condition ($p < .05$). Again the linear component of the main effect was significant $F(1, 72) = 6.96, p < .025$.

Table 2

Average total score from unstructured comments
divided by number of comments

	Speaker Uninformed	Informed Anonymous	Informed Face-to-face	Informed Audience	
Male Judges	−1.3	−0.5	−1.1	−0.2	−0.8
Female Judges	−1.1	−0.3	0.2	0.2	−0.3
	−1.2	−0.4	−0.4	0.0	

Judges' Reactions to the Task of Evaluating

None of the five scales showed any effects.

Discussion

Two different sources were used to measure the judges' tendency to be critical of the speakers: unstructured comments and rating scales. These two sources produced total scores which correlated .59. This correlation is high enough to suggest that both measures are tapping the same underlying process. Effects common to both measures should, therefore, indicate robust findings.

The average level of criticism per response was the measure which yielded differences across conditions for both types of criticism. In each case Duncan's test indicated that more critical levels of response were given in the speaker uninformed condition than in the informed audience condition. Inspection of the means shows the responses in the informed anonymous and informed face-to-face conditions falling about mid-point between these two extremes. Indeed the linear component across the four conditions was significant for both measures, accounting for more than 84% of the between cells effect in each case.

This pattern of results would appear to confirm the hypotheses about face-saving made in the introduction with two qualifications. The first is that the measure most likely to show consistent sensitivity to the face manipulations was not the number of criticisms or the total level of criticism but rather the average level of criticism per response. This result parallels results from the person perception area where an averaging model has proved more successful than a summation model in predicting final impressions formed.[18] The present results suggest that we may send our impressions in the same way we receive them.

The second qualification is that there was no difference in the level of criticism between the informed anonymous and face-to-face conditions across both sexes. However, examination of Tables 1 and 2 shows males and females giving opposite patterns of results across these two conditions. Resolution of this question must await further research.

What contrast then might account for the pattern of results? Fear of counter-attack does not seem adequate to explain the reduction in criticism for two reasons. First, judges are less critical in the informed anonymous condition where no counter-attack was possible. Second, judges are less critical in the informed audience condition than the face-to-face condition even though the potential for counter-attack was the same in both situations.

Increasing empathy[19] seems a much more reasonable explanation for the increasing moderation of criticism seen across conditions. Such empathy would have been absent in the speaker uninformed condition as the judges knew that the speaker would not have access to the evaluations. Hence there was no fear of hurting the speaker with their criticism. In the informed anonymous and informed face-to-face conditions, however, the speaker would possibly have suffered as a result of the judge's criticisms and so the criticisms were moderated. In the informed audience condition, the criticisms would have become public, extending beyond the judge-speaker dyad. Here the potential for loss of face and embarrassment of the speaker was magnified.

[18]N. H. Anderson, Adding versus averaging as a stimulus combination rule in impression formation. *Journal of Experimental Psychology*, 1965, *70*, 394–400.

[19]E. Stotland, Exploratory investigations of empathy. In L. Berkowitz (ed.), *Advances in experimental social psychology* (Vol. 4). New York: Academic Press, 1965.

The judge's empathy for the speaker was correspondingly greater, and so the criticisms were moderated further.

This empathetic concern was shown in many of the written comments made by judges in the informed conditions following the experiment. One subject wrote, "I am worried that the speaker will be unhappy when he reads my comments and hope he doesn't take them too seriously, because after all he had no time for preparation and the situation was strange. I hope he doesn't mind." (informed anonymous condition). Another wrote, "I don't want my criticisms to hurt another's confidence and self-concept." (informed audience condition). These, and other similar comments, indicate the judges' worry about the possible effects of their comments on the speakers.

Despite such examples of solicitude, none of the post-experimental questions relating to a concern for the speaker's possible reactions showed any differences across conditions. An analysis of the comments written by the judges after the experiment suggests why no differences were found.

The most striking feature of these comments was the judges' desire to be "good" evaluators by providing "objective", "accurate", and "reliable" feedback to the speakers and to the experimenter. Despite the attempt to ensure subjects that their personal perceptions were valuable, the judges repeatedly saw their own comments as "too subjective" or "too biased" and described themselves as "unskilled" or as "inexperienced".

Part of this general reaction reflects the subjects' reluctance to criticize others, even strangers. By pointing to their lack of expertise, the judges were in effect qualifying the criticisms they were required to make as experimental subjects.

The comments also indicate that subjects saw themselves as participating in a scientific enterprise requiring objective responses from them. This concern of the judges for providing accurate evaluations probably explains why none of the post-experimental measures tapping concern for the speaker's reactions showed any differences across experimental conditions. The judges after all had to maintain their own "face" as responsible and truthful observers, uninfluenced by personal considerations.

Despite the press for objectivity, the basic dilemma involved in all evaluation still existed. As one judge put it, "If the speaker is not good, I must simply tell him so, even though I can't get rid of my uneasy feeling." Fortunately, the criteria for evaluation in this situation were sufficiently imprecise that consideration of the speaker's face could operate to temper the criticism despite the demands for objectivity. As one judge wrote, "To criticize a speech is not an easy thing, but there are no accepted standards, so we often add in our subjectivity when evaluating." Face can be given as long as the criteria for evaluation remain flexible.

These results suggest possible hypotheses for future research. First, it could be argued that any instructional set which increases an observer's empathy for the performer will moderate criticism of the actor's performance. Secondly, any personality variable relating to an objective or impersonal approach to evaluating others' behaviour should lead to increased criticalness and lowered responsiveness to variables affecting face-saving. Finally, variations in the assessment instruments which allow for greater flexibility of interpretation should result in greater responsiveness to variables influencing face-saving. These questions are currently being explored.

Cross-culturally, replications of the experiment reported here would be most illuminating. Extensions of the present study across cultures might explore the relative strength of criticism made by judges of higher and lower status than the performers or made in front of an audience whose members are higher or lower in status than the performer. Given the argument which introduced this study, these variations should produce differences in face-saving behaviour across societies having unequal levels of concern for order-maintenance.

Methodological Problems in Data Collection and Questionnaire Construction in Hong Kong*

Betty J. Chung and Zack-kuen Kwok

The Research Problem

Introduction

As with many other places, social scientists have encountered numerous problems in their research in Hong Kong. However, very little attempt has been made to examine these problems in any systematic way, or to bring these problems to the attention of other social researchers in Hong Kong. Because of this lack of documentation, most researchers, in planning their research, have to depend on their intuition and move about blindly, possibly committing the same blunders previous researchers have committed. It is strongly felt by the authors of this paper that this situation impedes the development of research in Hong Kong. It is for the purpose of bridging this gap that the present paper was planned and written. In addition, it is the aim of this paper to stimulate the interest of other researchers in Hong Kong on this topic.

In order to collect data on some of the problems of doing research in Hong Kong, an attempt was made to conduct a survey of some interviewers about their perceptions of problems encountered in interviewing. The survey sample consisted of interviewers who participated in the study of "The impact of industrialization on fertility in Hong Kong".[1] Their responses were based on their experience of interviewing for the study and their use of the question-

*The authors wish to thank all the interviewers who participated in this study for their patience and cooperation. Also, the authors are most grateful to Asia Foundation and staff of the Social Research Centre. In addition, our warmest thanks must also be extended to Miss Betty Chen and Miss Anna Law for their invaluable assistance in supervising the fieldwork. Finally, but not the least, we are indebted to East-West Population Institute, East-West Center, Hawaii for making it possible for the paper to be written.

[1] The study was directed by Drs. C. Y. Choi and Betty Chung of the Social Research Centre at The Chinese University of Hong Kong in collaboration with Mr. K. C. Chan of the Hong Kong Family Planning Association in 1972. The project was funded by Asia Foundation.

naire. For this reason, it is necessary to become familiar with the project in which the interviewers participated, its objectives, its sample, and its methodology, in order to fully understand the problems they encountered.

The Project on "The Impact of Industrialization on Fertility in Hong Kong"

The purpose of the project was to examine the relationship between certain socio-economic and social psychological factors and fertility behaviour of women in Hong Kong, and also to understand the practice of contraceptive methods among people in Hong Kong so as to provide information to the Family Planning Association for the planning and implementation of their programmes.

Respondents of the study were currently married women (excluding divorcees, widows, or those not living with their husbands) between ages of 15 and 49. The sample was a representative sample of Hong Kong prepared by the Census and Statistics Department. The sample was stratified by housing types, namely, private housing, resettlement estates, low-cost housing, and squatter huts, and then by areas, Kowloon, New Kowloon, the New Territories, and Hong Kong Island. The original sample was 3,388 household units including households with or without married women of reproductive ages. At the end of the survey, 2,270 women were successfully interviewed. The non-response rate (including not-at-home's, refusals, and language problems) of eligible respondents was 10.56%, with the refusal rate, 2.76%.

A letter was sent before the interview to each household unit describing the project and also soliciting cooperation from the household head. Female interviewers (university and college students), were instructed to visit household units assigned to them, and interview all eligible respondents in each of the units. In case of unsuccessful interviews (excluding household units without eligible respondents) they were instructed to re-visit up to a maximum of eight times before closing the case. Also, more experienced interviewers were usually sent to interview unsuccessful cases. Before the interviewers went into the field, they were given a five-day training session, including training in interviewing techniques, and practice sessions in using the questionnaire.

A field-station was set up for the fieldwork, and there were two supervisors present who would give assignments to the interviewers and check their returned questionnaires to ensure that the questionnaires were completed without omissions.

The Study on Interviewers

As mentioned earlier, researchers encounter numerous problems in their research in Hong Kong, and a large number of these problems are the result of the operation of certain factors in Hong Kong.

In spite of the rapid spread of education in the last two decades, still almost one quarter of the inhabitants of Hong Kong have never had schooling, the majority of whom are women and people of older age groups.[2] With the relatively low level of education in Hong Kong, particularly among women and older people, it is not surprising to find that most people living here do not understand what social research means. Although various research projects have been done in Hong Kong using students or the public as respondents, people in general are not familiar with, nor knowledgeable about, social research. Because of this attitude toward social research, researchers usually encounter numerous difficulties, particularly when the research requires cooperation of the general public.

Furthermore, the complicated and delicate political situation in Hong Kong creates a reluctance in people to be interviewed. Although people in Hong Kong are not politically oriented—in fact most of them tend to be apathetic—they are well aware of the complexity of the political situation in Hong Kong. Hong Kong is a British Colony perched on the coast of Communist China, and its inhabitants are mainly refugees from China. A large piece of Hong Kong land—the New Territories and the northern part of Kowloon—are leased from China. The lease will expire in the year 1997. People are deeply concerned that the Communist Chinese Government may decide to recover Hong Kong. In the meantime, there is also a continuous struggle here between the Communists and the Kuomintang through a variety of organizations such as trade unions. The National days of both the Communist and the Nationalist governments are celebrated by people in Hong Kong. All these factors contribute to the creation of a very delicate political atmosphere. Thus, people are usually suspicious when they are being interviewed. Usually they conclude that the interviewers are from the government but under disguise and are trying to get information the possible use of which is unknown and possibly "threatening". This suspicious attitude, of course, increases people's reluctance to cooperate with the interviewers. This is even more true when the interviewers are inexperienced.

Another inhibiting factor is the reserved personality of most Chinese. They are not open about their personal matters. They do not like talking about themselves—revealing themselves to other people. All these are especially true when the "other people" are strangers who come to their door and ask various kinds of questions. Interviewing may be very easily viewed as interrogation.

An additional problem which has recently become more acute in Hong

[2]Census and Statistics Department of the Hong Kong Government, *Hong Kong Population and Housing Census 1971, Basic Tables*, Hong Kong Government Printer, 1972.

Kong and which inevitably affects interviewing, is the increased number of crimes in Hong Kong. People do not feel free and safe to open the door to strangers, out of fear that they may be burglars or robbers.

All these facts make interviewing difficult in Hong Kong. It is hoped that by understanding the practical problems involved in interviewing in a situation like Hong Kong through the experience of interviewers, one can find insights into the means of resolving some of them. It is, therefore, the aim of this study to collect and analyze some of the perceptions and experience of interviewers in Hong Kong, and on the basis of these make recommendations on some of the practical aspects of interviewing.

For the purpose of collecting data on interviewers, a survey was conducted on interviewers who participated in the fieldwork of the Fertility Study. A total of 60 female interviewers participated in the fieldwork which lasted two months. After the fieldwork was completed, each interviewer was given a questionnaire in which they were asked their experience of interviewing, and problems they encountered in interviewing and in the use of the questionnaire. Of the 60 questionnaires distributed, 45 were returned. In addition, at the end of each of the questionnaires that the interviewers used in their fieldwork, questions asking the interviewers' impression of the cooperation of the respondent were included and interviewers were required to complete them after each interview, making a total of 2,270 responses. On the basis of data collected from these two questionnaires, various aspects of interviewing in Hong Kong will be discussed in the next section of this paper. The fundamental factors of interviewing, namely, the interviewer, the respondent, and the questionnaire will form the board guideline of this paper around which the discussion will revolve.

The Major Findings

The Interviewers

One of the major concerns of researchers who collect data by interviews is the recruitment of competent interviewers. They are interested in such questions as who can interview? How can potentially competent interviewers be selected? It is not the intention of the authors of this paper to answer these questions here. In this section, on the basis of data collected, interviewer characteristics will be discussed in connection with interviewers' perception of problems in interviewing. Such a discussion may, however, lead to suggestions about interviewer selection.

A major problem of doing research in Hong Kong is the lack of experienced and qualified interviewers, which makes recruitment of interviewers hard. The reason for this difficulty is that it is often desirable for interviewers to have a fair amount of knowledge of social science, and thus social science students are often sought as interviewers. However, they are mostly unavailable during the term because they are too busy with their academic work, and therefore not very interested in earning money, for fear this would interfere with their studies. One can understand this work consciousness if one realizes how competitive education is in Hong Kong, and how students have been trained both by teachers and parents since grade one to put great emphasis on their school work.

In addition to this study consciousness, there is another factor operating. Some of the university students in Hong Kong are from "better-off" families and are supported by parents, and those students whose parents cannot afford to do so usually get a bursary, a scholarship or a regular part-time job. A large number of them work as private tutors or part-time teachers in secondary schools. Therefore, students who are not already working usually do not need the money, and those who need the money usually already have a steady job. Therefore, most students are not interested in short-term part-time jobs.

In view of the above problems, it is advisable to conduct interviews during a holiday. In the Fertility Study, for example, the first pre-test was carried out at Christmas break, the second pre-test in the Eastern vacation, and the main survey during the summer holidays. But still, there were some "delinquents" (e.g., drop-outs or taking a long time to complete assignments) during the fieldwork and some additional new interviewers had to be recruited.

In the following paragraphs, a comparison will be made of interviewers of different colleges, majors, years and interviewing experience, and their reactions to and perception of the questionnaire and the interviews.

64% of the interviewers for the Fertility Study, i.e., the sample of this study, were students from The Chinese University of Hong Kong, and the rest were from two post-secondary colleges. It was found that a little over half (64.4%) of the interviewers were sociology or social work students, and the others were mainly social science students. About 11.1% were fourth year students, 44.4% were second year students going to their third year, and 40.0% were first year students going to their second year. Nearly 90% of the interviewers were aged from 19 to 22. About 44% of the interviewers have had interviewing experience with class projects or projects with voluntary social welfare organizations while the rest have not had interviewing experience. About 29.5% of them participated in the Fertility Project in order to gain a better understanding of the "real world" as they called it, 22.7% to gain interviewing experience, 31.8% to earn money, and only 15.9% to past time.

When asked to rate the difficulty of the different parts of the questionnaire and the forms of the questions, students of the Chinese University seemed to attribute greater difficulty to the various parts of the questionnaire and the different forms of the questions than interviewers from the other two colleges, particularly those parts of the questionnaire and forms of questions that were agreed upon by the majority of the interviewers as being difficult. Again, this same trend was found among second and first year students, with the former attributing a higher level of difficulty to the questionnaire and the forms of the questions than the latter. Students with research experience also perceived greater difficulty with the questionnaire. Moreover, sociology and social work students found the parts of the questionnaire which were generally agreed to be easier less difficult than students of other disciplines, but found the difficult parts of the questionnaire more difficult. Similarly, interviewers who stated that they participated in the fieldwork for money and/or as a past-time also attributed greater difficulty to the different parts of the questionnaire than those who gave a different reason for participating. These findings seem to indicate that greater exposure to social science and social research increased the difficulty which interviewers found with the questionnaire. This, however, can be interpreted in a different way. The increase in the perceived difficulty is, perhaps, a result of a greater awareness, due to greater exposure, of the problems involved in interviewing and the use of the questionnaire, and of the reactions of the respondents. In this sense, interviewers with greater exposure to social sciences may be better interviewers than those with less exposure.

In comparing students of Chinese University and those from the other two colleges, it was found that the former did not have more research experience than the latter. 44.8% of Chinese University students as compared to 43.7% of the other colleges had research experience. 42.8% of students of Chinese University claimed to have participated for money whereas 43.7% and 37.5% of students of other colleges claimed respectively to have participated to gain research experience and to have a better understanding of 'society'. Also, it was felt that students from the other colleges worked very hard. This belief was partially supported by the data showing the number of hours interviewers worked each day. Chinese University students generally worked 5 to 6 hours a day while students of the other colleges worked 7 to 8 hours.

As expected, first year students were the least experienced interviewers. There were 72.22% of the first year students who had no research experience as compared to 45% of second year students and 40% of fourth year students. The data also show that first year students claimed to have been motivated to participate in the project mainly by the desire for knowledge and experience, whereas for the more senior students, especially the second year students, money was mentioned frequently as the motivational force. In view of the high proportion of interviewers, particularly senior students who participated in the survey for money, it would be advisable to use monetary incentive as a means of recruiting more and better interviewers.

From the above discussion, it can be seen that different groups of interviewers tended to have different perceptions of problems in interviewing. This leads to a very interesting question whether interviewer characteristics which were shown to be related to interviewers' perception of interviews would also in turn affect the interview product. Various studies on the effect of interviewer characteristics on interview product have shown that there is a substantial interviewer effect operating in any interview situation.[3] It would be interesting to replicate some of these studies in Hong Kong.

One possible way of conducting such a research would be to compare interviews done by different types of interviewers such as interviewers who are first year university students and those who are upper year students or interviewers of different age groups, and try to examine the extent to which the interviews or responses given are related to differences between the types. Results would be most useful for researchers in Hong Kong who at the moment have no access to such information at all.

The Respondents

This section will be devoted to the discussion of the cooperativeness of the respondents in relation to the following aspects:

(a) housing type
(b) religion
(c) educational level
(d) place of origin
(e) urban-rural experience
(f) working status
(g) income
(h) occupation

The non-response rate and the refusal rate in Hong Kong are generally quite high for reasons already discussed. For the Fertility Project, the non-response rate of eligible respondents was 10.56% including not-at-home's, language problems and refusals. The not-at-home rate was 7.68% and the refusal rate was 2.76%. In fact, these rates are not high in comparison with other similar studies done in Hong Kong.

One of the reasons for these relatively low rates was that interviewers revisited up to a maximum of eight times households where there was no

[3] See, for instance, D. Katz, "Do Interviewers Bias Poll Results," *Public Opinion Quarterly*, V. 6, 1942, pp. 248-268; H. Hyman, et al., *Interviewing in Social Research*, Chicago: University of Chicago Press, 1954; M. Benny, D. Riseman and S. A. Star, "Age and Sex in the Interview," *American Journal of Sociology*, V. 62, 1956, pp. 143-152.

response either because the eligible respondent was not at home, because the language or dialect spoken by the respondent could not be understood by the interviewer, or because the respondent refused. An additional measure introduced to curb refusal rate could also account partially for these low rates. In the first pre-test, the refusal rate was extremely high, up to 50% for the whole sample, and 90% for private housing. In the second pre-test, a letter describing briefly the purpose of the survey was sent to the respondent before the interview, and this seemed to have been very effective in lowering the refusal rate to about 15% for the whole sample and 25% for private housing. In view of the effectiveness of the letter, the same was done in the main survey. The refusal rate of eligible respondents for the final sruvey was only 2.76% (3.48% for private housing).

(a) Housing type

It is the general belief among researchers in Hong Kong that the most cooperative, and easily accessible respondents for interviews are people living in public housing, i.e., resettlement estates and low-cost housing. Data from this survey on interviewers lent support to this general belief. The majority of the interviewers cited people living in low-cost housing and people living in resettlement estates as being the easiest to interview, and those living in private housing and squatter huts as being less easy. This was further supported by the differential non-response rates of the different housing types. The refusal rate of eligible respondents for private housing was 3.5% whereas that for the other three housing types was between 1.1% and 1.4%. The not-at-home rate again was higher for private housing, 10.6%, and lower for the other housing types, 5.7% for squatter huts, and less than 2.5% for both resettlement estates and low-cost housing. These data can be easily explained by the situation or the nature of the different types of housing.

The resettlement estates were built by the Hong Kong Government to shelter people, mainly refugees from China, who lived in squatter huts on hillsides or rooftops, or in other types of buildings which had to be demolished or were destroyed by natural disasters. Two of the six types of resettlement estates (Mark I and II) are so constructed that the doors of the different units face a common open corridor which is also the major source of lighting for the units. This corridor also serves as the cooking place for the residents. In additon, washrooms are shared by units on the same floor and are located at the centre of the floor. In other words, many activities of the residents take place outside the dwelling unit itself, and therefore, the majority of the residents know each other and tend to keep their doors open. Consequently, gaining admittance to these units is fairly easy. Admittance into the other four types of estates (Mark III, IV, V and VI) is slightly more difficult because they are more similar to regular apartment houses where the units share a closed hallway. Each unit has its own kitchen, and is a complete, independent unit. As a consequence, residents do not have to leave their doors open, nevertheless a considerable number do so. (It is possible that because the fieldwork was done in the summer residents had tended to leave their doors open in order to get better ventilation.)

Low-cost housing is another type of public housing provided for the low income group. This type of housing is financed either by the Government or by a Government Development fund loan and rental revenue, and is managed by the Housing Society and the Housing Authority. In order to be able to interview respondents living in low-cost housing, it is necessary to get permission from the individual organizations which notify their offices at the respective estates. Because of the tight control over "solicitors" in these estates, those who are allowed to "solicit" are generally easily accepted by the residents. Indeed the Housing Society even notifies the household units before the interview, and asks them to cooperate with the interviewer. In addition, residents of low-cost housing are accustomed to being interviewed by their housing assistants who visit them regularly, and the relationship between residents and the housing assistants is generally good. Consequently, in low-cost housing cooperation was almost total.

There was less cooperation from private housing for various reasons. It seems that most people who live in private apartment buildings tend to lack any sense of being part of a community or a neighbourhood. They view themselves as independent household units, and, being in a city, residents have learned to become indifferent and blasé about happenings around them. They "mind their own business," so to speak. For these reasons, most of the private household units keep their doors locked. This made admittance into the respondents' homes fairly difficult. The recent increase in crime added to this difficulty. In addition, most of the household units in private housing have a "viewing window" at the door through which they can see who the caller is without opening the door. This makes it easier for people to refuse interviewers or pretend that the household head or the respondent is not at home.

In squatter areas, the main problem is locating the desired hut. Most of them are on hillsides which do not have street names or numbers. Interviewers had to spend a great deal of their time locating these squatter huts, and very often when they had done so the eligible respondents were not at home. They were probably at work, since most of the residents of squatter huts are poor, and often the wives have to go to work in order to make ends meet. Another problem is that since most of the squatter huts are located on dark and rather inaccessible hillsides, it could be unsafe for female interviewers to visit alone, particularly, at night. But, when the squatter huts could be located and people were at home, it was not difficult getting cooperation, for again most of them have their doors open.

Contrary to expectations, however, in rating respondents' cooperativeness, sincerity, initial reaction, and difficulty in understanding the questions, interviewers seemed to present a slightly different picture. Respondents living in low-cost housing were most frequently rated as extremely cooperative, most sincere, most interested in the project, and having the least difficulty in understanding the questions and the questionnaire, but, instead of people living in resettlement estates being ranked second with respect to these attributes, people from private housing ranked second, squatter huts ranked third, and resettlement estates ranked last. In other words, the relative ease of gaining an interview and the relative degree of interest, etc. of the interviewee did not correlate. Why was this?

A closer examination of the data shows that they are not necessarily contradictory. In rating respondents of the four different types of housing about who were the easiest to be interviewed, interviewers might be evaluating the availability or accessibility of the respondents, and the ease of admittance into the house rather than the ease of the interview itself, whereas in rating the cooperativeness of the respondents, interviewers were evaluating the cooperation during the actual interview. Probably, it was easy for interviewers to be admitted into the house or unit of those living in resettlement estates, but the respondents were not necessarily cooperative in answering the questions. Although the structure of the resettlement estate buildings made admittance easy for interviewers, there were factors which might have introduced a negative element to the cooperativeness of the resisdents. The mere fact that the resettlement estates are government projects could have made the residents very cautious about what they would say to the interviewers, and they might have considered any kind of interviews as being done for the Government in order to check on them. Also, the less than harmonious relationship between the residents and the resettlement assistants might also have intensified this feeling of doubt.[4]

Again, differences were found in interviewees' reactions to the topic of employment and income. Respondents who lived in resettlement estates and even more those who lived in low-cost housing were less reluctant to answer questions pertaining to this topic, whereas respondents from private housing were most reluctant. This, of course, does not necessarily have any bearing on the truth of the information given. It is possible that people living in resettlement estates and low-cost housing are accustomed to being asked

---

[4] See Andrew L. C. Lu and Z. K. Kwok, *Housing in Hong Kong: An Anatomy of the Government's 10-Year Housing Programme*, Hong Kong: Research and Development Centre, 1973, pp. 20-38.

about their income, particularly people living in low-cost housing where one of the major criteria of eligibility for this type of housing is income. In a certain sense their "claimed" income is an open secret. They had no reason to hide this "claimed" income from the interviewers. However, there is in most cases a tendency for residents to understate their income to match the income criterion so as to remain qualified for such housing. Also, respondents who live in public housing belong to the lower middle and upper lower classes, and they are usually less sensitive about such personal matters as income, on the other hand a high proportion of the people living in private housing belong to the middle and upper classes, and they do not like other people, particularly strangers, asking them questions about their income.

(b) Religion

The religion of the respondents did not seem to be related to their interview behavior. Despite this, there was a tendency for Catholics and Protestants to react similarly, and those who worship ancestors and traditional deities to react similarly also. The former groups were interested in the interview, very cooperative, and most sincere, and had the least difficulty in understanding the questions, whereas the latter groups reacted very differently, almost in the opposite direction. Those who worship traditional deities and ancestors were the least interested, least cooperative, least sincere, and had the greatest difficulty in understanding the questions asked when compared to other religious groups.

The effect of religious affiliation might have been a concomitant of education. Both Catholics and Prostestants are generally better educated than those who worship deities and ancestors. Consequently one could argue that Catholics and Protestants were more positive toward the interview in the same way as the highly educated respondents were and those who worshipped deities and ancestors had a less favorable attitude toward the interview as the less educated respondents did.

Furthermore because Christianity is a relatively new religion for Chinese people whereas worshipping deities and ancestors are traditional Chinese practices, it is likely that those who practise Christianity are more modern and thus may have a better understanding of what social research is than those who worship deities and ancestors.

(c) Education Level

As we would expect, the level of education of the respondents seemed to discriminate respondents' reaction to the interview very successfully. Generally speaking, respondents with higher education reacted more positively to the interview than those with less education. They were more interested, more cooperative, more sincere and had less difficulty in understanding the questions than respondents with less education. This may be because respondents who had little or no education could not really understand the letter sent to them and were therefore puzzled about what the interviewer wanted from them. Also, respondents who had little education may have had difficulty understanding some of the questions, and the interviewer had to elaborate. This would make the interview more lengthy and boring, and the respondents impatient and less attentive. This might then give the interviewer the impression of lack of interest, and insincerity on the part of the respondents. Respondents who had had more education could understand the letter, and were therefore perhaps less suspicious of the interviewers and thus more cooperative. In addition, respondents who were literates could read the questions and understand what the interviewers wrote down if they so desired. They might, therefore, find the interview less lengthy and less boring, giving the interviewer an impression of being interested.

(d) Place of Origin

When respondents of different places of origin were compared, those from Shanghai could be singled out as a distinct group. The Shanghai-Chinese were interested in the interview, least uncooperative, least insincere, and had the least difficulty in understanding the questions. This observation is not surprising, if one considers the nature of the city of Shanghai. Shanghai being the largest, most highly urbanized and modernized centre, its residents were generally more highly educated than residents of most of the other cities or provinces of China. Also, because it is situated so far away from Hong Kong, people who were able to migrate from there to Hong Kong were the "cream" of the crowd. Therefore, Shanghai-Chinese in Hong Kong are generally modernized and well-to-do. In view of this fact, it could be expected that people from Shanghai would be more positive toward being interviewed. However, with such a small number of Shanghainess in the sample, one should not be too hasty in one's conclusion.

Chiu Chow and Fukien women are usually less educated, and a great number of them are originally from rural areas. People from these two places show close solidarity. They perceive people from the same place of origin as belonging to the "in" group, and all others as "outsiders". Consequently it is not surprising that they were not very cooperative with interviewers who in most cases obviously belonged to the "out" group. It was reported by some interviewers that these respondents became more friendly when they found that the interviewer could speak their own dialects.

(e) Urban-rural Experience

One of the most interesting factors is the rural-urban background of the respondents. Respondents with different rural-urban backgrounds reacted very differently to the interviews. In general, respondents with a rural background (i.e., those who stated that they grew up in a small town or a village) reacted less favorably to the interview than those who had an urban background (i.e., those who stated they grew up in a city). For example, respondents from a village were least interested in the interview, those from a town a little less interested, those from a small city a little more interested and those from a big city very much interested. This same pattern was found in other kinds of reactions of the respondents toward the interview, namely, the cooperativeness of the respondents, their sincerity, and the amount of difficulty they had in understanding the questionnaire. This finding, which was paralleled by data on reactions of respondents from the rural and urban areas of Hong Kong, seems to illustrate the nature of urban social relationships. Urbanism is said by sociologists to increase the superficiality, anonymity and transitory characteristics of social relationships, and urban dwellers usually develop a blasé attitude toward things around them. If this is true, then it is not surprising that the respondents with urban backgrounds, being more superficial, sophisticated and capable of handling situations of meeting strangers, should give a positive impression when interviewed, whereas respondents with a rural background might not have developed a way of handling situations like interviews, and therefore, faced with a completely strange situation might try to take avoiding action by refusing the interview or refraining from answering certain questions, thus giving the interviewer an impression of being uncooperative, insincere or uninterested. Hower, urban women are generally better educated than rural women, and therefore it is expected that women with rural backgrounds would have more difficulty in understanding the questions than those with urban background.

(f) Working Status

The working status of the respondents was not successful in discriminating reactions to the interview. However, the distinction between full-time and part-time workers was found to be more discriminating. Full-time workers had greater interest in the interview, and less difficulty in understanding the questions and were more cooperative but less sincere than part-time workers. Of course, a confounding factor here is the education of the respondents. Respondents who had a higher education were more likely to be working full-time rather than part-time and vice versa.

Another possible explanation is that those who worked full-time tended to be more exposed to people, and thus might have developed more sophistication in dealing with strangers. Those who worked part-time tended to be less exposed, and therefore less confident in handling situations like interviews. Consequently, they appeared to be not interested and not cooperative. This explanation seems to be supported by data on respondents who worked at home and those who worked outside of home, with the latter also being more exposed to other people and the former less so. Respondents who worked at home reacted to the interview similarly to those who worked part-time, and those who worked outside reacted similarly to those who worked full-time. There is, of course, the factor that in most cases those who worked full-time worked outside, and those who worked part-time worked at home.

(g) Income

In general, higher income groups had the tendency to react more favorably to the interview than lower income groups. This seems to contradict the earlier finding that admittance into houses of people who live in wealthy residential areas was difficult, but in fact there is no contradiction because although interviewers found that getting admittance into houses in the more wealthy residential areas was indeed difficult, once they were admitted, the respondents were cooperative.

The factor of income is, of course, highly correlated with education. The high income group reacted similarly to the high education group and the low income group to the low education group. It is also possible that respondents with low income were more likely to be working part-time at home or busy with house work, and therefore less willing to spend their time being interviewed. They might consequently be impatient and show less interest and cooperation, giving an impression of being unfavorably inclined toward the interview.

(h) Occupation

Comparing respondents from different industries, we found that respondents who were in the field of education were the most interested, most cooperative, most sincere and had the least difficulty in understanding the questions. This, perhaps, was because these respondents were better educated and also, being in the field of education, they might have a better understanding of what research was. In addition, since this project on fertility was sponsored by a university, they might feel committed to cooperate.

When respondents of different occupations were compared, professionals such as teachers and nurses, and junior executives and administrators were found to be the most cooperative, most interested, and most sincere. This probably can be explained by differences in educational level of people in the various occupations.

(i) Summary

In short, the data seem to indicate that residents from low-cost housing were the most cooperative. Also, people who are better educated and have a higher income tended to be cooperative. Again, Catholics and Protestants seemed to be cooperative, and so were those respondents who worked full-time and those who lived in the urban areas of Hong Kong or who have an urban background.

Since a researcher cannot omit certain fractions of the population simply because they are not cooperative enough, it may seem that these findings have no direct implication for conducting research in Hong Kong. However, this is not so. On the contrary, they are extremely relevant. We have seen that respondents with certain characteristics were less cooperative than respondents with other characteristics. It is possible that this attitude of the respondents toward the interviews in this survey may have systematically influenced the way they responded and the answers they gave, and biased the results accordingly. Thus, in conducting research in Hong Kong, researchers should be alert to this possible bias and try to understand and overcome it when possible.

It would also be useful and interesting to study the extent to which respondents' attitudes toward an interview affect the answers they give in the interview. An appropriate question to ask is whether respondents' answers are affected by their attitude toward the interview, and, if so, how and why. This would not only help in the understanding of this effect but also throw light on how to minimize the effect. One possible way of answering this question would be to match respondents on certain criteria so as to obtain a homogeneous group of respondents, and induce in them two different attitudes toward the interview, a favorable and an unfavorable one. Then compare responses of these two groups of respondents. Another way of exploring this issue might be to compare the responses of respondents who were rated by interviewers as cooperative with those who were rated as uncooperative while controlling factors like education, religion and type of residence.

Many other questions can be asked in connection with this topic, and the above are only some examples of ideas for future research.

The Questionnaire

In this section, the discussion will concentrate on problems connected with particular parts of the questionnaire and with the format of certain particular questions.

Interviewers found certain parts of the questionnaire difficult to ask. These were the sections on knowledge, attitude and practice of contraception (KAP), husband-wife interaction, costs and satisfaction of children, time horizon and attitudes towards having children. For the KAP section, 37.8% of the interviewers found it difficult as compared to 15.6% who found it easy; for the husband-wife interaction section, 37.8% as compared with 24.4%; for costs and satisfaction of children, 51.1% as compared with 17.8%; for time horizon,

51.1% as compared with 31.1%; and for attitudes towards having children, 66.7% as compared with 6.7%. In addition, interviewers commented that respondents had difficulty in understanding the sections on costs and satisfaction of children, time horizon, and attitudes towards having children, 48.9%, 60% and 78.8% rating these three sections respectively as being difficult. When asked to name parts of the questionnaire which they believed bothered the respondents, the most frequently mentioned sections were KAP, husband-wife interaction, costs and satisfaction of children, and attitudes towards having children. The most frequently mentioned parts of the questionnaire which respondents were said to be reluctant to answer were KAP, and the section on employment and income. An examination of the problems raised by interviewers in connection with the questionnaire, and they type and form of questions which they considered difficult, will reveal partially their reasons for finding the above mentioned parts of the questionnaire difficult.

The interviewers criticized the questionnaire as being too long, and having too many hypothetical questions. The design of the questionnaire was also said to be too complicated. In addition, a large proportion of the interviewers commented that respondents found hypothetical questions and scales difficult to understand. It is possible that this is because most Chinese are not accustomed to think about abstract things or concepts or to imagine as in the case of hypothetical questions.

As shown earlier in the section describing the questionnaire, sections on KAP, husband-wife interaction, and costs and satisfaction of children had some factual items, but a substantial part of each of these sections consisted of hypothetical questions. In addition, each of these sections had a fair number of questions in the format of scales. A possible reason for the difficulty with scales is that Chinese respondents, particularly those who are not highly educated, may not possess the concept of rating scales, and therefore find it difficult to use them in expressing their attitudes. In view of the difficulty respondents had with hypothetical questions and scales, it is understandable why these sections were considered difficult.

One other section which was stated as being difficult for the interviewers to ask and the respondents to answer was that on time-horizon. It is possible that because the questions included in this section are abstract and require the respondents to project to the future respondents found them difficult to handle. An example of a question in this section is "Nowadays, do you think it is possible to predict the future?"

There was one section in the questionnaire which the respondents were reluctant to answer, and this was the section on employment status and income. The interviewers also indicated that the reluctance was generally about revealing income and not about revealing employment status. This reluctance in connection to questions on income is found to be true in many other countries.

In general, it can be said that respondents in Hong Kong feel at ease with factual questions (except those on income), questions in the form of dichotomized scales and multiple choice and open-ended questions. Basically, respondents found it difficult to answer hypothetical questions and questions in the form of a scale of more than three points. Any questions dealing with the abstract such as time horizon also posed problems.[5]

All the problems just discussed are particularly true for respondents who have not had very much education. Respondents with less education, less urban background, and less income had more difficulty in understanding the questionnaire than those with high education, more urban background and higher income.

The data discussed above show that certain types of questions and certain forms of questions are problematic for respondents in Hong Kong. But, since this present study is of an exploratory nature and the questionnaire used was so simple, problems in connection with the forms and types of questions could only be detected but not examined. Therefore, it seems reasonable to examine each of these types and forms of questions in greater depth and also to discover reasons for such difficulties. For example, the reason for respondents' difficulty in answering hypothetical questions may be due to the way the questions were phrased or it may be due to the nature of the questions asked, and so forth. A clarification of such issues would have strong implications for future questionnaires.

Conclusion and Suggestions

As stated earlier, one of the intentions of this paper is to find means of solving some of the problems of research in Hong Kong, such as those connected with the availability and training of interviewers, cooperation of respondents, safety of interviewers, questionnaires and fieldwork. On the basis of the above discussion, the following suggestions are offered.

One of the major problems connected with interviewers is the scarcity and unavailability of interviewers during the academic year. It seems that the only solution for this is to plan the research so that both the major pilot study and the fieldwork are scheduled during holidays.

Another factor which is likely to affect the willingness of interviewers to participate is the monetary incentive involved. As shown by the data collected,

[5] Z. K. Kwok, "Interviewers' Study—A Methodological Note on Hong Kong Public Housing Project," *The Sociological Review* (Journal of the Sociology and Social Work Society, Chu Hai College), 1973, V. 3, pp. 2-8.

a high proportion of interviewers participated for money. It may be advisable to offer a reasonably high monetary incentive to the interviewers.

Data seem to suggest that senior university students are better interviewers, particularly those in the second year going to their third year.

Training is especially important, indeed essential, for successful fieldwork. Role playing and actual experience in interviewing using the questionnaire are particularly helpful. Although five days were spent in training for the Fertility Study, it is felt that the period was not long enough. It seems that the interviewers should have been given a longer practice period to get familiarized with the questionnaire and to know how to handle the interviewing situation. Even interviewers with experience need the practice because each questionnaire is different and consequently creates a different interviewing atmosphere.

It can be seen from the earlier discussion of problems connected with respondents that one of the major problems is to gain admittance into the house and cooperation from the respondents, particularly those who live in private housing. Sending a letter in advance seems to have helped a great deal in these respects. This may suggest that publicizing the survey or project beforehand may be advantageous for the fieldwork. Publicizing the survey in newspapers or on radio or television may inspire trust concerning the project, and thus may reduce people's reluctance to accept the interview. Publicity may also help to reduce a respondent's fear of opening the door to strangers. In the Fertility Study, each interviewer was given an identification card with her picture attached and she was required to show her card to the respondents.

In this particular project, female interviewers were used. This apparently helped to reduce respondents' reluctance to open the door. However, the use of female interviewers created another problem that of security for the interviewers themselves. For example, in the Fertility Study, female interviewers were reluctant and at times refused to visit places which were far from the city and to visit during the evenings. This was one of the reasons why some of the follow-up cases were delayed. This problem of security for interviewers, particularly female interviewers, is very difficult to handle. One possible way is to organize the fieldwork during the summer when the days are quite long, and visits can still be made in the early evenings till about eight o'clock. There are a few possible solutions but they all create other problems. For example, it is possible to have a male escort for the interviewer but this is not practical for two reasons. Firstly, it is a very expensive operation, and secondly, the fact of having a male escort may increase people's reluctance to open the door. Another possible way is to have a group of interviewers visit the same block or building at the same time thus offering protection for each other. But this is only feasible when the fieldwork first starts; it is difficult for follow-ups. This problem of the security of interviewers is a very serious one, and should be considered most carefully before one starts field-work.

It was shown that residents in public housing seemed to be better respon-dents. Naturally it is very unlikely that any survey can concentrate on residents in public housing alone unless the project is specifically to study these residents. However, it is possible for researchers to plan the fieldwork so as to concentrate on private housing first and then turn to public housing which is a little bit less complicated.

It was indicated by interviewers that the best time during the day and evening for visiting was between 3 and 4 in the afternoon and between 7 and 8 in the evening. It is, perhaps, advisable to have interviewers follow this time schedule (or any time schedule which is most convenient for the group of respondents). This would ensure better cooperation from the respondents and also less time loss for the interviewers.

With regard to the questionnaire, it is perhaps wise not to make it lengthy. The questionnaire used in this project took about 45 minutes to an hour to be administered. Some respondents found it too long, and interviewers commented on this point. Hypothetical questions should be avoided, if possible, and scale should be dichotomized whenever possible. It was found, for example, in this project that by dichotomizing a five-point scale into a two-point bipolar scale and then further dichotomizing it into two points representing the strength of the response that the respondents chose, respon-dents were able to answer with ease, whereas respondents were unable to do so when the scale was in a 5-point scale format. An example of such a dicho-tomized scale is as follows:

"Compared to the last generation, do you think that children nowadays are more or less willing to support their parents?"

_____ more willing   _____ much more willing

                                     _____ more willing

_____ less willing   _____ less willing

                                     _____ much less willing

_____ the same

Also, in another study, instead of using numbers to represent points on a scale, stars were used to signify the strength of an opinion or an attribute. Respondents were found to be able to choose the number of stars which best represented their opinion. One possibe reason for this is that there is a practice among some film critics in Hong Kong of using stars to indicate the quality of the movies, with a larger number of stars signifying a better movie and fewer stars a poorer movie. With hypothetical questions, it is best not to use them in connection with situations which are unlikely to happen to the respondents, and consequently seem "unreal" to them.

It was expressed by interviewers that in tackling the question of income, the best way was to give respondents a range to choose from rather than ask for the exact amount. They felt that by so doing, more truthful answers could be obtained.

As far as the administration of the fieldwork is concerned, it is important to have more supervisors to check the returned questionnaires and to keep track of the various assignments. Unless a strict control can be kept over the fieldwork, it is very difficult to have good interviews produced. In addition, a very important, though often neglected, human factor should be taken into consideration: it is essential for the morale of the interviewers to have a researcher or a senior staff member of the project present at the field station to show concern for the interviewers, and give encouragement, if and when necessary. Very often, the interviewers need encouragement to continue, and also need consolation when they encounter problems.

From the experience of the Fertility Study, it is felt that keeping the same interviewers for the pre-tests and the final fieldwork proved very useful and helpful. Interviewers who participated throughout the project were great assets to the fieldwork in the sense that they were more experienced and were able to serve as resource persons for the other less experienced interviewers and help them.

These findings have raised a few interesting points with respects to interviewing in Hong Kong in connection with interviewers, respondents and questionnaires, and have also provided some insight into possible solutions for problems in research. However, in view of the simplicity of the questionnaire used for this present study, the data collected can only provide basic information on the various aspects and problems of interviewing in Hong Kong.

As was indicated at the beginning of this paper, this present study is only an exploratory exercise. It is to be hoped that suggestions for possible solutions and for future research will arise from the findings of this study. Much more sophisticated research is necessary.

Appendix B

Sociological and Related Studies of Hong Kong: A Selected Bibliography

Rance P. L. Lee, Tak-sing Cheung and Oi-ping Wong

[Occasional papers of the Social Research Centre, The Chinese University of Hong Kong are marked with an asterisk *; Research reports of the same Centre by a dagger †.]

(1) General

Hopkins, Keith, ed. 1971. *Hong Kong: The Industrial Colony*. Hong Kong: Oxford University Press.

Javie, I. C. and Joseph Agassi, ed. 1969. *Hong Kong: A Society in Transition*. London: Routledge and Kegan Paul.

Lethbridge, H. J. 1978. *Hong Kong: Stability and Change—A Collection of Essays*. Hong Kong: Oxford University Press.

Lin, T. B., Rance P. L. Lee, and U. E. Simonis, eds. 1979. *Hong Kong Economic, Social and Political Studies in Development*. N. Y.: M. E. Sharpe.

(2) Communication and Mass Media

Allen, C. L. 1970. *Communication Patterns in Hong Kong*. Hong Kong: The

Chinese University of Hong Kong.

Jarvie, I. C. 1977. *Window on Hong Kong: A Sociological Study of the Hong Kong Film Industry and Its Audience.* A Monograph of the Centre of Asian Studies, University of Hong Kong.

Lee, Wing-yee. 1969. *Youth and The Media: A Mass Media Study of Hong Kong Secondary School Students.* Lutheran World Federation Broadcasting Service, Hong Kong.

Mitchell, R. E. 1969. "How Hong Kong Newspapers Have Responded to 15 Years of Rapid Social Change." *Asian Survey* 9 (9): 669-681.

Shen, James C. Y. 1972. "The Law and Mass Media in Hong Kong." *Chung Chi Journal* 2 (1): 60-125.

Ward, B. E. 1979. "Not Merely Players: Drama, Art and Ritual in Traditional China." *Man* 14 (1): 18-39.

Weakland, John H. 1971. "Real and Reel Life in Hong Kong: Film Studies of Cultural Adaptation." *Journal of Asian and African Studies* 6 (3 & 4): 238-243.

Wei, Michael. 1970. *A Survey of the Reading Habits among Post-secondary Students in Hong Kong.* New Asia College, The Chinese University of Hong Kong. (in Chinese)

Wei, Michael and Timothy Light. 1973. *A Newspaper's Vocabulary: A Raw Frequency Count of the Words in the South China Morning Post.* Hong Kong: The Chinese University of Hong Kong.

Yu, L. M. coordinator. 1975. *An Annotated Bibliography of Mass Communication in Hong Kong and Macau: 1945-1973.* Centre for Communication Studies, The Chinese University of Hong Kong.

(3) *Education*

Anderson, Maurice John. 1969. "The Survival Strategies of a Complex Western-type Educational-religious Organization in an Eastern Culture: A Case Study of the Hong Kong Baptist College." Ph.D. Thesis, Louisiana State University, Baton Rouge.

Arbuthnott, Anne R. 1967. "Wider Educational Aims: Two Reports on Hong Kong Education." *Journal of Education* 34: 36-42.

Berrien, Marcia Taft and R. C. Barendsen. 1960. *Education in Hong Kong.* Washington D. C.: United States Office of Educational Studies in Comparative Education.

*Chan, Benjamin Y. 1980. "Evaluating the Effectiveness of Activity Approach in the Lower Primary Grades in Hong Kong."

Chan, Fook-kwan. 1972. *The Struggling for Survival in Primary Schools: A Study of Resettlement Families with Educationally Retarded Children.* Hong Kong: Research Subcommittee, Neighborhood Advice-action Council.

Chan, Kam-ngau. 1966. "The Two Universities in Hong Kong: An Analysis of Their Aims and Contributions to Our Bi-cultural Community." *Journal of Education* 23.

Chan, Te. 1977. "Students Movement." Pp. 27-36 in *A Quarter-Century of Hong Kong 1951-1976: Chung Chi College 25th Anniversary Symposium.* Chung Chi College, The Chinese University of Hong Kong. (in Chinese)

Cheong, George S. C. 1970. "Attitudes of Chinese Parents and Pupils Towards Studying in the Chinese Type of High Schools in Hong Kong." *Journal of Asian and African Studies* 5 (3): 202-208.

Davies, Derek and Raymond Yao.1974. "Hong Kong: Restricting Education." *Far Eastern Economic Review* 84 (18): 26-27.

*Delaney, Joan and C. W. Chan. 1971. "The Education and Professional Training of Secondary School Teachers in Hong Kong."

Engel, J. M. 1960. "Higher Education for Women in Hong Kong and Scope for Employment for Highly-educated Woman." *Journal of Education* 18: 9-13.

Etherton, A. R., B. J. Ong, and J. Lee. 1974. "Parental Motivation in the Choice of Secondary Schools." *Chung Chi Journal* 13 (1): 52-64.

Fehl, N. E. 1966. *History in Hong Kong Middle and Secondary Schools.* A Research Project of The Chinese University of Hong Kong, Hong Kong.

Fisher-short, W. 1966. "Some Thoughts on Educational Testing in Hong Kong." *Journal of Education* 23: 40-50.

Henderson, N. K. 1963. *Educational Development and Research: With Special Reference to Hong Kong.* Hong Kong: The Hong Kong Council for Educational Research.

————. 1964. *The Education of Handicapped Children: Recent Trends and Research, with Implications for Hong Kong.* Hong Kong: The Hong Kong Council for Educational Research.

————. 1966. "Education for Enlightened Leaderships and Community Awareness: An Analysis of One of Hong Kong's Future Needs." *Journal of Education* 23: 34-43.

————. 1967. *Recent Educational Research: An Analysis of Progress and Prospects in Hong Kong.* Hong Kong: The Hong Kong Council for Educational Research.

————. 1968. *Educational Research in Hong Kong: A Reference Book.* Hong Kong: The Hong Kong Council for Educational Research.

————. 1968. *Social and Educational Development of Chinese Children in Various Areas.* Hong Kong: Department of Education, University of Hong Kong.

————. 1973. *Educational Problem and Research: A Hong Kong Introduction.* Hong Kong: Educational Research Unit.

Hinton, Arthur. 1967. "Education and Social Problems in Hong Kong." *Journal of Education* 24: 29-35.

————. 1977. "Secondary Education." Pp. 145-162 in *A Quarter-Century of Hong Kong 1951-1976: Chung Chi College 25th Anniversary Symposium*. Chung Chi College, The Chinese University of Hong Kong.

Lai, Betty Lai-ling. 1969. "An Experimental Study of the Streaming of Pupils by Examination Results in Certain Hong Kong Secondary School." *Journal of Education* 26: 1-33.

Lee, Rance P. L. and P. S. Ng. 1972. "Social Class and Educational Aspiration among Chinese Secondary School Students in Hong Kong." *Chung Chi Journal* 2 (Apr./May): 160-165.

Leong, Che-kan. 1969. "Motives for the Choice of the Teaching Profession." *Journal of Education* 26: 67-84.

Lethbridge, H. J. 1971. "A Chinese Association in Hong Kong: The Tung Wah." *Contributions to Asian Studies* 1: 144-158.

Li, A. K. n.d. "Parental Attitudes, Test Anxiety and Achieved Motivation— A Study of Fifth and Sixth Grade Children." Ph.D. Thesis, University of Hong Kong.

Meclevie, J. G. 1966. "Teachers' Aims in Education: A Questionnaire Survey in Hong Kong Anglo-Chinese Schools." *Journal of Education* 23:11-19.

Mellor, Bernard. 1977. "Higher Education." Pp. 163-177 in *A Quarter-Century of Hong Kong 1951-1976: Chung Chi College 25th Anniversary Symposium*. Chung Chi College, The Chinese University of Hong Kong.

Mitchell, Robert E. 1972. *Pupil, Parent and School—A Hong Kong Study*. Taipei: The Orient Cultural Service.

Myers, Ramon H. 1964. "Education, Technology and the Economic Development of Hong Kong." *Chung Chi Journal* 3 (May): 190-201.

*Ng, Pedro P. T. 1975. "Access to Educational Opportunity: The Case of Kwun Tong."

*Pierson, Herbert D., Gail S. Fu, and Sik-yum Lee. 1980. "An Analysis of the Relationship between Language Attitudes and English Attainment of Secondary Students in Hong Kong."

Rowe, Elizabeth. 1966. *Failure in School: Aspect of the Problem in Hong Kong*. Hong Kong: The Hong Kong Council for Educational Research.

Shii, Winnie. 1970. *Primary School Dropouts*. Hong Kong: Hong Kong Council of Social Service.

Simpson, R. F. 1959. *Graduate Employment in Hong Kong and the Problems of University Expansion*. Hong Kong: Hong Kong University Press.

————. 1963. "Some Economic Aspects of Educational Planning in Hong Kong." *Journal of Education* 21: 22-30.

————. 1966. *Comparative Statistics on Economic and Educational Develop-*

ment in Asian Countries. Hong Kong: The Hong Kong Council for Educational Research.

————. 1966. *Economic Growth and Educational Resources.* Hong Kong: The Hong Kong Council for Educational Research.

————. 1966. *Future Development in Secondary Education.* Hong Kong: The Hong Kong Council for Educational Research.

————. 1966. *Increasing Educational Efficiency.* Hong Kong: The Hong Kong Council for Educational Research.

————. 1966. *Manpower and Employment Problems. Background to Educational Planning Series: Research Studies No. 4.* Hong Kong: The Hong Kong Council for Educational Research.

————. 1966. *The Methodology of Educational Planning. Background to Educational Planning Series: Research Studies No. 1.* Hong Kong: The Hong Kong Council for Educational Research.

————. 1966. *Perspectives in University Development.* Hong Kong: The Hong Kong Council for Educational Research.

————. 1966. *Population Projection, Economic Resources and Enrolments.* Hong Kong: The Hong Kong Council for Educational Research.

————. 1966. *Problems of Educational Planning in Hong Kong: An Introductory Booklet to a Series of Research Studies.* Hong Kong: The Hong Kong Council for Educational Research.

————. 1966. *Social Factors and Educational Efficiency.* Hong Kong:. The Hong Kong Council for Educational Research.

————. 1966. *Teacher Productivity and Professional Training.* Hong Kong: The Hong Kong Council for Educational Research.

————. 1966. "The Teacher Training Demand and Supply Paradox: Problems Arising in a Plural Society." *Journal of Education* 23: 51-55.

————. 1966. *Technical Education and Economic Development.* Hong Kong: The Hong Kong Council for Educational Research.

————. 1967. *A Comparative Study of Educational Development in Various Asian Cities.* Hong Kong: The Hong Kong Council for Educational Research.

————. 1967. *The Development of Education in Hong Kong: Problems and Priorities.* London: University of London.

————. 1967. *Educational Standards, Salary Structure and Finance.* Hong Kong: The Hong Kong Council for Educational Research.

————. 1967. *Priorities for Educational Development in Hong Kong: A Summary Report of Conclusions and Recommendations.* Hong Kong: The Hong Kong Council for Educational Research.

————. 1968. *Educational Planning in Hong Kong.* Hong Kong: Department of Education, University of Hong Kong.

*Siu, Ping-kee, et al. 1980. "The Effects of the Medium of Instruction on Student Cognitive Development and Academic Achievement."

To, Cho-yee. 1965. "The Development of Higher Education in Hong Kong." *Comparative Education Review* 9 (Feb.): 74-80.

Wong, F. M. 1971. "Study Report of the Methodist Primary Schools" in *Study of Methodist Social Services*. Hong Kong: Social Research Centre, The Chinese University of Hong Kong.

(4) *Ethnic Groups and Communities*

Aijmer Göran. 1967. "Expansion and Extension in Hakka Society." *Journal of the Hong Kong Branch of the Royal Asiatic Society* 7: 42-79.

Anderson, E. N., Jr. 1970. *The Floating World of Castle Peak Bay*. Washington: American Anthropological Association.

————. 1972. *Essays on South China's Boat People*. Taipei: The Orient Cultural Service.

Baker, H. 1966. "The Five Great Clans of the New Territories." *Journal of the Hong Kong Branch of the Royal Asiatic Society* 6: 25-48.

Berkowitz, Morris I. and Eddie K. K. Poon. 1969. "Political Disintegration of Hakka Village: A Study of Drastic Social Change in the New Territories of Hong Kong." *Chung Chi Journal* 8 (2): 16-31.

Berkowitz, Morris I. 1970. "Ecology and Human Behavior: A Comparison of Rural and Urban Environments and Their Effects on Resettled Hakka Villagers." In *Conservation and Development of the Countryside*, edited by J. A. Prescott. Hong Kong: Hong Kong University Press.

Blake, C. Fred. 1975. "Negotiating Ethnolinguistic Symbols in a Chinese Market Town." Ph.D. Thesis, University of Illinois, Urbana-Champaign.

Bracey, Dorothy H. 1967. "The Effects of Emigration on a Hakka Village." Ph.D. Thesis, Harvard University.

Campbell, G. 1912. "Origin and Migration of the Hakka." *The Chinese Recorder* 43: 473-480.

Chau, Lam-yam. 1979. "Power Bifurcation in a Changing Chinese Village of Hong Kong." Master Thesis, The Chinese University of Hong Kong.

Cheung, C. P. 1969. *A Study of Selected Folk Literature in the New Territories of Hong Kong: Marriage and Funeral Folk Songs*. Hong Kong: Yau Wah Publisher. (in Chinese)

Cohen, Myron. 1968. "The Hakka, a 'Guest People'—Dialect as a Socio-Cultural Variable in Southeast China." *Ethnohistory* 15 (3): 237-292.

Community Development Committee, ed. 1974-present. *Community Development Resource Book*. Hong Kong: Hong Kong Council of Social Service.

Da Silvia, Armando. 1972. *Tai Yu Shan: Traditional Ecological Adaptation in a South Chinese Island.* Taipei: The Orient Cultural Service.

Guldin, Gregory E. 1977. "Little Fujian (Fukien): Subneighborhood and Community in North Point, Hong Kong." *Journal of the Hong Kong Branch of the Royal Asiatic Society* 17: 112-129.

————. 1977. "Overseas at Home: The Fujianese of Hong Kong." Ph.D. Thesis, University of Wisconsin.

Hayes, James W. 1962. "The Pattern of Life in the New Territories in 1898." *Journal of the Hong Kong Branch of the Royal Asiatic Society* 2: 75-102.

————. 1968. "Itinerant Hakka Weavers." *Journal of the Hong Kong Branch of the Royal Asiatic Society* 8: 162-165.

————. 1970. "Old Ways of Life in Kowloon: The Cheung Sha Wan Villages." *Journal of Oriental Studies* 8 (Sept.): 154-188.

————. 1977. *The Hong Kong Region 1850-1911: Institutions and Leadership in Town and Countryside.* Connecticut: Archon Books.

†Hsieh, Jiann. 1980. "Voluntary Associations and Cultural Persistence: A Study of the Wai-chau Hakka Associations in Hong Kong." (in Chinese)

Johnson, Elizabeth L. 1976. " 'Patterned Bands' in the New Territories of Hong Kong." *Journal of the Hong Kong Branch of the Royal Asiatic Society* 16: 81-91.

Johnson, Graham E. 1977. "Leaders and Leadership in an Expanding New Territories Town." *The China Quarterly* No. 69: 109-125.

Kani, Hiroaki. 1967. *A General Survey of the Boat People in Hong Kong.* A Monograph of the Southeast Asia Studies Section, New Asia Research Institute, Hong Kong.

————. 1972. "The Boat People in Shatin, New Territories, Hong Kong— The Settlement Pattern in 1967 and 1968." *Chung Chi Journal* 11 (2): 57-65.

King, Frank H. 1954. "Pricing Policy in a Chinese Fishing Village." *Journal of Oriental Studies* 1 (1): 215-226.

*Lee, Rance P. L. 1976. "The Fading of Earthbound Compulsion in a Hong Kong Village: Population Mobility and Its Economic Implication."

Lethbridge, H. J. 1975. "Condition of the European Working Class in Nineteenth Century Hong Kong." *Journal of the Hong Kong Branch of the Royal Asiatic Society* 15: 88-112.

McCoy, J. 1965. "The Dialects of Hong Kong Boat People: Kau Sai." *Journal of the Hong Kong Branch of the Royal Asiatic Society* 5: 46-64.

Menard, Wilmon. 1969. "The Boat People of Hong Kong." *Michigan Quarterly Review* 8: 189-193.

Morland, J. Kenneth. 1969. "Race Awareness among American and Hong Kong Chinese Children." *American Journal of Sociology* 75 (Sept.): 360-374.

Nakagawa, Manabu. 1975. "Studies on the History of the Hakkas: Reconsidered." *The Developing Economies* 13: 208-223.

Osgood, Cornelius. 1975. *The Chinese: A Study of a Hong Kong Community, Vol. I, II, and III*. Tuscon: The University of Arizona Press.

Potter, Jack. 1974. "Cantonese Shamanism." Pp. 207-243 in *Religion and Ritual in Chinese Society*, edited by Arthur P. Wolf. Stanford: Stanford University Press.

Pratt, Jean A. 1960. "Emigration and Unilineal Descent Groups: A Study of Marriage in a Hakka Village in the New Territories, Hong Kong." *The Eastern Anthropologist* 13 (4): 147-158.

Riches, G. C. P. 1973. *Community Development in Hong Kong: Sau Mau Ping, a Case Study*. A Monograph of the Centre of Asian Studies, University of Hong Kong.

Sparks, Douglas W. 1976. "Interethnic Interaction—A Matter of Definition: Ethnicity in a Housing Estate in Hong Kong." *Journal of the Hong Kong Branch of the Royal Asiatic Society* 16: 57-80.

————. 1976. "The Teochiu: Ethnicity in Urban Hong Kong." *Journal of the Hong Kong Branch of the Royal Asiatic Society* 16: 25-56.

Sung, Hok-p'ang. 1973. "Legends and Stories of the New Territories: Kam Tin." *Journal of the Hong Kong Branch of the Royal Asiatic Society* 13: 111-132.

Topley, Majorie, ed. 1965. *Aspects of Social Organization in the New Territories*. Hong Kong: The Hong Kong Branch of the Royal Asiatic Society.

Vaid, K. N. 1972. *Overseas Indian Community in Hong Kong*. A Monograph of the Centre of Asian Studies, University of Hong Kong.

†Wang, Sung-hsing. 1980. "Interpersonal Interaction in Pluralistic Societies: The Case of Cheung Chau."

Ward, B. E. 1954. "A Hong Kong Fishing Village." *Journal of Oriental Studies* 1 (1): 195-214.

————. 1959. "Floating Villages: Chinese Fishermen in Hong Kong." *Man* 59 (62): 44-45.

————. 1965. "Varieties of the Conscious Model: The Fishermen of the South China." Pp. 113-137 in *The Relevance of Models for Social Anthropology*, edited by M. Banton. London: Tavistock Publications.

————. 1966. "Sociological Self-awareness of the Conscious Models." *Man* (New Series) 1 (2): 201-215.

————. 1967. "Chinese Fishermen in Hong Kong: Their Post-peasant Economy." Pp. 271-288 in *Social Organization: Essays Presented to Raymond Firth*, edited by Maurice Freedman. London: Frank Cass & Co.

————. 1968. "Temper Tantrums in Kau Sai: Some Speculations Upon Their Effects." Pp. 109-125 in *Socialization: The Approach from Social*

Anthropology, edited by Philip Mayer. A Monograph of the Association of Social Anthropologists, Tavistock.

Watson, James Lee. 1972. "A Chinese Emigrant Community: The Main Lineage in Hong Kong and London." Ph.D. Thesis, Berkeley: University of California.

————. 1975. *Emigration and the Chinese Lineage: The Mans in Hong Kong and London*. Berkeley: University of California Press.

Williams, B. V. 1967. "The Chan Clan of Tseung Kwan O, New Territories." *Journal of the Hong Kong Branch of the Royal Asiatic Society* 7: 158-160.

*Wong, S. L. 1975. "A Chinese Village in Transition: Some Preliminary Findings."

(5) *Family and Marriage*

Aijmer, Göran. 1967. "A Structural Approach to Chinese Ancestor Worship." *Bijdragen tot de Tall-Land-en Volkenkunde* Pt. 124: 91-98.

Anderson, E. N., Jr. 1970. "Lineage Atrophy in Chinese Society." *American Anthropologist* 72 (2): 363-365.

Baker, Hugh D. R. 1968. *A Chinese Lineage Village: Sheung Shui*. London: Frank Cass and Co. Ltd.

Chaney, David and David Podmore. 1974. "Family Norms in a Rapidly Industrializing Society: Hong Kong." *Journal of Marriage and the Family* 36 (May): 400-407.

Chau, C. K. Y. 1967. "Hong Kong Women and Society: A Study." *Phillipine Educational Forum* 16 (3): 32-38.

Cheng, Irene. 1976. *Clara Ho Tung: A Hong Kong Lady, Her Family and Her Times*. Hong Kong: The Chinese University Press.

Greenfield, D. E. 1958. "Marriage by Chinese Law and Customs in Hong Kong." *International and Comparative Law Quarterly* 7 (July): 437-451.

Hong, Lawrence K. 1970. "The Chinese Family in a Modern Industrial Setting: Its Structure and Functions." Ph.D. Thesis, University of Notre Dame.

————. 1972. "The Association of Religion and Family Structure: The Case of Hong Kong Family." *Sociological Analysis* 33 (Spring): 50-57.

————. 1972. "A Comparative Analysis of Extended Kin Variables, Cohabitation and Anomia in Rural and Urban Hong Kong." *Sociology and Social Research* 57: 43-54.

————. 1973. "A Profile Analysis of the Chinese Family in an Urban Industrialized Setting." *International Journal of Sociology of the Family* 3 (1): 1-9.

Johnson, Elizabeth C. 1975. "Women and Childbearing in Kwan Mun Hau Village." Pp. 215-241 in *Women in Chinese Society*, edited by Margery

Wolf and Roxane Witke. Stanford: Stanford University Press.

†Lam, M. C. 1980. "Changing Pattern of Child Rearing Practices Among Urban Low-income Families in Hong Kong."

*Lau, S. K. 1978. "From Traditional Familism to Utilitarianistic Familism: The Metamorphosis of Familial Ethos Among the Hong Kong Chinese."

————. 1978. "Utilitarianistic Familism: The Basis of Political Stability in Hong Kong."

Lee, Chiung-ying. 1978. "Modernization and Marriage Attitude: A Hong Kong Case Study." Master Thesis, The Chinese University of Hong Kong. (in Chinese)

Liu, William T. 1966. "Family Interactions among Local and Refugee Chinese Families in Hong Kong." *Journal of Marriage and the Family* 28 (3): 314-323.

Liu, William T., Ira W. Hutchison, and Lawrence K. Hong. 1973. "Conjugal Power and Decision Making: A Methodological Note on Cross-Cultural Study of Family." *American Journal of Sociology* 79 (1): 84-98.

Mading, Klaus. 1968. "Research in Family Values and Culture Change in Hong Kong's Modern Chinese Novels." *Journal of the Hong Kong Branch of the Royal Asiatic Society* 8: 154-156.

Mitchell, Robert E. and Irene Lo. 1968. "Implication of Changes in Family Authority Relations for the Development of Independence and Assertiveness in Hong Kong Children." *Asian Survey* 8 (4): 309-322.

Mitchell, Robert E. 1971. "Changes in Fertility Rates and Family Size in Response to Changes in Age at Marriage, the Trend Away from Arranged Marriages, and Increasing Urbanization." *Population Studies* 25 (Nov.): 481-489.

————. 1971. "Some Social Implications of High Density Housing." *American Sociological Review* 29: 210-217.

————. 1972. *Family Life in Urban Hong Kong Vol. I and II.* Taipei: The Orient Cultural Service.

————. 1972. "Husband-wife Relations and Family-planning Practices in Urban Hong Kong." *Journal of Marriage and the Family* 34 (1): 139-146.

————. 1972. "Residential Patterns and Family Network I." *International Journal of Sociology of the Family* 2: 212-214.

Mok, Bong-ho. 1977. "A Survey of Parental Attitudes and Marital Satisfaction in Chaiwan: Implications for Family Life Education Programme." *The Hong Kong Journal of Social Work* 11 (2): 23-29.

*Ng, Pedro P. T. 1976. "The Family and Family Planning in Kwun Tong, Hong Kong: An Overview of the Findings."

Pegg, Leonard. 1975. "Chinese Marriage, Concubinage and Divorce in Contemporary Hong Kong." *Hong Kong Law Journal* 5 (1): 4-38.

Podmore, David and David Chaney. 1972. "Attitudes Towards Marriage and the Family among Young People in Hong Kong and Comparisons with the United States and Taiwan." *Journal of Comparative Family Studies* 3: 228-238.

————. 1973. "Parental Influence on the Occupational Choice of Young Adults in Hong Kong and Comparisons with the United States, the Phillipines and Japan." *International Journal of Comparative Sociology* 14 (1 and 2): 104-113.

Rosen, Sherry. 1976. *Mei Foo Sun Chuen: Middle Class Chinese Families in Transition.* Taipei: The Orient Cultural Service.

————. 1978. "Sibling and In-law Relationships in Hong Kong: The Emergent Role of Chinese Wives." *Journal of Marriage and the Family* 40 (3): 621-628.

Salaff, Janet W. 1976. "The Status of Unmarried Hong Kong Women and the Social Factors Contributing to Their Delayed Marriage." *Population Studies* 30 (Nov.): 391-412.

————. 1976. "Working Daughters in the Hong Kong Chinese Family: Female Filial Piety or a Transformation in the Family Power Structure?" *Journal of Social History* 9 (June): 439-465.

Stoodley, Bartlett H. 1967. "Normative Family Orientations of Chinese College Students in Hong Kong." *Journal of Marriage and the Family* 29 (4): 773-782.

Watson, James Lee. 1975. "Agnates and Outsiders: Adoption in a Chinese Lineage." *Man* (New Series) 10 (2): 293-306.

White, Henry E., Jr., ed. 1973. *An Anthology of Seminar Papers: The Changing Family, East and West.* Hong Kong: The Hong Kong Baptist College.

Wong, Aline K. 1973. "Rising Social Status and Economic Participation of Women in Hong Kong—Review of a Decade." *Southeast Asian Journal of Social Science* 1 (2): 11-28.

Wong, F. M. 1969. "Modern Ideology, Industrialization and the Middle Class Chinese Family in Hong Kong." Ph.D. Thesis, University of California, Santa Barbara.

————. 1970. "Current Dating and Love Patterns among College Students in Hong Kong." *Chung Chi Bulletin* No. 49 (Dec.): 18-22. (in Chinese)

*————. 1972. "Maternal Employment and Family Task-Power Differentiation among Lower Income Chinese Families."

————. 1972. "Modern Ideology, Industrialization and Conjugalism: The Hong Kong Case." *International Journal of Sociology of the Family* 2 (2): 139-152.

*————. 1974. "Industrialization and Family Structure in Hong Kong."

————. 1974. "The Family and Household Structure in Hong Kong." In *Monograph on Family and Household Structure*. Manila: Organization of Demographic Associates.

————. 1975. "Industrialization and Family Structure in Hong Kong." *Journal of Marriage and the Family* 37 (Nov.): 985-1000.

————. 1977. "Effects of the Employment of Mothers on Marital Role and Power Differentiation in Hong Kong." *International Journal of Sociology of the Family* 7 (2): 181-196.

————. 1977. "Modernization and Family Change." Pp. 47-68 in *A Quarter-Century of Hong Kong 1951-1976: Chung Chi College 25th Anniversary Symposium*. Chung Chi College, The Chinese University of Hong Kong. (in Chinese)

*————. 1977. "Family Structure and Processes in a New Industrial Town."

Wong, S. L. 1965. "Adjustment Problem between Two Generations Arising from the Changes of Social Values in Hong Kong." *Chung Chi Journal* 5 (1): 31-39. (in Chinese).

————. 1970. "Social Change and Parent-child Relations in Hong Kong." Pp. 167-174 in *Families in East and West*, edited by R. Hill and R. Konig. The Hague: Mouton and Co.

Wright, B. R. 1964. "Social Aspect of Changes in the Chinese Family Pattern in Hong Kong." *Journal of Social Psychology* 63 (1): 31-39.

(6) *Health*

Anderson, E. N. 1968. "Folk Medicine in Rural Hong Kong." *Etnoiatria* 2 (1): 22-28.

Anderson, E. N. and M. L. Anderson. 1975. "Folk Dietetics in Two Chinese Communities, and Its Implications for the Study of Chinese Medicine." Pp. 143-176 in *Medicine in Chinese Cultures*, edited by Arthur Kleinman, et al. Washington, D. C.: U. S. Department of Health, Education, and Welfare.

Au, K. K. 1977. "Trends of Infant Mortality in Hong Kong over the Past Two Decades." *Journal of the Society of Community Medicine, Hong Kong Branch* 8: 94-101.

————. 1978. "Childhood Mortality in Hong Kong over the Past Twenty-five Years." *Journal of the Society of Community Medicine, Hong Kong Branch* 9: 94-100.

*Chan, Y. K. 1978. "Life Satisfaction in Crowded Urban Environment."

————. 1978. "Life Satisfaction in Crowded Urban Environment." Pp. 187-196 in *Proceedings of the 4th Asian Pacific Social Development Seminar, A.S.P.A.C.* Korea: Seoul.

Cheng, Irene. 1962. "The Development of the Mental Health Movement in

Hong Kong." *Overseas Education* 34 (July): 63-70.

Cheung, Fanny M. 1979. "Residential Rehabilitation: Evaluation of Half-Way House for the Mentally Ill." *Hong Kong Journal of Mental Health* 8 (3): 17-22.

†————. 1980. "Adjustment and Social Behavior in the Community."

Choa, Gerald H. 1967. "Chinese Traditional Medicine and Contemporary Hong Kong." Pp. 31-35 in *Some Traditional Chinese Ideas and Conceptions in Hong Kong Social Life Today*, edited by Majorie Topley. Hong Kong: Hong Kong Branch of the Royal Asiatic Society.

————. 1967. "Some Ideas Concerning Food and Diet Among Hong Kong Chinese: The Constitution and Food Therapy." Pp. 54-59 in *Some Traditional Chinese Ideas and Conceptions in Hong Kong Social Life Today*, edited by Majorie Topley. Hong Kong: Hong Kong Branch of the Royal Asiatic Society.

————. 1977. "Medical and Health Services." Pp. 123-132 in *A Quarter-Century of Hong Kong 1951-1976: Chung Chi College 25th Anniversary Symposium*. Chung Chi College, The Chinese University of Hong Kong.

Colbourne, M. J. 1976. "Mortality Trends in Hong Kong." *Journal of the Society of Community Medicine, Hong Kong Branch* 8: 18-42.

————. 1979. "Developments in Medical Education in Hong Kong in the Last 25 Years." Pp. 7-16 in *Recent Development in Medical Education*, edited by G. H. Choa. Hong Kong: The Chinese University Press.

Higa, Sister Mary Louise. 1975. "Community Nursing in Hong Kong." *Impact* 10 (5): 169-171.

Hodge, Peter. 1973. "Community Development and Mental Health." *Hong Kong Journal of Mental Health* 2 (1): 2-7.

*Lee, Rance P. L. 1972. "Organizational Complexity and Industrial Health Services: A Study of Kwun Tong."

*————. 1972. "Population, Housing and the Availability of Medical and Health Services in an Industrializing Chinese Community."

*Lee, Rance P. L., and Grace Y. C. Chiu. 1972. "Spatial Distribution of Modern Western and Traditional Chinese Medical Practitioners in an Industrializing Chinese Town."

*Lee, Rance P. L. 1972. "Study of Health Systems in Kwun Tong: Preliminary Research Report No. I: Health Attitudes and Behavior of Residents."

*————. 1972. "Study of Health Systems in Kwun Tong: Preliminary Research Report No. II: General Health Care Units and Physicians."

*————. 1972. "Study of Health Systems in Kwun Tong: Preliminary Research Report No. III: Organizations and Attitudes of Western-trained and Traditional Chinese Medical Personnel in an Industrial Community of

Hong Kong."

————. 1973. "Population, Housing and the Availability of Medical and Health Services in an Industrializing Chinese Community." *Journal of The Chinese University of Hong Kong* 1: 191-208.

*————. 1974. "Problems of Integrating Chinese and Western Health Services in Hong Kong: Topia and Utopia."

*————. 1974. "The Stratification between Modern and Traditional Professions: A Study of Health Services in Hong Kong."

————. 1975. "Health Services System in Hong Kong: Professional Stratification in a Modernizing Society." *Inquiry* Supplement to Vol. XII (June): 51-62.

————. 1975. "Interaction between Chinese and Western Medicine in Hong Kong: Modernization and Professional Inequality." Pp. 219-240 in *Medicine in Chinese Cultures: Comparative Studies of Health Care in Chinese and Other Societies*, edited by A. Kleinman et al. Washington, D. C.: U.S. Department of Health, Education and Welfare.

————. 1975. "Toward a Convergence of Modern Western and Traditional Chinese Medicine Services in Hong Kong." Pp. 393-412 in *Topias and Utopias in Health*, edited by S. R. Ingman and A. E. Thomas. The Hague: Mouton and Co.

*————. 1976. "Sex and Social Class Differences in Mental Illness: The Case of Hong Kong."

————. 1976. "Social Psychological Correlates of Psychiatric Impairment in Hong Kong." *Hong Kong Nursing Journal* 21 (Nov.): 33-49.

*Lee, Rance P. L., Tak-sing Cheung, and Yuet-wah Cheung. 1978. "Material and Non-material Considerations in the Life Satisfaction of Urban Residents in Hong Kong."

Lee, Rance P. L. and Y. K. Chan. 1978. "Personal Happiness in Hong Kong." *Journal of the Hong Kong Society of Community Medicine* 9 (2): 68-72.

*Lee, Rance P. L. 1979. "High Density Effects in Urban Hong Kong: What Do We Know and What Should We Do?"

Lee, Rance P. L. and Suet-ming Hsu. 1979. "Stress as a Function of the Inconsistency Between Education and Economic Status." *Hong Kong Journal of Mental Health* 8 (3): 1-7.

Lee, Rance P. L. 1980. "Perceptions and Uses of Chinese Medicine among the Chinese in Hong Kong." *Culture, Medicine and Psychiatry: An International Journal of Comparative Cross-Cultural Research* 4: 1-31.

————. 1980. "Sex Roles, Social Status and Psychiatric Symptoms in Urban Hong Kong." In *Normal and Deviant Behavior in Chinese Cultures*, edited by Tsung-yi Lin and Arthur Kleinman. D. Reidel Publishing Co.

Lethbridge, H. J. 1971. "A Chinese Association in Hong Kong: The Tung

Wah." *Contributions to Asian Studies* 1: 144-158.

MacLean, Una. 1977. "Behavioral Sciences in the Training of Medical Under-graduates." *Journal of the Society of Community Medicine, Hong Kong Branch* 8: 86-93.

Millar, S. E. 1976. "Health and Well-being in Relation to High Density Living in Hong Kong." Ph.D. Thesis, Australian National University.

Mitchell, Robert E. 1971. "Some Social Implications of High Density Housing." *American Sociological Review* 29: 210-217.

Mitchell, Robert E. and Barbara M. Wong. 1972. *Levels of Emotional Strain in Southeast Asian Cities: A Study of Individual Responses to the Stresses of Urbanization and Industrialization, Vol. I and II.* Taipei: The Orient Cultural Service.

Potter, Jack. 1974. "Cantonese Shamanism." Pp. 207-243 in *Religion and Ritual in Chinese Society*, edited by Arthur P. Wolf. Stanford: Stanford University Press.

Priestley, K. E. and Peryl R. Wright. 1956. *Mental Health and Education in Hong Kong*. Hong Kong: Hong Kong University Press.

Tang, Donna. 1978. "Regionalization of the Medical and Health Services." *Journal of the Society of Community Medicine, Hong Kong Branch* 9: 101-104.

Topley, Majorie. 1970. "Chinese and Western Medicine in Hong Kong: Some Social and Cultural Determinants of Variation, Interaction and Change." Pp. 241-271 in *Medicine in Chinese Cultures*, edited by Arthur Kleinman, et al. Washington, D. C.: U.S. Department of Health, Education and Welfare.

————. 1970. "Chinese Traditional Ideas and the Treatment of Disease: Two Examples from Hong Kong." *Man* 5 (3): 421-437.

————. 1976. "Chinese Traditional Etiology and Methods of Cure in Hong Kong." Pp. 243-265 in *Asian Medical Systems*, edited by Charles Leslie. Berkeley: University of California.

Worth, R. M. 1963. "Urbanization and Squatter Resettlement as Related to Child Health in Hong Kong." *American Journal of Hygiene* 78: 338-348.

Yap, P. M. 1965. "Koro, a Culture-bound Depersonalization Syndrome." *British Journal of Psychiatry* 3 (470): 43-50.

————. 1967. "Ideas of Mental Health and Disorder in Hong Kong and Their Practical Influence." Pp. 73-85 in *Some Traditional Chinese Ideas and Conceptions in Hong Kong Social Life Today*, edited by Majorie Topley. Hong Kong: Hong Kong Branch of the Royal Asiatic Society.

————. 1972. "Mental Illness among Western Expatriates in a Plural Society: An Exploratory Study." Pp. 344-363 in *Transcultural Research in Mental Health*, edited by William P. Lebra. Honolulu: East West Center Book, University of Hawaii Press.

(7) Housing

Aijmer, Göran. 1975. "An Enquiry into Chinese Settlement Patterns: The Rural Squatters of Hong Kong." *Man* (New Series) 10 (4): 559-570.

Chan, Hung-kwan. 1970. "The Provision of Public Housing in Hong Kong." Master Thesis, University of Sidney.

*Choi, C. Y. 1977. "Housing Policy and Internal Movement of Population: A Study of Kwun Tong, A Chinese New Town in Hong Kong."

*Choi, C. Y. and Y. K. Chan. 1978. "Public Housing Development and Population Movement: A Study of Kwun Tong, Hong Kong."

Chung, Y. P. 1972. "Residential Changes of Households in Kowloon, Hong Kong." Ph.D. Thesis, University of Minnesota.

Drakakis-Smith, D. W. 1971. "Housing Needs and Planning Policies for the Asian City—The Lessons from Hong Kong." *International Journal of Environmental Studies* 1: 115-128.

————. 1972. "Tenement Slums in Hong Kong." *Pacific Viewpoint* 13 (2): 155-168.

————. 1973. *Housing Provision in Metropolitan Hong Kong*. A Monograph of the Centre of Asian Studies, University of Hong Kong.

————. 1973. "Housing Needs and Policies for Cities in Developing Countries with Special Reference to Hong Kong." Ph.D. Thesis, University of Hong Kong.

Dwyer, D. J. 1965. "The Problems of In-migration and Squatter Settlement in Asian Cities: Two Case Studies, Manila and Victoria Kowloon." *Asian Studies* 2: 145-169.

————. 1970. "Urban Squatters: The Relevance of the Hong Kong Experience." *Asian Survey* 10 (7): 607-613.

Fung, Chee-keung. 1973. "Commuting Patterns of Resettled Squatters in Hong Kong: A Geographical Study." Master Thesis, University of Hong Kong.

Golger, Otto Johnson. 1968. "An Environmental Study of Squatter and Resettlement Housing in Hong Kong, Vol. I, II, and III." Ph.D. Thesis, University of Hong Kong.

————. 1972. "Hong Kong: A Problem of Housing the Masses." *Ekistics* 32 (196): 173-177.

Hassan, Riaz. 1975. "Social and Psychological Implications of High Density in Hong Kong and Singapore." *Ekistics* 39 (235): 382-386.

Hopkins, Keith. 1973. *Public Housing Policy in Hong Kong*. A Monograph of the Centre of Asian Studies, University of Hong Kong.

Hui, C. S., W. F. Maunder, and J. Tsao. 1959. *Hong Kong's Resettled Squatters: The Final Report of the 1957 Sample Survey of Resettlement Estates.* Hong Kong: Hong Kong University Manuscript.

Johnson, Sheila K. 1967. "Hong Kong's Resettled Squatters: A Statistical Analysis." *Asian Survey* 6 (11): 643-656.

*Kan, Angela W. S. and Pedro P. T. Ng. 1974. "The Hostel Need of the Students of The Chinese University of Hong Kong."

*Kan, Angela W. S. 1974. "A Study of Neighborly Interaction in Public Housing: The Case of Hong Kong."

*————. 1975. "Implications of Concentrated Utilization of Local Facilities and Services in Public Housing Estates in Hong Kong."

Kehl, Frank. 1975. "Environmental Health: Hong Kong Squatters and Engles' Remarks on the Housing Question." Pp. 253-266 in *Topias and Utopias in Health*, edited by S. R. Ingman and A. E. Thomas. The Hague: Mouton and Co.

Lai, C. Y. 1975. "Human Crowding in Hong Kong: A Study of Its Earliest Type of Public Housing." Pp. 141-180 in *Themes on Pacific Lands*, edited by M.C.R. Edgell and B. H. Farrell. Victoria, B.C.: University of Victoria.

*Lee, Rance P. L. 1972. "Population, Housing and the Availability of Medical and Health Services in an Industrializing Chinese Community."

Leeds, P. F. 1966. "Housing in Hong Kong—Postwar Problems." *Journal of Local Administration Overseas* 5 (July): 184-193.

Lu, Lo-chung and Z. K. Kwok. 1973. *Housing in Hong Kong: An Anatomy of the Government's Ten Year Housing Programme.* A Monograph of the Research and Development Centre, Hong Kong. (in Chinese)

Mitchell, Robert E. 1971. "Some Social Implications of High Density Housing." *American Sociological Review* 36 (Feb.): 18-29.

————. 1972. *Housing, Urban Growth and Economic Development.* Taipei: The Orient Cultural Service.

Pryor, E. G. 1971. "An Assessment of the Need and Scope for Urban Renewal in Hong Kong." Ph.D. Thesis, University of Hong Kong.

————. 1972. "A Historical Review of Housing Conditions in Hong Kong." *Journal of the Hong Kong Branch of the Royal Asiatic Society* 12: 89-129.

————. 1973. *Housing in Hong Kong.* Hong Kong: Oxford University Press.

————. 1975. "Environmental Quality and Housing Policy in Hong Kong." *Pacific Viewpoint* 16 (Nov.): 195-207.

Richmond, G. M. 1971. "Urban Housing in Hong Kong." Master Thesis, York University.

Rudduck, Grenfell and Kenneth H. C. Fung. 1959. "Housing in Malaya and Hong Kong—A Contrast." *Ekistics* 8 (July): 16-23.

Sparks, Douglas W. 1976. "Interethnic Interaction—A Matter of Definition:

Ethnicity in a Housing Estate in Hong Kong." *Journal of the Hong Kong Branch of the Royal Asiatic Society* 16: 57-80.

Wong, Luke S. K. 1968. "Squatters of Urban Hong Kong: Their Distribution, Morphology, Functions and Evolutions." Ph.D. Thesis, University of Hong Kong.

————. 1970. "Squatters in Pre-war Hong Kong." *Journal of Oriental Studies* 8: 189-205.

————, ed. 1978. *Housing in Hong Kong: A Multidisciplinary Study*. Hong Kong: Heinemann Educational Books (Asia) Ltd.

Yeung, Yue-man and D. E. Drakakis-Smith. 1974. "Comparative Perspectives on Public Housing in Singapore and Hong Kong." *Asian Survey* 13 (8): 763-775.

(8) *Industrial Relations*

But, Ho-ming. 1979. "Orientation to Work and Union Commitment: A Case Study of the Union of Midwives in Hong Kong." Master Thesis, The Chinese University of Hong Kong.

Carr, N. 1973. "Employee Attitudes Survey in a Hong Kong Engineering Company." *Journal of Industrial Relations* 15 (2): 108-111.

*Chin, Ai-li. 1972. "Hong Kong Managerial Styles: Chinese and Western Approaches to Conflict Management."

Chung, C. Y. 1971. "A Study of the Leisure Activities of Youth Labourers in Hong Kong." An Occasional Paper of Sociology and Social Work Department, Hong Kong Baptist College, Hong Kong.

England, Joe and John Rear. 1975. *Chinese Labour under British Rule*. Hong Kong: Oxford University Press.

Fung, W. M. 1977. "The Labour Union Movement." Pp. 37-40 in *A Quarter-Century of Hong Kong 1951-1976: Chung Chi College 25th Anniversary Symposium*. Chung Chi College, The Chinese University of Hong Kong. (in Chinese)

Hetherington, R. M. 1963. "Industrial Labor in Hong Kong." *Hong Kong Economic Papers* 2: 28-41.

*King, Ambrose Y. C. and Peter J. L. Man. 1974. "The Role of Small Factory in Economic Development: The Case of Hong Kong."

*King, Ambrose Y. C. and Davy Leung. 1975. "The Chinese Touch in Small Industrial Organizations."

*Lau, S. K. 1977. "Managerial Attitudes Toward Employees: Traditionalistic or Modern?"

Law, Yu-fai. 1975. "Tradition and Modernity: A Study of Factory Organization in a New Territories Temporary Area." Master Thesis, The Chinese University of Hong Kong.

*Lee, Rance P. L. 1972. "Organizational Complexity and Industrial Health Services: A Study of Kwun Tong."

*———. 1972. "Organizational Size, Structural Differentation and the Man at the Top in Hong Kong."

Leung, Tat-shing. 1975. "Review of Social and Economic Development Planning in Hong Kong through the Eye of Workers." Pp. 93-99 in *One World Only: Social Aspect of Economic Development Planning in Asia*. An International Forum under the Auspices of the Friedrich-Ebert-Stiftung, Bangkok, Jan. 3-9. Bangkok, FES.

*Mok, Victor. 1973. "The Organization and Management of Factories in Kwun Tong."

*———. 1974. "The Small Factories in Kwun Tong: Problems and Strategies for Development."

Ng, Wing-cheung. 1974. "A Sociological Study of the Apprenticeship System in Hong Kong." Master Thesis, The Chinese University of Hong Kong.

Silin, Robert H. 1972. "Marketing and Credit in a Hong Kong Wholesale Market." Pp. 327-352 in *Economic Organization in Chinese Society*, edited by W. E. Willmott. Stanford: Stanford University Press.

†Ting, Theodora. 1978. "The Socio-psychological Factors of Labor Turnover in Hong Kong."

Ward, B. E. 1972. "A Small Factory in Hong Kong: Some Aspects of Its Internal Organization." Pp. 353-385 in *Economic Organization in Chinese Society*, edited by W. E. Willmott. Stanford: Stanford University Press.

(9) *Politics and Social Order*

Au, William Ka-hing. 1978. "An Exploratory Study of Police Attitude and Behaviour in Hong Kong." Master Thesis, The Chinese University of Hong Kong.

Carr, Neil. 1975. "Report of Hong Kong: Quality of Life Means Political and Social Change." Pp. 139-156 in *One Way Only: Industrialization and Environment*. An International Forum under the Auspices of the Friedrich-Ebert-Stiftung, Tokyo, Nov. 25–Dec. 1, 1973. Tokyo, FES.

Catron, G. W. 1971. "China and Hong Kong 1945-1967." Ph.D. Thesis, Harvard University.

———. 1972. "Hong Kong and Chinese Foreign Policy 1955-60." *The China Quarterly* No. 51: 405-424.

Chau, Lam-yam. 1979. "Power Bifurcation in a Changing Chinese Village of Hong Kong." Master Thesis, The Chinese University of Hong Kong.

Cheng, Tung-tsai. 1969. "Chinese Unofficial Members of the Legislative and Executive Councils in Hong Kong up to 1941." *Journal of the Hong Kong Branch of the Royal Asiatic Society* 9: 7-30.

Clark, David. 1979. "The Policeman's Duties: Problems of Definition and Enforcement." *Hong Kong Journal of Public Administration* 1 (1): 30-56.

Cooper, John. 1970. *Colony in Conflict: The Hong Kong Disturbances May 1967-January 1968.* Hong Kong: Swindon Book Co.

Covin, David Leroy. n.d. "Political Culture as an Analytical Instrument: An Examination of Refugees in Hong Kong." Ph.D. Thesis, Washington State University.

Endacott, G. B. 1956. "Proposals for Municipal Government in Early Hong Kong." *Journal of Oriental Studies* 3 (1): 75-82.

————. 1964. *Government and People in Hong Kong 1841-1962: A Constitutional History.* Hong Kong: Hong Kong University Press.

————. 1973. *A History of Hong Kong.* Revised Edition. Hong Kong: Oxford University Press.

Endacott, G. B. and Alan Birch. 1978. *Hong Kong Eclipse.* Hong Kong: Oxford University Press.

Freedman, Maurice. 1950. "Colonial Law and Chinese Society." *Journal of Royal Anthropological Institute* 89: 97-126.

————. 1966. "Shift of Power in the Hong Kong New Territories." *Journal of Asian and African Studies* 1 (1): 3-12.

Fung, Yee-wang. 1973. "Some Contributory Factors to Student Movement in Hong Kong." *Asia Quarterly* 4: 287-311.

Hambro, E. I. 1955. *The Problem of Chinese Refugees in Hong Kong.* Leyden: A. W. Sijthoff.

Harris, P. B. 1974. "The Frozen Politics of Hong Kong." *World Today* 30 (6): 259-267.

————. 1974. "Sources of Stability and Instability in Hong Kong." *Southeast Asian Spectrum* 3 (1): 42-50.

————. 1975. "Representative Politics in a British Dependency: Some Reflections on Problems of Representation in Hong Kong." *Parliamentary Affairs* 28 (2): 180-198.

————. 1978. *Hong Kong: A Study in Bureaucratic Politics.* Hong Kong: New Kwok Printing Press Co. Ltd.

————. 1979. "Government and Politics." Pp. 69-86 in *A Quarter-Century of Hong Kong 1951-1976: Chung Chi College 25th Anniversary Symposium.* Chung Chi College, The Chinese University of Hong Kong.

Hayes, James W. 1977. *The Hong Kong Region 1850-1911: Institution and Leadership in Town and Countryside.* U.S.A.: Archon Books.

Heaton, William. 1970. "Maoist Revolutionary Strategy and Modern Colonialism: the Cultural Revolution in Hong Kong." *Asian Survey* 10 (9): 840-857.

Heinl, Robert D. 1966. "Hong Kong: Communism and Colonialism in Collision." *U.S. Naval Institute Proceedings* 92 (July): 72-81.

Ho, H. C. Y. 1979. *The Fiscal System of Hong Kong*. London: Croom Helm.

Ho, Mary Kwai-wah. 1976. "Social Action and Political Activities—A Case Study: The Movement to Eliminate Sex and Violence in Children's Comic Books in Hong Kong." *The Hong Kong Journal of Social Work 10* (2): 18-23.

Hoadley, J. S. 1967. "Political Attitudes among Chung Chi College Students." *Chung Chi Bulletin* 43: 43-48.

————. 1968. "The Government and Politics of Hong Kong: A Descriptive Study with Special Reference to the Analytical Framework of G. Almond." Ph.D. Thesis, University of California, Santa Barbara.

————. 1970. "Hong Kong is the Lifeboat: Notes on Political Culture and Socialization." *Journal of Oriental Studies* 8: 206-218.

————. 1973. "Political Participation of Hong Kong Chinese: Patterns and Trends." *Asian Survey* 13 (6): 604-616.

*————. 1980. "Planned Development and Political Adaptability in Rural Hong Kong."

Hughes, Richard. 1976. *Hong Kong: Borrowed Time, Borrowed Place*. London: Deutsch.

Johnson, Graham E. 1972. "Hong Kong: Colonial Anarchronism." *The China Quarterly* No. 51: 554-557.

————. 1977. "Leaders and Leadership in an Expanding New Territories Town." *The China Quarterly* No. 69: 109-125.

*King, Ambrose Y. C. 1972. "The Political Culture of Kwun Tong: A Chinese Community in Hong Kong."

————. 1972. "A Political-administrative Response to Urban Growth." Pp. 201-233 in *Social Science Research for Urban Development in Southeast Asia*, edited by Kasem Suwanagul, Jacques Amyot, and Kramol Tongdhamachart. Southeast Asian Social Science Association.

*————. 1973. "The Administrative Absorption of Politics in Hong Kong: With Special Emphasis on the City District Officer Scheme."

————. 1975. "Administrative Absorption of Politics in Hong Kong: Emphasis on the Grass Roots Level." *Asian Survey* 15 (5): 422-439.

————. 1977. "The Political Culture of Kwun Tong: A Chinese Community in Hong Kong." *Southeast Asian Journal of Social Science* 5 (1 & 2): 123-141.

*Kuan, Hsin-chi and S. K. Lau. 1979. "Development and Resuscitation of Rural Leadership in Hong Kong—The Case of Neo-indirect Rule."

*Lau, S. K. 1978. "Utilitarianistic Familism: The Basis of Political Stability in Hong Kong."

*Lau, S. K. and Kam-fai Ho. 1980. "Social Accommodation of Politics: The

Case of the Young Hong Kong Workers."

Lethbridge, H. J. 1971. "The District Watch Committee: The Chinese Executive Council of Hong Kong." *Journal of the Hong Kong Branch of the Royal Asiatic Society* 11: 116-141.

————. 1978. *Hong Kong: Stability and Change: A Collection of Essays*. Hong Kong: Oxford University Press.

Liu, William T., Ira W. Hutchison, and Lawrence K. Hong. 1973. "Conjugal Power and Decision Making: A Methodological Note on Cross-Cultural Study of Family." *American Journal of Sociology* 79 (1): 84-89.

Lorenzo, M. 1959. "Attitude of Communist China Towards Hong Kong." Master Thesis, University of Chicago.

Mills, Lennox Algernon. 1970. *British Rule in Eastern Asia: A Study of Contemporary Government and Economic Development in British Malaya and Hong Kong*. N. Y.: Russell and Russell.

Miners, N. J. 1975. *The Government and Politics of Hong Kong*. Hong Kong: Oxford University Press.

————. 1975. "Hong Kong: A Case Study in Political Stability." *Journal of Commonwealth Comparative Politics* 13 (1): 26-39.

Podmore, David. 1971. "Localization in the Hong Kong Government Service." *Journal of Commonwealth Political Science* 9: 36-51.

Riberio, R. A. 1977. *The Law and Practice of the Hong Kong Labor Tribunal: A Socio-legal Study on the Problem of Legal Access*. A Monograph of the Centre of Asian Studies, University of Hong Kong.

*Shively, Stanley. 1972. "Political Orientations in Hong Kong—A Socio-psychological Approach."

Smith, Carl. 1971. "The Emergence of a Chinese Elite in Hong Kong." *Journal of the Hong Kong Branch of the Royal Asiatic Society* 11: 74-115.

Speak, C. M. 1969. *Hong Kong and the World Today*. Hong Kong: Oxford University Press.

Tang, Stephen Lung-wai. 1973. "The Power Structure in a Colonial Society—A Sociological Study of the Unofficial Members of the Legislative Council in Hong Kong 1948-1971." B.S.Sc. Thesis, The Chinese University of Hong Kong.

Wong, Aline K. 1970-71. "Political Apathy and Political System in Hong Kong." *United College Journal* 8: 1-20.

*————. 1972. "Higher Non-expatriate Civil Servants in Hong Kong."

Yang, T. L. 1977. "Law and Legislation." Pp. 87-100 in *A Quarter-Century of Hong Kong 1951-1976: Chung Chi College 25th Anniversary Symposium*. Chung Chi College, The Chinese University of Hong Kong.

(10) *Population and Fertility Planning*

Aijmer, Göran. 1973. "Migrant into Hong Kong's New Territories: On the

Background of Outsider Vegetable Farmers." *Ethnos* 1 (4): 57-70.

Anderson, E. N., Jr. 1972. "Some Chinese Methods of Dealing with Crowding." *Urban Anthropology* 1: 141-150.

Au, K. K. 1977. "Trends of Infant Mortality in Hong Kong over the Past Two Decades." *Journal of the Society of Community Medicine, Hong Kong Branch* 1: 94-101.

————. 1978. "Childhood Mortality in Hong Kong over the Past Twenty-five Years." *Journal of the Society of Community Medicine, Hong Kong Branch* 9: 94-100.

Barnett, A. D. 1953. "Social Osmosis—Refugees in Hong Kong." *American Universities Fieldstaff Report* 2 (2): 1-8.

Berkowitz, Morris I. 1968. "Plover Cove Village to Taipo Market: A Study of Forced Migration." *Journal of the Hong Kong Branch of the Royal Asiatic Society* 8: 96-108.

Census and Statistics Department. 1978. *Hong Kong Population: A 20-Year Projection.* Hong Kong Government.

Chan, K. C. 1971. "Hong Kong Oral Contraceptive Follow-up Study." *Studies in Family Planning* 2 (3): 70-74.

————. 1971. "Hong Kong: Report on the IUD Reassurance Project." *Studies in Family Planning* 2 (11): 225-233.

————. 1976. "The Role of the Family Planning Association in Hong Kong's Fertility Decline." *Studies in Family Planning* 7 (10): 284-289.

Chan, Y. K. 1979. "Urban Density and Social Relation." *Journal of The Chinese University of Hong Kong* 5 (1): 315-322.

*Choi, C. Y. and K. C. Chan. 1973. "The Impact of Industrialization on Fertility in Hong Kong: A Demographic, Social and Economic Analysis."

Choi, C. Y. 1973. "Population Movement in Hong Kong 1961-1971." *United College Journal* 11: 147-154.

————. "Some Consequences of Future Population Trends in Hong Kong." *The Hong Kong Journal of Social Work* 8 (1): 6-12.

*————. "The Impact of Industrialization on Fertility in Hong Kong: Some Psychological Aspects."

————. 1975. "Urbanization and Redistribution of Population in Hong Kong—A Case Study." In *Patterns of Urbanization: Comparative Country Studies,* edited by Goldstein and Sly. Liege: Ordina Edition for IUSSP.

*————. 1977. "Housing Policy and Internal Movement of Population: A Study of Kwun Tong, A Chinese New Town in Hong Kong."

*Choi, C. Y. and Y. K. Chan. 1978. "Public Housing Development and Population Movement: A Study of Kwun Tong, Hong Kong."

Colbourne, M. J. 1976. "Mortality Trends in Hong Kong." *Journal of the*

Society of Community Medicine, Hong Kong Branch 8: 18-42.

Cottle, T. F. 1967. "Comparative Evaluation of Occupations by English-speaking Refugee, and Local Hong Kong Adolescents." *Sociological Review* 15 (1): 21-31.

Coughlin, Richard J. and Margaret M. Coughlin. 1963. "Fertility and Birth Control among Low Income Chinese Families in Hong Kong." *Journal of Marriage and Family Living* 25 (2): 171-177.

Chun, W. C. 1964. "Hong Kong: The Family Planning Association." *Eastern World* 18 (2): 13-14.

Chung, Betty Jamie. 1974. "Social and Psychological Aspects of Fertility in Hong Kong." Reprint Paper of the East-West Population Institute, Honolulu.

Davis, S. G. 1959. *Population Growth and Pressure in South China and Hong Kong*. Tokyo: Kasai Publishing & Printing Co.

————. 1962. "The Rural-Urban Migration in Hong Kong and Its New Territories." *The Geographical Journal* 128 (3): 328-333.

Fan, Shuh-ching. 1974. *The Population of Hong Kong*. Hong Kong: Swindon Book Co.

————. 1974. "The Population Projection of Hong Kong." *Southeast Asian Journal of Social Science* 2 (1 & 2): 105-117.

Freedman, Maurice. 1979. "Emigration from the New Territories." Pp. 223-231 in *The Study of Chinese Society*, edited by G. William Skinner. Stanford: Stanford University Press.

Freedman, R. and A. L. Adlakha. 1968. "Recent Family Declines in Hong Kong: The Role of the Changing Age Structure." *Population Studies* 22 (2): 181-198.

Freedman, R., D. N. Namboothiri, A. L. Adlakha, and K. C. Chan. 1969. "Hong Kong: The Continuing Fertility Decline, 1967." *Studies in Family Planning* 44: 8-15.

————. 1970. "Hong Kong's Fertility Decline, 1961-1968." *Population Index* 36 (1): 3-18.

Freedman, R. 1973. "A Comment on 'Social and Economic Factors in Hong Kong's Fertility Decline' by Sui-ying Wat and R. W. Hodge." *Population Studies* 27 (3): 589-595.

Hayes, James W. 1963. "Movement of Villages on Lantau Island for Fung Shui Reasons." *Journal of the Hong Kong Branch of the Royal Asiatic Society* 3: 143-144.

Johnson, Graham E. 1973. "In-migration and Community Expansion in Hong Kong: The Case of Tsuen Wan." *Journal of Oriental Studies* 11 (1): 107-114.

*Lee, Rance P. L. 1972. "Population, Housing and the Availability of Medical and Health Services in an Industrializing Chinese Community."

*————. 1976. "The Fading of Earthbound Compulsion in a Hong Kong Village: Population Mobility and Its Economic Implication."

Lo, Chor-pang. 1968. "Changing Population Distribution in the Hong Kong New Territories." *Annals of the Association of the American Geographers* 58 (2): 273-284.

————. 1972. "A Typology of Hong Kong Census District: A Study in Urban Structure." *Journal of Tropical Geography* 34: 34-43.

Millar, S. E. 1976. "Health and Well-being in Relation to High Density Living in Hong Kong." Ph.D. Thesis, Australian National University.

Mitchell, Robert E. 1968. "Hong Kong: An Evaluation of Field Workers and Decision Making in Family Planning Programs." *Studies in Family Planning* 30 (May): 7-12.

————. 1971. "Changes in Fertility Rates and Family Size in Response to Changes in Age at Marriage, the Trend Away from Arranged Marriages, and Increasing Urbanization." *Population Studies* 25 (Nov.): 481-489.

*Ng, Pedro P. T. 1976. "The Family and Family Planning in Kwun Tong, Hong Kong: An Overview of the Findings."

*————. 1978. "Family Planning, Fertility Decline, and Family Size Preference in Hong Kong: Some General Observations."

Pryor, E. G. 1967. "Population Changes in Hong Kong between 1961 & 1966." *Australian Planning Institute Journal* 5 (4): 99-102.

Saw, See-hock. 1967. "Errors in Chinese Age-statistics." *Demography* 4 (2): 859-875.

Saw, See-hock and K. C. Chan. 1971. "Family Planning Acceptance in Hong Kong." *The Journal of Family Welfare* 18 (1): 16-25.

Saw, See-hock and W. K. Chiu. 1975. "Population Growth and Redistribution in Hong Kong, 1844-1975." *Southeast Asian Journal of Social Science* 4 (1): 123-131.

Schmitt, R. C. 1963. "Implications of Density in Hong Kong." *Journal of the American Institute of Planners* 29 (Aug.): 210-217.

Taeuber, Irene B. 1972. "Chinese Population in Transition: The City-states." *Population Index* 38 (1): 3-34.

Traver, Harold. 1976. "Privacy and Density: A Survey of Public Attitudes Towards Privacy in Hong Kong." *Hong Kong Law Journal* 6 (3): 327-343.

United Nations. 1974. *The Demographic Situation in Hong Kong.* ESCAP Country Monograph Series No. 1.

Uttley, K. H. 1938. "The Chinese Urban Death Rate in Hong Kong." *Transaction of Royal Society Academy of Tropical Medicine and Hygiene* 31 (Jan.): 457-468.

Vaughn, T. D. 1966. "Some Aspects of Postwar Population Growth in Hong

Kong." *Economic Geography* 42 (1): 37-51.

Ward, B. E. 1964. "The Surge to the Towns." *UNESCO Courier* 9 (Sept.): 5-6.

Wat, Siu-ying and R. W. Hodge. 1972. "Social and Economic Factors in Hong Kong's Fertility Decline." *Population Studies* 26 (3): 455-464.

Watson, James Lee. 1972. "A Chinese Emigrant Community: The Main Lineage in Hong Kong and London." Ph.D. Thesis, University of California, Berkeley.

————. 1975. *Emigration and the Chinese Lineage: The Mans in Hong Kong and London*. Berkeley: University of California Press.

(11) *Religion and Folk Tradition*

Aijmer, Göran. 1968. "Being Caught by a Fishnet: On Fengshui in Southeast China." *Journal of the Hong Kong Branch of the Royal Asiatic Society* 8: 74-81.

Berkowitz, Morris I., F. P. Brandauer, and J. H. Reed. 1968. "Study Program on Chinese Religious Practices in Hong Kong—A Progress Report." *Ching Feng* 11 (3): 5-19.

————. 1969. "Folk Religion in an Urban Setting: A Study of Hakka Villagers in Transition." *Ching Feng* 12 (3 & 4): 1-167.

————. 1969. *Folk Religion in An Urban Setting: A Study of Hakka Villagers in Transition*. Christian Study Centre on Chinese Religion and Culture, Hong Kong.

Berkowitz Morris I. and J. H. Reed. 1971. "Research into the Chinese Little Tradition: A Progress Report." *Journal of Asian and African Studies* 6 (3 & 4): 233-238.

Berkowitz, Morris I. 1975. "The Tenacity of Chinese Folk Tradition—Two Studies of Hong Kong Chinese." An Occasional Paper of the Institute of Southeast Asian Studies, Singapore.

Boxer, Baruch. 1968. "Space, Change and Feng-shui in Tsuen Wan's Urbanization." *Journal of Asian and African Studies* 3 (3 & 4): 226-240.

Brim, John A. 1974. "Village Alliance Temples in Hong Kong." Pp. 93-104 in *Religion and Ritual in Chinese Society*, edited by Arthur P. Wolf. Stanford: Stanford University Press.

Buck, S. 1952. "Chinese Temples in Hong Kong." *The Orient* 20 (7): 27-29.

Chuang, Shen. 1978. *Chinese Temples in Hong Kong Island, Hong Kong*. A Monograph of the Centre of Asian Studies, University of Hong Kong.

Delaney, Sister Joan. 1975. *A Report on a Survey of Religious Women in Hong Kong*. The Association of the Major Superiors of Religious Women, Hong Kong.

Delaney, Sister Joan and Y. K. Chan. 1975. "A Study of the Role of Religious

Organization in the Kwun Tong Community." *United College Journal* 12 & 13 (Feb.): 253-280.

Freedman, Maurice. 1979. "Chinese Geomancy: Some Observations in Hong Kong." Pp. 189-211 in *The Study of Chinese Society*, edited by G. William Skinner. Stanford: Stanford University Press.

Hayes, James W. 1963. "Movement of Villages on Lantau Island for Fung Shui Reasons." *Journal of the Hong Kong Branch of the Royal Asiatic Society* 3: 143-144.

Hong, Lawrence K. 1972. "The Association of Religion and Family Structure: The Case of Hong Kong Family." *Sociological Analysis* 33 (Spring): 50-57.

King, Rex et al. 1974. "The School Systems, Social Values and the Church: A Disucssion." *Ching Feng* 17 (4): 199-218.

Lau, Tat-ching. 1972. "A Political, Economic and Social Analysis of the Buddhist Career in Hong Kong." Master Thesis, The Chinese University of Hong Kong. (in Chinese)

Lee, Wing-yee. 1969. *Youth and Religion: A Religious Attitude Study of Hong Kong Secondary School Students*. Lutheran World Federation Broadcasting Service, Hong Kong.

Liu, Chih-p'ing. 1970. "The Indigenization of Church and Its Institutions in Hong Kong." *Ching Feng* 13 (1): 3-5.

March, A. L. 1968. "An Appreciation of Chinese Geomancy." *Journal of Asian Studies* 27: 253-267.

*Myers, John T. and Davy Leung. 1974. "A Chinese Spirit-medium Temple in Kwun Tong: A Preliminary Report."

Myers, John T. 1975. "A Hong Kong Spirit-medium Temple." *Journal of the Hong Kong Branch of the Royal Asiatic Society* 15: 16-27.

Potter, J. M. 1970. "Wind Water, Bones and Souls: the Religious World of the Cantonese Peasants." *Journal of Oriental Studies* 13 (1): 139-153.

Sha, Anita. 1970. "A Study of Religious Attitudes of First Year Students in The Chinese University of Hong Kong." *Ching Feng* 13 (3): 18-23.

Smith, Carl T. 1973. "Notes on Chinese Temples in Hong Kong." *Journal of the Hong Kong Branch of the Royal Asiatic Society* 13: 133-139.

————. 1974. "The Chinese Church in a Colonial Setting: Hong Kong." *Ching Feng* 12 (2 & 3): 75-89.

Stevens, Keith. 1972. "Three Chinese Deities." *Journal of the Hong Kong Branch of the Royal Asiatic Society* 12: 169-195.

Stoodley, Bartlett H. 1965. "Christian Preference and Western Cultural Influence Among Chinese College Youth in Hong Kong." *Chung Chi Journal* 5 (1): 21-30.

Topley, Majorie. 1963. "The Great Way of Former Heaven: A Group of Chinese Secret Religious Sects." *Bulletin of the School of Oriental and*

African Studies 26 (pt. 2): 362-392.

————, ed. 1967. *Some Traditional Chinese Ideas and Conceptions in Hong Kong Social Life Today*. Hong Kong: The Hong Kong Branch of the Royal Asiatic Society.

————, ed. 1975. *Hong Kong: The Interaction of Traditions and Life in the Towns*. Hong Kong: The Hong Kong Branch of the Royal Asiatic Society.

Ward, B. E. 1977. "Readers and Audiences: An Exploration of the Spread of Traditional Chinese Culture." Pp. 181-203 in *Text and Context: The Social Anthropology of Tradition*, edited by R. Jain. Essays in Social Anthropology Vol. 2; Association of Social Anthropologists. ISHI.

————. 1979. "Not Merely Players: Drama, Art and Ritual in Traditional China." *Man* 14 (1): 18-39.

Welch, Holmes. 1960-61. "Buddhist Organizations in Hong Kong." *Journal of the Hong Kong Branch of the Royal Asiatic Society* 1: 98-114.

————. 1962. "Buddhist Career." *Journal of the Hong Kong Branch of the Royal Asiatic Society* 2: 37-48.

Wilson, B. D. 1960-61. "Chinese Burial Customs in Hong Kong." *Journal of the Hong Kong Branch of the Royal Asiatic Society* 1: 115-123.

(12) *Social Problems and Welfare*

Barnett, A. D. 1953. "Social Osmosis—Refugees in Hong Kong." *American Universities Fieldstaff Report* 2 (2): 1-8.

Caritas, Hong Kong and Hong Kong Christian Service, ed. 1972. *Report of Seminar on Care for Old Age in Hong Kong*.

Census and Statistics Department. 1979. *Crime and Its Victims in Hong Kong: A Report on the Crime Victimization Survey Conducted in January 1979*. Hong Kong: Government Printer.

Chan, Fook-kwan. 1973. *The Road to Delinquency: A Study of Juvenile Crime in Hong Kong*. Hong Kong: Research Sub-committee, Neighborhood Advice-action Council.

Cheng, Chi-ho. 1974. "The Study of Criminal Organization of Hong Kong through the Structure and Subculture of Triad Societies." Master Thesis, The Chinese University of Hong Kong. (in Chinese)

Cheung, Fanny M. 1979. "Care for Rape Victims." *Hong Kong Journal of Mental Health* 8 (1): 39-45.

————. 1979. "Self-perception, Cultural Norm and Development—Case Studies of 36 Chinese Women." *Journal of The Chinese University of Hong Kong* 5 (1): 355-362.

Ch'ien, James M. N. 1973. "Drug Abuse and Young People." *The Hong Kong Journal of Social Work* 8 (2): 23-29.

Cho, Revin. 1968. "Kaifong Welfare Association in Hong Kong." *Hemisphere* 12 (July) 28-31.

Choa, Gerald H. 1976. "Some Observations on the Phenomenon of Drug Addiction." *Journal of the Society of Community Medicine, Hong Kong Branch* 8: 6-17.

Choi, C. Y. 1973. "Some Consequences of Future Population Trends in Hong Kong." *The Hong Kong Journal of Social Work* 8 (1): 6-12.

*Chow, Nelson W. S. 1979. "The Feasibility of Contributory Social Security Schemes in Hong Kong: A Study of Employers' and Employees' Opinions."

Dial, Oliver Eugene. 1964. "An Evaluation of the Impact of China's Refugee in Hong Kong on the Structure of the Colony's Government in the Period Following World War II." Ph.D. Thesis, University of California, Claremont.

Downey, Berbard. 1976. "Combating Corruption: The Hong Kong Solution." *Hong Kong Law Journal* 6 (1): 27-66.

Dwyer, D. J. 1969. "Problems of Urbanization: The Example of Hong Kong." *Ekistics* 28 (168): 334-343.

Elliot, Elsie. 1971. *The Avarice, Bureaucracy and Corruption of Hong Kong.* Hong Kong: Friends Commercial Printing Factory.

Faulkner, R. J. and R. A. Field. 1975. *Vanquishing the Dragon: The Law of Drugs in Hong Kong.* A Monograph of the Centre of Asian Studies, University of Hong Kong.

Gardner, T. G. P. 1970. *Drug Addiction in Hong Kong.* Hong Kong Prisons Department.

Goodstadt, Leo. 1974. "Rejected Immigrants—The Chinese Connection." *Hong Kong Law Journal* 4 (3): 223-241.

Hambro, E. I. 1955. *The Problem of Chinese Refugees in Hong Kong.* Leyden: A. W. Sijthoff.

Harris, Peter. 1978. "The Bus and Its Riders: An Approach to the Problem of Corruption in Hong Kong." Pp. 140-161 in *Hong Kong: A Study in Bureaucratic Politics* by Peter Harris. Heineman Asia.

Haywood, S. 1972. "Poverty in Hong Kong: Some Reflections." *Chung Chi Journal* 11 (1): 138-149.

Hess, Albert Gunter. 1965. *Chasing the Dragon: A Report on Drug Addiction in Hong Kong.* Amsterdam: North-Holland Publishing Co.

Hinton, Arthur. 1967. "Education and Social Problems in Hong Kong." *Journal of Education* 24: 29-35.

Hodge, Peter. 1973. "Social Policy: An Historical Perspective as Seen in Colonial Policy." *Journal of Oriental Studies* 11 (2): 207-219.

————. 1976. "The Poor and the People of Quality: Social Policy in Hong Kong." *The Hong Kong Journal of Social Work* 10 (2): 2-17.

Holzner, Anne S. and L. K. Ding. 1970. "White Dragon Pearls in Hong Kong:

A Study of Young Woman Drug Addicts." A Report of The Methodist Church, Hong Kong.

(The) Hong Kong Committee of the International Council on Social Welfare. 1972. *Developing Social Policy in Conditions of Rapid Change: The Role of Social Welfare.* Hong Kong: The Hong Kong Council of Social Service.

—————. 1970. *New Strategies for Social Development: Role of Social Welfare.* Hong Kong: The Hong Kong Council of Social Service.

(The) Hong Kong Council of Social Service. 1978. *Report of the Study on the Social Service Needs of the Elderly in Hong Kong.* Hong Kong: The Hong Kong Council of Social Service.

Hu, Yueh (pseudo). 1962. "The Problem of the Hong Kong Refugee." *Asian Survey* 2 (1): 28-37.

Ikels, Charlotte. 1975. "Old Age in Hong Kong." *The Gerontologist* 15 (3): 230-235.

—————. 1978. "Urbanization and Modernization: The Impact on Aging in Hong Kong." Ph.D. Thesis, University of Hawaii.

—————. 1980. "The Coming of Age in Chinese Society: Traditional Patterns and Contemporary Hong Kong." In *Aging in Culture and Society: Comparative Viewpoints and Strategies,* edited by Christine L. Fry. New York: Bergin Publishers, Inc.

*Jones, John F. 1978. "Government Funding of Voluntary Social Services."

Kao, Mary and Bernard Downey. 1974. "Patterns of Homicide of Hong Kong." *Hong Kong Law Journal* 4 (1): 5-21.

King, Ambrose Y. C. 1979. "An Institutional Response to Corruption: The ICAC of Hong Kong." A Paper presented at The Conference on Hong Kong: Dilemmas of Growth, December 10-14, at the Australian National University, Canberra.

Lau, M. P. 1967. *An Epidemiological Study of Narcotics Addiction in Hong Kong.* Hong Kong: Government Printer.

*Lau, S. K. and Kam-fai Ho. 1980. "Social Accommodation of Politics: The Case of the Young Hong Kong Workers."

*Lee, H. M. 1972. "Social Welfare Organization in Kwun Tong."

Lee, Peter Nan-shong. 1979. "The Patterns and Causes of Police Corruption in Hong Kong." *Hong Kong Journal of Public Administration* 1 (1): 2-18.

Lee, Rance P. L. and Y. K. Chan. 1978. "Personal Happiness in Hong Kong." *Journal of the Hong Kong Society of Community Medicine* 9 (2): 68-72.

* —————. 1979. "High Density Effects in Urban Hong Kong: What Do We Know and What Should We Do?"

—————, ed. 1981. *Corruption and Its Control in Hong Kong.* Hong Kong: The Chinese University Press.

————. 1981. "The Folklore of Corruption in Hong Kong." *Asian Survey* 21 (3).

Lee, T. S. 1977. "Delinquency and Crime." Pp. 101-122 in *A Quarter-Century of Hong Kong 1951-1976: Chung Chi College 25th Anniversary Symposium.* Chung Chi College, The Chinese University of Hong Kong.

Lethbridge, H. J. 1972. "Penal Policy and Crime Rates: The Hong Kong Experience." *Hong Kong Law Journal* 2 (1): 54-68.

————. 1972. "The Evolution of a Chinese Voluntary Association in Hong Kong: The Po Leung Kuk." *Journal of Oriental Studies* 10 (1): 33-50.

————. 1974. "The Emergence of Bureaucratic Corruption as a Social Problem in Hong Kong." *Journal of Oriental Studies* 12 (1 & 2): 17-29.

————. 1976. "Corruption, White Collar Crime and the ICAC." *Hong Kong Law Journal* 6 (2): 150-178.

————. 1978. "Prostitution in Hong Kong: A Legal and Moral Dilemma." *Hong Kong Law Journal* 8 (2): 149-173.

Liang, C. S. 1975. "Overcrowding and Environmental Deterioration: The Case of Hong Kong." *Journal of The Chinese University of Hong Kong* 3 (1): 219-253.

Low, Daphne Nai-ling. 1974. "Dimensions in the Identity Profile of the American Educated Hong Kong Chinese." Ph.D. Thesis, Chicago: Illinois Institute of Technology.

Mcdouall, J. C. and K. Keen. 1966. "The Kaifong Welfare Association." Pp. 246-254 in *A Casebook of Social Change,* edited by Arthur H. Niehoff. Chicago: Aldine Publishing Co.

*Mok, Bong-ho. 1979. "Community Programme Evaluation: A Study of the Demand and Existing Practice of Evaluation in the Summer Youth Programme in Hong Kong."

Morgan, W. P. 1960. *Triad Societies in Hong Kong.* Hong Kong: Government Printer.

Murray, Leo. 1969. *Chaiwan Social Needs Study: A Report of a Survey Carried out among Organizers and Residents in the Chaiwan District of Hong Kong.* A Monograph of The Hong Kong Council of Social Service, Hong Kong.

*Ng, Agnes. 1975. "Social Causes of Violent Crimes among Young Offenders in Hong Kong."

See, Ying-yan. 1971. *A Report on Forced and Voluntary Prostitution in Hong Kong.* Hong Kong: Hong Kong Christian Emmanuel Church.

————. n.d. *Report on Drugs.* Hong Kong: Hong Kong Christian Emmanuel Church.

*Sugg, Michael L. 1975. "Adolescent Aggression in Hong Kong."

Topley, K. W. J. 1961. "Hong Kong's Immigrant Problem in 1960." *Interna-*

tional Union of Local Authorities Quarterly 13 (Spring-Summer): 122-125.

Tse, N. Q. 1968. "Industrialization and Social Adjustment in Hong Kong." *Sociology and Social Research* 52 (Apr.): 237-251.

Tsui, C. L. 1968. *Male Adolescent Delinquency in Britain and Hong Kong.* Britain: University College of Swansea Press.

United Nations. 1977. *The Aging in Slums and Uncontrolled Settlements.* Department of Economic and Social Affairs.

Walker, J. 1972. *Under the Whitewash.* Second Edition. Hong Kong.

Way, Edward Leong. 1965. "Control and Treatment of Drug Addiction in Hong Kong." Pp. 274-289 in *Narcotics*, edited by Daniel M. Wilmer and Gene G. Kassebaum. New York.

Webb, Paul R. 1977. "Voluntary Social Welfare Services." Pp. 133-144 in *A Quarter-Century of Hong Kong 1951-1976: Chung Chi College 25th Anniversary Symposium.* Chung Chi College, The Chinese University of Hong Kong.

Whisson, Michael G. 1965. *Under the Rug: The Drug Problem in Hong Kong.* A Monograph of the Hong Kong Council of Social Service, Hong Kong.

Williams, Gertrude. 1966. *Report on the Feasibility Survey into Social Welfare Provision and Allied Topics in Hong Kong.* Hong Kong: Government Printer.

Wong, Chee-ham. 1979. *Study of Closed Cases of Criminal & Law Enforcement Injuries Compensation Scheme April 1978-March 1979.* A Report of the Research & Statistics Section, Social Welfare Department, Hong Kong Government.

Wong, Aline K. 1970. "The Kaifong (Neighborhood) Association in Hong Kong." Ph.D. Thesis, University of California, Berkeley.

————. 1971. "Chinese Voluntary Associations in Southeast Asian Cities and the Kaifongs in Hong Kong." *Journal of the Hong Kong Branch of the Royal Asiatic Society* 11: 62-73.

————. 1972. "Chinese Community Leadership in a Colonial Setting: The Hong Kong Neighborhood Associations." *Asian Survey* 12 (7): 587-601.

————. 1972. *The Kaifong Associations and the Society of Hong Kong.* Taipei: The Orient Cultural Service.

Wong, F. M. 1960. "The Chinese Refugee Problem in Hong Kong." *Chung Chi Student* 8 (March): 26-31. (in Chinese)

————. 1971. "Study Report of the Day Nursery, Yang Social Service Centre." in *Study of Methodist Social Services.* Hong Kong: Social Research Centre, The Chinese University of Hong Kong.

————. 1971. "Study Report of the Home Nursing Problem, Yang Social Service Centre." in *Study of Methodist Social Serivces.* Hong Kong: Social Research Centre, The Chinese University of Hong Kong.

————. 1972. "The Impact of Social and Family Change upon Social Service in Hong Kong." *Journal of the Hong Kong Council Service* No. 40 (Spring): 11-18.

————. 1975. "The Aged—An Integral Part of the Society." Pp. 7-11 in *Report of the Seminars on Care for the Elderly*. Hong Kong: The Hong Kong Council of Social Service.

Wong, S. L. 1965. "Adjustment Problems between Two Generations Arising from the Change of Social Values in Hong Kong." *Chung Chi Journal* (Nov.): 31-39.

————. 1970. "Social Change and Parent Child Relations in Hong Kong." Pp. 167-174 in *Families in East and West*, edited by R. Hill and R. Konig. The Hague: Mouton and Co.

Yao, Raymond. 1974. "Refugees: A Question of Rights." *Far Eastern Economic Review* 84 (25): 15-16.

Yap, P. M. 1958. *Suicide in Hong Kong*. Hong Kong: Hong Kong University Press.

(13) *Social Research and Statistics*

Berkowitz, M. I. and Eddie K. K. Poon, ed. 1969. *Hong Kong Studies: A Bibliography*. Department of Extramural Studies, The Chinese University of Hong Kong.

Braga, J. M. 1965. *A Hong Kong Bibliography*. Hong Kong: Government Printer.

Breese, Gerald, et al., ed. 1973. *Urban Southeast Asia: A Selected Bibliography of Accessible Research, Reports & Related Materials on Urbanism and Urbanization in Hong Kong, Indonesia, Malaysia, the Philippines, Singapore, Thailand, and Vietnam*. N. Y.: Southeast Asia Development Advisory Group of the Asia Society.

Census & Statistics Department. 1969. *Hong Kong Statistics 1947-1967*. Hong Kong Government.

————. 1973. *Hong Kong Social & Economic Trends 1968-1972*. Hong Kong Government.

————. 1975. *Hong Kong Social & Economic Trends 1964-1974*. Hong Kong Government.

————. 1978. *Hong Kong Annual Digest of Statistics 1967-1977*. Hong Kong Government.

*Chan, Y. K. 1972. "Sampling in the Kwun Tong Industrial Community Research Programme."

Cheng, C. K., compiled. 1971. "Social Research Index, June 1971." A Report of the Research Department of the Hong Kong Council of Social Service.

Cheung, Chan Fai, compiled. 1976. *Directory of Current Hong Kong Research on Asian Topics 1976*. Hong Kong: Centre of Asian Studies, University of Hong Kong.

Cheung, T. S., et al. 1980. *An English-Chinese Glossary of Sociological Terms*. Hong Kong: The Chinese University Press.

*Chung, Betty J. and Z. K. Kwok. 1974. "Methodological Problems in Data Collection and Questionnaire Construction in the Social Context in Hong Kong—A Sub-study of the Impact of Industrialization of Fertility in Hong Kong."

Freedman, Maurice. 1976. "A Report of Social Research in the New Territories of Hong Kong 1963." *Journal of the Hong Kong Branch of the Royal Asiatic Society* 16: 191-261.

Ip, David F. K., Chi-keung Leung, and Chung-tong Wu, compiled. 1974. *Hong Kong: A Social Sciences Bibliography*. Hong Kong: Centre of Asian Studies, University of Hong Kong.

*Lee, Rance P. L. 1975. "Growth and Limitations of Social Science Research Institutions in Asia: The Hong Kong Experience."

————. 1977. "Growth and Limitations of Social Science Research Institutions in Hong Kong, with Special Reference to the Social Research Centre of The Chinese University of Hong Kong." Pp. 9-38 in *Social Sciences and National Development: The Southeast Asian Experience*, edited by S. S. Hsueh. New Delhi: Abhinav Publications.

————. 1979. "Survey on the Social Science Resources in Hong Kong." *Social Sciences in Asia* Vol. 4. UNESCO.

————. Forthcoming. "Sociology in Hong Kong." In Man Singh Das, ed. *Sociology in Asia Today*. Vikas Publishing House.

Leung, Margaret, compiled. 1973. *Directory of Current Hong Kong Research on Asian Topics 1973*. Hong Kong: Centre of Asian Studies, University of Hong Kong.

Li, A. K. 1966. "The Cantonese Semantic Differential Scales." *Journal of Education* 23: 27-33.

Mitchell, Robert E. 1966. "Research Centres: The Social Science Research Centre of The Chinese University of Hong Kong." *Social Sciences Information* 5 (4): 117-118.

Ng, E. W., compiled. 1978. *Directory of Current Hong Kong Research on Asian Topics 1978*. Hong Kong: Centre of Asian Studies, University of Hong Kong.

Podmore, David, David Chaney, and Paul Golder. 1975. "Don't Know Responses among Young Adults in Hong Kong." *Journal of Social Psychology* 96 (Aug.): 307-308.

Pong, Wai-ming, et al. 1974. *Youths in Hong Kong: A Statistical Profile*. Research Department, The Hong Kong Council of Social Service.

Rydings, H. Anthony and Nellie Childe, compiled. 1970. *Directory of Current Hong Kong Research on Asian Topics 1969-70*. Hong Kong: Centre of Asian Studies, University of Hong Kong.

Topley, Majorie, ed. 1969. *Anthropology and Sociology in Hong Kong, Field Projects and Problems of Overseas Scholars: Proceedings of a Symposium Feb. 8-9, 1969*. A Monograph of the Centre of Asian Studies, University of Hong Kong.

—————, compiled. 1970. "Published and Unpublished Materials on Hong Kong by Overseas Affiliated Scholars." *Journal of Oriental Studies* 8 (1): 219-225.

Urban Council Libraries of Hong Kong. 1975. *Hong Kong Bibliography: A Preliminary Draft*. Hong Kong: Urban Council.

(14) *Social Stratification*

Cheng, Irene. 1976. *Clara Ho Tung: A Hong Kong Lady, Her Family and Her Times*. Hong Kong: The Chinese University Press.

Chung, Fung-chi. 1977. "Ranking Occupational Prestige in Hong Kong: A Popular Evaluation." An Occasional Paper of the Social Research Centre, Hong Kong Baptist College, Hong Kong.

Cottle, T. F. 1967. "Comparative Evaluation of Occupations by English-speaking Refugee, and Local Hong Kong Adolescents." *Sociological Review* 15 (1): 21-31.

Hetherington, R. M. 1963. "Industrial Labor in Hong Kong." *Hong Kong Economic Papers* 2: 28-41.

*Lee, Rance P. L. 1974. "The Stratification between Modern and Traditional Professions: A Study of Health Services in Hong Kong."

*—————. 1976. "Sex and Social Class Differences in Mental Illness: The Case of Hong Kong."

—————. 1977. "Social Stratification and Psychiatric Disorder in Hong Kong." *Journal of The Chinese University of Hong Kong* 4 (1): 89-101. (in Chinese)

Rosen, Sherry. 1976. *Mei Foo Sun Chuen: Middle Class Chinese Families in Transition*. Taipei: The Orient Cultural Service.

Smith, Carl T. 1971. "The Emergence of a Chinese Elite in Hong Kong." *Journal of the Hong Kong Branch of the Royal Asiatic Society* 11: 74-115.

Wong, Aline K. 1973. "Rising Social Status and Economic Participation of Women in Hong Kong—Review of a Decade." *Southeast Asian Journal of Social Science* 1 (2): 11-28.

(15) *Socializaton and Social Values*

*Bond, Michael H. 1978. "Dimensions Used in Perceiving Peers: Cross-cultural Comparisons of Hong Kong, Japanese, American and Filipino University

Students."

*Bond, Michael H. and Peter W. H. Lee. 1978. "Face Saving in Chinese Culture: A Discussion and Experimental Study of Hong Kong Students."

Chaney, David and David Podmore. 1973. *Young Adults in Hong Kong*. A Monograph of the Centre of Asian Studies, University of Hong Kong.

Cheung, T. S. 1977. "Establishing a Self-image in a Fragmentary World." Ph.D. Thesis, University of New York, Buffalo.

*————. 1978. "The Socially Malnourished Children: An Anatomy of the Self-image of a Student Population in Hong Kong."

————. 1979. "The Structure of the World of Significant Others of a Student Population in Hong Kong." *Journal of The Chinese University of Hong Kong* 5 (1): 323-335.

Chung, Betty Jamice Yu-juen. 1967. "Studies in Adolescent Behavior and Culture Patterns in Hong Kong." Master Thesis, University of Hong Kong.

Dawson, John L. M., Henry Law, Andrew Leung, and Richard E. Whitney. 1971. "Scaling Chinese Traditional-modern Attitudes and the GSR Measurement of 'Important' Versus 'Unimportant' Chinese Concepts." *Journal of Cross-cultural Psychology* 2 (1): 1-27.

Dawson, John L. M. and William W. C. Ng. 1972. "Effects of Parental Attitudes and Modern Exposure on Chinese Traditional-modern Attitude Formation." *Journal of Cross-cultural Psychology* 3 (2): 201-207.

Field, C. E. and Flora Baber. 1973. *Growing up in Hong Kong: A Preliminary Report on a Study of the Growth, Development and Rearing Children in Hong Kong*. Hong Kong: Hong Kong University Press.

Li, A. K. n.d. "Parental Attitudes, Test Anxiety and Achieved Motivation—A Study of Fifth and Sixth Grade Children." Ph.D. Thesis, University of Hong Kong.

Liu, William T. 1965. "Achievement Motivation among Chinese Youth in Southeast Asia." *Asian Survey* 5 (5): 186-196.

————. 1966. "Chinese Value Orientations in Hong Kong." *Sociological Analysis* 27: 53-66.

Liu, Y. H. and Gerald M. Meredith. 1966. "Personality Structure of Chinese College Students in Taiwan and Hong Kong." *Journal of Social Psychology* 70 (Oct.): 165-166.

Low, Daphne Nai-ling. 1974. "Dimension in the Identity Profile of the American Educated Hong Kong Chinese." Ph.D. Thesis, Chicago: Illinois Institute of Technology.

Lyczack, R., G. S. Fu, and A. Ho. 1976. "Attitudes of Hong Kong Bilinguals Towards English and Chinese Speakers." *Journal of Cross-cultural Psychology* 7 (4): 425-438.

Morland, J. K. 1969-70. "Race-awareness among American and Hong Kong Chinese Children." *American Journal of Sociology* 75: 360-374.

*Shively, Stanley and Aliza Shively. 1972. "Value Change During a Period of Modernization—The Case of Hong Kong."

Spergel, Irving A. 1972. *Planning for Youth Development: The Hong Kong Experience.* United Nations Programme of Technical Co-operation; Department of Economic and Social Affairs.

Su, Cheung-jen. 1967. "China's Assimilation of Western Cultures through Hong Kong." *East Asian Cultural Studies* 6 (1): 73-81.

Traver, Harold. 1976. "Privacy and Density: A Survey of Public Attitudes towards Privacy in Hong Kong." *Hong Kong Law Journal* 6 (3): 327-343.

Ward, B. E. 1968. "Temper Tantrums in Kau Sai." Pp. 109-125 in *Socialization: The Approach from Social Anthropology*, edited by Philip Mayer. A Monograph of the Association of Social Anthropologists, Tavistock.

Wong, F. M. 1964. "An Empirical Study of the Relationship between Attitude and Scale Values: With Chinese College Students as the Study Sample." *Chung Chi Journal* 4 (1): 85-94.

(16) Urban and Industrial Development

Brim, John Anthony. 1970. "Local System and Modernizing Change in the New Territories of Hong Kong." Ph.D. Thesis, Stanford University.

Carr, Neil. 1975. "Report of Hong Kong: Quality of Life Means Political and Social Changes." Pp. 139-156 in *One World Only: Industrialization and Environment.* An International Forum under the Auspices of the Friedrich-Ebert-Stiftung, Tokyo, Nov. 25-Dec. 1, 1973. Tokyo, FES.

*Chan, Y. K. 1972. "The Growth Pattern of Organizations in Kwun Tong."

*————. 1972. "The Spatial Distribution of Organizations in Kwun Tong."

*————. 1973. "The Rise and Growth of Kwun Tong: A Study of Planned Urban Development."

*————. 1977. "The Development of New Towns in Hong Kong."

*————. 1978. "Life Satisfaction in Crowded Urban Environment."

————. 1978. "Life Satisfaction in Crowded Urban Environment." Pp. 187-196 in *Proceedings of the 4th Asian Pacific Social Development Seminar*, A.S.P.A.C. Korea: Seoul.

————. 1979. "Urban Density and Social Relation." *Journal of The Chinese University of Hong Kong* 5 (1): 315-322.

Cheng, Tong-yung. 1977. *The Economy of Hong Kong.* Hong Kong: Far East Publications.

Cho, Revin. 1968. "Kaifong Welfare Association in Hong Kong." *Hemisphere* 12 (July): 28-31.

Community Development Committee, ed. 1974-present. *Community Development Resource Book*. The Hong Kong Council of Social Service.

Drakakis-Smith, D. W. 1971. "Traditional and Modern Aspects of Urban System in the Third World: A Case Study in Hong Kong." *Pacific Viewpoint* 12 (May): 21-40.

————. 1976. "Urban Renewal in an Asian Context: A Case Study in Hong Kong." *Urban Studies* 13 (3): 295-306.

Dwyer, D. J. 1969. "Problems of Urbanization: The Example of Hong Kong." *Ekistics* 28 (168): 334-343.

————, ed. 1971. *Asian Urbanization: A Hong Kong Casebook*. Hong Kong: Hong Kong University Press.

————, ed. 1971. *The City as a Centre of Change in Asia*. Hong Kong: Hong Kong University Press.

Endacott, G. B. 1973. *A History of Hong Kong*. Revised Edition: Hong Kong: Oxford University Press.

Geiger, Theordore and Frances M. Geiger. 1973. *Tales of Two City-states: The Development Progress of Hong Kong and Singapore*. Washington, D. C.: National Planning Association.

Hodge, Peter. 1973. "Social Policy: An Historical Perspective as Seen in Colonial Policy." *Journal of Oriental Studies* 11 (2): 207-219.

————. 1976. "The Poor and the People of Quality: Social Policy in Hong Kong." *The Hong Kong Journal of Social Work* 10 (2): 2-17.

Hong Kong Committee of the International Council on Social Welfare, ed. 1976. *Symposium on Social Planning In a New Town—Case Study: Shatin New Town, April 30-May 1, 1976*. The Hong Kong Council of Social Service, Hong Kong.

Hu, Chia-chien and Aline K. Wong. 1968-69. "A Preliminary Report on the Kaifong Study." *United College Journal* 7: 27-48.

Hughes, R. H. 1951. "Hong Kong: An Urban Study." *Geographical Journal* 117 (1): 1-23.

Johnson, Graham E. 1973. "In-migration and Community Expansion in Hong Kong: The Case of Tsuen Wan." *Journal of Oriental Studies* 11 (1): 107-114.

————. 1971. "From Rural Committee to Spirit Medium Cult: Voluntary Association in the Development of a Chinese Town." *Contributions to Asian Studies* 1: 123-143.

————. 1971. "Natives, Migrants and Voluntary Associations in a Colonial Chinese Setting: A Study of Tsuen Wan." Ph.D. Thesis, Cornell University.

————. 1977. "Leaders and Leadership in an Expanding New Territories Town." *The China Quarterly* No. 69: 109-125.

*Jones, John F., K. F. Ho, B. Lo Chau, M. C. Lam, and B. H. Mok. 1978. "Neighborhood Association in a New Town: The Mutual Aid Committee in Shatin."

*King, Ambrose Y. C. and Y. K. Chan. 1972. "A Theoretical and Operational Definition of Community: The Case of Kwun Tong."

*King, Ambrose Y. C. and Peter J. L. Man. 1974. "The Role of Small Factory in Economic Development: The Case of Hong Kong."

*Kuan, Hsin-chi and S. K. Lau. 1980. "Planned Development and Political Adaptability in Rural Hong Kong."

Lai, David, C. Y. and D. J. Dwyer. 1964. "Tsuen Wan: A New Industrial Town in Hong Kong." *Geographical Review* 54 (2): 151-169.

————. 1965. "Kwun Tong, Hong Kong: A Study of Industrial Planning." *Town Planning Review* 35 (4): 299-310.

Lau, S. K. 1975. "Patterns of Urban Differentiation in Hong Kong: A Reexamination of Shevky's Theory of Urban Development." *Southeast Asian Journal of Social Science* 4 (1): 87-97.

*————. 1976. "Patterns of Urban Differentiation in Hong Kong: A Reexamination of Shevky's Theory of Urban Development."

Lee, Rance P. L. 1974. "The State of Affairs in a Chinese Satellite Town: the Case of Kwun Tong." *Chung Chi Bulletin* No. 57 (Dec.): 17-20.

*Lee, Rance P. L., Tak-sing Cheung, and Yuet-wah Cheung. 1978. "Material and Non-material Considerations in the Life Satisfaction of Urban Residents in Hong Kong."

Leeming, Frank. 1975. "The Earlier Industrialization of Hong Kong." *Modern Asian Studies* 9 (pt. 3): 337-342.

Leung, Joe Cho-bun. 1977. "The Community Development Drama, 1968-77." *The Hong Kong Journal of Social Work* 11 (2): 17-22.

Leung, Wai-tung. 1972. "Tsuen Wan: A Study of a New Town in Hong Kong." Master Thesis, University of Hong Kong.

Liang, C. S. 1962. "Growth of Satellite Towns in Hong Kong." *Chung Chi Journal* 1 (2): 200-241.

————. 1966. "Urban Land Use in Hong Kong & Kowloon, Part I: Tsim Sha Tsui District." *Chung Chi Journal* 6 (1): 1-24.

————. 1968. "Urban Land Use in Hong Kong and Kowloon, Part II: The Central Business District: Its Structure and Development Trend." *Chung Chi Journal* 8 (1): 107-132.

————. 1975. "Overcrowding and Environmental Deterioration: The Case of Hong Kong." *Journal of The Chinese University of Hong Kong* 3 (1): 219-253.

Lo, Chor-pang. 1968. "Changing Population Distribution in the Hong Kong New Territories." *Annals of the Association of the American Geographers* 58 (2): 273-284.

————. 1972. "A Typology of Hong Kong Census District: A Study in

Urban Structure." *Journal of Tropical Geography* 34: 34-43.

*Lu, Andrew L. C. and H. K. Tsoi. 1972. "Hawkers and Their Relocation in Hong Kong: Preliminary Report I."

*————. 1973. "Hawkers and Their Relocation in Hong Kong: Preliminary Report II."

Mcdouall, J. C. and K. Keen. 1966. "The Kaifong Welfare Associations." Pp. 246-254 in *A Casebook of Social Change*. Edited by Arthur H. Niehoff. Chicago: Aldine Publishing Co.

McGee, T. G. 1973. *Hawkers in Hong Kong: A Study of Planning and Policy in a Third World City*. A Monograph of the Centre of Asian Studies, University of Hong Kong.

Mitchell, Robert E. 1969. "How Hong Kong Newspapers Have Responded to 15 Years of Rapid Social Changes." *Asian Survey* 9 (9): 669-681.

*Mok, Victor. 1972. "The Nature of Kwun Tong as an Industrial Community: An Analysis of Economic Organizations."

*————. 1974. "The Small Factories in Kwun Tong: Problems and Strategies for Development."

Murray, Leo. 1969. *Chaiwan Social Needs Study: A Report of a Survey Carried out among Organizers and Residents in the Chaiwan District of Hong Kong*. A Monograph of The Hong Kong Council of Social Service, Hong Kong.

Potter, J. M. 1968. *Capitalism and the Chinese Peasant: Social and Economic Change in a Hong Kong Village*. Berkeley: University of California Press.

Riches, G. C. P. 1973. *Community Development in Hong Kong: Sau Mau Ping, a Case Study*. A Monograph of the Centre of Asian Studies, University of Hong Kong.

————. 1973. *Urban Community Centres and Community Development: Hong Kong and Singapore*. A Monograph of the Centre of Asian Studies, University of Hong Kong.

Riedel, James. 1972. "The Industrialization of Hong Kong." Ph.D. Thesis, University of California, Davis.

————. 1973. *The Hong Kong Model of Industrialization*. Kiel: Kiel Institute of World Economics.

————. 1974. *The Industrialization of Hong Kong*. Tubingen: J. C. B. Mohr (Paul Sieback).

Roberts, Philip James. 1975. *Valuation of Development in Hong Kong*. Hong Kong: Hong Kong University Press.

Saw, See-hock and W. K. Chiu. 1975. "Population Growth and Redistribution in Hong Kong, 1844-1975." *Southeast Asian Journal of Social Science* 4 (1): 123-131.

*Shively, Stanley and Aliza Shively. 1972. "Value Change During a Period of Modernization—The Case of Hong Kong."

Steward, G. O. W. 1962. "Post-war Development in Hong Kong." *Asian Review* 58 (Apr.): 128-131.

Sutu, H. 1968. "Industrialization in Hong Kong." *California Management Review* 11 (Fall): 85-90.

Topley, Majorie, ed. 1973. *Chinese Tradition and the Development of a City*. Hong Kong: Hong Kong University Press.

*Tse, F. Y. 1974. "Market and Street Trading—A Conceptual Framework."

*————. 1974. "Street Trading in Hong Kong: Part I—Population, Role and Characteristics."

*————. 1974. "Street Trading in Hong Kong: Part II—A Spatial Economy."

*————. 1974. "Street Trading in Hong Kong: Part III—An Examination of Government Policy."

Tse, N. Q. 1968. "Industrialization and Social Adjustment in Hong Kong." *Sociology and Social Research* 52 (Apr.): 237-251.

Ward, B. E. 1960. "Cash or Credit Crops?" *Economic Development and Cultural Change* 8: 148-163.

————. 1964. "The Surge to the Towns." *UNESCO Courier* 9 (Sept.): 5-6.

Wigglesworth, J. M. 1965. "Planning in Hong Kong." *Journal of the Town Planning Institute* 51 (7): 283-289.

Wong, Aline K. 1970. "The Kaifong (Neighborhood) Association in Hong Kong." Ph.D. Thesis, University of California, Berkeley.

————. 1971. "An Analytical Study of the Development of Hong Kong Society in the Light of Contemporary Theories of Social Change." *United College Journal* 9: 113-124. (in Chinese)

————. 1971. "Chinese Voluntary Associations in Southeast Asian Cities and the Kaifongs in Hong Kong." *Journal of the Hong Kong Branch of the Royal Asiatic Society* 11: 62-73.

————. 1972. "Chinese Community Leadership in a Colonial Setting: The Hong Kong Neighborhood Associations." *Asian Survey* 12 (7): 587-601.

————. 1972. *The Kaifong Associations and the Society of Hong Kong*. Taipei: The Orient Cultural Service.

*Wong, F. M. 1974. "Industrialization and Family Structure in Hong Kong."

————. 1977. "Modernization and Family Change." Pp. 47-68 in *A Quarter-Century of Hong Kong 1951-1976: Chung Chi College 25th Anniversary Symposium*. Chung Chi College, The Chinese University of Hong Kong.

————. 1979. "Rapid Urbanization and Family Adaptation." *The Hong Kong Journal of Social Work* 13 (1): 10-14.

*Wong, S. L. 1975. "A Chinese Village in Transition: Some Preliminary Findings."

Wong, Sidney Sik-yu. 1972. "Life Pattern of Hawkers: Case Study of Vegetable Hawkers in Yaumatei." Master Thesis, The Chinese University of Hong Kong.

Wu, Chung-tong. 1973. "Societal Guidance and Development: A Case Study of Hong Kong." Ph.D. Thesis, University of California, Los Angeles.